Between Worlds

Worlds

A Reader, Rhetoric, and Handbook

FIRST CANADIAN EDITION

Susan Bachmann
El Camino College

Melinda Barth
El Camino College

Karen Golets Pancer
Humber College

Editorial Advisers:
Crystal Hurdle, Capilano College
Ron Bonham, Malaspina University College

 **Addison-Wesley**

An imprint of Addison Wesley Longman Ltd.

Don Mills, Ontario • Reading, Massachusetts • Harlow, England
Melbourne, Australia • Amsterdam, The Netherlands • Bonn, Germany

Publisher: Brian Henderson
Managing Editor: Linda Scott
Editor: Suzanne Schaan
Permissions Editor: Madhu Ranadive
Cover Design, Design, and Layout: Anthony Leung
Production Coordinators: Linda Allison, Alex Odulak
Manufacturing Coordinator: Sharon Latta Paterson

Pages 505–506 constitute an extension of this copyright page. The publishers will gladly receive information enabling them to rectify any errors in references or credits.

Canadian Cataloguing in Publication Data
Pearson Education Canada
Bachmann, Susan
  Between worlds: a reader, rhetoric, and handbook

1st Canadian ed.
Includes index.
ISBN 0-673-98432-X

1. College readers.   2. English language—Rhetoric.   3. English language—Grammar—Handbooks, manuals, etc.   I. Barth, Melinda.   II. Pancer, Karen Golets.
III. Title.

PE1417.B47 1998   808'.0427   C97-932643-5

ISBN 0-673-98432-X

Printed and bound in Canada.

9 10 11 DPC 10 09 08

CONTENTS

PREFACE

Between Worlds is a reader, rhetoric, and handbook that offers students and instructors a variety of materials that support their writing courses. A diverse reader with thematically arranged selections includes writing prompts that encourage students to write about each reading in isolation as well as in relation to other texts. A concise rhetoric and handbook follow the reader. They are designed to help students through every aspect of the writing process and through some of the most common writing assignments, including the research paper. Although each section of this textbook can be used independently, both instructors and students will find the cross-referencing of material between the parts an advantage for teaching and learning.

THE READER

All the readings in this text reflect the conflicting realms—the "between worlds"—in which most of us live. Like us, the individuals in these readings are caught between balancing the burdens of work and school, satisfying family obligations and meeting personal needs, and defining themselves while relating to others. These "others" may be from different generations and cultures, may be of the opposite sex, or may have diverse self-perceptions and values. Rather than focusing on the extremes of these experiences or their exclusivity, we include readings that explore the overlapping worlds where most of us find ourselves.

The between-worlds experience is the substance of our five reading chapters: "Between Generations," "Between Genders," "Between Cultures," "Between Perceptions," and "Between Values." We have included numerous selections so that instructors can vary their readings (if they prefer) without changing books each semester, and so that students may be inspired to read unassigned material.

Each chapter contains essays, plus a short story and a poem, that are deliberately paired or grouped to prompt critical thinking, class discussion, and focused writing. The writing topics encourage students to use multiple materials and genres for support and to see how the concerns expressed in an essay can be succinctly captured in a poem or illustrated in a short story.

The essays are of varying complexity and length, from documented analytical studies to shorter pieces that have appeared in periodicals.

Each reading is followed by questions ("Thinking about the Text") so that students can review the content of the piece prior to class discussion. In addition, "Writing from the Text" sections provide students with writing topics for each work. Most valuable of all for the college writer are the writing assignments ("Connecting with Other Texts") that link related readings in each chapter *and* throughout the book. Students have the opportunity in the connecting assignments to examine multiple perspectives critically and then use diverse materials to support their points in papers. Also, because students may be using more than one source, they will have practice incorporating and documenting ideas before a longer research paper is assigned. In addition to those topics that relate to readings in the text, we have included assignments that will send students to other sources—including research sources in the library—for longer, more developed papers.

THE RHETORIC

We have designed the Rhetoric as a *focused guide to the entire writing process*. In order to demonstrate a process students might use when writing a college essay, we follow student writers through multiple stages of various assignments. Therefore, the Rhetoric can be used in class by instructors or stand on its own as a how-to for the students. Because we recognize that writing is a discovery process, we emphasize the following: numerous prewriting strategies; practical advice for considering audience; ideas about arrangement, outlines, drafting, and revision; and tips for constructing and revising the thesis (Chapters 6–8). In the Rhetoric, we show that writing is not a step-by-step process; it involves concurrent and recursive activities.

An important part of the Rhetoric is a guide to developing specific assignments (Chapter 9). We discuss strategies and methods for writing papers commonly assigned in college courses and provide discussion, models, and exercises for each. We teach how to write an in-class essay. We also explore the techniques of professional writers and examine how they use multiple strategies to analyse and argue their points. Many of our examples draw from themes, works, and assignments in the Reader.

Although early in the Rhetoric we introduce the skills necessary for incorporating others' ideas and words in shorter papers, we devote an entire chapter to the research paper (Chapter 10). This chapter includes instruction and an annotated student paper that is a response to a between-worlds topic. We also provide a clear guide to MLA and APA documentation. Throughout the Rhetoric, we offer plenty of illustrations and practice exercises to reinforce our conviction that we learn to write by actually writing . . . and rewriting.

THE HANDBOOK

We are convinced that control of grammar and punctuation gives the writer power over ideas and audience. Therefore, the Handbook is intended to empower students but not overwhelm them. We briefly explain how sentences work so that students can better organize and revise their writing (Chapter 11). Then we focus on the most common errors that persistently appear in student writing (Chapter 12). We include a list of marginal symbols for this correction guide so students can interpret their instructors' comments.

We also focus on understanding punctuation (Chapter 13) and word choice (Chapter 14) to help students become efficient editors of their own work, and we include an alphabetical list of words that are confused or misused by many writers (Chapter 15). The final chapter in the Handbook (Chapter 16) offers exercises for students to practise correcting common errors. The Handbook is designed to help students write, revise, and edit essays and understand their instructors' comments and corrections.

APPLAUSE

The first Canadian edition of *Between Worlds* would not have been possible without the generosity of many fine people.

First of all, I offer my warmest thanks to Susan Bachmann and Melinda Barth, for trusting me to revise and supplement their text for Canadian students and for approving of the results.

I also extend my appreciation to the professional and student writers who so kindly agreed to have their work included in this book, and whose names appear with their contributions. Several other students at Humber College contributed to this project as well, and each deserves acknowledgment: Anthony Aquino, Darrell Assiniwe, Erin Bittschwan, Megan Cameron, Peter Goodwin, Sylvie Haché-Cloer, Erin Harvey, Phill Kim, Jason Lunn, Suzanne Malcolm, Marija Pavkovic, Mark Scott, Sandy Silveira, and Jeny Zanfir.

Many colleagues at Humber College, especially Joe Aversa, Patricia Burke, Chris Coleman, Noreen Moran, Barb Morris, and Joan Pilz, offered just-in-time advice and support. Special recognition is due as well to the indispensable library staff at both Humber College and Conestoga College.

I am particularly grateful to Ronald Bonham of Malaspina University College for his prompt e-mail messages and constructive comments; to Crystal Hurdle of Capilano College for her meticulous, insightful, and good-humoured suggestions; and to Alice Oliveira, who was always available, often at short notice, with perceptive editorial advice and encouraging words.

A sincere thank-you goes to friends and acquaintances across the country and beyond for their time, responses, and suggestions: Robert Chodos; Susan Dobra; Susan Drain, Mount Saint Vincent University; Eric Hamovitch; Allan Hepburn; Jana Karger, University of Waterloo; Andrea Leis, Conestoga College; Andrea Lunsford, Ohio State University; S. Mark Pancer, Wilfrid Laurier University; Margaret Procter, University of Toronto; Judy Segal, University of British Columbia; Barb Sibley; Lyle Stewart; Eileen Wood, Wilfrid Laurier University; and Sandra Woolfrey, Wilfrid Laurier University Press. Jim Streeter of Seneca College and David O'Rourke of Centennial College reviewed the manuscript in the early stages of the project.

I owe a special debt of gratitude to three extraordinary editors at Addison Wesley Longman, whose infinite patience and diligence deserve a standing ovation. Thank you Brian Henderson, Suzanne Schaan, and Linda Scott.

Finally, I thank my family and friends for always understanding why I had to get back to work. Most of all, though, I thank Jordie and Matt for being themselves, and for constantly reminding me about what is most important in life. Thanks, guys.

Karen Golets Pancer
(First Canadian Edition)

This textbook could never have been written without the help of many people who have been particularly supportive and generous with their time as we worked on this book. A superb librarian, Judy Harris, searched computer screens and stacks to find what we needed. We are especially grateful to Rïse Daniels and Bill Bachmann for their talented teamwork on this book and for putting aside their own projects when we needed their expertise. Over the years, colleagues at El Camino College, Marymount College, the State University of New York at Buffalo, the University of Wisconsin at Madison, the University of Illinois at Champaign, and California State University at Dominguez Hills have shared teaching strategies and writing ideas that inspired portions of this book. Nancy Hennessy Swanby meticulously prepared parts of the manuscript. We are pleased that some of our students became published writers with the printing of this text; they merit hearty applause.

Special thanks must go to a number of fine reviewers who brought insights from their teaching to improve our efforts in creating this text. We wish to thank these supportive critics: Chris Anderson, Oregon State University; Richard Batteiger, Oklahoma State University; Joseph Boles, Northern Arizona University; Patricia Bridges, Mount Union College; Bruce E. Coad, Mountain View College; Lynda R. Corbin, San Diego Mesa College; Timothy Dekin, Loyola University of Chicago; William D. Dyer, Mankato State University; Gabrielle Gautreaux, University of New Orleans; Patricia H. Graves, Georgia State University; Stephen Hahn, William Paterson College; Aija Hoover, Odessa College; Ellen Redding Kaler, University of Kansas; Phoebe Mainster, Wayne State University; Jack Miller, Normandale Community College; Jane Bowman Smith, Winthrop University; Carol Wershoven, Palm Beach Community College; and Elizabeth Wood, Santa Barbara City College.

We are grateful to our new friends at HarperCollins: Patricia A. Rossi, senior acquisitions editor, who was immediately and continuously enthusiastic about our project; and Marisa L. L'Heureux, developmental editor, whose judgment, support, and sense of humor helped us revise and improve this book.

Finally, we want to try to thank the men in our lives who lived *Between Worlds* with us. Walter and Ron rescued us from computer chaos and kept our children from feeling they had been banished to another world. Ryan and Adam and Dylan and Evan helped as well—sometimes with hugs, often with humor, and occasionally by simply disappearing! Other family members and friends sent us relevant articles, offered their help, and understood when we turned down invitations and did not answer letters or phone calls. They all believed this project was worth their being temporarily "displaced" . . . and we applaud their willingness to live "between worlds" with us.

Susan Bachmann
Melinda Barth
(U.S. Edition)

PART I
The Reader

The readings in this text have been chosen to reflect the interests of college students like you, who are juggling school and work as well as balancing social lives and family expectations. The selections have been arranged thematically into five chapters. These chapters describe the multifaceted worlds that all of us live in and the tensions that pull us between the realms of generations, genders, cultures, perceptions, and values. We chose these readings to stimulate your thinking so that you can write meaningful essays—the goal of your composition course.

Each chapter contains essays, a short story, and a poem, all arranged to parallel or contrast with each other. After each reading you will find a section called "Thinking about the Text." These questions are designed for you to use as a study review prior to class and for small-group discussions during class. We follow these questions with "Writing from the Text," a section of writing assignments that spring from the readings and from your own experience. These topics may be assigned by your instructor, or they can be used for practice writing in a journal. You will find help for writing these assignments in the Rhetoric, Part II of this text.

A third section, "Connecting with Other Texts," will help you if your instructor asks you to compare two or more readings in this book. Some assignments in this section will encourage you to find extra material in the library, and these assignments can be used if your instructor assigns a paper that requires research. You will find instruction on how to write research papers of various lengths in the Rhetoric.

Some of the authors in this book are caught between generations and, like you, are trying to understand themselves in relation to parents and grandparents. Just as you are examining the roles that define your gender, many of these authors argue for a re-examination of those roles that limit the lives of people of both sexes. Whether you are a newcomer to Canada, a second- or third-generation Canadian, or a Native, you may find that these writers describe what you have experienced living between cultures. Your perception of who you are inevitably is coloured by others' images of you. Yet your desire to be perceived as an individual, rather than a stereotype, is also the experience of many college students and of the authors who write about being between perceptions. The selections in the final chapter of the Reader encourage you to think about your identity and values—something you probably have done more seriously since you started college. You may want to examine the ideas of the authors in this last chapter in order to re-assess your own convictions.

One of our contributors, Wayson Choy, wrote recently about an important discovery he made as he was writing his book *The Jade Peony*. In examining the conflicts inherent in being Chinese and North American, he realized that "these 'between world' struggles are universal. In every human being there is 'the Other'—something that makes each of us feel how different we are to everyone else, even our family members. Yet, ironically, we are all the same, wanting the same security and happiness. I know this now" ("I'm a banana and proud of it," *Globe and Mail,* 18 July 1997: A14). We invite you to read, write, and learn more about the worlds you and the people around you inhabit, and to further your own insight into what it means to be "between worlds."

CHAPTER 1
Between Generations

The French writer André Malraux believed that, without family, the individual "alone in the world trembles with the cold." The family often nurtures its members and tolerates differences and failings that friends and lovers cannot accept. But as you may realize from your own experiences and observations, people also tremble with fear or anxiety even within the family unit. The writers in this chapter show the family as a source of both nurturing and trembling.

Judith Timson muses about how closeness and conflict are equally possible at family gatherings, and how families change over time. In looking back at her childhood, Madeleine Gagnon questions beliefs about the power structure in families and praises her own family's unconventional "healthy democracy." Moira Farr, in her essay, confronts current myths about family life with two disturbing examples of families where nurturing was scarce.

If you have a strong bond with one member of your family, you will value Wayson Choy's short story, Lorna Crozier's poem, and Roy MacGregor's essay. These works show how powerful positive relationships between family members can be. Yet the conflicts between generations can be as instructive, as you will see in the essays by Joy C. and another writer who wishes to remain anonymous. In the final essay of this chapter, Kerry Banks's desire to be a good parent prompts him to explore the meaning of fatherhood at a time when parental roles are not as clear as they might have been in the past.

Your awareness of gaps between and across generations, as well as a deeper sense of family connection, may inspire your own writing. The works in this chapter attest to the will of the human spirit to mitigate family tension, to smile at some of the chaos, to forge bonds, and to survive and thrive from one generation to the next.

Here's to Family Feasting

Judith Timson

1   One of the best family dinners I ever experienced was the time the adults in my husband's family catered an intimate 60th birthday dinner for my mother-in-law. We wore black tie, we hired a pianist to play Gershwin, and we were all on our best behaviour. But what pushed the dinner into genius was that my mother-in-law knew instinctively that her role was not to be the passive centre of attention (passivity, in her case, being a gene that was apparently bred out at least a generation before). Instead, at the candlelit table, she spoke movingly of each of us and what we meant to her. The glow lasted a long time.

2   One of the worst dinners, I'm sorry to say, was approximately the same set of characters, plus children, a hot night, and the wrong topic for discussion. I can't remember if it was pay equity or affirmative action, but it certainly confirmed Gloria Steinem's tart theory that women grow more radical with age while men become more conservative. Moreover, one man lost his temper, and at least one woman I know very well was hormonally challenged. Kids fidgeted, nobody seemed remotely interested in anything anyone else had to say, and not all the strawberry shortcake in the world could make it right. "Well, that was a disaster," said my husband amiably later.

3   It is certainly not news to anyone as we head into the entertaining season that the family get-together—with its potential for conflict, chaos and enough neurotic undercurrents to bring you to your knees—is a challenge that some people look forward to almost as much as gum surgery.

4   We can rehash Tolstoy's brilliant axiom that all happy families are alike, and each unhappy family is unhappy in its own way, or we can cut straight to the chase—recalling the time Uncle Henry grabbed his brother around the neck, got him in a stranglehold and yelled, "You are too a greedy bastard!" while the cranberry sauce toppled off the table, or the time cousin Louise announced she was pregnant—by her brother-in-law—or merely, because not all of us are so gloriously dysfunctional, the time your sister thought a can of toasted almonds was an adequate contribution to a dinner you had sweated over for two weeks.

5   I am a sucker for family gatherings. I get too excited about them, I work too hard at them, and then I sit there, either appalled or in heaven, as they progress to their inevitable end.

6   As I grow older, even setting the table takes on a certain poignancy.

The extended family groans, shifts and changes—through divorce, death, birth and even, wonderfully, adoption—in ways we had never imagined. On my husband's side, Nanny's chair is empty, and in many families I know, relatives who once commanded the room with the sheer force of their personalities have been physically shattered in ways that make it hard to look at them, and hard to look away.

7   Time plays amusing tricks as well: we who used to be the subversive element—snickering as the adults downed their furtive second (or fifth) drinks, or made yet another inane comment, have become the snickerees, while our children, growing alarmingly older, murmur "Oh, please" in our direction.

8   Through it all, my favourite family characters faithfully play their roles: there is my brother, who is so engagingly offensive that he can unite an entire dinner table against him, a certain brother-in-law who defuses many a family time bomb with a silly joke, a sister-in-law who generously keeps an eye out when I am the hostess, knowing I have a tendency to fade in the third act. ("Dessert? What dessert?") There is, of course, my husband, who has been known to leap up from the table after being so silent he seemed in need of life support, and rush to play the piano. (Maybe that is his life support.)

9   I used to rail at the confusion of these dinners, but recently I realized that along with the noise, intrigue and cranky pronouncements, it was the crapshoot itself that engaged me. What will it be—triumph or disaster?

10   There is a wonderful passage in American author Anne Tyler's latest novel, *Ladder of Years*, in which an older man looks at a photograph of a table set for a family holiday celebration—"chair after chair after chair, silverware laid just so, even a baby's high chair, all in readiness." The man, deep in his own family turmoil, contemplates this exquisitely ready table in an empty dining room and says: "I bet that's as good as it got, that day. From there on out, it was all downhill, I bet."

11   Maybe. But then again, maybe not.

Thinking about the Text

1. What made the celebration described in the opening paragraph "one of the best family dinners"? What made the dinner described in the second paragraph one of the worst?

2. What elements of family feasting does Timson find the most attractive?

3. In what ways does the passage of time change individual families and their family gatherings?

4. Why does Timson use sentence fragments to end her essay, despite the fact that fragments are considered to be grammatical errors?

Writing from the Text

1. Compare one of your family get-togethers that was wonderful with one that was not.

2. Family dinners are one of the traditions most families follow. Is it important for a family to have traditions? Why or why not? Write an essay in which you discuss the role of tradition in family life.

3. In paragraph 8, Timson discusses some of the roles members of her family play during family gatherings. Analyse the roles particular people in your family play, either during holiday celebrations or, more generally, throughout the year.

4. Timson writes that "the family get-together—with its potential for conflict, chaos and enough neurotic undercurrents to bring you to your knees—is a challenge that some people look forward to almost as much as gum surgery" (paragraph 3). In an essay, show how this statement is valid or not valid, using examples from your family and its holiday celebrations, or other families you know, for support.

5. The Russian novelist and social theorist Leo Tolstoy said that "all happy families are alike, and each unhappy family is unhappy in its own way." Write a brief analysis of a happy family you know, classifying the characteristics that in your opinion are common to all happy families.

Connecting with Other Texts

1. Use any of the *Between Worlds* depictions of family, including Madeleine Gagnon's "Respect and Balance in Our 'Tribe'" (p. 6), Lorna Crozier's "Paper Boy" (p. 24), or Kenneth J. Harvey's "Life After Cable" (p. 188), to write an essay that explains the positive features of family life. Use the texts for examples and specific support.

2. Use any of the *Between Worlds* depictions of family, including Moira Farr's "Welcome to FamilyValuesWorld!" (p. 9), Joy C.'s "The Phone Call" (p. 31), or Robyn Sarah's "Maintenance" (p. 69), to write an essay that explains the negative features of family life. Use the texts for examples and specific support.

Respect and Balance in Our "Tribe"

Madeleine Gagnon

1 According to a sociological theory long current in Quebec and Canada, traditional French-Canadian society was—and to a large extent still is—a matriarchy. The tenets of this theory are taken to be self-evident: the men of my people were weak and absent from the family unit, dominated by

women, even subjugated under their rule, which was no less implacable for being insidious.

2   In my view, nothing could be further from the truth. I am not a sociologist, but I have lived in Quebec for a good half-century and have observed and become acquainted with an impressive number of families covering no fewer than five generations.

3   My own family, like many other large families, offers a good sample on which to base an understanding and analysis of relations between the sexes. My paternal grandparents brought nineteen children of both sexes into the world, and my maternal grandparents brought eleven. Some of them died young, but enough survived to provide me with an imposing array of uncles and aunts, almost all of whom married and had their own large families. It's hard to believe, but I had eighty-two first cousins on my father's side and forty-five on my mother's. I knew each one by his or her first name; as a child, instead of counting sheep to fall asleep, I counted—and named—my uncles, aunts and cousins.

4   The clergy encouraged this phenomenon of large families, which was supposed to be our revenge—the "revenge of the cradle"—for the Conquest on the Plains of Abraham. But it fell apart in my generation. After the "Quiet Revolution," we no longer sought revenge in this way. First of all, the clergy lost a lot of its ideological control. And then, with the rise of feminism and wider access to higher education, women and their husbands refused to become reproductive machines.

5   In the huge family of my youth, and in the other families I saw all around me, I did not observe the consistent matriarchy the theory suggests. I saw strong women and weaker women, powerful men and men who were more feeble. These tendencies were distributed more or less equitably, according to temperament and psychic structure.

6   Of course, my own family was the one I knew best. I am the fifth of ten children—six girls and four boys. I think I can say that my father and mother (who are still alive, at eighty-seven and eighty-three respectively) were able to maintain a balance of forces between the male and female members of what they sometimes called their "tribe."

7   As in all families, to be sure, problems came up, but no one could say that one sex systematically dominated the other. The affection that developed among some members of the family was based on complete respect for individuals, whatever sex they belonged to. I see this same respect among my parents' grandchildren (there are twenty of them), between them and their spouses and among the great-grandchildren who are beginning to grow up.

8   Perhaps this is a result of the deep and affectionate understanding that characterized relations between my parents. They are strong and happy creatures and I don't remember one of them ever attacking the integrity of the other, even in the smallest way. Along with their love, they shared this obvious regard for each other and, it seems to me, a common conception of education, which involved taking everyone as a role model, sharing tasks equally and engaging in dialogue. Everything could be discussed in our house. And because of the size of our family, some decisions were taken by majority vote.

9   An example of this healthy democracy occurred around the Sunday dinner table, a favourite time for very important conversations. I was fourteen. My father, who had less schooling than my mother but believed just as strongly in the need for everyone to pursue higher education, told us of a conclusion he had reached, as he said, "in agreement with your mother." In essence, he wanted to communicate the result of one of his ruminations to us: "Your education will be our greatest legacy. If it should ever happen that I don't have enough money to pay for a classical-college and university education for all of you, we have decided to have the girls educated first."

10   "Why?" we asked in unison.

11   "Because in a family it is the women who are more likely to pass on moral and intellectual values. Men can always earn their living through the strength of their muscles."

12   He said this as if it were such an obvious truth that no vote was necessary on that particular Sunday.

13   It was my good fortune to have a father who was a feminist before his time—and that did not take anything away from his strength and authority. It was my brothers' good fortune that he had the financial means to pay for everyone's education. And it was all of our good fortune to have parents who supported and encouraged us in the varied and individual directions that we took.

Thinking about the Text

1. Gagnon says that her experience contradicts sociological theory about French-Canadian families. What does the theory say about families in French-Canadian society? What evidence does Gagnon give to contradict that theory?

2. Could it be argued that Gagnon's father was indeed "weak" and "dominated by women"? Use examples from the text to support your answer.

3. What were Gagnon's father's attitudes toward women's education? What other values did the Gagnon children learn from their parents?

4. List the details that indicate the author's family relationships were based on respect and balance.

Writing from the Text

1. Write an essay in which you discuss the way decisions are made in your family. Is your family a matriarchy, a patriarchy, a democracy, or some combination?

2. Gagnon's father believed that "in a family it is the women who are more likely to pass on moral and intellectual values. Men can always earn their living through the strength of their muscles" (paragraph 11). Write an essay in which you argue that Gagnon's father is correct (or incorrect) in this assumption.

3. Abstract qualities are important to understand but can be hard to define. Using examples from this essay and your personal experience, write an essay in which you define respect as it relates to family life or intergenerational relationships.

Connecting with Other Texts

1. In "Don't Let Stereotypes Warp Your Judgments" (p. 128), Robert L. Heilbroner cautions readers about believing in stereotypes. Write an essay in which you argue that theories of matriarchy or patriarchy stereotype (or do not stereotype) families unnecessarily.

2. Other works in this book examine parents' roles in raising children and some of the ensuing conflicts. Read Robyn Sarah's "Maintenance" (p. 69), Kerry Banks's "As a Dad, Will I Do Right by My Daughter?" (p. 37), and Kenneth J. Harvey's "Life After Cable" (p. 188). Then write an essay discussing the roles and conflicts inherent in parenting or being parented.

Welcome to FamilyValuesWorld!

Moira Farr

God, I hate families. —Mikal Gilmore, *Shot in the Heart*

1 It is a chilly autumn morning, and I am buying stamps for a letter to my sister, who lives a long way away. The postal clerk grins and asks if I'd

like the pretty stamps, and I smile back and say, "Why not?" He hands me a colourful five-panel strip with "International Year of the Family" running up the side of each stamp. Number one shows a woman cradling a naked infant. Stamp two pictures a kneeling man embracing two happy toddlers and, behind him, a casually dressed man and woman smiling at a group of children, one of them in a wheelchair. In the next, a little girl in a straw bonnet kisses an old woman's cheek, while in the background a man and boy carrying fishing rods stroll beside a calm lake. Next up, a classroom full of youngsters and oldsters are engrossed in computer screens; finally, the surreal tableau ends in the large figure of a black woman in lawyer's robes gazing gently down at a woebegone child clutching a Slinky. Further off to the side, a white woman crouched beside a rocking horse smiles broadly at the same wee nipper; behind them all, an elderly man using a walker is helped by another, younger man down a long, fluorescent-lit, institutional corridor.

2   Your basic birth-to-death scenario, Canadian-style, circa 1994. Special, don't you think? As I stood gaping at the stamps, I wondered how many civil servants it took to select and sanction these particular images, how much time they spent attempting to strike the precise note of governmental blandness to ensure that not a single stamp-buying citizen could possibly take offence: put in a mix of races, ages and genders, of course; show the men, as well as the women, in nurturing roles; then throw in a disabled person, a judge and a social worker to indicate that we're not totally divorced from reality.

3   There are a lot of these propaganda exercises going on around this, the International Year of the Family. Or maybe it's just that the long-standing use of sentimentalized images of the family as a cultural sedative has reached critical mass. Can't quite wrap your mind around what's happening in Rwanda? Tune in to the CBC's Family Hour for a soothing dose of *Road to Avonlea*. All those homeless people got you down? You could always bake a pie, just like Mom used to, only use that new low-cholesterol shortening. Yum, yum. Better yet, call your old Mom, long-distance, at a discount.

4   On newsstands, right up there with *Time* and *Newsweek*, you'll now find *Family Life*. There's a whole Family Channel, where nice folks can watch reruns of *Little House on the Prairie* and other swell programs depicting a world that's never been. Last summer, when Marie Osmond breezed into town headlining as Maria the singing nun in *The Sound of Music*, she warbled to interviewers about what a great introduction to the theatre this musical about "family values" is for kids.

5   Meanwhile, at the tumultuous population conference in Cairo, religious fundamentalists of all stripes squared off in defence of family values against the perceived evils of secular humanism. As Benazir Bhutto stood at a conference podium extolling the virtues of the family, snake-charmers in Bangladesh marched in the streets, calling for the death of Taslima Nasrin, the notorious feminist who dared critique the abuse of women within traditional marriages. Back in Canada, the term "family values" seemed to have become some kind of fervent mantra, routinely invoked by politicians in defence of retrograde spending cuts and policies more suited to the 1950s than the 1990s. The logic is brutally simple: Families are Good, Amen. Make them, stay in them, fulfil all of your emotional, physical and material needs within them, and if you can't, well, guess you're out of luck.

6   Although I hail from a family and like to think that I have values, whenever I hear the term "family values" used by Reform Party MPs and the like, I never feel as though they are talking about me, or about any other human beings I know. The kind of family they seem to uphold is one that consists solely of a Mom and a Dad and a couple of kids living under one snug roof, all kitted out in matching pastels, grinning inanely as they go out and spend their no doubt hard-earned money at Paramount Canada's Wonderland. I imagine that their RRSPs are well-stoked, their microwave ovens always issuing forth healthy lunches, their lovely homes adorned with delightful crafts made according to instructions in *Canadian Living* magazine.

7   Of course, there are a goodly number of us who would rather have freshly cut jalapeño peppers applied to the quick of our fingernails than spend time in FamilyValuesWorld, and who might conclude that *The Simpsons* and *Married . . . With Children* have more to do with the reality of contemporary families than do the cloying, church-and-state-generated visions rearing up with particular force during this special United Nations year. I have no idea what a family value is anyway, apart from jumbo-sized bottles of shampoo you can buy on sale at Shopper's Drug Mart. Those who talk about them seem to make a distinction between the kind of high-toned, squeaky clean values espoused by their blessed selves and the bottom-dwelling, scum-sucking values (or complete lack of values, period) of everyone else.

8   The modern family may well appear to be in rickety, perilous shape. The Canadian government can fashion an inoffensive series of stamps, but it has declined to use its census data to come up with a universal definition of what forms of living arrangements and relationships constitute a

family. The United Nations proclaimed the year (after 14 years of debate), but decided against holding a conference on the subject of the family, deeming it too controversial.

9   Yet it would be a shame if the only voices heard during the International Year of the Family were those of a vocal few who seek to deal with the apparent chaos by appropriating moral virtue and freeze-framing the family into desiccated stereotypes. There are good families and bad families, and sometimes the good ones look like nothing the planet's ever seen before and the bad ones live in lovely homes and have lots of RRSPs. Fortunately, there are those in our culture who seek to unearth and explore the way families really are, not the way they exist in the aggressively (yet impotently) nostalgic conservative mind-set.

10   As Mormon Marie Osmond was whimsically whipping the singing von Trapp children into shape on the stage of the Royal Alexandra Theatre here in Toronto, I was reading journalist Mikal Gilmore's memoir *Shot in the Heart*. Gilmore is the youngest brother of Gary Gilmore, who became famous in the late seventies when he chose to be shot by a firing squad in Mormon Utah for the vicious murders of two young men, and is the subject of Norman Mailer's acclaimed book, *The Executioner's Song*. Gary Gilmore was not a nice person. After reading his brother's stunningly honest and painful memoir, it is easy to understand why.

11   While the sensational aspects of *Shot in the Heart* were bound to get the most widespread media attention, and the Gilmore family certainly dwelt on the extreme edge of screwed up, what the book reveals is nothing if not archetypal. Gilmore delves deep into the heart of his own family's dysfunction and comes face-to-face with the usual suspects: a restless, violent, alcoholic father who mercilessly bullied his sons and his wife, and an embittered mother who pegged the fulfilment of her conventional hopes and dreams on her shiftless husband, and punished everyone in sight when the good life she felt entitled to failed to materialize. Gary in particular bore the brunt of his father's twisted wrath, while Mikal, the fourth and youngest son, born to an older, more sober father and a more materially sated mother, received at least the bare modicum of love and stability needed to enable him to function as an adult. That the fiercely battered Gary would realize himself as a murderer, while Mikal became merely an intense, depressive writer who has difficult relationships with women, seems in this hindsight account as rigidly and inexorably scripted as a Greek tragedy. (There were also two other brothers: Galen, who died in his twenties of injuries sustained in a squalid stabbing incident; and Frank, who disappeared after the death of his mother and became a

ghostly rooming-house dweller, finally tracked down by Mikal when he began writing his book.)

12 I leave it to *Hard Copy* and the *National Enquirer* to muck around in the more gruesome, pulpy elements of the Gilmore story. What is remarkable, ground-breaking even, about the book is that in revealing one family's secrets through the perceptions of one damaged but intact member/witness, it reveals much about every family: that destructive patterns can be deeply set in cultural history and internally generated myths (in this case, the mother's gnarled Mormon roots alongside the father's vague and shrouded beginnings) and so subtly unleashed, no one has a clue it's happening; that the rotten things parents do to children are so often and so predictably a doomed reprise of what was done to them that mere blame can only be a stop-over on the road to real understanding and self-awareness.

13 But Mikal Gilmore is no Sensitive New-Age Guy, and his book is not a chest-beating cry for pity. Wisely, he does not seek to judge or be judged. The extremity of his life's circumstances perhaps marked him for an unenviably dirty job; his goal as an author isn't, and shouldn't be, social work, but by plunging (if not entirely by choice) into the slimiest sewers underlying the American Dream (and the actions and consequences involved mean he explores more than his own family in this regard), he has come up with something that might well help others live more cleanly. I have rarely read a man's accounting of his own relationships, and how they have been relentlessly shaped by the parental power struggles of his childhood, that exhibited such naked candour and humility. In laying bare the grim anatomy of his personal past, Gilmore offers truths and articulates emotions that will resonate for those, particularly men, I imagine, who have experienced family alcoholism and violence. In writing his book, he has transcended an enormous weight of ugliness and hatred. As a redemptive document of our times, *Shot in the Heart* deserves a wide and respectful audience.

14 The Gilmore family played out its dramas in the forties and fifties; earlier this year, Canadians were able to witness their very own contemporary fuck-up in the making, on *The Fifth Estate*'s astonishing documentary, "The Trouble With Evan." Producers managed to persuade a southern Ontario couple participating in a parenting workshop to allow the installation of unobtrusive video cameras in their home as they attempt to raise their 11-year-old son, Evan, whose trouble is stealing, lying, schoolyard fighting and general recalcitrance at home. (There is also an eight-year-old daughter, who receives scant attention in the final program; I eagerly await "The Trouble With What's-Her-Name, Evan's Little Sister.") As a counterpoint to

the alarming family dramas caught by the at-home camera, the documentary also includes interviews with several young men, and one young woman, incarcerated at a detention centre for young offenders. The not-too-subtle, but still movingly presented subtext, as each one of them speaks of his or her own abusive family, tears spilling from bereft eyes onto the cloth masks that protect their identities, is that Evan could well be joining them soon.

15   Of course, the real trouble with Evan is revealed to be nothing if not the manifestly inadequate parenting of his confused, immature, at times infuriatingly obtuse and destructive mother and stepfather. Indeed, they often come across as two big kids bullying a smaller one. Oedipal tensions roiling, they intermittently shout, occasionally hit, whine, wheedle, cry, threaten, viciously taunt, withhold love and affection, then inexplicably beg forgiveness and pour it on, and more or less make the child feel like the most worthless human being ever conceived.

16   It's all woefully banal, and at the same time monumental; walk out of the room for one minute, and miss a parent–child interaction so subtly loaded it will probably indelibly scar the kid for life. Yet, if the NDP ever needs Ordinary Canadians for an ad campaign, Mr. and Mrs. Evan's Parents could be the actors. This is not meant as a slight—only that what the documentary does succeed in illuminating is that your typical abusive parents are not obvious psychopaths, but just folks in their modest bungalow (or monster home, or family estate), damaged themselves and obliviously passing on the torch of pain to the next generation, between episodes of *Roseanne* and *The Wonder Years*.

17   And these are the ones who realize there's a problem and have sought help. After the documentary aired, social workers at the Children's Aid Society removed Evan from his home; his fate is now before the courts. Whether his and his family's lives are further ruined or somehow enhanced by all the media attention remains to be seen, but if the program is to achieve anything beyond voyeurism of the most appalling kind, it needs to be used and recognized as a kind of lasting testament. Once efforts like this are in our faces, it's harder to deny that violence breeds violence (and because it's socially cheaper in the short term to think it doesn't, lawmakers and politicians continue to do so). With "The Trouble With Evan" and *Shot in the Heart* now in our midst, it is perhaps possible to burn up some demonic old patriarchal ways on the pyre of understanding, with the hope that something positive and healing might rise from the ashes.

18   When Mikal Gilmore says he hates families, we can all relate to why, but he also has the emotional wisdom and maturity to acknowledge that there is something broken and perverse about not being able to bond with others in a deep, lasting, undestructive way as an adult; that it's no laughing matter—what happens to children matters profoundly. At best, the legacy of childhood abuse is a life spent stoically bearing a burden of internal anguish that never really goes away, even in the midst of what looks like success. At worst, it means wreaking havoc beyond one's self; wounding, scarring and killing others. Tragedy. It's this widespread reality that none of us can afford to ignore, or gloss over with pretty stamps and atavistic political declarations.

19   For many, there's as much pain and despair in trying to conform to conventional family norms and expected roles that don't mesh with inner reality as there is in rejecting them. The truth is, healthy or unhealthy, nuclear or diffuse, no matter how much physical or psychological distance we might put between ourselves and our own families, they can't be escaped. (Gary Gilmore's last words, before being shot in the heart: "There will always be a father.") Their intimate failings and triumphs are harrowing and luminous, as awesome in their power as the tides. If we don't actively seek to understand our own home truths, we're doomed, as individuals and as a culture. What happens, or happened, in our families explodes within us as long as we live, propelling us forward and pulling us back, fueling us, depleting us, influencing whom and how we do or don't love, gently shaping or grossly distorting our identities, whether we reject and rebel against them or find ways to live more or less comfortably within their inevitable compromises.

20   Social work won't save everyone, and you'll probably find more wisdom about families in *Long Day's Journey into Night* by Eugene O'Neill than in a stack of theoretical textbooks. In the end, it comes back to the successful formation of a self, and a self can be a very crowded, yet numbingly lonely house. It takes a lot of moral virtue to make room for the diverse beings who dwell in a self, a family, a rapidly shifting society; as someone like Mikal Gilmore can attest, it takes courage, restraint and tolerance. In 1994, the International Year of the Family, we had better face the fact that most families don't resemble those of FamilyValuesWorld, a place a lot of people feel they learned how to do everything wrong; a place a lot of people want to challenge and demystify so they can do it right.

Thinking about the Text

1. How does this essay define a typical "family values" family? Why does Farr object to this image?

2. In what ways do the media contribute to the "sentimentalized images of the family"? List examples from the text.

3. Why did the Canadian government create a series of stamps rather than use census data to define what a family is (paragraph 8)? Why does the United Nations consider a conference on the subject of family "too controversial"?

4. According to the author, in what ways does the family affect the individual?

5. Why does Farr admire Mikal Gilmore?

Writing from the Text

1. Write a subject analysis of families you have seen in movies, television sit-coms, magazines, or advertisements. In what ways are families in these contexts idealized or sentimentalized?

2. Considering your own experience, analyse some of the implicit myths about family life that Farr says the "family values" movement perpetuates. In your conclusion, state whether you agree or disagree with Farr's position.

3. Reread Farr's essay. Underline any words that are unfamiliar to you, and look up the meaning of these words in a dictionary. Are there any examples of slang in the essay? Write a brief analysis of the range of vocabulary in the essay and comment on its effectiveness.

Connecting with Other Texts

1. Farr writes: "For many, there's as much pain and despair in trying to conform to conventional family norms and expected roles that don't mesh with inner reality as there is in rejecting them" (paragraph 19). Write an essay in which you explain the significance of this quotation for Joy C., author of "The Phone Call" (p. 31).

2. Find some current periodical articles on child abuse. Then write a problem analysis in which you discuss the problem of child abuse within families and offer possible solutions.

3. Research the history of the nuclear family. Has the "family values" family always been the norm? Write a persuasive essay in which you argue that the nuclear family is (or is not) the historic norm for family life.

4. Farr says governments shy away from defining family because the topic is too controversial. Write an essay in which you define the meaning of family in the late twentieth century. Use the families in "Welcome to FamilyValuesWorld!" as well as Judith Timson's "Here's to Family Feasting" (p. 4) and Madeleine Gagnon's "Respect and Balance in Our 'Tribe'" (p. 6) as examples.

The Jade Peony

Wayson Choy

1 When Grandmama died in 1940 at eighty-three, our whole household held its breath. She had promised us a sign of her leaving, final proof that her life had ended well. My parents knew that without any clear sign, our own family fortunes could be altered, threatened. Stepmother looked every day into the small cluttered room the ancient lady had occupied. Nothing was touched; nothing changed. Father, thinking that a sign should appear in Grandmama's garden, looked at the frost-killed shoots and cringed: *No, that could not be it.*

2 My two older teenage brothers and my sister, Liang, were embarrassed by my parents' behaviour. What would white people in Vancouver think of us? We were Canadians now, *Chinese-Canadians*, a hyphenated reality that our parents could never accept. So it seemed, for different reasons, we were all holding our breath, waiting for *something.*

3 I was nearly seven when Grandmama died. For days she had resisted going into the hospital . . . *a cold, just a cold* . . . and instead gave constant instructions to Stepmother on the boiling of ginseng root mixed with bitter extract. At night, between racking coughs and deadly silences, Grandmama had her back and chest rubbed with heated camphor oil and sipped a bluish decoction of an herb called Peacock's Tail. When all these failed to abate her fever, she began to arrange the details of her will. This she did with Father, confessing finally: "I am too stubborn. The only cure for old age is to die."

4 Father wept to hear this. I stood beside her bed: she turned to me. Her round face looked darker, and the gentleness of her eyes, with the thin, arching eyebrows, seemed weary. I brushed a few strands of grey, brittle hair from her face; she managed to smile at me. Being the youngest, I had spent nearly all my time with her and knew that she would be with me forever. Yet when she spoke, and her voice hesitated, cracked, the sombre shadows of her room chilled me. Her wrinkled brow grew wet with fever, and her small body seemed even more diminutive.

5 "You know, Little Son, whatever happens I will never leave you," she said. Her hand reached out for mine. Her palm felt plush and warm, the slender, old fingers bony and firm; so magically strong was her grip that I could not imagine how she could ever part from me. Ever.

6 Her hands *were* magical. Long, elegant fingers, with impeccable nails, a skein of fine barely visible veins, and wrinkled skin the colour of light

pine. Those hands were quick when she taught me, at six, simple tricks of juggling, learnt when she was a village girl in southern Canton; a troupe of actors had stayed on her father's farm. One of them, "tall and pale as the whiteness of petals," fell in love with her, promising to return. "My juggler," she said, "he never came back to me from Honan . . . perhaps the famine . . ." In her last years, his image came back into her life. He had been a magician, an acrobat, a juggler, and some of the things he taught her she had absorbed and passed on to me through her stories and games.

7   Most marvellous for me was the quick-witted skill her hands revealed in making windchimes for our birthdays: windchimes in the likeness of her lost friend's parting present to her, made of bits of string and the precious jade peony, a carved stone the size of a large coin, knotted with red silk to hang like a pendant from the centre, like the clapper of a sacred bell. This wondrous gift to her had broken apart years ago, in China, but Grandmama kept the jade pendant in a tiny red silk envelope, and kept it always in her pocket, until her death.

8   Hers were not ordinary, carelessly made chimes, such as those you now find in our Chinatown stores, whose rattling noises drive you mad. But the making of her special ones caused dissension in our family, and some shame. Each one that she made was created from a treasure trove of glass fragments and castaway costume jewellery. The problem for the rest of the family lay in the fact that Grandmama looked for these treasures wandering the back alleys of Keefer and Pender Streets, peering into our neighbours' garbage cans, chasing away hungry, nervous cats and shouting curses at them.

9   "All our friends are laughing at us!" Second Brother Jung said at last to Father, when Grandmama was away having tea at Mrs. Lim's.

10   "We are not poor," First Brother Kiam declared, "yet she and Sek-Lung poke through garbage as if—" he shoved me in frustration and I stumbled against my sister "—they were beggars!"

11   "She will make Little Brother crazy!" Sister Liang said. Without warning, she punched me sharply in the back; I jumped. "You see, look how *nervous* he is!"

12   I lifted my foot slightly, enough to swing it back and kick Liang in the shin. She yelled and pulled back her fist to punch me again. Jung made a menacing move towards me.

13   "Stop this, all of you!" Father shook his head in exasperation. How could he dare tell the Old One, his ageing mother, that what was appropriate in a poor village in China was shameful here? How could he prevent me, his youngest, from accompanying her? "She is not a beggar

looking for food. She is searching for—for . . ."

14   Stepmother attempted to speak, then fell silent. She, too, was perplexed and somewhat ashamed. They all loved Grandmama, but she was *inconvenient*, unsettling.

15   As for our neighbours, most understood Grandmama to be harmlessly crazy, others conceded that she did indeed make lovely toys, but for what purpose? *Why?* they asked, and the stories she told to me, of the juggler who had smiled at her, flashed in my head.

16   Finally, by their cutting remarks, the family did exert enough pressure that Grandmama no longer openly announced our expeditions. Instead, she took me with her on "shopping trips," ostensibly for clothes or groceries, while in fact we spent most of our time exploring stranger and more distant neighbourhoods, searching for splendid junk: jangling pieces of a broken vase, cranberry glass fragments embossed with leaves, discarded glass beads from Woolworth necklaces. We would sneak them all home in brown rice sacks, folded into small parcels, and put them under her bed. During the day when the family was away at school or work, we brought them out and washed the pieces in a large black pot of boiling lye and water, dried them carefully, and returned them, sparkling, to the hiding place under her bed.

17   Our greatest excitement occurred when a fire gutted the large Chinese Presbyterian Church, three blocks from our house. Over the still-smoking ruins the next day, Grandmama and I rushed precariously over the blackened beams to pick out the stained glass that glittered in the sunlight. Her small figure bent over, wrapped against the autumn cold in a dark blue quilted coat, she happily gathered each piece like gold, my spiritual playmate: "There's a good one! *There!*"

18   Hours later, soot-covered and smelling of smoke, we came home with a carton full of delicate fragments, still early enough to smuggle them all into the house and put the small box under her bed.

19   "These are special pieces," she said, giving the box a last push, "because they come from a sacred place."

20   She slowly got up and I saw, for the first time, her hand begin to shake. But then, in her joy, she embraced me. I buried my face in her blue quilted coat, and for a moment, the whole world seemed perfect.

21   One evening, when the family was gathered in their usual places in the parlour, Grandmama gave me her secret nod of warning: a slight wink of her eye and a flaring of her nostrils. There was *trouble* in the air. Supper had gone badly, school examinations were approaching. Father had failed to meet an editorial deadline at the *Chinese Times*.

22   A huge sigh came from Sister Liang. "But it is useless, this Chinese they teach us!" she lamented, turning to First Brother Kiam for support.

23   "I agree, Father," Kiam began. "You must realize that this Mandarin only confuses us. We are Cantonese speakers . . ."

24   "And you do not complain about Latin, French or German in your English school?" Father rattled his newspaper, a signal that his patience was ending.

25   "But Father, those languages are *scientific*." Kiam jabbed his brush in the air for emphasis. "We are now in a scientific, logical world."

26   Father was silent. He wanted his children to have both the old ways and the new ways.

27   Grandmama went on rocking quietly in her chair. She complimented Stepmother on her knitting, made a remark about the "strong beauty" of Kiam's brushstrokes which, in spite of himself, immensely pleased him.

28   "*Daaih ga tohng yahn*," Grandmama said. "We are all Chinese." Her firm tone implied that this troubling talk about old and new ways should stop.

29   "What about Sek-Lung?" Second Brother Jung pointed angrily at me. "He was sick last year, but this year he should have at least started Chinese school, instead of picking over garbage cans!"

30   "He starts next year," Father said, in a hard tone that immediately warned everyone to be silent. Liang slammed her book shut.

31   The truth was, I was sorry not to have started school the year before. I knew going to school had certain privileges. The fact that my lung infection in my fifth and sixth years gave me a reprieve only made me long for school the more. Each member of the family took turns on Sunday, teaching me. But Grandmama taught me most. Tapping me on my head, she would say, "Come, Sek-Lung, we have *our* work," and we would walk up the stairs to her small crowded room. There, in the midst of her antique shawls, the ancestral calligraphy and multicoloured embroidered hangings, beneath the mysterious shelves of sweet-smelling herbs and bitter potions, we would continue making windchimes.

32   "I can't last forever," she declared, when she let me in on the secret of the chime we had started this morning. "It will sing and dance and glitter." Her long fingers stretched into the air, pantomiming the waving motion of her ghost chimes. "My spirit will hear its sounds and see its light and return to this house to say goodbye to you."

33   Deftly, she reached into the carton she had placed on the chair beside me. She picked out a fish-shaped amber piece, and with a long needlelike tool and a steel ruler, she scored it. Pressing the blade of a cleaver against

the line, she lifted up the glass until it cleanly snapped into the exact shape she required. Her hand began to tremble, the tips of her fingers to shiver, like rippling water.

34   "You see that, Little One?" She held her hand up. "That is my body fighting with Death. He is in this room now."

35   My eyes darted in panic, but Grandmama remained calm, undisturbed, and went on with her work. I got out the glue and uncorked the jar for her. Soon the graceful ritual movements of her hand returned to her, and I became lost in the magic of her task: she dabbed a secret mixture of glue on one end and skilfully dropped the braided end of a silk thread into it. This part always amazed me: the braiding would slowly, *very* slowly, unwind, fanning out like a prized fishtail. In a few seconds, as I blew light-ly over it, the clear, homemade glue began to harden, welding to itself each separate silk strand.

36   Each jam-sized pot of glue was treasured; each large cork stopper had been wrapped with a fragment of pink silk. We went shopping at the best stores in Chinatown for the perfect square of silk she required. It had to be a deep pink, blushing towards red. And the tone had to match, as closely as possible, her precious jade carving, the small peony of white and light-red jade, her most lucky possession. In the centre of this semi-translucent carving, no more than an inch wide, was a pool of pink light, its veins swirling out into the petals of the flower.

37   "This colour is the colour of my spirit," Grandmama said, holding it up to the window so I could see the delicate pastel against the broad strokes of sunlight. She dropped her voice, and I held my breath at the wonder of the colour. "This was given to me by the young acrobat who taught me how to juggle. He had four of them, and each one had a centre of this rare colour, the colour of Good Fortune." The pendant seemed to pulse as she turned it: "Oh, Sek-Lung! He had white hair and white skin *to his toes!* It's true—I saw him bathing." She laughed and blushed, her eyes softened at the memory. The silk had to match the pink heart of her pendant, for the colour was magical for her: it held the unravelling strands of her memory.

38   Six months before she died, we began to work on her last windchime. Three thin bamboo sticks of varying length were steamed and bent into circlets; twenty exact lengths of silk thread, the strongest kind, were cut and braided at both ends and glued to pieces of the stained glass. Her hands worked on their own command, each hand racing with a life of its own: cutting, snapping, braiding, knotting. Sometimes she breathed heav-ily, and her small body, growing thinner, sagged against me. *Death*, I thought, *is in this room*, and I would work harder alongside her. For weeks

Grandmama and I did this every other evening, a half-dozen pieces each time. The shaking in her hand grew worse, but we said nothing. Finally, after discarding a hundred, she told me she had the necessary twenty pieces. But this time, because it was a sacred chime, I would not be permitted to help her tie it up or have the joy of raising it.

39   "Once tied," she said, holding me against my disappointment, "not even I can raise it. Not a sound must it make until I have died."

40   "What will happen?"

41   "Your father will then take the centre braided strand and raise it. He will hang it against my bedroom window so that my ghost may see it, and hear it, and return. I must say goodbye to this world properly or wander in this foreign land forever."

42   "You can take the streetcar!" I blurted, suddenly shocked that she actually meant to leave me. I thought I could hear the clear chromatic chimes, see the shimmering colours on the wall: I fell against her and cried, and there in my crying I knew that she would die. I can still remember the touch of her hand on my head, and the smell of her thick woollen sweater pressed against my face. "I will always be with you, Little Sek-Lung, but in a different way . . . You'll see."

43   Weeks went by, and nothing happened. Then one late September evening, Grandmama was preparing supper when she looked out our kitchen window and saw a cat—a long, lean white cat—jump into our garbage pail and knock it over. She ran out to chase it away, shouting curses at it. She did not have her thick sweater on and when she came back into the house, a chill gripped her. She leaned against the door: "That was not a cat," she said, and the odd tone of her voice caused Father to look with alarm at her. "I cannot take back my curses. It is too late." She took hold of Father's arm. "It was all white and had pink eyes like sacred fire."

44   Father started at this, and they both looked pale. My brothers and sister, clearing the table, froze in their gestures.

45   "The fog has confused you," Stepmother said. "It was just a cat."

46   But Grandmama shook her head, for she knew it was a sign. "I will not live forever," she said. "I am prepared."

47   The next morning she was confined to her bed with a severe cold. Sitting by her, playing with some of my toys, I asked her about the cat: "Why did Father jump when you said the cat was white with pink eyes? He didn't see it, you did."

48   "But he and Stepmother know what it means."

49   "What?"

50   "My friend, the juggler, the magician, was as pale as white jade, and

he had pink eyes." I thought she would begin to tell me one of her stories, a tale of enchantment or wondrous adventure, but she only paused
to swallow; her eyes glittered, lost in memory. She took my hand, gently
opening and closing her fingers over it. "Sek-Lung," she sighed, "*he* has
come back to me."

51   Then Grandmama sank back into her pillow and the embroidered
flowers lifted to frame her wrinkled face. She placed her hand over mine,
and my own began to tremble. I fell fitfully asleep by her side. When I
woke up it was dark and her bed was empty. She had been taken to the
basement of St. Paul's Hospital, where the sick Chinese were allowed to
stay. I was not permitted to visit her.

52   A few days after that, Grandmama died of the complications of pneu-
monia. Immediately after her death, Father came home. He said nothing
to us but walked up the stairs to her room, pulled aside the drawn lace
curtains of her window, and lifted the windchimes to the sky.

53   I began to cry and quickly put my hand in my pocket for a handkerchief. Instead, caught between my fingers, was the small, round firmness
of the jade peony. In my mind's eye I saw Grandmama smile, and heard,
softly, the pink centre beat like a beautiful, cramped heart.

Thinking about the Text

1. Describe what Sek-Lung and Grandmama do together. Although he is six
    and she is eighty-three, in what ways does their relationship resemble that
    of siblings?

2. What tangible and intangible things did the juggler give Grandmama?

3. Why does Grandmama build windchimes? Why does she want Sek-Lung to
    help her?

4. Discuss the significance of the story's title.

5. What does this story have to say about the scientific, logical world com-
    pared to the magical world? What other worlds are contrasted in this story?

Writing from the Text

1. We usually associate inheritances with money, yet grandchildren inherit
    other things from their grandparents: physical characteristics, personality
    traits, interests, and so on. Consider your relationship with each of your
    grandparents. What have they handed down to you that makes you the per-
    son you are today? Write an essay classifying their legacies to you.

2. Write an essay about Chinese beliefs about magic as they are presented in
    this story. How do these beliefs relate to the story's theme?

3. The narrator says that his father "wanted his children to have both the old ways and the new ways" (paragraph 26), which in effect requires the children to live between worlds. Write an essay exploring how Sek-Lung and his siblings find themselves caught between generations, genders, cultures, perceptions, and values.

Connecting with Other Texts

1. Compare the ways this story and Wallace Stegner's essay "In Search of Whitemud" (p. 160) deal with the issue of memory. According to these two works, where do our memories "live"?

2. Read Archibald J. Crail's "Affirmative Action" (p. 145) and Yeshim Ternar's "Ajax Là-Bas" (p. 110). Using examples from these stories as well as from "The Jade Peony," write an essay on the way immigrants to Canada are forced to change or compromise in order to survive here. If you wish, include examples from your own, or your family's, experience as well.

Paper Boy
Lorna Crozier

Just before sunrise
the snow is blue as flax.
Down our street, only one
other house with its windows lit.
5 Next door the paper boy
climbs the steps, the pompom
on his red tuque bobbing.
Behind him, waiting with his bag
on a wooden sled, a little girl
10 who could only be his sister,
she looks so proud and happy
to be there. Without his friends around
he doesn't seem to mind,
seems pleased to have her,
15 the two of them the only ones
on this long blue street
beneath the morning moon.

It could be my brother and me.

How I loved to be with him
20 even in the cold, even when
he didn't want me there.
I'd sneak out the back
and follow his whistle,
hopping from track to track,
25 fitting my feet inside his
across the snow.

Finally, his route almost done,
he'd wait for me,
lift me up and put me in his bag
30 on top of the papers he had left,
carry me home like a kangaroo
nestled in the pouch, warmed
by his body, my eyes barely open,
as if I'd slipped out of him
35 seven years after he was born,
he, as much as my mother,
giving me this life.

Thinking about the Text

1. Who is the speaker in this poem? What specific facts do you learn about her? What can you infer about her?

2. Poetry depends on words and imagery to convey meaning to readers. List and then compare the images in the first stanza with images in the last two stanzas. In what ways are they different?

3. How do the images define the mood and tone here? List specific examples from the text.

4. Describe the diction Crozier has chosen to use in this poem. In what ways does her word choice relate to the poem's theme?

Writing from the Text

1. Think about a sibling you are particularly close to or anyone else who has fulfilled that role for you. Then write a narrative about an event that illustrates that person's qualities and your feelings for each other.

2. Explore the meaning of the final two lines of the poem: "he, as much as my mother, / giving me this life."

3. Families give us our first opportunity to learn how to relate to people of the opposite sex. Analyse the relationship between each brother and sister pair in the poem. Then write a cause-and-effect essay on how the brother–sister relationship, or another pairing in the family, is (or is not) a training ground for future male–female relationships. Refer to the poem's brother–sister relationships in your essay.

Connecting with Other Texts

1. This poem begins with an external reality, the sight of a paper boy and his sister, and moves to an internal reality, the narrator's memory of her brother. Write about the ways perception and memory interact in "Paper Boy." Then compare the perception and memory interaction in the poem with the similar interaction in Wallace Stegner's essay "In Search of Whitemud" (p. 160).

2. Consider how the character pairs in this poem, older brothers and younger sisters, behave toward each other. Would there be any differences if the sister were older and the brother were younger? Research the role birth order plays in families, and then write an essay in which you explain how birth order research would explain the familial relationships in "Paper Boy."

3. The section "The Gardens Within Us" in Lorna Crozier's book *Inventing the Hawk* contains other poems about family relationships. Read "Facts About My Father," "Repetitions for My Mother," and other poems in the section. Then write an essay on how this fictional family is and is not like other families.

Fathers, Sons and Hockey
Roy MacGregor

1 The relationship between fathers and sons is too complicated for language. Walt Disney once pointed out how few songs were written about fathers and then went back to work at his empire that portrayed fathers as essentially ineffectual, bumbling and usually absent. And British philosopher Bertrand Russell once said, "The fundamental defect of fathers is that they want their children to be a credit to them." Fathers can't help themselves, particularly when it comes to sports, even more particularly when it comes to *their* sport. "To show a child what has once delighted you," the British writer J.B. Priestley wrote, "to find the child's delight added to your own, so that there is now a double delight seen in the glow of trust and affection. This is happiness."

2   What makes the parent–child relationship special in hockey is necessity as much as anything else. The circumstances are simply different from those associated with most other North American sports. Ken Rappoport has covered all sports for the Associated Press out of New York City for more than three decades. He has also written nearly twenty books on sports, all of them aimed at a young audience, each of them concerned with team values and family values and personal values. An American, Rappoport long ago came to the conclusion that he liked the Canadian game best. Not so much because of the way it is played—though that, too, matters a great deal to him—but because of those who play it: their politeness, their manner, the values they carry. Ken Rappoport's theory is that it all has to do with family—usually Canadian families, so often small-town or rural families—and that hockey players have a need of family that is unmatched in any other team sport.

3   "They've got to make those 5 a.m. practices," says Rappoport. "Someone's got to make those drives. If there's no family support, they won't have the right equipment and they won't be able to afford to play the game. There has to be that family environment or they don't become hockey players."

4   Part of the story is, unfortunately, economic. The great players of the past—Maurice Richard, Gordie Howe, Bobby Orr, Guy Lafleur, even Wayne Gretzky—all came out of the working class where a happy combination of idle time and few other distractions produced the best and most creative players for generations. For some time now, hockey has been a sport that would, in all likelihood, be out of reach today for a Gordie Howe, if he were today growing up in Saskatoon in near poverty. The family of modern hockey too often means two parents, two cars, money for registration, money for equipment, money for ice time, tournaments, jackets, parties and snack bars.

5   And yet, in an odd way, perhaps it is precisely this deepening involvement that makes it even more a *family* sport in the 1990s than it was in the 1940s, when Gordie Howe was first enraptured by the game and stuck to it despite a father who had precious little involvement and thought his son "clumsy and backward and bashful."

6   It would be an impossible task to spend much time around the National Hockey League and not be aware that there exists something very special between sons who play this game for a living and their parents. Sports fans who move to Canada from other countries, the United States included, are often taken aback by the corny "Hockey Night in Canada" player interviews where the scarred, stitched-up, gap-toothed player seems to be forever asking, or being asked, if he could say hello to his folks back

home in Kamloops or Moose Jaw or Sudbury or Trois-Rivières. Each relationship is, obviously, entirely its own, but there are so many parallels in hockey that it is undeniable that there is something about fathers and sons and hockey worthy of examination.

7   Rarely has the father–son link been better described than in a diary goaltender John Tanner kept for journalist Robert Olver, who in 1989–90 was working on his book on junior hockey, *The Making of Champions*. Tanner recorded what he felt at the moment his team reached the Memorial Cup: "The feeling's great. You look up in the stands and Dad was there. I held up the trophy and just looked at him. That's the culmination of everything I've ever done, winning that trophy. And he's a part of it, just because he was there. I couldn't have been more happy. My uncle was there, friends were there, but I didn't see anyone in the stands except him."

8   If the young players gathered here today in the Hartford Civic Center were asked to identify their best friend, a surprising number would name the older man sitting beside them or directly behind them—their father. The total would be entirely out of proportion to any other gathering of eighteen-year-old males. Take an established NHL player aside and ask him about his goal scoring, his slump, his injuries, his team, and the answers will be short, polite but sometimes impatient, the ground being covered so familiar it is regarded as a slightly irritating detour between the dressing-room and the bus and the afternoon nap before the evening game. Ask an NHLer about his dad—even if those relationships were far removed from the sentimental—and the conversation might go on for days. The link between fathers and sons and hockey is so established, so significant among players, that at times it can take on absurd, even pathetic, tones. Members of the Montreal Canadiens of the mid-1980s still shake their heads over the insecure player who gave out cigars and bragged about his wife giving birth to their first son, when in fact it was a second daughter.

9   Such desperation is rare in hockey. Robert Bly, the American poet and author of *Iron John*, and the renowned advocate of such New Age notions as "male mothers" and the necessity of forced male bonding, would find little empathy in hockey circles. When Bly says, "One could say that the father now loses his son five minutes after birth," he does not speak to those men standing around the boards with their styrofoam cups of coffee at six o'clock in the morning. When he talks of the need for "ritual spaces" he does not know the hockey dressing-room. When he tells of group sessions where grown men gather to chant the words "Dad," "Father" and "Daddy" until they begin to cry, he should know that when Marty McSorley, the NHL's toughest player, arrived late to join Wayne Gretzky's

1994 European tour, he greeted his father, Bill, with a kiss.

10   Olga Silverstein and Beth Rashbaum wrote in their 1994 book, *The Courage to Raise Good Men*, that there exists in America a "cult of father hunger" and cited as proof such movies as *Field of Dreams*, *Star Wars*, *Indiana Jones* and *Hook*; they would find some, but surprisingly little, such hunger in hockey. Most élite hockey players, having been raised in a team-and-coach atmosphere since ages seven or eight and often having to leave home at fifteen or sixteen to play junior hockey, never did go through the traditional rebellion–separation–reconciliation that is the substance of the prototype father–son relation.

11   Perhaps it is because so many of them learned the game from their fathers. Perhaps because it was the father got them up, got them dressed, drove them to the rink, waited through the practices, argued with them, fought with them, comforted them, rationalized with them, believed in them or didn't believe in them, perhaps for these reasons the father–son relationship in hockey tends to have a different intensity than that of the player and his mother. Mothers tend generally to be worshipped by hockey players—and surely, are worthy of their own study. So often they have given undying support no matter what—no matter if the husband was challenging the very core of their child with his criticisms and with his own personal frustrations. It is, generally speaking, how "the home team" operates in hockey, and obviously in other endeavours in this huge and cold country. It is significant to note that a 1994 survey of twenty-two thousand thirteen- and sixteen-year-olds determined that Canadian teens idolize their parents far more than traditional sports and media heroes.

12   Hockey is a highly conservative sport, not given to change, not open to challenge. The traditions in hockey often lag behind the realities of society by decades. When most players talk of their mothers, it is of someone who was usually at home, waiting, always positive, supportive, quick with meals and comfort and applause. The image of 1950s television. Mothers might drive them, but fathers usually *drove* them—in as many different ways as there are sons playing this game. Sometimes, as in Brett Hull's case, the father didn't even need to be there to have the most profound effect on his son's career. To all this mothers have been witnesses, spectators, sometimes participants, but they know better than any that there are matters that come into play between a man, his boy and this game that is as much environment as it is invention.

13   Rappoport's observations are well founded. What other sport would dedicate a section of its Hall of Fame to the family living-room, a national shrine on a cold winter's Saturday night? Furniture and fashion may

change—the 1950s black-and-white TV may now be a full-colour giant-screen home entertainment centre—but the experience and values have a stronger link than that of tube to transistor. The Hockey Hall of Fame's Household Family Zone is as legitimate a display as Howie Morenz's skates.

Thinking about the Text

1. What is MacGregor's thesis?
2. Why does the American sports writer Ken Rappoport like Canadian hockey best? What specifically does he like about it?
3. According to MacGregor, why is there little "father hunger" in hockey?
4. How do hockey players tend to view their mothers? Why do they view their mothers this way?

Writing from the Text

1. Using examples from the text or from your own experience, write an essay in which you discuss the role of family in hockey today.
2. MacGregor cites the work of Ken Rappoport, whose books connect team values, family values, and personal values. What is the relationship between team sports and these three types of values? Write an essay in which you discuss the defining features of each of these types of values and show how they are related.
3. Do you agree with philosopher Bertrand Russell that fathers "want their children to be a credit to them," and that this wish is their "fundamental defect"? Are mothers less likely to want their children to be a credit to them? Write an essay in which you explore the issue of parents' expectations for their children, and the validity of such expectations. Use examples from your own experience as support.

Connecting with Other Texts

1. Both Roy MacGregor and David Evans, author of "What Do Men Want?" (p. 44) refer to the work of Robert Bly, a leading figure in the men's movement. Write an essay in which you relate MacGregor's and Evans's assessment of Bly's ideas about fathers and sons.
2. This passage ends with an image of a television set as a central feature in the family living room, and, by implication, as a central feature in family life. Using examples from "Fathers, Sons and Hockey" and Kenneth J. Harvey's "Life After Cable" (p. 188), write an essay discussing the role of television in family life.
3. Read Roy MacGregor's book The Home Team: Fathers, Sons and Hockey. Analyse other ways hockey has shaped families and write an essay on your findings.

The Phone Call
Joy C.

1 When I look into our photo albums, I often wonder at the innocence and trust apparent in my old photographs. How is it that the baby I was has become the person I am now? It almost seems pointless to ask. Looking at the dozens of photographs, I take note of what I look like: I have my father's hands and his smile, I have the broad powerful frame of both my parents. We are so alike, yet so different. Our similarities are only on the surface, and I think my parents may wonder where this daughter of theirs has come from. I can almost note to the day when I began to diverge from the path they expected of me, or rather, when they noticed that I was headed somewhere they could not follow. I was expected, like my brothers before me, to go to college where I would meet someone (of the opposite gender) to marry. However, by the time I was fifteen, I had realized that I would not be following in my brothers' footsteps, and at this point my parents began to notice that I was not communicating my hopes for the future.

2 Both my brothers moved away when I was little, and my mom, dad, younger sister, and I live in separate worlds, spheres actually, that occasionally intersect but rarely meet for long. Part of this is due to my independence; I resent asking for anything and rarely do, even when I desperately need help or advice. They did not understand my world, my path, and I did not want them to. Therefore, when I was thirteen I began to withdraw from my parents, stopped talking to them much, except about silly superficial things, like, "How was your day?" "Fine." That was my reply to nearly every question, except for the big one; the question that seemed to tear my entire world apart.

3 It was my junior year, and I had just turned sixteen in August. School had been in session for a couple of months, and, in general, my life was miserable. Everyone seemed on my back. My relationship with my parents became worse as I began to withdraw more and more. I was trying to drown myself in work in order to keep out of my head. I didn't mind the stress. As long as I didn't have to deal with myself I was okay. Then, as I was passing by the administration office between classes, the school secretary gave me a message. "Your Mom wants you to call, she says it's important." I didn't really think much about the message. I just figured that she wanted me to run to the store or go to the pharmacy, so when I got a chance I went over to the phone in the office. Standing there staring at

the spare, white phone, I suddenly got a strange feeling that this was really not a phone call that I wanted to make. The phone seemed to stare up at me threateningly. I steeled my nerves; it was just a phone call—no reason to worry. Slowly I reached for the phone and dialed. The ring of the phone was unnaturally loud, breaking the silence.

4   "Hello."

5   A slightly out of breath voice picked up on the other line.

6   "Hi Mom, it's me. They said you wanted me to call."

7   "I went into your room today." At that moment I wanted to sink into the brown carpet beneath me. Every square inch of my being longed to run as far away from that phone as possible. My hand clenched the bone-white receiver in a painful grip and I clung to the edge of the desk like a sailor clinging to a life raft. With that brief statement, I knew that what I had been trying to hide for so long was out. She knew. There was nothing I could do about it. Through my own carelessness I would never be able to face my parents again.

8   I keep journals obsessively. They help me organize my feelings. They are an outlet for everything I cannot say to anyone. With those words I knew that mom had done the unthinkable: she had read my thoughts. I glanced at the clock; "Mom, I have math. I really have to go. Please."

9   "No, I need to know something; when I went into your room to open the curtain, I found something, and I need to know if it's true." Her words were choppy and pained. Slowly I spoke.

10   "What?" The room seemed to be getting smaller, and my breath quickened as I clenched my fist and felt my fingernails dig into my palm. Everything seemed to spin about me as she read my own words back to me verbatim. I could vividly remember writing that page in my journal and at that moment I regretted ever laying pen to paper, ever living, ever breathing, ever thinking.

11   "It says here 'I'm a lesbian' and I want to know if that's true."

12   I released the breath that had turned stale in my lungs. Shakily I spoke into the receiver.

13   "Mom, I have class, I have to go." What could I say? I clenched my fist harder, rocking back and forth in my shoes.

14   "No, I need to know. No matter what I still love you." I could almost hear the tears in her voice and I, too, was close to the edge.

15   "No . . . Mom, I have to go, I'm on the school phone." I felt my voice grow firm as I struggled to regain control.

16   "Then why did you write it?"

17   "Mom, I have to go." Then, for the first time in my life, I hung up on her. Conversation over. Picking up my books I rushed out of the room, her words echoing again and again throughout my head, driving out thought of all else. As I looked out at the brilliant blue sky I felt so small, and the world outside seemed so big. It was a beautiful view that left no escape. I knew that I could not hide forever, and the rest of my life stretched out before me—a new era.

18   The next few weeks were hard on all of us as my mom searched for a concrete reason for my lesbianism. I was grounded for several months and sent to a psychiatrist in hopes that I would change. Because I was not prepared to come out to my parents, I was unable to explain to my mother that my sexuality was not anybody's fault. Several of our discussions dissolved into screaming matches as she accused me of tearing our family apart. My dad, on the other hand, pretended nothing had happened and refused to even say the word "lesbian." My parents did not want me to tell my sister or brothers, and I agreed because I was not ready to deal with their reactions.

19   Since the initial day of my mom's discovery, we've talked a lot, and now, more than a year and a half later, my mom still has difficulty accepting my sexuality. But, coming to terms with being out to my parents has taught me to respect the strength it takes to be myself when so many stand against me. Gradually I have learned to love and respect myself for the strengths I have. I never want to have to hide again.

20   Maybe someday my mom will be able to see me as my friends do: opinionated, verbose, feminist, bookworm, writer, philosopher, actress, and idealist who also happens to have a crush on Melissa Etheridge. Maybe someday she will realize that my lesbianism is just one part of a very complex whole—something that has contributed to my identity and broadened my horizons. Whether or not "someday" ever comes, I know that I have the strength to continue to be who I am. So, on the first day of the fall semester, listen for my contagious laugh and look for the rainbows I wear with pride.

Thinking about the Text

1. Consider Joy's comment about her parents: "They did not understand my world, my path, and I did not want them to" (paragraph 2). In what ways does Joy create a distance between herself and her family that may have blocked communication between them?

2. During the phone call, the author's mother tries to reassure Joy: "No matter what I still love you" (paragraph 14). However, what evidence does Joy give

that her parents are unable to extend that love to the point of accepting her lesbianism?

3. Was Joy ready to "come out" at the age of sixteen? Use details from the text to support your answer.

4. Comment on the lack of parallelism in the final paragraph. Why does faulty parallelism work in this context?

Writing from the Text

1. Write a narrative about a time that you feared a family member's response to some revelation about you—something you had done, a choice you made, or one of your beliefs or values. Show the responses to your revealing this truth.

2. Based on your own or a friend's experience in telling some important truth, argue for or against revealing the truth to others.

3. What can parents do to make it easier for their teens to talk to them about serious issues? Write a process essay advising parents of teenagers about the steps they can follow to improve the channels of communication between the two generations.

Connecting with Other Texts

1. Although Joy is apparently a member of a typical nuclear family, there are important differences between the public picture and the private reality. Discuss this discrepancy in light of Moira Farr's essay "Welcome to FamilyValuesWorld!" (p. 9).

2. What agencies or groups offer emotional support for gay and lesbian teens in your community? Research this topic and summarize the information on available resources in a short research essay. You may also wish to revise the format and submit the finished article to your school newspaper.

The Shackles of Everyday Lies

Anonymous

1   I'm trying to come out of the closet, but the door keeps closing in my face.

2   As a member in good standing of the establishment, I continue, amongst my peers anyway, to support values dear to their hearts. For the most part, I am in agreement with these values: honesty (except for fudging a little on tax returns and the like); fidelity (perhaps overlooking an

occasional dalliance, as long as it's discreet); generosity toward the less privileged (except unmarried mothers on welfare who brought it on themselves); and compassion (several of my acquaintances don a pink smock to volunteer their services in a hospital, providing they are not in contact with AIDS patients, who are in the same category as unmarried mothers).

3   The trouble is, I really hate cheaters, tax or marital; my sympathies lie with single mothers on welfare; I am desperately sorry for AIDS victims; and my son is gay.

4   For the record, he is in his mid-40s, tall, good-looking in a masculine way, athletic, successfully self-employed, funny, warm, kind-hearted to a fault, popular, and has lived quite happily with another man for the past 10 years.

5   His father and I, after experiencing the typical reaction of establishment parents ("How could you do this to me!"—Mother. "You could change if you want to"—Father), eventually came face to face with reality: love him or lose him. We chose the former.

6   His partner (I will call him Roger) is a familiar face at our dinner table, whether there is just the four of us, or whether our daughters, sons-in-law and grandchildren have joined us. Roger's presence is by now a given—he is a likable, trustworthy member of the family. The irony of the situation seldom occurs to me anymore.

7   So what, you may be thinking, is the lady's problem? Let me try to explain. Because of my husband's business, we entertain rather frequently—usually eight or so for dinner. Politics is a favourite topic, followed by local gossip—harmless enough as a rule. But then, all too often lately, the H-word is introduced. Someone at the table heard that so-and-so, the son of a well-known corporate head, is gay. Invariably, this leads to opinions piously delivered, a general expression of complacent satisfaction that this tragedy did not (could not?) happen to any of us present. Usually a gay joke or two follows, enjoyed by all, then the conversation shifts direction. Mercifully.

8   Do these people wonder about my son? I think not. I am adept at inventing plausible stories: He is pining for a lost love; he has a live-in girlfriend, a career woman whose business often takes her far afield; he recently ended a relationship of long standing; or his true love lives in another city. Variations on the theme are trotted out, depending on the circumstances. Whatever the story, a "mystery woman" is implanted in the minds of my guests. So far so good.

9   Perhaps I am being complacent. Perhaps a few of my acquaintances are in fact sceptical about my stories. But as some infamous character once

said: "Tell the same lie often enough and eventually everyone will believe it. Including the perpetrator."

10   Oh, I sometimes manage to emerge part way out of my closet. A family picture prominently displayed in my house includes a snapshot of Roger and my son, along with daughters and spouses and grandchildren. (My son put it there. When guests visit, I exchange it for one of my grandchildren.) And Roger recently attended an extended family get-together. Smiling, I made a point of introducing him to those he had not met. "Ben's (not his real name) friend, Roger" was how I put it.

11   The truth is, I secretly hated it when Roger came to this party, resented having to introduce him to cousins and worried inwardly that the absence of visible reaction was just good manners. But most of all, I hate the times when I sit calmly back while my guests exchange gay jokes, churning inside, yet joining in the laughter at the punch line. What makes it worse is that the hatred I feel is directed at myself.

12   I so want out of that closet. I want to introduce the real Ben to my acquaintances, my cousins, my friends. I want to say: "This is my beloved son, a gay man in whom I am well pleased." Perhaps one day soon I will. Until then, sign me Anonymous.

Thinking about the Text

1. What assumptions does the author make about social attitudes toward gays and lesbians?

2. Discuss the significance of the title. In what ways and to whom does the author lie? Give specific examples from the text. How do her lies become shackles?

3. Does membership in a "higher" social class mean tighter social constraints? Would the author have an easier time resolving her conflict if she were not "a member in good standing of the establishment"? Why or why not?

4. The author begins by saying, "I'm trying to come out of the closet, but the door keeps closing in my face." Who is closing this metaphorical door? What does the author reveal about her own character in this essay? How does the conclusion tie in with the introduction?

Writing from the Text

1. Does the author deserve sympathy or censure? Write an essay in which you argue your case, using examples from the text for support.

2. Write a companion essay from the author's son's point of view. What would Ben want his parents and friends to know about him? What would he have to say about his mother's attitude toward him?

Connecting with Other Texts

1. The authors of "The Shackles of Everyday Lies" and "The Phone Call" (p. 31) do not use their real names. Why not? Research mainstream newspaper and magazine coverage of gay and lesbian issues over the past year to see the proportion of positive and negative attitudes reflected there. Then write an essay arguing that Joy C. and Anonymous are wise (or unwise) in preserving their anonymity.

2. Several essays in this book explore the personal conflicts that arise from social constraints based on gender. Read Warren Farrell's "Men as Success Objects" (p. 50), Pam Withers's "The Babysitters Club: No Boys Allowed" (p. 54), Naomi Wolf's "The Beauty Myth" (p. 57), or Catherine Pigott's "Adding Weight to an Image of Beauty" (p. 152), and write an essay classifying gender-based social restrictions.

As a Dad, Will I Do Right by My Daughter?

Kerry Banks

1 My daughter's first word was "Da-Da." At least, that's how I remember it. Her mother, Anne, insists it was actually "dog." Whatever the true order, it was a thrill to hear her identify me by name. I think the bond between us grew a little closer at that moment. I know the weight of responsibility suddenly gained several pounds.

2 Riley is our first child and she is full of surprises. As she nears one year of age, we are amazed to discover how much she enjoys books, how quickly she can ransack a room and how deeply she is attached to the TV remote control. The first surprise, though, was her sex.

3 Both Anne and I come from families dominated by male progeny, and the odds seemed to suggest a son. When he turned out to be a she, it immediately struck me how little I knew about girls. With a son, I would be on familiar turf; I would instinctively know where he was heading and how he would feel when he got there. With a daughter, I would only be guessing. Each stage of her development would be a mystery to me.

4 Being a first-time parent is never easy, but I think it is especially tough for fathers these days. Our role is in flux. The "good provider" and "stern father" figures are as out of style as the hula hoop. Modern dads are expected to be more actively involved in child-rearing. We are supposed

to change more diapers, spend more time at home, be more sensitive and avoid gender stereotyping of our children at all costs.

5   Unfortunately, we have no role models on whom to base our behaviour. It is hard to feel confident when you are making things up as you go along. Pressured by society to be different from our own fathers and struggling to achieve domestic equilibrium with our wives, we cannot help but feel anxious. So, as I confronted the reality of having a daughter, I could only wonder: what sort of father was I going to be?

6   As I was mulling over this conundrum, a book entitled *Women and Their Fathers: The Sexual and Romantic Impact of the First Man in Your Life* came across my desk. Contrary to popular wisdom, the author, New York journalist Victoria Secunda, contends it is the father, not the mother, who has the more profound impact in shaping a daughter's self-image. According to Secunda, the way dad and daughter get along largely determines how the daughter will see herself as an adult, and what she will expect from men.

7   Secunda classifies fathers into categories—"templates for their daughters' future attachments," she calls them. Fathers are doting, distant, demanding, absent or seductive. She classifies daughters too. A particular type of father does not necessarily produce a single type of daughter, but the way the relationship plays out produces daughters who are favoured, good, competitive, fearful or maverick. As I read the sobering litany of the ways in which each father type can damage his daughter's psyche, little Riley began to assume the fragility of a package of gelignite. Did so much of what she would become really depend on me?

8   I began questioning women I knew about the impact of their fathers on their lives. Few of their relationships fit Secunda's categories precisely, but some patterns were evident. It was, for example, not difficult to find examples of the **distant father**—most of the women I spoke with had fathers who were remote in some way. But it was harder to correlate cause and effect. According to Secunda, distant fathers can produce a myriad of emotional consequences. Their daughters may or may not become sexually promiscuous, suffer from anorexia nervosa, be unable to achieve orgasm or marry men who don't notice them.

9   Sometimes, women raised by distant fathers deliberately seek out men who are diametrically different. Terrie Orr is a case in point. Orr, a soft-spoken but strong-willed 39-year-old Vancouver homemaker, says she has always been drawn to men with dynamic outgoing characters—men quite unlike her own father, who is a quiet, unemotional reserved man. Orr refers to her dad as an "armchair father." His main interest, she recalls, was

his job on the Canadian Pacific Railway. He occupied most of his leisure time with solitary pursuits, such as watching TV, doing carpentry and gardening. Orr says it was her effervescent mother who kept the family's five kids in line. "It was strange. Even though Dad was around a lot, you never had the feeling that he was really there."

10   Orr's most vivid memory of her father was one rare occasion when he stepped out of character. On Mother's Day, when Orr was 10, her father suggested that his wife sleep in as a treat while he took the kids out for a stroll in the woods near their home in Winnipeg. "We walked for two or three hours. I remember sunshine and open fields and laughing and skipping along. It was one of the only times he initiated something with the family."

11   Orr still finds her father an enigma, although she knows that her own reserved personality somewhat resembles his. Ironically, her relationship with her sales manager husband, Laurie Stein, is in some respects a mirror image of her own parents' merger of opposites. But, in this case, it is her husband who is the socializer.

12   Orr says that one of the things that attracted her to Laurie was his natural affinity for children: "He likes to play and fool around with our two boys and be naughty."

13   Orr's distant father does not sound much like me, but I do tend to be the introspective type. In fact, my wife does not hesitate to describe me as "moody." And truth be told, I exhibit other "distant father" danger signs— obsession with my work and a reluctance to discuss my feelings on personal subjects openly. Uptight, macho, WASP, self-obsessed: as I read Secunda's book, these psychological buzzwords began doing a noisy dance in my male psyche.

14   Maybe it's just self-justification, but I think some of the distance that exists between fathers and daughters is a product of our sexual blueprints. Men tend to deal with their emotions differently from women. It does not mean we do not have any. The challenge I will face with Riley is to make sure our differences never destroy the bonds between us.

15   At the other end of the emotional spectrum is the **doting father**—the daddy who makes everything all right. Annemarie Beard, 35, a stylish, sassy production manager with a Vancouver advertising firm, says she was "always the light in my father's eye." In sharp contrast to her two brothers, she was "spoiled and treated like a princess." Beard says her father, a chemical engineer, was always physically affectionate and ready to play. Only when she reached puberty did "the bubble burst," as her father began to pull away.

16   This is evidently a common reaction among fathers, according to Vancouver family therapist Mary Trokenberg. "As daddy's little girl grows into womanhood and becomes more sexually aware, many men don't know how to handle it. When men feel fragile and in doubt, they withdraw, and as a result, children feel abandoned."

17   Today, Annemarie Beard says the bond with her father has been restored. Yet, she admits that her early idealization of him had its consequences. "It took me a long time to grow up. I had to discover that not all men are like my father."

18   Author Secunda says many women with doting fathers are drawn to men who resemble their fathers—men who will protect them and keep them in the pampered style to which they are accustomed. Often, they tend to be older men. This is certainly true of Beard. "I had my first date at 15," she says. "He was 35." Today, she continues to feel most comfortable with older men. She likes their secure nature and the attentive manner in which they treat her. "Older men seem delighted just to have a younger woman around."

19   Doting and distant are polar opposites. Logically, therefore, I can't possibly be the doting type. So, why is it that Anne and I are already divided over the issue of protectiveness, which is one of the characteristics Secunda attributes to doting dads? I think Anne is too carefree with Riley; she feels I worry too much. And yet, how can I not worry? Our once benign household has suddenly become a nest of dangers—electrical outlets, open staircases, hot liquids, bottled poisons. So, if I am doting now, it is only for Riley's own good. This stage will surely pass. Once she is old enough to take care of herself, I will let her climb trees and play tackle football. Maybe.

20   Another of Secunda's archetypes, the **demanding father**, casts a dual-edged shadow over his daughter's life. Secunda says the best sort of demanding fathers are those who are stern but fair—they inspire confidence and ambition in their daughters. But when the sternness is not balanced by tenderness and support, daughters may be left with painful legacies.

21   Bonita Thompson, a vivacious, high-energy, 45-year-old Vancouver lawyer, traces much of what she has accomplished in life to her demanding father's influence. A chartered accountant, he was wrapped up in his career and spent little time with her three sisters and one brother. But Thompson forged a bond with him through sports. "From age 6 to 16, I was dad's caddie on the golf course. He taught me a sense of gentlemanly conduct, sportsmanship, ethics and setting high standards for yourself."

22   But some of his standards were impossibly high. "I'd bring home my

report card with an average of 94 percent, and he'd say, 'Why isn't it 100 percent?' He was joking, but there was a barb underneath it."

23 As far back as she can recall, Thompson always had a strong desire to achieve. Yet, even as her law career flourished, she sensed there was something lacking. "After each of my achievements, I'd feel empty." Eventually, Thompson realized that "all I had done in life was a continuing effort to elicit my father's praise."

24 Thompson's failed first marriage was to a man very similar to her father. Her current husband is the antithesis. "He's a free spirit, a warm, outgoing humorous person. And he's a bit of a rascal and a rule breaker. He's the nurturer in our family. He stayed home and raised our child."

25 The problem of fathers who are grudging with praise often surfaced in my conversations with women. I may be in dangerous waters here too. Neither of my parents expressed support easily, and it's going to be hard for me to break the mould.

26 The discussions with my female friends did little to relieve my angst. I kept seeing bits of my character reflected in the darker side of their fathers' images. As for Secunda's book, I was left wondering whether a healthy relationship between a father and a daughter is possible at all.

27 Mary Trokenberg, the therapist, helped me put it in perspective: "Some of the ways in which daughters develop has to do with their fathers, but not all. The danger with these sorts of self-help books is that people will think one-dimensionally. When you divide people into categories, you lose the nuances and fail to see other possibilities."

28 This makes sense to me. While I will undoubtedly have a major influence on Riley, I suspect her view of men will also be shaped by what she sees in the relationship between my wife and me, and in her mother's attitudes toward men generally.

29 As for being distant, doting or demanding, I will try to keep my conflicting impulses in balance. Like any new parent, I have hopes. I want Riley to be an independent thinker, confident and creative. I want her to be a woman who is involved in the world, a woman who likes men and who can tell a joke. Most of all, I want her to be happy.

30 I don't know yet how I will deal with the familiar crises of fatherhood, such as when Riley begins dating boys with green hair and nose rings. But there is time to learn, and I will need to trust my instincts. For now, I am content simply to share the extraordinary discoveries of Riley's young life—her awe at seeing the night stars for the first time, the giddy tingle of walking barefoot on a freshly mown lawn, the magical spell of a street musician's guitar. For now, just being Da-Da is enough.

Thinking about the Text

1. What are the main differences between the three types of fathers Banks describes?

2. What anxieties does Banks have about being a good father? What hopes does he have for his daughter? Are these anxieties and hopes common to all fathers? Why or why not?

3. Do you agree with Victoria Secunda's contention, paraphrased in this essay, that it is the father who has more input than the mother in shaping his daughter's self-image? Why or why not?

4. Are there any inherent dangers in classifying fathers the way Banks does in this essay? Does classification oversimplify or help us better understand complex family relationships?

Writing from the Text

1. The term "bonding" describes the intense attachment a newborn baby and its mother form shortly after birth. However, bonding can extend into childhood, when children form strong attachments to their parents. Write an essay describing the activities either or both of your parents undertook to ensure that you formed strong attachments to them. If your parents were not able to make such efforts, what would you like to do with your own children to foster bonding?

2. Write an essay parallelling this one in which you discuss the mother–son or mother–daughter relationship and classify three types of mothers.

3. Banks says: "Men tend to deal with their emotions differently from women" (paragraph 14). Compare and contrast the ways men and women deal with their emotions, using examples from your own experience. Suggest what complications in parenting these gender differences might create.

Connecting with Other Texts

1. Both Banks and David Evans in "What Do Men Want?" (p. 44) allude to the interconnections between masculinity and fatherhood. Describe the role models Banks's and Evans's fathers presented to their sons. In what ways have our role expectations for fathers changed since these two authors were boys? Would Evans say that Banks has compromised his masculinity by expressing his anxieties? Why or why not?

2. Banks confesses that he may have trouble giving praise to his daughter because "neither of [his] parents expressed support easily." In an essay, compare the concept of how difficult it is "to break the mould" as it is discussed in this essay and in Moira Farr's "Welcome to FamilyValuesWorld!" (p. 9).

3. Look in current magazines geared toward parents (such as *Today's Parent*) for articles on fathers as nurturers. What programs or courses are available to help men become nurturing fathers?

CHAPTER 2
Between Genders

As you can imagine, if women and men were completely satisfied with their lives, this chapter of readings probably would be quite different. Essays would show that gender conflicts were issues of the past, poems would celebrate gender equality, and memoirs would attest to universal self-acceptance.

But as the work in this chapter reveals, many lives are still riddled with tensions related to gender. The women's movements of the last four decades have helped to identify and address these tensions, and the men's movement of the last decade has raised questions that also disturb the status quo. Some individuals embrace this disturbance, others fear it, and many feel caught in between. You and your friends may be in the process of exploring or resolving some of the same gender issues that the writers in this chapter discuss.

The writers here show how social conditioning about gender affects both men and women. David Evans reflects on current developments in the men's movement and the possibility for change, while Warren Farrell analyses the burden placed on men to be "success objects." In her essay, Pam Withers discusses the messages men and boys receive about their trustworthiness as caregivers to children.

Clearly, women do not escape the effects of social conditioning either. Naomi Wolf outlines specific myths that keep women confined and Brenda Austin-Smith criticizes the sexism inherent in technology in general and the Internet in particular. Robyn Sarah's poem details the numbing reality of a homemaker's life. These writers question the messages that women receive about gender and gender roles, and the limitations such messages establish.

Finally, three writers explore pressures that can affect men and women equally. Lauren Griffin questions the necessity of turning every skirmish between men and women into a full-scale battle. The impact of AIDS on young people's sexuality is at issue in John DeMont's report; the impact of disfigurement on a couple's relationship is the subject of Andrew Pyper's short story.

You will find these writers addressing problems that you may also have considered. You undoubtedly have found that gender problems are central concerns, showing up in such diverse places as the lyrics of popular music and the feature articles of newspapers and magazines. These authors re-examine gender roles, expose myths, and pose solutions that may help both sexes reach accord between genders.

What Do Men Want?

David Evans

1 On a brilliant weekend in early fall, I flew to Indianapolis, Indiana, to learn about being a man. The flight was uneventful. I mention this because uneventful flights have always been important to my understanding of what it means to be a man. When I was younger, my father, who was in business, would periodically fly off to places like Kansas City, Missouri, Pittsburgh, Pennsylvania, or Indianapolis. Upon his return, my mother would ask him how his flight had been, and my father would always reply, "Oh, uneventful." Somehow, this word struck me as terribly manly. I used to practise it alone in my room. "Un-e-*vent*-ful."

2   Since growing up, I have discovered that my father is actually a nervous flier. When he said that his flight was uneventful, he didn't mean that he'd slept or read all the way. He meant that none of the engines had fallen off in midflight. With my father's knees clamped together and his fingers strangling both armrests, the plane had defied gravity long enough to bring him home. The flight had been uneventful: Nothing Had Gone Wrong.

3   Unlike my father, I am a fairly relaxed flier. And I was flying to Indianapolis because, in the minds of thousands of North American men, something has gone terribly wrong. The definition of what it means to be a man has been changing, almost as fast as the idea of what it means to be a woman, and the result has been universal confusion. Some 200 men were gathering in Indianapolis to try to sort it all out.

4   This men's "gathering" was to be supervised by Robert Bly, undeclared leader of what has come to be known as the Mythopoetic Men's Movement. When I'd first heard about the meeting, I figured that the main topic of conversation would be women and the aftershocks of the feminist revolution. But on the plane, I browsed through some of Robert Bly's

books and realized that, at least according to him, the problem went deeper than that.

5   It seemed to have a lot to do with the example a generation of fathers had set for their sons in terms of being a man. The problem was that we had believed our fathers when they said flights were uneventful, when they said that everything was all right at work, that they were "fine." Our fathers never mentioned the turbulence over the Alleghenies, or being passed over for promotion twice in a row, or that sometimes, lying awake at night and watching the headlights sweep across the ceiling, they knew they'd made a hash of things.

6   In fact, they'd hardly said much of anything. And now that we were grown up, we'd call home, and if our fathers answered the phone, after "Hello" they'd tend to say, "Did you want to speak to your mother?"

7   Now, thousands of middle- and working-class men were finding their fathers' silence maddening enough to flock to gatherings like the Indianapolis conference. The week before, Robert Bly had met 90 men in the woods north of Minneapolis; the week after, he was to be somewhere else again. Meanwhile, an energetic "being a man" cottage industry was pumping out Bly's books, magazines and cassettes. He has been featured in *The New York Times Magazine* and interviewed by broadcaster Bill Moyers. He is, you might say, on a roll.

8   Bly is an unlikely role model for North American males. Competing with Arnold Schwarzenegger, Clint Eastwood and Sylvester Stallone, Bly is the 98-pound weakling, albeit a 98-pound weakling with heavy credentials. Bly is a poet: as a young man, he was a fixture of the civil rights and antiwar movements; in 1968, he won the National Book Award for his book of poems entitled *The Light Around the Body*. In the decades since, he has turned out volume after volume of accomplished verse, earning himself a place among the best American poets of his generation. But somewhere along the line, Bly crossed from the literary to the sociological; readers became followers; and followers became a movement—a movement of men.

9   Suddenly, men who normally wouldn't be caught dead reading poetry were snapping up Bly's manly verse, subscribing to newspapers and magazines with titles like *Wingspan*, and forking out $220 plus to travel to "gatherings" like the Indianapolis weekend.

10   While shorter than most (two days instead of three or four) and smaller than most (200 men, not 400), in most aspects, the Indianapolis gathering was typical. Upon our arrival at a suburban theatre centre, we were urged down a dimly lit corridor to emerge in an auditorium through a

gauntlet of whooping, grunting, drumming savages. Not savages, actually—most of these members of the Indianapolis Men's Gathering Steering Committee were (like the rest of us) accountants and lawyers and salesmen. But there they were flailing wildly at bongos and tambourines to set the tone, to bring out a little of the primitive in us, to replace the silence of our fathers with the exuberance of the wild.

11   We new arrivals leapt easily, if self-consciously, into the spirit of the thing, prancing and capering into our plush seats, where we spent most of the weekend listening to Bly and a procession of other speakers offering up testaments to parental abuse, fatherly neglect and emotional uncertainty. Uncertainty, above all.

12   Just 50 years ago, a man's home was his castle, and women were his handmaids. Then, everything changed. There were women on the assembly line and in the corner office. Tolerance and mildness replaced violence and bluster as hallmarks of the ideal woman's ideal man. At first, many men were compliant, hanging their heads at Betty Friedan's accusations of a domineering patriarchy and muttering "guilty" before falling on their nine irons. Later, some men became angry. Hostile hard-eyed guys, who'd lost a child-custody battle or two, formed a "men's rights" movement to fight what they saw as a rising tide of castrating women.

13   Today, some men are trying to find a new identity, not in opposition to the feminist movement but (they claim) parallel to it. And the first task is self-discovery.

14   Modern men, Bly told us, have learned about life—learned how to be men—from their mothers. When our fathers came home from work, they were tired shadowy figures whom we never learned to know and whom we have never forgiven for their distance.

15   The result: we have never learned how to have close trusting relationships with other men. Our fathers never initiated us into manhood, as older men in traditional cultures do, and even though our women have recently taught us to express some of our more "feminine" feelings, we still have a mass of uniquely "masculine" feelings buried deep inside us waiting to be released.

16   These are the desires of what Bly calls the "wild man" who sleeps inside every man—the strong man who takes forceful action "not with cruelty but with resolve" to "protect the earth," to strive "for the infinite," to court "the woman at the edge of the world," to find "the treasure at the bottom of the sea."

17   To awaken the wild man inside us, Bly told us, we must tap the stories of more primitive men. But first, we must resolve our problems with

our fathers.

18   A pretty young man with long blond hair stood in the audience, uninvited, and began to talk. At first, his voice was too soft to be heard a few rows away.

19   "Speak up, speak up," came the calls from around the auditorium.

20   He sighed, looked around and began again. "I was molested by my mother when I was a child," he said simply. Both his parents had been alcoholics. His father had done nothing to stop the abuse.

21   It had taken many years, but the young man had finally confronted his father about his passivity. "I was just so damned angry with him," the young man told us through gritted teeth. Suddenly, he was sobbing, swaying on his feet, and the room was very quiet.

22   Then, off in a far corner, someone started thumping a drum. Soon, the whole room was shaking with stamping feet and wild cheering. The young man looked up, startled at first, and then, his face changed to pride. On behalf of us all, he had joined the battle.

23   Throughout it all, Bly sat in an ornate wing chair onstage, as befits the elder of the tribe, wearing a flowered vest and white trousers, white hair spilling over his shoulders. He recited poetry. He told folk fairy tales embellished by pop sociology. Across his knees, he cradled a stringed instrument that he played purposefully, if not musically, between verses of poetry.

24   During breaks, we'd head outside to a nearby football field. There, arranged in a huge ragged circle, we swayed awkwardly to drum rhythms. It was a beautiful fall day in middle America, perfect for throwing the ball around or doing a little hunting. But our eyes were fixed on Bly, who patrolled the inside of the circle, bouncing and shifting on his toes like a cat on a wet floor.

25   Every now and then, he'd click the castanet in his right hand. Then, he'd lift his head and cry out the name of an animal.

26   "Lion!"

27   Four hundred hands shot into the air, fingers curled like claws. Growling from deep in our throats, we stalked inward, rolling and menacing to the beat in lion imitations that would be the pride of *Romper Room*. As we crowded together, the growling and drumming reached a deafening crescendo. Then, we turned and retreated, still lion-like, to the perimeter, where we allowed ourselves a few minutes of clapping and whooping in congratulation before Bly called "Snake!" and in we went again.

28   Before lunch hour was out, we'd also perform as kangaroos, eagles and horses.

29   As the weekend wore on, through obscure diagrams of The Four

Components of the Male Psyche (the warrior, the lover, the magician and the king), through manly diets of fried chicken and fried bread (no quiche here), through the midnight screening of *The Great Santini*, I couldn't help thinking that my father would have hated every minute. Sitting in the back, listening to the umpteenth middle-aged man congratulate himself on forgiving his father, I realized that when my father had told us his flight had been uneventful, he hadn't been lying to us but merely protecting his wife and kids from unnecessary fears. His stoicism had been an acceptance of what he saw as his burden as a man—to make everything seem easier for his family than it really was.

30   On the other hand, these men seemed determined to make their lives more complicated than they really were. Like schoolyard bullies, they wanted you to be impressed by their emotional scars, to reach out and touch them, to marvel at how they didn't flinch from scrutiny.

31   Take Dennis, for example. A white sweater set off his perma-tan; between his linen pants and his Italian slip-ons, two telltale blue polo players adorned his socks. Dennis is a very wealthy man, he was glad to tell me as we chatted in the dying moments of the gathering, but that "doesn't mean shit" to him anymore. Now, he was ready to "re-evaluate his life from the bottom up." More important, he was determined to tell me about it.

32   It happened this way: a month ago, Dennis left his wife for the mistress he'd been seeing for a couple of years. At the time, it seemed like the right thing to do, he says, but then, without warning, the mistress dumped him. Dennis seemed upset not so much by the loss of either woman as dumbfounded that something like this could happen to him, something he hadn't planned. A friend suggested he join a local men's group and immediately things began to look up. He got in contact with his wife, although he hung on to his own apartment for the moment, and they have a "rejuvenated relationship" now. "She is truly my best friend," he said proudly.

33   "And your mistress?" I asked.

34   "She's out of the picture," he said.

35   "What does your wife say about that now?" I asked.

36   Dennis looked shocked. He glanced around the room, perhaps trying to discern why, among this convention of the self-obsessed, he'd picked the one guy who didn't get it. "She doesn't know about her!" he hissed. "I could never tell her. She would *kill* me." He strode off to buy a drum.

37   On the flight back to Toronto, it took me a long time to straighten out my feelings about the dancing and the drumming and the fairy tales. And about Dennis. I wondered whether Bly's disciples, and their sons, would

turn out to be very different from their fathers. They put a lot of energy into their thumping and whooping and sharing, but where will it get them? Are they really interested in changing the way they are—or just in feeling better about the way they are?

38   Back home, my girlfriend looked up from her paper as I set down my bags, and asked: "How was your trip?"

39   "Oh, you know," I said. "Uneventful."

Thinking about the Text

1. What does men's movement leader Robert Bly believe are the key characteristics of the "wild man"? According to Bly, what are the four components of the male psyche?

2. Compare and contrast the effect the gathering had on the "pretty young man with long blond hair" with that on Dennis, the man described at the end of the essay. How significant are the differences between the two reactions?

3. Discuss Evans's tone. What is his attitude toward his topic? Give concrete examples from the text to support your assertion.

Writing from the Text

1. Using specific details from "What Do Men Want?" write an essay comparing Evans's description of manhood as it was defined 50 years ago, Robert Bly's version, and your own version. Do you agree that the definition of what it means to be a man today is changing so fast that the result is "universal confusion"? Why or why not?

2. Consider the question in Evans's title: What *do* men want? Write an essay in which you focus on and develop the specific issues.

3. What do women really want in men? Does the answer to this question vary according to the age of the people involved? Write an essay in which you focus on and develop the specific qualities.

Connecting with Other Texts

1. Using details from Evans's essay as well as from Warren Farrell's "Men as Success Objects" (p. 50) and Kerry Banks's "As a Dad, Will I Do Right by My Daughter?" (p. 37), write about the pressures on a male to find an identity of his own.

2. Argue that men should (or should not) join the men's movement and give specific support for your argument from "What Do Men Want?" and Warren Farrell's essay "Men as Success Objects" (p. 50).

Men as Success Objects

Warren Farrell

1 For thousands of years, marriages were about economic security and survival. Let's call this Stage I in our culture's conception of marriage. Beginning in the 1950s, marriages became focused on personal fulfillment and we entered into the era of the Stage II relationship. In Stage II, love was redefined to include listening to each other, joint parenting, sexual fulfillment, and shared decision making. As a result, many traditional marriages consummated in Stage I failed under the new Stage II expectations. Thus we had the great surge of divorces beginning in the '60s.

2   The increasing incidence of divorce altered the fundamental relationship between women, men, and the workplace. Before divorce became common, most women's income came from men, so discrimination in favor of a woman's husband benefited her. But, as the divorce rate mushroomed, the same discrimination often hurt her. Before divorce became a common expectation, we had two types of inequality—women's experience of unequal rights in the workplace and men's experience of unequal responsibility for succeeding in the workplace. To find a woman to love him, a man had to "make his mark" in the world. As women increasingly had to provide for themselves economically, we confined our examination of inequality between the sexes to inequality in the workplace. What was ignored was the effect of inequality in the homeplace. Also ignored was a man's feeling that no woman would love him if he volunteered to be a full-time househusband instead of a full-time provider. As a result, we falsely assumed that the experience of inequality was confined to women.

3   Because divorces led to a change in the pressures on women (should she *become* a doctor, marry a doctor, or have a career and marry a doctor?), that change became "news" and her new juggling act got attention in the media. Because the underlying pressures on men did not change (women still married men who earned more than they did), the pressure on men to succeed did not change, and, therefore, received no attention. With all the focus on discrimination against women, few understood the sexism directed against men.

4 The feminist perspective on relationships has become like fluoride in water—we drink it without being aware of its presence. The complaints about men, the idea that "men are jerks," have become so integrated into our unconscious that even advertisers have caught on. After analyzing

1,000 commercials in 1987, researcher Fred Hayward found that when an ad called for a negative portrayal in a male–female interaction, an astonishing 100 percent of the time the "bad guy" was the man.

5   This anti-male bias isn't confined to TV commercials. A sampling of the cards in the "Love and Friendship" section of a greeting card store revealed these gems:

6   "If they can send one man to the moon, why can't they send them all?"

7   "When you unzip a man's pants . . . his brains fall out."

8   "If we can make penicillin out of moldy cheese . . . maybe we can make men out of the low-lifes in this town."

9   A visit to the bookstore turns up titles like *No Good Men. Imagine No Good Women* or *No Good Jews*. And what do the following titles have in common? *Men Who Can't Love*; *Men Who Hate Women and the Women Who Love Them*; *Smart Women/Foolish Choices*; *Successful Women, Angry Men*; *Peter Pan Syndrome*.

10   Feminism-as-fluoride has left us acknowledging the working mother ("Superwoman") without even being aware of the working father. It is by now well recognized that, even among men who do more housework or more childcare than their wives, almost never does the man truly share the 24-hour-a-day psychological responsibility of ministering to everyone's needs, egos, and schedules.

11   But it is not so widely recognized that, despite the impact feminism has had on the contemporary family, almost every father still retains 24-hour-a-day psychological responsibility for the family's financial well-being. Even women who earn more than their husbands tell me that they know their husbands would support their decision to earn as much or as little as they wish. If a woman marries a successful man, then she knows she will have an option to work or not, but not an obligation. Almost all men see bringing home a healthy salary as an obligation, not an option.

12   A woman today has three options:

> *Option 1:* Full-time career.
> *Option 2:* Full-time family.
> *Option 3:* Some combination of career and family.

13   A man sees himself as having three "slightly different" options:

> *Option 1:* Work full time.
> *Option 2:* Work full time.
> *Option 3:* Work full time.

14   The U.S. Bureau of the Census explains that full-time working males

work an average of eight hours more per week on their jobs than full-time working females.

15   Since many women now earn substantial incomes, doesn't this relieve the pressure on men to be a wallet? No. Why? Because successful women do exactly what less-successful women do—"marry up," that is, marry a man whose income is greater than her own. According to statistics, if a woman cannot marry up or marry someone with a high wage-earning potential, she does not marry at all. Therefore, a man often reflexively backs away from a woman he's attracted to when he discovers she's more successful than he is because he senses he's only setting himself up for rejection. Ultimately, she'll dump him for a more successful man. She may sleep with him, or live with him, but not marry him unless she spots "potential." Thus, of top female executives, 85 percent don't get married; the remaining 15 percent almost all marry up. Even successful women have not relaxed the pressure on men to succeed.

16 Ask a girl in junior high or high school about the boy whom she would "absolutely love" to ask her out to the prom and chances are almost 100 percent that she would tell you her fantasy boy is *both* good-looking *and* successful (a jock or student leader, or someone who "has potential"). Ask a boy whom he would absolutely love to ask out to the prom and chances are almost 100 percent his fantasy girl is good-looking. Only about 25 per-cent will also be interested in a girl's "strong career potential" (or her being a top female jock). His invisible curriculum, then, taught him that being good-looking is not enough to attract a good-looking girl—he must be suc-cessful *in addition* to being good-looking. This was his experience of inequality: "Good-looking boy does not equal good-looking girl." Why are boys willing to consider themselves unequal to girls' attention until they hit their heads against 21 other boys on a football field?

17   In part, the answer is because boys are addicted. In all cultures, boys are addicted to the images of beautiful women. And in American culture this is enormously magnified. Boys are exposed to the images of beautiful women about 10 million times per year via television, billboards, maga-zines, etc. In the process, the naturally beautiful girl becomes a *genetic celebrity*. Boys become addicted to the image of the quasi-anorexic female. To be the equal of this genetic celebrity, the adolescent boy must become an *earned celebrity* (by performing, paying on dates, etc.). Until he is an earned celebrity, he feels like a groupie trying to get a celebrity's attention.

18   Is there an invisible curriculum for girls and boys growing up? Yes. For girls, "If you want to have your choice among boys, you had better be beautiful." For boys, it's "You had better be handsome *and* successful." If

a boy wants a romantic relationship with a girl he must not only be successful and perform, he must pay and pursue—risk sexual rejection. Girls think of the three Ps—performing, paying, and pursuing—as male power. Boys see the three Ps as what they must do to earn their way to female love and sexuality. They see these not as power, but as compensations for powerlessness. This is the adolescent male's experience of inequality.

Thinking about the Text

1. How do Farrell's historical descriptions of marriage relate to the point of his essay? What is the cause-and-effect relationship that he describes?

2. What inequalities does Farrell perceive for both sexes, and how are the inequalities relevant to the men's movement? What is Farrell's thesis?

3. According to Farrell, how are men depicted in popular culture? What has the culture failed to address?

4. How do men's and women's "options" for making a living compare? Do you agree with Farrell's perceptions? What is the "invisible curriculum" (paragraph 16)? Does he overlook anything in his reasoning?

5. How does each sex's perceptions of a desirable date influence the perception of power or powerlessness that each sex has?

Writing from the Text

1. Interview male and female acquaintances of your age to see if adults' views of the desirable date or mate are consistent with the views Farrell cites for junior-high and high-school students. Write an essay to present your views.

2. Who has more options in the dating/mating and work worlds—women or men? Support your assertion with specific examples.

3. A psychological/sociological study that was done twenty years ago determined that, generally, women felt limited by what they were *allowed* to do and men felt limited by what they felt *required* to do. After discussing this perception with friends, write an essay to show what the sexes feel today.

4. Paragraphs 6–8 in this essay cite some examples of politically *in*correct humour. Write an essay in which you discuss whether this type of humour is offensive or harmless fun.

Connecting with Other Texts

1. Write an analysis of the "invisible curriculum" for women and men using the work of current feminist writers and Farrell's books (such as *Why Men Are the Way They Are* and *The Myth of Male Power*) to support your points.

2. Do some research on the men's movement to learn about the main grievances of the men, such as Warren Farrell and Robert Bly, who are involved in it. Discuss and evaluate the movement and its goals.

The Babysitters Club: No Boys Allowed

Pam Withers

1 With the sweet innocence only a seven-year-old can muster, my son recently asked me to hire a male rather than female babysitter for his after-school child care.

2 "I can try, but I don't think I'll be able to find one," I said.

3 To the inevitable "Why not?" I fumbled for a way to weave gently between three truths: that males are considered potential pedophiles, that males are considered inadequate at child care, and that child-care wages are so low that most males find better things to do.

4 The "inadequate" label he already knows to be untrue, for he enjoys a special relationship with his dedicated and nurturing father, who has changed his diapers, fed him, played with him and guided his social growth at least as much as I have, from birth. His special bond with Dad is undoubtedly the key to his request in the first place. Besides, at age 7, his priorities are well formed: soccer, basketball and computer games. Already, he knows such interests are shared primarily by males, although his favourite female babysitter is a bona-fide enthusiast of all three.

5 The "pervert" issue is, for me, more troubling. Let's face it: males don't apply in great numbers to child-care programs for the simple reason that widespread suspicion of their motives chokes the opportunity for employment—never mind the poor wages, potential ridicule, and cold-shoulder treatment on the part of child-care teaching programs.

6 Very few of my friends will hire the teenaged sons of their best friends for an evening out, never mind strangers for full-time positions. One says she'd consider doing so if she had a son, but absolutely not for her daughter. The assumption that boys are not at risk is foolhardy. One study indicates that more pedophiles prey on boys than girls (50 percent prey on boys, 30 percent on girls and 20 percent on both).

7 Although another reports that one in two girls and one in three boys are abused, JoAnne Fahr, program co-ordinator of the Red Cross Child Abuse Prevention Program for Adults in Vancouver, says the discrepancy is most likely explained by under-reportage on the part of boys.

8 Another friend with two boys admits there is irony in the inadvertent message she's giving her sons by never hiring males, but due to a "bad experience" in her own childhood, she would never consider a male babysitter. Although I'm in full sympathy with her feelings and support her right to make such a decision, her comment reminds me of a male friend

who once hired a female manager who didn't work out. Feeling justified in having tried, he refuses to hire a female manager again.

9   In the babysitting co-op to which my husband and I belong—where we were screened before acceptance, and where members are all parents and neighbours—several members routinely request "female only" sitters. One explained, "I think it's reasonable if they're babies." Why? Because men are presumed unable to change diapers? (Surely those with diaper or baby phobia will decline that job anyway.)

10   Or because babies can't report abuse, and all males are guilty until proven innocent (and females vice versa)?

11   Another explained to me, "I think my children would freak out if a man babysat them." To which I respond: Do they freak out when their father spends time with them—or doesn't he? And have they ever been given the chance to not freak out, to experience one of those unusual men who happen to be good with children, and doesn't abuse that role?

12   While I salute the freedom of every parent to make a "female babysitters only" decision, I worry about the implications of large numbers tilting to this bias. Since more males than females sexually abuse children (90 percent are said to be male, although Ms. Fahr warns that little research has been done on female offenders), and since checking references is hard work and no guarantee of safety, it's easier to hire females only.

13   But by turning our backs on male babysitters—those who have a talent for relating well to children, whose motives are honest, whose records are clean and who are willing to apply—we are broadcasting two dangerous messages to three generations of males, including our husbands, teenaged boys and young sons: All males have perverted sexual urges that they cannot be expected to control. All males lack the skills required for child care. These messages work against society's need for more nurturing fathers, who could use some early training, never mind the need to break down rigid stereotyping.

14   The statistics are sobering, but nowhere do they indicate that hiring females only, or protecting girls more than boys, is the answer. Just because most pedophiles are male does not mean that most males are pedophiles. Ms. Fahr says only a "minute" number of males abuse children.

15   In fact, statistically speaking, babysitters are hardly a concern; in 97 percent of reported cases of physical abuse, parents are the perpetrators. Surely, boycotting male babysitters is a poor substitute for carefully screening a caregiver of any gender, "people proofing" children old enough to talk, and listening hard when they express dislike of an individual.

16   In my son's request, I see hope: He trusts and values male companionship, without subscribing to stereotypes that would stunt his own growth as a male who happens to relate well to younger children. In fact, he eagerly aspires to babysit when he's a teen. I hope someone will hire him with all the trust he deserves.

Thinking about the Text

1. What reasons does Withers give her son to explain the shortage of male babysitters?

2. Why does Withers comment that "all males are guilty until proven innocent (and females vice versa)" (paragraph 10)? What evidence does she give in the essay that parents are biased against male babysitters?

3. How does the author support her views that hiring only females as caregivers or "protecting girls more than boys" will not solve the problem of child abuse? List examples from the text.

Writing from the Text

1. When parents hire female babysitters exclusively, are they also reinforcing gender stereotypes? Why or why not? Write an essay on gender stereotyping and include examples from this essay or from your own experience.

2. What can men do to change perceptions that all men "have perverted sexual urges that they cannot be expected to control" (paragraph 13)? Propose a solution to the problem of such misperceptions.

Connecting with Other Texts

1. In his essay "Men as Success Objects" (p. 50), Warren Farrell notes that men are often maliciously depicted in popular culture. Besides greeting cards and self-help books, where else are men or fathers maligned that would lead parents to mistrust male babysitters? Write an essay describing the specific examples you cite and proposing reform or discussing the consequences.

2. Withers writes that her husband is a "dedicated and nurturing father" (paragraph 4). Do you agree with Withers that *society* will also benefit from more nurturing fathers? Use some of the fathers mentioned in readings in this book to support your thesis.

The Beauty Myth

Naomi Wolf

1 At last, after a long silence, women took to the streets. In the two decades of radical action that followed the rebirth of feminism in the early 1970s, Western women gained legal and reproductive rights, pursued higher education, entered the trades and the professions, and overturned ancient and revered beliefs about their social role. A generation on, do women feel free?

2 The affluent, educated, liberated women of the First World, who can enjoy freedoms unavailable to any women ever before, do not feel as free as they want to. And they can no longer restrict to the subconscious their sense that this lack of freedom has something to do with—with apparently frivolous issues, things that really should not matter. Many are ashamed to admit that such trivial concerns—to do with physical appearance, bodies, faces, hair, clothes—matter so much. But in spite of shame, guilt, and denial, more and more women are wondering if it isn't that they are entirely neurotic and alone but rather that something important is indeed at stake that has to do with the relationship between female liberation and female beauty.

3 The more legal and material hindrances women have broken through, the more strictly and heavily and cruelly images of female beauty have come to weigh upon us. Many women sense that women's collective progress has stalled; compared with the heady momentum of earlier days, there is a dispiriting climate of confusion, division, cynicism, and above all, exhaustion. After years of much struggle and little recognition, many older women feel burned out; after years of taking its light for granted, many younger women show little interest in touching new fire to the torch.

4 During the past decade, women breached the power structure; meanwhile, eating disorders rose exponentially and cosmetic surgery became the fastest-growing medical specialty. During the past five years, consumer spending doubled, pornography became the main media category, ahead of legitimate films and records combined, and thirty-three thousand American women told researchers that they would rather lose ten to fifteen pounds than achieve any other goal. More women have more money and power and scope and legal recognition than we have ever had before; but in terms of how we feel about ourselves *physically*, we may actually be worse off than our unliberated grandmothers. Recent research consistently shows that inside the majority of the West's controlled, attractive,

successful working women, there is a secret "underlife" poisoning our freedom; infused with notions of beauty, it is a dark vein of self-hatred, physical obsessions, terror of aging, and dread of lost control.

5   It is no accident that so many potentially powerful women feel this way. We are in the midst of a violent backlash against feminism that uses images of female beauty as a political weapon against women's advancement: the beauty myth. It is the modern version of a social reflex that has been in force since the Industrial Revolution. As women released themselves from the feminine mystique of domesticity, the beauty myth took over its lost ground, expanding as it waned to carry on its work of social control.

6   The contemporary backlash is so violent because the ideology of beauty is the last one remaining of the old feminine ideologies that still has the power to control those women whom second wave feminism would have otherwise made relatively uncontrollable: It has grown stronger to take over the work of social coercion that myths about motherhood, domesticity, chastity, and passivity, no longer can manage. It is seeking right now to undo psychologically and covertly all the good things that feminism did for women materially and overtly.

7   This counterforce is operating to checkmate the inheritance of feminism on every level in the lives of Western women. Feminism gave us laws against job discrimination based on gender; immediately case law evolved in Britain and the United States that institutionalized job discrimination based on women's appearances. Patriarchal religion declined; new religious dogma, using some of the mind-altering techniques of older cults and sects, arose around age and weight to functionally supplant traditional ritual. Feminists, inspired by Friedan, broke the stranglehold on the women's popular press of advertisers for household products, who were promoting the feminine mystique; at once, the diet and skin care industries became the new cultural censors of women's intellectual space, and because of their pressure, the gaunt, youthful model supplanted the happy housewife as the arbiter of successful womanhood. The sexual revolution promoted the discovery of female sexuality; "beauty pornography"— which for the first time in women's history artificially links a commodified "beauty" directly and explicitly to sexuality—invaded the mainstream to undermine women's new and vulnerable sense of sexual self-worth. Reproductive rights gave Western women control over our own bodies; the weight of fashion models plummeted to 23 percent below that of ordinary women, eating disorders rose exponentially, and a mass neurosis was promoted that used food and weight to strip women of that sense of

control. Women insisted on politicizing health; new technologies of invasive, potentially deadly "cosmetic" surgeries developed apace to re-exert old forms of medical control of women.

8   Every generation since about 1830 has had to fight its version of the beauty myth. "It is very little to me," said the suffragist Lucy Stone in 1855, "to have the right to vote, to own property, etcetera, if I may not keep my body, and its uses, in my absolute right." Eighty years later, after women had won the vote, and the first wave of the organized women's movement had subsided, Virginia Woolf wrote that it would still be decades before women could tell the truth about their bodies. In 1962, Betty Friedan quoted a young woman trapped in the Feminine Mystique: "Lately, I look in the mirror, and I'm so afraid I'm going to look like my mother." Eight years after that, heralding the cataclysmic second wave of feminism, Germaine Greer described "the Stereotype": "To her belongs all that is beautiful, even the very word beauty itself . . . she is a doll . . . I'm sick of the masquerade." In spite of the great revolution of the second wave, we are not exempt. Now we can look out over ruined barricades: A revolution has come upon us and changed everything in its path, enough time has passed since then for babies to have grown into women, but there still remains a final right not fully claimed.

9   The beauty myth tells a story: The quality called "beauty" objectively and universally exists. Women must want to embody it and men must want to possess women who embody it. This embodiment is an imperative for women and not for men, which situation is necessary and natural because it is biological, sexual, and evolutionary: Strong men battle for beautiful women, and beautiful women are more reproductively successful. Women's beauty must correlate to their fertility, and since this system is based on sexual selection, it is inevitable and changeless.

10   None of this is true. "Beauty" is a currency system like the gold standard. Like any economy, it is determined by politics, and in the modern age in the West it is the last, best belief system that keeps male dominance intact. In assigning value to women in a vertical hierarchy according to a culturally imposed physical standard, it is an expression of power relations in which women must unnaturally compete for resources that men have appropriated for themselves.

11   "Beauty" is not universal or changeless, though the West pretends that all ideals of female beauty stem from one Platonic Ideal Woman; the Maori admire a fat vulva, and the Padung, droopy breasts. Nor is "beauty" a function of evolution: Its ideals change at a pace far more rapid than that of the evolution of species, and Charles Darwin was himself unconvinced by

his own explanation that "beauty" resulted from a "sexual selection" that deviated from the rule of natural selection; for women to compete with women through "beauty" is a reversal of the way in which natural selection affects all other mammals. Anthropology has overturned the notion that females must be "beautiful" to be selected to mate: Evelyn Reed, Elaine Morgan, and others have dismissed sociobiological assertions of innate male polygamy and female monogamy. Female higher primates are the sexual initiators; not only do they seek out and enjoy sex with many partners, but "every nonpregnant female takes her turn at being the most desirable of all her troop. And that cycle keeps turning as long as she lives." The inflamed pink sexual organs of primates are often cited by male sociobiologists as analogous to human arrangements relating to female "beauty," when in fact that is a universal, nonhierarchical female primate characteristic.

12   Nor has the beauty myth always been this way. Though the pairing of the older rich men with young, "beautiful" women is taken to be somehow inevitable, in the matriarchal Goddess religions that dominated the Mediterranean from about 25,000 B.C.E. to about 700 B.C.E., the situation was reversed: "In every culture, the Goddess has many lovers. . . . The clear pattern is of an older woman with a beautiful but expendable youth—Ishtar and Tammuz, Venus and Adonis, Cybele and Attis, Isis and Osiris . . . their only function the service of the divine 'womb.'" Nor is it something only women do and only men watch: Among the Nigerian Wodaabes, the women hold economic power and the tribe is obsessed with male beauty; Wodaabe men spend hours together in elaborate make-up sessions, and compete—provocatively painted and dressed, with swaying hips and seductive expressions—in beauty contests judged by women. There is no legitimate historical or biological justification for the beauty myth; what it is doing to women today is a result of nothing more exalted than the need of today's power structure, economy, and culture to mount a counteroffensive against women.

13   If the beauty myth is not based on evolution, sex, gender, aesthetics, or God, on what is it based? It claims to be about intimacy and sex and life, a celebration of women. It is actually composed of emotional distance, politics, finance, and sexual repression. The beauty myth is not about women at all. It is about men's institutions and institutional power.

14   The qualities that a given period calls beautiful in women are merely symbols of the female behavior that that period considers desirable: *The beauty myth is always actually prescribing behavior and not appearance.* Competition between women has been made part of the myth so that

women will be divided from one another. Youth and (until recently) virginity have been "beautiful" in women since they stand for experiential and sexual ignorance. Aging in women is "unbeautiful" since women grow more powerful with time, and since the links between generations of women must always be newly broken: Older women fear young ones, young women fear old, and the beauty myth truncates for all the female life span. Most urgently, women's identity must be premised upon our "beauty" so that we will remain vulnerable to outside approval, carrying the vital sensitive organ of self-esteem exposed to the air.

15   Though there has, of course, been a beauty myth in some form for as long as there has been patriarchy, the beauty myth in its modern form is a fairly recent invention. The myth flourishes when material constraints on women are dangerously loosened. Before the Industrial Revolution, the average woman could not have had the same feelings about "beauty" that modern women do who experience the myth as continual comparison to a mass-disseminated physical ideal. Before the development of technologies of mass production—daguerreotypes, photographs, etc.—an ordinary woman was exposed to few such images outside the Church. Since the family was a productive unit and women's work complemented men's, the value of women who were not aristocrats or prostitutes lay in their work skills, economic shrewdness, physical strength, and fertility. Physical attraction, obviously, played its part; but "beauty" as we understand it was not, for ordinary women, a serious issue in the marriage marketplace. The beauty myth in its modern form gained ground after the upheavals of industrialization, as the work unit of the family was destroyed, and urbanization and the emerging factory system demanded what social engineers of the time termed the "separate sphere" of domesticity, which supported the new labor category of the "breadwinner" who left home for the workplace during the day. The middle class expanded, the standards of living and of literacy rose, the size of families shrank; a new class of literate, idle women developed, on whose submission to enforced domesticity the evolving system of industrial capitalism depended. Most of our assumptions about the way women have always thought about "beauty" date from no earlier than the 1830s, when the cult of domesticity was first consolidated and the beauty index invented.

16   For the first time new technologies could reproduce—in fashion plates, daguerreotypes, tintypes, and rotogravures—images of how women should look. In the 1840s the first nude photographs of prostitutes were taken; advertisements using images of "beautiful" women first appeared in mid-century. Copies of classical artworks, postcards of society

beauties and royal mistresses, Currier and Ives prints, and porcelain figurines flooded the separate sphere to which middle-class women were
confined.

17   Since the Industrial Revolution, middle-class Western women have
been controlled by ideals and stereotypes as much as by material constraints. This situation, unique to this group, means that analyses that trace
"cultural conspiracies" are uniquely plausible in relation to them. The rise
of the beauty myth was just one of several emerging social fictions that
masqueraded as natural components of the feminine sphere, the better to
enclose those women inside it. Other such fictions arose contemporane-
ously: a version of childhood that required continual maternal supervision;
a concept of female biology that required middle-class women to act out
the roles of hysterics and hypochondriacs; a conviction that respectable
women were sexually anesthetic; and a definition of women's work that
occupied them with repetitive, time-consuming, and painstaking tasks
such as needlepoint and lacemaking. All such Victorian inventions as these
served a double function—that is, though they were encouraged as a
means to expend female energy and intelligence in harmless ways, women
often used them to express genuine creativity and passion.

18   But in spite of middle-class women's creativity with fashion and
embroidery and child rearing, and, a century later, with the role of the suburban housewife that devolved from these social fictions, the fictions' main
purpose was served: During a century and a half of unprecedented feminist agitation, they effectively counteracted middle-class women's dangerous new leisure, literacy, and relative freedom from material constraints.

19   Though these time- and mind-consuming fictions about women's natural role adapted themselves to resurface in the post-war Feminine
Mystique, when the second wave of the women's movement took apart
what women's magazines had portrayed as the "romance," "science," and
"adventure" of homemaking and suburban family life, they temporarily
failed. The cloying domestic fiction of "togetherness" lost its meaning and
middle-class women walked out of their front doors in masses.

20   So the fictions simply transformed themselves once more: Since the
women's movement had successfully taken apart most other necessary fictions of femininity, all the work of social control once spread out over the
whole network of these fictions had to be reassigned to the only strand
left intact, which action consequently strengthened it a hundredfold. This
reimposed onto liberated women's faces and bodies all the limitations,
taboos, and punishments of the repressive laws, religious injunctions and
reproductive enslavement that no longer carried sufficient force.

Inexhaustible but ephemeral beauty work took over from inexhaustible but ephemeral housework. As the economy, law, religion, sexual mores, education, and culture were forcibly opened up to include women more fairly, a private reality colonized female consciousness. By using ideas about "beauty," it reconstructed an alternative female world with its own laws, economy, religion, sexuality, education, and culture, each element as repressive as any that had gone before.

21   Since middle-class Western women can best be weakened psychologically now that we are stronger materially, the beauty myth, as it has resurfaced in the last generation, has had to draw on more technological sophistication and reactionary fervor than ever before. The modern arsenal of the myth is a dissemination of millions of images of the current ideal; although this barrage is generally seen as a collective sexual fantasy, there is in fact little that is sexual about it. It is summoned out of political fear on the part of male-dominated institutions threatened by women's freedom, and it exploits female guilt and apprehension about our own liberation—latent fears that we might be going too far. This frantic aggregation of imagery is a collective reactionary hallucination willed into being by both men and women stunned and disoriented by the rapidity with which gender relations have been transformed: a bulwark of reassurance against the flood of change. The mass depiction of the modern woman as a "beauty" is a contradiction: Where modern women are growing, moving, and expressing their individuality, as the myth has it, "beauty" is by definition inert, timeless, and generic. That this hallucination is necessary and deliberate is evident in the way "beauty" so directly contradicts women's real situation.

22   And the unconscious hallucination grows ever more influential and pervasive because of what is now conscious market manipulation: powerful industries—the $33-billion-a-year diet industry, the $20-billion cosmetics industry, the $300-million cosmetic surgery industry, and the $7-billion pornography industry—have arisen from the capital made out of unconscious anxieties, and are in turn able, through their influence on mass culture, to use, stimulate, and reinforce the hallucination in a rising economic spiral.

23   This is not a conspiracy theory; it doesn't have to be. Societies tell themselves necessary fictions in the same way that individuals and families do. Henrik Ibsen called them "vital lies," and psychologist Daniel Goleman describes them working the same way on the social level that they do within families: "The collusion is maintained by directing attention away from the fearsome fact, or by repackaging its meaning in an

acceptable format." The costs of these social blind spots, he writes, are destructive communal illusions. Possibilities for women have become so open-ended that they threaten to destabilize the institutions on which a male-dominated culture has depended, and a collective panic reaction on the part of both sexes has forced a demand for counterimages.

24   The resulting hallucination materializes, for women, as something all too real. No longer just an idea, it becomes three-dimensional, incorporating within itself how women live and how they do not live: It becomes the Iron Maiden. The original Iron Maiden was a medieval German instrument of torture, a body-shaped casket painted with the limbs and features of a lovely, smiling young woman. The unlucky victim was slowly enclosed inside her; the lid fell shut to immobilize the victim, who died either of starvation or, less cruelly, of the metal spikes embedded in her interior. The modern hallucination in which women are trapped or trap themselves is similarly rigid, cruel, and euphemistically painted. Contemporary culture directs attention to imagery of the Iron Maiden, while censoring real women's faces and bodies.

25   Why does the social order feel the need to defend itself by evading the fact of real women, our faces and voices and bodies, and reducing the meaning of women to these formulaic and endlessly reproduced "beautiful" images? Though unconscious personal anxieties can be a powerful force in the creation of a vital lie, economic necessity practically guarantees it. An economy that depends on slavery needs to promote images of slaves that "justify" the institution of slavery. Western economies are absolutely dependent now on the continued underpayment of women. An ideology that makes women feel "worth less" was urgently needed to counteract the way feminism had begun to make us feel worth more. This does not require a conspiracy; merely an atmosphere. The contemporary economy depends right now on the representation of women within the beauty myth. Economist John Kenneth Galbraith offers an economic explanation for "the persistence of the view of homemaking as a 'higher calling'": the concept of women as naturally trapped within the Feminine Mystique, he feels, "has been forced on us by popular sociology, by magazines, and by fiction to disguise the fact that woman in her role of consumer has been essential to the development of our industrial society. . . . Behavior that is essential for economic reasons is transformed into a social virtue." As soon as a woman's primary social value could no longer be defined as the attainment of virtuous domesticity, the beauty myth redefined it as the attainment of virtuous beauty. It did so to substitute both a new consumer imperative and a new justification for economic unfairness

in the workplace where the old ones had lost their hold over newly liberated women.

26   Another hallucination arose to accompany that of the Iron Maiden: The caricature of the Ugly Feminist was resurrected to dog the steps of the women's movement. The caricature is unoriginal; it was coined to ridicule the feminists of the nineteenth century. Lucy Stone herself, whom supporters saw as "a prototype of womanly grace . . . fresh and fair as the morning," was derided by detractors with "the usual report" about Victorian feminists: "a big masculine woman, wearing boots, smoking a cigar, swearing like a trooper." As Betty Friedan put it presciently in 1960, even before the savage revamping of that old caricature: "The unpleasant image of feminists today resembles less the feminists themselves than the image fostered by the interests who so bitterly opposed the vote for women in state after state." Thirty years on, her conclusion is more true than ever: That resurrected caricature, which sought to punish women for their public acts by going after their private sense of self, became the paradigm for new limits placed on aspiring women everywhere. After the success of the women's movement's second wave, the beauty myth was perfected to checkmate power at every level in individual women's lives. The modern neuroses of life in the female body spread to woman after woman at epidemic rates. The myth is undermining—slowly, imperceptibly, without our being aware of the real forces of erosion—the ground women have gained through long, hard, honorable struggle.

27   The beauty myth of the present is more insidious than any mystique of femininity yet: A century ago, Nora slammed the door of the doll's house; a generation ago, women turned their backs on the consumer heaven of the isolated multiapplianced home; but where women are trapped today, there is no door to slam. The contemporary ravages of the beauty backlash are destroying women physically and depleting us psychologically. If we are to free ourselves from the dead weight that has once again been made out of femaleness, it is not ballots or lobbyists or placards that women will need first; it is a new way to see.

Thinking about the Text

1.   According to Wolf, what prevents apparently liberated women from feeling free?

2.   In this introductory chapter of her book *The Beauty Myth*, Wolf juxtaposes gains for women in the last decades of the twentieth century with specific problems that mitigate the triumphs for women. What are the problems, and to what does she attribute their existence?

3. How does Wolf defend her assertion that "'beauty' is not universal or changeless" (paragraph 11)? Think of additional examples from your own experience or awareness of anthropology, history, or art to support her point.

4. Why is the beauty myth a "fairly recent invention" (paragraph 15)?

5. What is the original Iron Maiden? How is Wolf using the term?

6. What does Wolf believe will be the only way for women to free themselves from the insidious myth?

Writing from the Text

1. Have you or your friends experienced any of the pressures to believe in the beauty myth? Compare your experiences with Wolf's examples in this reading.

2. Discuss Wolf's assertion: "The beauty myth is not about women at all. It is about men's institutions and institutional power" (paragraph 13). Use examples from this reading and your own experience in your essay.

3. What will be the "new way to see" that will liberate women from the beauty myth? Write an analysis of the problems facing women today, and propose a reform.

Connecting with Other Texts

1. Take any one of the issues Wolf discusses, such as eating disorders, cosmetic surgery, the economics of beauty, or pornography, and write your own researched analysis of that topic. You will find information in Wolf's book *The Beauty Myth*, as well as in popular periodicals.

2. Compare the problems that faced women in your mother's or grandmothers' generation with those facing women in your own time. Research the corresponding "waves" of feminism at the time, or interview representatives of the two older generations, in order to write this paper.

The Internet and Gender

Brenda Austin-Smith

With attention focused on the impact of computing and other technologies on daily life, the phrase "information super-highway" now dominates public descriptions of the phenomenon created when two or more computers are connected for the purposes of communication.

*But the Internet is not a neutral asphalt construction,
and the use of highway language to describe it obscures its
very real social dimension. . . .*

1 Considered as a social arena or forum rather than a highway, the Internet is an electronic space in which people using computers gather to send and receive information as varied as recipes, articles, virtual movies, erotica, and Seinfeld trivia. In the social field of the Internet, as in all other social areas, however, power is exchanged along with information. Who has access to that information and that power, how is it distributed or made accessible, and in what kind of virtual world or society does it circulate?

2   As the Internet grows and changes, answers to these questions will also change. At present, though, the world of the Internet is a male-dominated one, and many of its elements partake of the sexism of the real world in which it was originally designed as a military communications system. Only 20–30 percent of Internet users are women. This is not all that surprising, given that in this culture, men rather than women are associated with machines and technology, and men rather than women are encouraged to explore and "master" technology.

3   Women are not physically prevented from gaining access to computers and so entering the Internet. But what they often find there is an electronic culture so saturated with what real-world culture defines as "masculinity" that the experience is discouraging in the extreme.

4   Besides the comparison of the Internet to a superhighway, itself an example of defining the net in terms of men's stereotypical attachment to and identification with cars, there is the way in which netters interact. "Newbies," or newcomers to the net, are especially vulnerable to hazing by more experienced netters, as if the net were a college fraternity requiring an initiation. And any verbal exchange of opinion on the net runs the risk of igniting a "flame war": torrents of insult and abuse flung from one netter to another. This sort of verbal aggressiveness is difficult for many women who use the net to stomach, as the real world is already a place where language is used violently against women. Nor are most women socialized to joust verbally with others, particularly men, for some kind of social dominance.

5   Women who enter the net, say to participate in a newsgroup discussion, often find that as soon as they identify themselves as female, they are immediately sexualized by other users. It's as if a woman had walked into a smoky men's bar, and conversation stops as all heads turn in her direction. Women are subject to unwanted attention of a specifically sexual

nature, such as requests for phone numbers and dates. And as with the real world, so with the virtual one: women have found themselves "stalked" electronically by netters who find out who they are from their signature on the net, follow them from group to group, or harass them through e-mail.

6   All this is not to claim that the Internet is essentially "male" in some biological way, or that women can't hope to become equal users of the system. But the culture of the Internet is not at present very woman-friendly. Change must come not only from women becoming more of a presence on the net, but from the male users who currently dominate it.

7   Redefining the Internet as a public space where you don't need to drive fast in order to fit in would be a good first step.

Thinking about the Text

1. What evidence does Austin-Smith give to support her argument that the Internet is sexist?

2. Do you agree that in North American culture men, not women, "are associated with machines and technology, and . . . are encouraged to explore and 'master' technology" (paragraph 2)? Why or why not?

3. The issue of access to technology is an important one. What other barriers to access to technology, besides sexism, can you think of?

Writing from the Text

1. Austin-Smith outlines a problem with current technology. In an essay, summarize her position and propose possible solutions.

2. If you have used the Internet, do you agree or disagree with Austin-Smith's bar metaphor? Is the Internet a "social arena" where "power is exchanged along with information"? Write a persuasive essay on the nature of gender power as it presents itself on the Internet.

3. Write a persuasive essay in which you argue the contrary position, that the Internet is as neutral a medium as a telephone or television.

Connecting with Other Texts

1. Using both print and electronic sources (including the Internet), research the issue of technology, gender, and power. Has much been written on the subject? Summarize your findings.

2. Write a research essay on ways women are putting their own stamp on technology. Search as wide a range of print and electronic sources as possible.

Maintenance

Robyn Sarah

Sometimes the best I can do
is homemade soup, or a patch on the knee
of the baby's overalls.
Things you couldn't call poems.
5 Things that spread in the head,
that swallow
whole afternoons, weigh down the week
till the elastic's gone right out of it—
so gone
10 it doesn't even snap when it breaks.
And one spent week's
just like the shapeless bag
of another. Monthsful of them,
with new ones rolling in and
15 filling up with the same junk: toys
under the bed, eggplant slices sweating
on the breadboard, the washing machine
spewing suds into the toilet, socks
drying on the radiator and falling down
20 behind it where the dust lies furry and
full of itself . . . The dust!
what I could tell you about
the dust. How it eats things—
pencils, caps from ballpoint pens,
25 plastic sheep, alphabet blocks.
How it spins cocoons
around them, clumps up and
smothers whatever strays into
its reaches—buttons,
30 pennies, marbles—and then
how it lifts, all of a piece,
dust-pelts
thick as the best velvet
on the bottom of the mop.

35   Sometimes
        the best that I can do
        is maintenance: the eaten
        replaced by the soon-to-be-eaten, the raw
        by the cooked, the spilled-on
40 by the washed and dried, the ripped
        by the mended; empty cartons
        heaved down the cellar stairs, the
        cans stacked on the ledge, debris
        sealed up in the monstrous snot-green bags
45 for the garbage man.

        And I'll tell you what
        they don't usually tell you: there's no
        poetry in it. There's no poetry
        in scraping concrete off the high chair tray
50 with a bent kitchen knife, or fishing
        with broomhandle behind the fridge
        for a lodged ball. None in the sink
        that's always full, concealing its cargo
        of crockery under a head
55 of greasy suds. Maybe you've heard
        that there are compensations? That, too's
        a myth. It doesn't work that way.
        The planes are separate. Even if there are
        moments each day that take you by the heart
60 and shake the dance back into it, that you lost
        the beat of, somewhere years behind—even if
        in the clear eye of such a moment you catch
        a glimpse of the only thing worth looking for—
        to call this compensation, is to demean.
65 The planes are separate. And it's the
        other one, the one called maintenance,
        I mostly am shouting about.
        I mean the day-to-day,
        that bogs the mind, voice, hands
70 with things you couldn't call poems.
        I mean the thread that breaks.
        The dust between
        typewriter keys.

Thinking about the Text

1. Who are "they" (line 47)? What myths have "they" perpetrated? Who or what is demeaned by these myths?

2. Who is the speaker in this poem? How would you describe the speaker's tone? Explain whether the speaker is actually "shouting" or not (line 67).

3. What are the two separate planes the speaker is talking about?

4. What motivates the speaker to tell us about her life? Is anything about her life going to change?

Writing from the Text

1. Write an essay about the domestic images in "Maintenance." How do these images contribute to the poem's tone and the theme of being caught between worlds?

2. Discuss the levels of significance of the word "maintenance" in this poem. Exactly what things, customs, or values are being maintained, and by whom?

3. Is there any irony in the narrator's claim that there is no poetry in the mundane events of everyday life, given that this claim is in a poem on that very topic? Use examples from the text as support.

Connecting with Other Texts

1. Naomi Wolf writes in "The Beauty Myth" (p. 57) that, over the years, "the gaunt, youthful model supplanted the happy housewife as the arbiter of successful womanhood" (paragraph 7). Write an essay in which you discuss the ways "Maintenance" and Pamela Erens's essay "Bodily Harm" (p. 155) question idealized concepts of successful womanhood.

2. Relate the ideas underlying "Maintenance" to those in "Welcome to FamilyValuesWorld!" (p. 9).

3. Write an essay discussing "women's work" as it is presented in "Maintenance" and Yeshim Ternar's short story "Ajax Là-Bas" (p. 110).

Making Big Deals out of Little Deals

Lauren Griffin

1 Joe is a flirt. The first time I met him he was driving a truck as big and loud as he was, with his reflector sunglasses, imposing frame and baseball cap emblazoned with the logo of a heavy diesel equipment company. If I had had any qualms about moving up north, it was because I imagined I would end up meeting men like Joe.

2   In a small town, people like Joe have no hesitation about inviting themselves over to see what the new people in town are up to. In our first months in the country, we were up to our necks in trouble: broken well pumps, failing car brakes, rabid fox scares and chimney fires. The day Joe's big double-wheeled pickup truck pulled up in the yard, the problem was the roof. It was in a sorry state and we were trying to tear off the old roof while putting the new one on. Rain was on the way. I was not in the mood for visitors. He heaved his big frame out of the truck. "How'ya doing gorgeous?" he asked. "Is your old man around?"

3   Sixteen years earlier I had come of age in the thick of the WAVAW (Women Against Violence Against Women) movement. The week I turned eighteen I took my first shift on a twenty-four-hour Rape Crisis line. I was so apprehensive I spent the night sleeping on the floor by the phone in my parents' hallway. For five years I attended more night marches, rallies and conferences than I can remember. I did direct action. I discussed the negative implications of marriage, heterosexuality, male violence and even sexual penetration. When I met Charlie, who would become my husband, I was still wearing my "Don't Call Me Girl" button.

4   And now here I was, face to face with this guy who looked like he belonged far south of the Mason–Dixon Line and was doing the "little lady" routine with me. I wasn't quite sure what to do. Maybe because I was so surprised, maybe because he was so casual about it all, I was caught off guard. I had no speedy comeback. So I called the "old man."

5   Joe began by asking Charlie why he hadn't rigged up scaffolding and made a few jabs about "city boys." Then out of the bulky box of his pickup he began to haul ropes, bits of scaffolding and various indecipherable gadgets. Adjusting his three-inch-wide suspender straps, he took command of the situation. For the next three days, Joe hauled cartons of shingles up the side of our two-storey home, barked orders like a boot-camp sergeant, and fed us a steady stream of his famous barroom brawl stories. After three days we had a brand-new roof and I felt as if I had been inside every

cheesy bar along the Tijuana border.

6   As casually as he first invited himself onto our roof, Joe has invited himself into our lives. There have been days when the sound of that truck clanging into my driveway causes me to cringe, but often on those days he's dropping off some raspberry plants or some beets for my goats. It all comes out in the wash.

7   Over the years it has become clear that Joe doesn't come by just to bring me raspberry plants. He comes by because he is a relentless, and at times boorish, flirt. He craves the company of women, which takes him to my place or to the Tim Horton's on the highway with its bevy of waitresses. Like many men he is drawn to women because women make life more interesting and colourful. At times I have to get him back in line, and he always goes. Seen in the big scheme of things, his old-fashioned compliments and low-level flirtations aren't such unbearable things.

8   The other day I heard him telling my husband about an incident at the local adult education centre that had been set up to handle unemployed miners like Joe. He saw one of the teachers in the hall and greeted her with the greeting he uses on every woman he meets: "How'ya doing gorgeous?" Her response wasn't friendly. She passed him a pamphlet on sexual harassment. "Lady," he said "Look at me. I'm bald, I'm fat and I'm ugly, and I'm not about to become politically correct now."

9   When I heard him tell this story, I thought of how I would have once championed the woman's action. It was the powerless speaking out against the powerful. Men must be reminded that only a thin line separates the flirt from the rapist and the rapist from Marc Lepine. Only I don't think I believe that any more.

10   What I've learned from knowing Joe is that perhaps too much time and effort go into making big deals out of little deals. We are losing the casual distance and sparring that have always given men and women room to be with each other and yet separate. To be sure, the battle between the sexes has a long history, but never before has it been subjected to this degree of scrutiny and discussion. And to such little result. The estrangement remains, and sex war has become entrenched.

11   We are losing the everyday ways in which men can feel good about meeting women and vice versa. Women, sensing that righteousness is on their side, feel quite comfortable wielding a big stick. Men like Joe are often rapidly put back in their place, pegged as sexists and hung out to dry. On the other hand, men who feel threatened by the fast pace of social change can strike out with the same old putdowns at women who are the least likely to fight back. And so it goes.

12   Couples have waged domestic warfare since time immemorial. The difference is that the disputes are now charged with the sexual politics of the day. Unpleasant words like exploitation and misogyny have entered domestic vocabulary. Instead of couples co-operating, they see a long-term relationship as being a competition of needs. In the very sphere where we most need to be forgiving and loving, we are encouraged to be exacting and uncompromising.

13   The private realm, the space of tenderness, vulnerabilities and fragile intimacies, needs to be preserved. We all need a place to let down our guard with one another, and we all need to believe that the men and women in our lives enjoy us. In *The Culture of Narcissism*, Christopher Lasch provided an alternative view to the resolution of hostilities between the sexes: "The abolition of sexual tension is an unworthy goal in any case; the point is to live with them more gracefully than we have lived with them in the past."

Thinking about the Text

1. Describe Griffin's initial stereotype of "men like Joe." How did her perception change over time?

2. Is Joe one of "the powerful" (paragraph 9)? Why or why not?

3. Griffin notes that women's righteous actions can sometimes backfire. Explain how this can happen, giving examples from the text or from your own experience.

4. In your opinion, what kinds of male comments or behaviour are harmless flirtations? When do these actions become harassment?

5. Suggest some ways men and women can learn to live together more gracefully.

Writing from the Text

1. Is Griffin's statement that women "feel quite comfortable wielding a big stick" (paragraph 11) accurate? Argue that many women still feel uncomfortable speaking up for themselves. You may want to discuss their dependence on their more self-assured "sisters" to raise the public's consciousness about gender issues.

2. Write a narrative about a similar gender conflict you have experienced. Describe a time someone made inappropriate comments to you and explain how you handled the situation. Or write about a time your "politically incorrect" behaviour toward a member of the opposite sex met with hostility. As a class, exchange narratives and discuss if, and how, perceptions of social dynamics can differ between men and women.

Connecting with Other Texts

1. Today sexual harassment claims have become a media topic. Increasingly, women *and* men are daring to admit that they are being or have been sexually harassed. Research the history of charges of sexual harassment. Focus your paper on the changes in public consciousness and use specific examples from the reported cases to support your analysis.

2. Based on the arguments in this essay, would you expect Griffin to say that Brenda Austin-Smith, in "The Internet and Gender" (p. 66), is making "a big deal out of a little deal"? Write an essay in which you discuss this possibility and then explain your position on the issue of where to draw the line in gender issues.

Love and Fear in the Age of AIDS

John DeMont

1 The car speeds west along the Trans-Canada Highway as snowflakes swirl from an aluminum-coloured sky. "The worst thing is going home," Trudy Parsons says, huddled in the front passenger's seat, wearing a baggy men's overcoat. As the car nears Bay Roberts, the Newfoundland outport 100 kilometres west of St. John's where she spent her teen years, Parsons, now 22, recalls the wave of panic she felt when she returned to her old high school a year ago. There, in a crowded classroom, her voice quavered as she warned teenagers about the dangers of HIV, which is believed to cause acquired immune deficiency syndrome (AIDS); Parsons tested positive for the virus in November, 1991. Now, with another room full of students waiting at her old school, her anxiety again deepens. "I grew up with these people," says Parsons, who works full time for the Newfoundland AIDS Committee. "My family lives out there—and I fear that they will be judged because of a mistake that I made."

2 The place happens to be Bay Roberts, but it could be anywhere. From Newfoundland to British Columbia, Canadian teenagers are struggling with the urgent issue of how to conduct their lives in the shadow of AIDS, and assorted counsellors are warning: with utmost care. In fact, despite nation-wide AIDS education campaigns, only 38 percent of sexually active teens across Canada say that they use a condom every time they have sex, according to a *Maclean's*/Decima poll. In her work for the AIDS committee, travelling across the province to raise public awareness about the

disease, Parsons says that she finds most teens do use condoms, but not all the time. She also points out that Newfoundland has an HIV-infection rate among teens that is four times the national average. "These kids still think that it is a gay men's disease and they can't get it," she says.

3   Sitting one-third of the way up Conception Bay's west coast, Bay Roberts, a town of 5,000, is bordered by a narrow harbour on one side and barren, rocky hills on the other. Parsons, who was born in St. John's but moved to Bay Roberts eight years ago with her family, remembers teenage life there as dull, but generally happy. She babysat for relatives, sipped beer in the woods on weekends, went to dances. Then, when she was 19, Parsons contracted the HIV infection from a Bay Roberts–area man. He was her third sexual partner.

4   As she walks across the slushy pavement towards her old high school, there are no words of bitterness or anger—only a hint of sorrow. "I made my bed and I will sleep in it," she says. "But I wish that I had known someone like me when I was in high school. I like to believe that if I had had the opportunity, that maybe things would have turned out differently for me." With that, she opens the school's front door and steps into the lobby.

5 Ascension Collegiate's guidance counsellor, Mervin Clarke, says that education campaigns urging teens to use condoms have made an impact. When teens have sex, he says, "most of them take the correct precautions." But he adds: "There are some who understand the dangers, and still don't protect themselves. They think that they are immortal."

6   It is that kind of attitude that Parsons is fighting. She leans forward in her chair in the school's guidance office as she speaks. Of slender build, with a mane of thick black hair framing her thin, serious face, she hardly looks older than the two dozen 16- and 17-year-olds who sit in a tight circle around her. They are Ascension's peer counsellors—who receive special training to provide fellow students with advice on everything from study habits to personal relationships. And Parsons' message has captured their attention.

7   In fact, the dangers of AIDS are well known to them. In July, the Bay Roberts area was rocked by the report that Raymond Mercer, a 29-year-old man from nearby Upper Island Cove, was sentenced to 27 months in jail for infecting two young women with HIV by having unprotected sex in defiance of a court order. In fact, health department officials have found 30 HIV-positive cases around Conception Bay, 23 of them young women. Dr. Catherine Donovan, the medical officer for Newfoundland's Eastern Region, describes the incidence of infection in the area as "extraordinary."

8   Many teens in Bay Roberts claim to know someone who has tested HIV-positive—and they blame Mercer for what has happened to their friends and acquaintances. Parsons, however, warns that Mercer is only part of the problem. "Some people are just so arrogant that they know all about the disease but think it doesn't apply to them," she declares. "It is almost like you have to come in and die in front of them before they will believe you."

9   When the bell rings to change classes, the students are reluctant to leave. Tanya Craik, a 16-year-old from Bay Roberts, walks up to Parsons and embraces her. "You see her and you realize that if it can happen to her, it can happen to anybody," says Craik, clutching her schoolbooks to her chest. "It is not something you want to think about—but you have to."

10   Between classes, neat and tidy Ascension Collegiate teems with controlled mayhem. The hallways are a sea of permed and teased female hair and young men sporting Toronto Blue Jay shirts and jackets and high-topped running shoes. "Move to the right or you'll get trampled," Trudy Gosse, a 17-year-old Grade 12 student shouts above the din. About 900 students from Bay Roberts and surrounding settlements go to the school, which claims as its motto "Carpe Diem" (Seize the Day).

11   Romance blooms easily here, as the walls in the main-floor girl's washroom attest. Until the surfaces are repainted, "Jody loves Ellis" and "Tammy Loves Cory." For a while, it seems, Margaret and Christopher were an item, along with C.N. and P.N. One Ascension girl has scribbled: "Hope all your ups and downs are on a water bed." The consensus in the Bay Roberts area is that many students begin having sex when they are between 14 and 17—a finding that is consistent with the *Maclean's*/Decima poll showing that half of 17-year-olds across Canada say they have had sex. "They do it in houses," declares Keith Drover, 18, as he loiters with friends in an otherwise-empty hallway. "They do it in cars. They do it in trucks. They do it anywhere." Still, Drover maintains that the HIV scare has changed sexual patterns. "People stay together longer," he says.

12   Cindy Coombs, 18, says that condom use is also increasing. "Nowadays," says Coombs, "I'd say most people are pretty careful when it comes to sex." Not everyone is so sure. Susan Penney, 17, a cheerleader and peer counsellor, says that, while she and her boyfriend of a few months have not even talked about sex, "when a boy and girl have a one-night stand around here, 9 out of 10 times the boy does not wear a condom."

13   Age-old courting rituals continue. Behind Ascension's swimming pool, dozens of teens gather in small groups. Displays of macho maleness seem

unaffected by the cold weather: a boy with a sparse moustache bites off the top of a Pepsi can and holds it up for approval. Best friends Lori Francis, 16, and Samielle Hynes, 15, seem unimpressed. "A lot of guys, sex is all they want," says Francis. "And it doesn't matter if you do it or you don't. They'll tell all the boys that you do anyway."

14   Yet even the most popular boys have been affected by the HIV scare. The Ascension Astros—champions in their high-school hockey league last year—stand at the apex of the school's loose social pyramid. Most have steady girlfriends. "That one-night-stand stuff, it ain't no good for any of us," explains David Mugford, a 17-year-old forward. And going steady has other benefits. Says another player: "Around here, there is about a 99.9-percent chance that if you go out with a girl for a night, you will not get laid."

15 The Parsons' house is a white, wooden bungalow. In some ways, it is as if Trudy never left the warm, comfortable home. Beatles posters still hang in her old room. Photographs of her adorn the walls throughout the house—particularly in the carpeted family room where she and her mother sit one January day, drinking coffee. Minnie Parsons is slim like her daughter, and wears a flannel shirt and green chino pants that make her look younger than her 45 years. But the weariness around her eyes reflects some of her pain.

16   Minnie's smile fades as Trudy leaves to play cards in the kitchen. "I just fell apart," she says, recalling the terrible day when Trudy told her that she had tested HIV-positive. "Nothing mattered to me any more." As Minnie saw it, Trudy had been issued a death sentence, and she felt partially responsible. "We were open with each other about sexual matters," she explains. "But I didn't know anything about AIDS or HIV and didn't realize that it should have been part of her education."

17   It is late afternoon, and the cigarette she just lit flares orange in the darkening room. Speaking in a quiet voice, Minnie says that she has not gotten over her sense of unfairness at what happened to her daughter. "Trudy wasn't a wild girl," she explains, adding, almost in a whisper, "she was just unlucky."

18   Later, Trudy Parsons talks about her own self-doubts. "I really believed that I was a slut, even though I had had only three sex partners," she says. "And I thought about suicide. I never went into the actual process, but I had it planned—how I would do it and where, and the method I would use."

19 Shortly after supper, they begin arriving at a clearing in the woods on the Spaniard's Bay back road. At its most crowded, a few dozen teens congregate there, smoking, drinking a few beers and generally trying to figure

out what to do with their night. "It's sort of boring," says Jerome Greeley, 18. "But we have nowhere else to go." A handful of students have chosen another hideaway, a decrepit wooden building in the middle of a frozen field on the outskirts of Bay Roberts. Eight males and a female crowd around a potbellied iron stove as Led Zeppelin and The Doors blare from a tape machine.

20   Although it is still early, one member of the group has already smoked enough hashish to reduce his eyes to narrow slits. But the acknowledged leader of the pack, a wiry blond-haired 18-year-old, stands straight and sober. "Our bunch is sort of the outsiders around here," he explains. But there are limits to his rebelliousness. He expresses his disapproval of some of his friends' sexual habits. "Some of them don't give a shit, they never wear a rubber," he says. As for himself—"I've always got my Trojan on."

21   With all its latter-day complications, the dating game can still seem timeless, full of youthful hopes and innocence. Inside the Spaniard's Bay Recreational Centre, dozens of teens move to the taped music while couples, many of them holding hands, circle the dance floor. On the room's outskirts, Michael Badcock, a tall blond 16-year-old, sits embroiled in conversation with Maxine Drover, a 16-year-old brunette from Spaniard's Bay. For the past few weeks, the couple's on-again, off-again relationship has been off. But tonight, they talk earnestly about how much they missed each other. By the time the dance ends at 11:30, they decide to resume dating. "It seems like we can never stay apart for long," Badcock remarks cheerfully. The first thing he does after his mother drives him home is to phone Maxine. Then, until 1:30 a.m., the reunited couple speak happily of the night's events—and of the future that awaits them.

22 Trudy Parsons seems tired but relieved as she stretches out in the passenger's seat and Bay Roberts disappears in the distance behind her. Seeing her mother again has left her content, and she speaks, of all things, of her good fortune. Because of her own unfamiliarity with the virus, she thought that she had only a year to live when she first learned that she was HIV-positive—three years ago. And there has been another pleasant surprise: a six-month-old romantic relationship, even though she thought her dating days were over. "I have proven myself wrong on every count," she says.

23   Still, even during her happy moments, despair lurks beneath the surface. Parsons acknowledges that sometimes her work seems futile—all the speeches in tiny outports to people who sometimes hardly seem to listen. "I'm the only person doing this. And my going to a high school once a year is not going to reinforce anything," she says wearily. "You know you

are going to see some of them again, and that it is going to be at the AIDS clinic in St. John's—and it is going to be because they are HIV-positive."

Thinking about the Text

1. According to this magazine article, what attitudes prevent teens from using condoms on a regular basis?

2. How are people with AIDS and their families judged?

3. Study DeMont's descriptive style. What details of place does he add to make Trudy's trip back to Bay Roberts more immediate?

Writing from the Text

1. Part of the subtext of this article is that, given the shortage of things to do in small towns, sex often becomes a recreational activity for some young people. If you have grown up in such an environment, write a letter to your local officials suggesting that the problem of AIDS among young people could be solved if there were more for young people to do in small towns.

2. Write a short essay in which you argue that overconformity to masculine modelling—achieving "macho maleness"—can be destructive. Use and develop examples cited in this article and add others of your own.

Connecting with Other Texts

1. Interview the director of the student health centre at your college or the AIDS clinic at your local hospital, and ask to see the pamphlets or other educational material available to inform young people about AIDS. Write an essay about how effective or ineffective current efforts are in convincing young people to practise safe sex.

2. Research current periodicals to find out about recent developments in our understanding of AIDS. Does the public still consider AIDS to be a "gay disease"? How many HIV-positive people are living in Canada today? How is medical research progressing in the search for a cure?

Kiss Me

Andrew Pyper

1 Jasmine Broadhurst. First name like department store perfume and last name like a street. They say you always remember losing your virginity but I don't, not really. But I do remember the first time Jasmine Broadhurst transferred the gum in her mouth into mine, without warning, guiding it in with a tender flick of tongue. It was the loveliest thing, something new inside of me, a warm lump of strawberry rubber. So artificially flavoured and excessively sweet it didn't even pretend to taste like fruit, but somehow it wasn't too bad when worn down by the spit of the one you love. And her eyes too close to my own to look at them both at the same time so I move back and forth between them and try to express something deep straight into her pupils. And the whole time I know I'm kissing her, *kissing* her. Jasmine Broadhurst. The first person to teach me that some things that sound unpleasant are fantastic when you just relax and let them happen.

2 After what's happened, Jasmine Broadhurst stands not for love but for the memory of love. Not so much the memory of the thing itself, but the feeling that it's possible, inevitable, a right. The pleasure in fooling yourself by borrowing serious feelings without the burden of carrying them with you for real. The comfort that there will always be someone else to kiss you, somewhere down the line, no matter what. But my face, the way it looks now, shows how wrong this assumption is. Even with eyes closed you can feel its ugliness. To kiss me would be to taste the metallic sourness of mottled scars. The rough edge of an empty soup tin.

3 *I am repulsive.* That's a hell of a thing to say to yourself every day. I know it from seeing my face reflected in others', the way the edges of their mouths drop and then tremble back up to an awkward mask of indifference. I see it in their bulging eyes as they recall what vampires look like in the movies when they are finally exposed to the sun.

4 I am the face you turn from on the street because it's rude to stare, but you turn back to anyway, to feel again how lucky you are to live in the skin that you have. I appear in nightmares, bearing down with a crooked, open mouth and tongue moving around inside like a lizard in its hole. In this story I have made for myself I am the troll who lives under the bridge, sniffling in the shadows, closing my ears to the clamour of love as it passes over my head.

5 I burned my face lighting our third floor balcony barbecue.

6   It was the sort of day that provided no hints that a horrible disfigura-
tion was about to happen: bright, a light breeze swirling up St. Urbain
from the river, the Haitian kids on the ground floor sitting behind an
upturned grapefruit crate selling plastic cups of lemonade. The little girl
shouting "*C'est frais!* It's cold!" every couple of minutes.

7   It was the lighting fluid. Crazy stuff, it really goes up. It was my habit to
douse the hell out of the coals before lighting them so, when lit, they could
dazzle your audience with a thrilling *whhooosshhh* and a short-lived bonfire
that broiled cheeks from ten feet away. Another fun thing was to spray more
fluid on when the flames were lowering to blaze it up again, aiming the can
into the barbecue like a flamethrower. This is the dangerous part, there's
even a warning against it on the label if you read the print below the little
picture of an explosion. The problem is this: sometimes the flame follows the
trail of fluid up towards the can like a lit fuse, and if you don't cut off the
stream somehow you find yourself holding a live Molotov cocktail. When it
blows, the fluid remaining in the can goes everywhere. For whatever reason
on this particular occasion (being in flames I can't recall the exact physics
involved) most of it ended up splashing over my face, dripping down my
chin and over the tender part of my neck. I kept my eyes open and I remember the yellow flash and the black smoke rising off my skin before the heat
melted off my eyelashes and seared my eyelids into half-shut slits.

8   I was conscious the whole time, flapping my hands over my face and,
when the flames had gone out, opening the screen door and telling Leah
to call an ambulance. I didn't scream, focusing all of my energy on breathing in regular intervals. But the pain was something I'd rather not describe,
aside from saying it was what I imagine insanity to be like: consuming,
relentless, a world entirely apart from the one you were born into.

9   Leah was pretty calm too, but in the way that people who are terrified
become calm. After she got off the phone she came out the door carrying
a glass of water. (Was this meant to put out the flames or quench my
thirst?) When she looked at me she made a sound somewhere between a
gasp and a gag but carefully bent down to set the glass on the floor. She
said nothing but kept her eyes on me, her pupils the size of dimes in the
bright sunshine.

10   "Do I have any hair?" I asked her.

11   "Not a lot."

12   "It stinks. Burnt hair stinks."

13   She gave me a look that said that bad smells should be the last of my
worries. "You're bleeding."

14   "Am I?"

15   "Does it hurt?"

16   "Yes."

17   "Oh, baby."

18   Then she put her arm around my back and moved beside me on the tiny Juliet balcony to wait for the ambulance. It was during this time that I learned it's true what people in these situations always say: *The seconds felt like hours.*

19   "They'll be here soon," she said.

20   "Fucking barbecue. We were going to have a *barbecue*," I kept saying as we waited on the paint-flaky wood, holding each other in the sun. From a distance we would have looked like a couple making up after a fight, or consoling each other after receiving bad news.

21 When I was in the hospital Leah came to visit every day, sometimes twice, so that it seemed that when I wasn't knocked out on the dope they pumped into me she was always there. Even when the nurses came to change my bandages. A disgusting ritual. Three times a day layers of what used to be skin were removed and, slowly, the hardened ridges of my new face dried, thickened, emerged. Leah was there for all of it, watching. She was strong as hell, didn't flinch, but didn't go overboard on the sympathy either. Just stood there at the side of the bed and watched, taking my hand when I held it out. "Oh, baby," she'd say. "What are we going to do with you?"

22   We had moved in together at the beginning of that summer. The plan was that this move was the beginning of a complete life together. Finish degrees, work for a while, save, travel, attend other people's weddings, find careers we could live with, children. We were at the stage of actually talking about all of this out loud. We saw ourselves as separate from the relationships our friends were in, distinguished by our degree of frankness, pragmatism, and talent. I spoke seriously of feelings and intentions that, if said to any woman before her, would have made me feel foolish, unsophisticated, an anxious farm boy going crazy after the first good sex of his life.

23   In the hospital Leah never told me how bad I looked. They kept me well away from mirrors and (intentionally, I think) served my food with plastic cutlery and juice in ceramic mugs. Nothing that could reflect myself back at me. I have since learned that more than the preservation of vanity or good spirits is at stake in such manoeuvres. In fact, burn victims have been known to go into long and untreatable shock when shown their faces too early. The doctors had spoken to Leah about this, and she was careful to look me directly in the eye, her blinking disciplined into

consistency. She was cheerful, too, but never lied to me. Everybody else that drummed up the courage or guilt to visit dropped off magazines and lied their asses off, and who could blame them? But Leah never played down the situation if asked directly, which I rarely did, having had the question sufficiently answered the first time.

24   "So am I the Elephant Man, or more Phantom of the Opera?"

25   "The best parts of each."

26   One night when I was in a particularly pissy mood because they had taken away the IV full of the good stuff and put me on the puny distraction of maximum dosage Tylenol-3, I became weepy. More than weepy: I bawled, screeched, blubbered, choked. I cried from the pain, but also for how the rest of my life would be diminished, how nothing would ever be as simple or privileged. Leah was there, crying along with me, asking the nurses for more dope and being told they didn't have the authority.

27   "I won't leave you," she said, over and over.

28   At first I thought she meant *tonight. I won't leave you tonight before you get to sleep.* But the way she kept saying it, the intensity in her voice, made me realize she meant *after this. I won't leave you for being burned.* And even though she meant nothing but comfort in saying this, it struck me for the first time that such an event was a reasonable possibility. That she might *want* to leave me after this, that people have left others for similar reasons.

29   Leah was granting me the intimate favour of subtlety. Speaking about something without mentioning it directly, knowing it should be unnecessary to spell certain unpleasant thoughts out. She was reminding me of what I'd known all along from other people's lives but had yet to recognize as a possibility in my own: that, even under conditions of love, there are some events that change the rules entirely.

30 Leah's sympathy was not learned from the bedside scenes of daytime television. She knew something herself of how the failures of the body can get in the way of the anticipated patterns of life. That's why her presence at the hospital didn't embarrass or irritate me as it would if she were any other woman I've ever thought I could live with forever.

31   When Leah was twenty-two, before we met, she was the star of the university gymnastic team. I remember reading about her in the *McGill Daily*'s sports section where there was a buzz about her inclusion on the Canadian Olympic team. All of this was interrupted abruptly during a pre-dawn practice when her chalked feet missed the beam. As she fell her knee slammed against it, wrenching her leg out of its hip socket. The

immediate pain brought her to the edge of unconsciousness but did not quite push her over. Instead, it induced hallucinations of puppets. The coaches and ambulance attendants who jostled over her took the form of wobbly marionettes controlled by a complex web of strings, their joints hinged on loose screws that threatened to come apart altogether. When they picked her up and placed her on the stretcher she could see strings attached to her own slack limbs, each one drifting up high into the gymnasium ceiling floodlights. The coach told her later that she kept asking "Who's up there?" the whole time. She wanted to know who had failed her, who the puppet master was. Her question carried the stinging tone of betrayal: this whole thing was someone else's fault. She squinted up to see where all the strings led, but whoever controlled their movements was washed out in spheres of halogen light.

32   I met Leah shortly after her life had been changed by her vision of puppets. By that time the Olympics were over, and she would be too old by the time they came around again. Best-case scenarios now spoke of being able to walk one day without a noticeable limp, of scars that could be covered with black nylons or make-up when she wanted to wear a skirt. I was her boyfriend for the recovery period, going along for the visits to doctors, physiotherapists, consultations with orthopaedic surgeons who showed us menacing plastic hip joints and stainless steel knees. Instead of kisses over St. Denis café tables or walks in Parc Mont-Royal, we spent a lot of time sitting in out-patient waiting rooms holding hands.

33   Through all of this Leah was brave, where "brave" means covering your disappointment and anger with an ironic laugh and fatalistic shrug. It wasn't this alone that made me love her (can it ever be one thing?) but it was a part of it. I felt she was stronger than me, that all of this was a test that she was uniquely able to meet. When we made love Leah showed her scars, distorted angles and withered muscles with something close to pride, a womanliness. More than just making do with what you have, she turned the worst thing in her life into a claim of self-worth that went deeper than having straight and nearly Olympian legs.

34 Before, I used to daydream about breasts and legs and buttocks. Leah's body. Touching these places with my hands. Leah leading me into rooms, smile heavy with suggestion, fingers unbuttoning things. Now it's lips. Not sex, but tender, eyes-open kisses. When I became ugly I stopped dreaming of physical vigour, and wished instead for the restrained tremors of delicacy. Or at least this is how I rationalized the fact that Leah and I weren't sleeping together any more. I took her invitations as charity, a

gesture meant to bring me back into life. Desire, the simple wanting my body close to hers, had been ruled out.

35   "What's wrong?" she asks, her hand high on my thigh under the sheets.

36   "Please. Do we have to *talk* about it?"

37   "Just tell me what you'd like."

38   *My life back.* No, not my life. Give *me* back.

39   "Don't serve me."

40   "I'm not."

41   "I'm sorry—"

42   "It's all right, it's all right."

43   She holds me, buries her face in my neck. I almost tell her that I'm not sorry about anything except that she has to be here, now, with me, instead of someplace else where you don't need to feel embarrassed about a fucking thing.

44 Classes started again in the fall but I rarely showed up. Instead, I meticulously worked through the pile of magazines left for me at the hospital, reading *GQ* and *People* with the same careful attention as *Saturday Night* and the *New Republic*. I took to making messes, leaving stains, garbage and layers of clothing around the place. Made anxious by the idea of the grocery store's fluorescent lights, I stopped cooking altogether and relied on cheeseburgers supplemented by styrofoam tubs of *poutine*. I was fending for myself, a child left alone for the weekend, gorging on undeserved treats. Leah (whom I once loved to please with favourite meals) was left to warm tins of Habitant pea soup abandoned by the junkie couple who lived in the apartment before we moved in. By then it was the middle of winter, dark by five, and we ate in front of the TV with the lights off.

45   "You don't have to go *completely* to hell, you know," Leah tells me on her way out the bedroom door in the morning.

46   "It's not hell. Consider it a lifestyle choice."

47   "Walk with me to school? You don't even have to go yourself. Just walk to the gates, turn around, and come straight home. It's called exercise."

48   "No, it's called being patronized."

49   "What do you want from me?"

50   "What have I asked you for?"

51   She pauses in the door frame, engulfed in instantaneous shafts of sunlight. Like Nosferatu, I raise my arm from the crypt to shield my eyes.

52   "I think we should get counselling," she says.

53 "Oh. We've come to that. How long could we go before counselling was suggested? She thinks we should get counselling."

54 "Please don't refer to me in the third person. That really pisses me off. I'm right here."

55 "Right, OK. Then who should we call? 1-800-BURN VICTIM?"

56 Leah looks at me with her eyes set and square, willing herself to keep looking to prove she is not afraid. I look back at her as long as I can, but I am always the first to drop my eyes. Since the hospital I've caught enough Halloween flashes of myself in mirrors, silver kettles and polished knives to know exactly what she sees when she looks at me. It is the face of bad luck, and it looks back at her, blinks, tries to smile.

57 "I love you," she says.

58 "Don't."

59 "Don't what?"

60 "Just don't."

61 She blows me a kiss and leaves. Holds her palm flat before her chin, kisses the air and exhales through her perfectly round mouth. I imagine it, tangible and warm, travelling in my direction through the space of the bedroom. But it must have missed me, because although I raise my head to meet it, I feel only the cool disturbance caused by the closing of the bedroom door.

62 "Kiss me," she said and closed her eyes, just like Tina Louise from *Gilligan's Island* when she wanted to seduce somebody into rescuing her from the clumsy, numbskull castaways she got stuck with. Jasmine Broadhurst. A strange name compared to those of the other girls. Smelled a little strange, too. A combination of lemon deodorant and insect repellent, but this wasn't entirely bad. In fact I liked the way it prickled and made her seem sharp and tangy instead of the flowery bundles of *potpourri* the rest of them suggested.

63 "Kiss me," she said, just like that, the strawberry gum lurking in her molars.

64 Love, was that it? Was that the feeling that moistened the eyes, sent gentle currents through the discs of the spine? No, not love, just a kiss outside the Stratford Arena in December, the Junior B team playing their Friday night game inside. Fourteen years old and nowhere else to go to stay warm. The smell of cherry Chap-Stick and father-borrowed splashes of musk Lectricshave on the collar. Giant snowflakes whispering around us, confetti clinging to eyelashes. Not love but definitely something close.

65 Spring arrives with a week of warm rain and sidewalks blocked by rivers of brown slush. I'm writing exams off the top of my head, picking away at listless essays. Professors can offer no more extensions. "You're still a *student* here, right?" is how one of them puts it.

66 . For a while now Leah has been spending her days in the library, usually staying in the humid cafeteria for dinners of tortilla chips and machine-made hot chocolate. This routine has become so reliable that I am surprised to come home after my Fascism in Film exam to find her standing in the middle of the living room.

67 "What's up?"

68 She says nothing, but bends down to pick up her suitcase. How could I not immediately recognize something as obvious as Leah's giant orange suitcase?

69 "Separate vacations?" I ask.

70 "I meant to be gone before you got back. I didn't want this."

71 "What's 'this'?"

72 "This fucking sarcastic, self-pitying exchange."

73 "Oh. Well, were you at least going to leave me a note?"

74 "No. I thought it would be clear."

75 "Yes. I guess it would've been."

76 I back away from the door, give her room to pass. *Don't go*, I say, but only think I say. *I'm still here inside this mask and I can't take it off.*

77 She lugs the suitcase to the door and moves close enough to me that I can smell how good she smells. I could reach out to her without raising my arm, I could whisper and she'd hear, but nothing happens.

78 "Just to make this whole scene clear, I'm leaving. You've already chosen the reasons why," she says without looking. I respond with a nod and another step back.

79 I watch her go.

80 Move over to the front window and stand beneath the underwatered spider plant, Leah bumping and spiralling her way down the wonky wrought-iron stairs. *You need her. You're not enough on your own.* I watch her reach the street and head down toward St. Joseph without looking up to see if I'm there. *Don't let this happen.* I think this, knowing I'm wrong, this whole thing is hugely wrong, but nothing happens. *She's not leaving because of your charbroiled face, she's leaving because of you.* I think this. *You are going to be monstrous and alone. You will hate being monstrous and alone.* I think this, too. *You don't believe in anything, not fate or Jesus, but she's the closest thing.*

81 I think all of these things, but nothing happens.

Thinking about the Text

1. What "failures of the body" do the narrator and Leah experience? How do these "get in the way of the anticipated patterns of life" (paragraph 30) for each character?

2. Contrast the roles Jasmine and Leah play in the narrator's life.

3. Why are kisses so important in this story?

4. In what ways is the narrator like other men? In what ways is he different?

Writing from the Text

1. Analyse the role food plays in this story. In what ways is food a symbol, and what does it symbolize?

2. Write an essay discussing the significance of the narrator's vision that he is "the troll who lives under the bridge, sniffling in the shadows, closing [his] ears to the clamour of love as it passes over [his] head" (paragraph 4).

Connecting with Other Texts

1. As Lauren Griffin points out in "Making Big Deals out of Little Deals" (p. 72), relationship conflicts often originate in the differences between the ways men and women experience the world. Write an essay comparing the relationship conflicts in Griffin's essay and "Kiss Me." Argue that the conflicts the narrator and Leah face in the story are human-to-human conflicts, rather than being gender-based.

2. Using this story and Janice Giavedoni's essay "Jerry Lewis and the MDA Telethon" (p. 136), write an essay on the challenges people with disabilities face in learning to separate the image they present to the world from their self-perception and knowledge of who they really are.

CHAPTER 3
Between Cultures

anada is a country shared by Native people and the generations of immigrants who chose it as their home, and your classrooms undoubtedly reflect this diversity. After class, you may find yourself enjoying sushi or tacos, digesting cultural diversity as easily as you munch a burger and fries. Or you may find yourself perplexed by cultural pluralism, unsure of its merits. The readings in this chapter illustrate the joy and stress of adapting to the cultural differences within North America today.

This chapter begins with an essay by Sonnet L'Abbé, who grapples with our longstanding uncertainty of how we as Canadians should define ourselves when our nearest neighbours dominate our continent's population and the world's perception of us. Robert Chodos also writes from the point of view of a minority, about the discomfort he as a Jew feels during the month of December, when the trappings of Christmas are inescapable.

Julia Nunes, whose mother was from England and whose father was from India, probes her dual identity and examines how it has developed and changed over her lifetime. Similarly, Sean Kelly's essay continues this theme of being caught between worlds; in his case, his feelings of isolation encapsulate what it means to grow up as a Native in white society.

Three works in this section document how language has the power to place us uncomfortably between cultures. In Rita Joe's poem, we read of enforced loss of the narrator's native language in a residential school. Sun-Kyung Yi describes the tension arising from her efforts to master the frustrating intricacies of the English language. The central character in Yeshim Ternar's short story is clearly articulate, but not in the language of her adopted country.

Cultural characteristics are important because they define who we are, but they can also lead to misunderstanding and a narrowing, rather than broadening, of options for our own identity as Canadians. At one time Michael Ignatieff accepted the myth of a bicultural Canada without question, even though he had never met any Francophones to confirm this belief; his trip to Quebec forces him to concede that the differences between Quebec and Canada may be greater than he ever imagined. Montrealer Carl Wilson advocates an expansion of cultural identity, and so refuses to be labelled as being a member of any cultural group.

As you will discover reading this section, identity, assimilation, and rejection are issues not only for immigrants but for longtime residents who experience the psychological, political, and economic realities of living between cultures.

Hello, We're Not American!

Sonnet L'Abbé

1 Like many people my age, daunted by the prospects for the future after finishing university, I decided to escape for awhile, see a bit of the world, learn something about other people of the planet. I took off, pack on back, to see Indonesia, Singapore and Malaysia. And, taking the advice I had heard many times, I had a Canadian flag sewn visibly onto my backpack.

2 A Canadian traveller is counselled to do this, supposedly, to avoid being mistaken for an American while abroad. Americans, I was told, have a horrendous reputation worldwide as obnoxious, loud, demanding tourists, and that Canadians, on the other hand, are known to be laid back, generous and friendly visitors. I had heard many stories of Canadians receiving cold or even hostile reactions from locals of some countries until the confusion over their nationality had been cleared up, at which point smiles and a much warmer reception were offered. And I had one similar experience a few years ago, when visiting England, so subsequent flag-bearing seemed well advised. However, after a few weeks in Asia, I came to see the whole practice in a different light. The flag on my back seemed so unnecessary it began to embarrass me.

3 When a Western tourist shows up in Asia, it is fairly obvious that he or she is not from that country. Even if you are a North American of Asian descent, there are many other things to give you away: clothing, accent, even body language betrays your origin, not to mention your big, cumbersome pack that swings dangerously back and forth as you stare up at road signs, then at your map, then back up at the road signs. You will be asked where you are from. Ad nauseam. But at least you will be asked, and so will have many opportunities to say proudly, "Canada."

4 Now shouldn't the flag pre-empt such questions? Well, sometimes I wasn't wearing it, sometimes people didn't see it, but also, ego-shatteringly, often people didn't recognize it. To be honest, I only know Malaysia and Singapore's flags from having looked them up once I got home. So

why did I assume that Canada's flag ranks among the iconographic flags of such high-profile countries as Japan, the former Soviet Union or, say, the States? I soon observed that the "worldwide" tourist reputation Canada enjoys actually exists only within the boundaries of "Western" countries. Where I was, a Canadian was a Westerner was a rich Westerner. Period.

5   Except that the Canadians were the ones who wore the flags on their backs. Good thing for me—I could recognize my fellow countrypersons a mile away, the inevitable flags bobbing with their every step, beacons of familiarity on crowded sidewalks or jungle paths. I crossed a busy Malaysian street to say hello to three young men that I couldn't help noticing. They had seven flags of varying sizes between them. But more than once I was asked by other Western tourists, "Why do all of you have those flags?"

6   The Europeans and Australians I met were ignorant of the American notoriety. But the Canadians knew it, and the Americans I met also were apologetically aware of their reputation. Could it be that we keep the stereotypes alive among ourselves? I ask this because without a solid, reality-based reason to promote our "un-Americanness," the glaring red leaves plastered all over our gear are in fact an unnecessary announcement, perilously close to arrogance.

7   Before I left home, I thought I could always tell the difference between a Canadian and an American, by accent if by nothing else. This is perhaps true if one hears my Québécoise grandmother next to a Texan cowgirl, but I was surprised by the number of times I heard a North American accent and guessed wrong. After awhile, I began approaching people who were obviously from this continent by asking: "Are you from Canada or the States?"

8   One woman I asked, named Shelley, was from Seattle. She came up to me the day after we met to thank me for phrasing the question in a way that acknowledged that it was not always so easy to tell. While travelling with a woman from Toronto, she explained to me, they met another man from Vancouver. The usual questions about origin were exchanged, and the man nodded when Shelley said her home was Seattle, but exclaimed with joy on hearing that her companion was "from Canada!" and proceeded to engage her friend in animated conversation while virtually ignoring Shelley. The man obviously felt he had more in common with the woman who lived in the same country, thousands of kilometres away, rather than the one who lived three hours away, across a border.

9   Shelley said it was not the first time that she'd run across Canadians who were reluctant to engage in conversation with her, as if by simply being in her proximity they might be judged American by association. So

much for the friendly, laid-back Canadian.

10   The question is how different are we, really, from our neighbours? There are certainly important distinctions to be made, but when I tried to explain Canada versus the United States to a young Sumatran woman who has never left her native island, I was hard-pressed to come up with traits that would solidly identify our country to her. I quipped that we have more cold and fewer guns. Obviously, when speaking to someone who has no idea about Canadians and only a vague idea about American culture, one of the best ways I could describe my own culture to them was to say yes, I am quite like an American.

11   As for my own observations on who was more obnoxious, I can say in all honesty that some of the most generous, gentle people I met were American, and that the two men I remember most for their pretentiousness and impatience turned out to be Canadian.

12   The Insensitive American Tourist is as much a stereotype as any other. Wearing our flags for the wrong reasons only endorses the myth. Do we really want to identify ourselves by a negation, by stating loudly what we are not? Our pride in being Canadian should stem from a pride in what we are, even if what we are bears a striking resemblance to Americans.

Thinking about the Text

1. What events prompted L'Abbé to change her views on the differences between Canadians and Americans?

2. Is her turnaround ironic? Why or why not?

3. Infer why some Canadians want to be seen as different from Americans and why others do not.

Writing from the Text

1. Write a narrative about how you have been received as a Canadian travelling abroad. In your experience, is the reputation of American and Canadian tourists justified?

2. In an essay, answer L'Abbé's question: "How different are we, really, from our neighbours?" (paragraph 10). Be sure to include concrete examples to support your position.

3. Does L'Abbé's age have any bearing on her perceptions of Canadians and Americans? Ask people who are older than L'Abbé, such as your parents or grandparents, about their perceptions of the differences between Canadians and Americans. Write an essay comparing and contrasting the viewpoints of the different age groups.

Connecting with Other Texts

1. Read Robert L. Heilbroner's essay "Don't Let Stereotypes Warp Your Judgments" (p. 128), and write an analysis of the stereotypes L'Abbé describes. Are "positive" stereotypes as impoverishing as negative ones?

2. Many Canadians have published books and essays about their experiences in foreign countries. Read a work such as Karen Connelly's *Touch the Dragon*, Gwendolyn MacEwen's *Mermaids and Ikons: A Greek Summer*, or Kildare Dobbs's anthology of essays *Away from Home: Canadian Writers in Exotic Places*, and write an essay about what the author learned in his or her travels.

Being a Jew at Christmas

Robert Chodos

1 For eleven months of the year, I consider myself a full participant in Canadian society. I pay taxes. My children go to public schools. I vote. I even have the *chutzpah* to comment in print on this country's politics.

2 And then there is December. December for most Canadians means Christmas. I do not celebrate Christmas. In December, I am hardly more integrated into Canadian society than my grandparents were when they got off the boat from Lithuania at the turn of the century.

3 At first glance, the statement that I do not celebrate Christmas seems a simple one, based on a simple reason. After all, Christmas is a Christian holiday that expresses Christians' joy at the birth of Jesus, their Saviour. Since I am a Jew, Jesus is not my Saviour, and therefore it would be inappropriate for me to celebrate a holiday devoted to rejoicing at his birth.

4 However, neither the act of not celebrating Christmas nor Jews' reason for not celebrating it is as simple as it first appears. How does one not celebrate Christmas? You can avoid actively observing Christmas, but you cannot avoid passively absorbing it: Christmas is all around you from late November on. All the public institutions that I participate in and support with my taxes celebrate Christmas. (Very rarely in Canada, and only slightly less so in the United States, do they celebrate any of the holidays that are specific to my own faith and culture.) Government offices—along with almost everything else—are closed on December 25. Public schools stage Christmas concerts. Towns put up Christmas decorations on their main streets.

5 Last Christmas, my wife and two children and I were in Washington, D.C., on a sightseeing trip. We planned our activities around the fact that

all the museums would be closed on December 25 and decided to spend Christmas day walking through the Mall and looking at the White House (with the giant Christmas tree on the lawn), the Washington Monument, the Lincoln Memorial and the Vietnam wall. With a few phone calls we even found two indoor things that would be open: the head office of B'nai B'rith, which had a special children's program, and the Islamic Center.

6   We enjoyed our monument tour, but by early afternoon we were cold and hungry. After a fruitless search for a restaurant that was not closed, we ended up at B'nai B'rith. In marked contrast to the all but deserted streets of the city, it was swarming with people. We made camp on the floor of a room where cookies and juice were available. We felt like refugees who had just come ashore. Christmas has a way of doing that to you, if you're not part of it.

7   But before I start sounding like the proverbial Grinch, I should confess what has hitherto been something of a secret passion of mine. I love Christmas. My first direct experience of Christmas, beyond observation and passive absorption, occurred in my early twenties when I visited friends in St. John's, Newfoundland. We decorated the tree, ate T-bone steaks and sang *Come all ye*'s until the early hours of the morning. I was enchanted. And yet I have never felt any desire to adopt Christmas as my own celebration or envy towards people who do have Christmas as part of their background. Like the classical poetry of Ireland or the carnival costumes of Trinidad, it is something from another culture whose beauty and power have an impact on me.

8   The question of why Jews don't celebrate Christmas is complex because the question of to what extent Christmas is a Christian holiday is complex. And this question is made still more complicated for me by the circumstance that it is precisely the specifically Christian aspects of Christmas that I find most appealing, from the Gospel narratives to the themes of peace and goodwill to the incomparable music. It is "O Holy Night" sung by Kathleen Battle that makes Christmas enticing, not "Rudolph the Red-Nosed Reindeer" played by Mantovani. But the religious and secular elements in Christmas are intricately intertwined. Early last December, I was in The Bay. If there is a place in Canada where Christmas is purely secular, surely it is The Bay. What music was being played to create a suitable atmosphere for shopping? "It Came upon a Midnight Clear" . . . "Hark the Herald Angels Sing" . . . "O Come All Ye Faithful." . . .

9   Nevertheless, not being a Christian does not appear even to begin to disqualify a person from celebrating Christmas. One friend of mine, who grew up in a militantly atheistic Communist household, has celebrated

Christmas all his life without the slightest notion that he was taking part in a religious festival. Another friend, who was raised in the United Church but has since become a Unitarian, says that when she rejected organized Christianity it never crossed her mind to reject Christmas.

10   In a discussion in my daughter's enrichment class last December, it emerged that she was the only one who didn't celebrate Christmas, even though one of her classmates was a Buddhist and another a Hindu: their families, recently arrived from Asia, celebrated Christmas because it was a "Canadian" thing to do. In the movie *The Outside Chance of Maximilian Glick*, about a Jewish boy growing up in a small Manitoba town, Max says that Christmas is like a gigantic party and he's wearing a big neon sign on his head that reads "NOT INVITED." But Jews' isolation from Christmas is, to some extent at least, self-imposed. Indeed, not celebrating Christmas is one of the chief distinguishing characteristics of Jews in North American society and one of the most intentionally Jewish things that many Jews do.

11   Nowhere do the issues surrounding Christmas hit closer to home than in the public school system. At least in Ontario where I live (and in Quebec where I grew up), the public school system has firm Christian roots, which it has never fully reconciled with its responsibility to provide education for all children in the society, Christian or not. It is in December that this tension is most difficult to manage.

12   In one school, the music program last December consisted of learning carols and preparing to sing them in a church; there was no sense that this curriculum might be inappropriate for a Jewish child. It is more common, however, for there to be some effort at accommodation. Some teachers and principals limit Christmas observance to its secular aspects, but as we have seen this robs Christmas of most of its beauty and meaning without really solving the problem. An especially uncreative and insecure principal might take Christmas out of the school entirely, but this only makes people who do celebrate Christmas angry and deprives them of the legitimate right to have an important event in their lives recognized in the school.

13   A more promising approach where Jewish children are present is to introduce Chanukah, the Jewish festival that occurs around the same time, as part of the December program. Unfortunately, that is often done in a way that makes the Jewish child feel singled out rather than included. It also tends to leave the impression in non-Jewish children's minds that Chanukah is the "Jewish Christmas," when in fact it is a completely different holiday—ironically, one that celebrates fierce Jewish resistance to accommodation with Greek religion and culture in the second century B.C.E. (the story is told in the book of 1 Maccabees).

14   My Unitarian friend, despite the joy and authenticity with which she celebrates Christmas, nevertheless wishes that the school her children go to would take a more detached attitude towards the holiday. She would like to see the school handle Christmas more in a spirit of "This is what people do" than of "Let's all celebrate." Even though the atmosphere that pervades the school in December does not present a problem to her personally, she appreciates the extent to which it could present a problem to others.

15   Interreligious marriages represent the front lines of the struggle between the desire of a majority Christian (or at least nominally Christian) society to have a common celebration at Christmas and the desire of religious minorities to opt out of the celebration while remaining part of the society. Each mixed Jewish/Christian family works out its own accommodation, based on its own particular circumstances and inclinations. When such families do observe Christmas, they often find themselves in an uncomfortable position within the Jewish community, many of whose members regard not celebrating Christmas as an integral part of Jewish identity.

16   And yet, one friend of mine who is Jewish by birth and is married to a Ukrainian who converted to Judaism regards the fact that their family celebrates both Chanukah and Christmas as enriching. Sharing celebrations with one another, he says, can only encourage mutual tolerance and understanding. He is no doubt right, and it works for his family. But it has only limited application to the wider society because the "sharing" tends to be overwhelmingly one-way.

17   So Jews who without a second thought send their kids out trick-or-treating on the eve of All Saints' Day and write each other love notes on St. Valentine's Day will continue to agonize over the "December Dilemma." It is probably inevitable. But Christians can help by not making assumptions. In a multicultural society, something that is near and dear to you may be perceived differently by someone else. Yes, even Christmas.

Thinking about the Text

1. Based on your reading of this essay, explain the personal discomfort Jews feel in December.

2. Describe the author's observations about Christmas and its commercialism. What are some of the contradictions between the religious and secular nature of Christmas?

3. What does Chodos like about Christmas?

4. Explain the author's contention that cultural "'sharing' tends to be overwhelmingly one-way" (paragraph 16).

Writing from the Text

1. Have you ever felt "like a refugee," excluded from the majority because of your cultural differences in celebrating holidays or rituals? Write a short narrative about your experience.

2. Put yourself in Chodos's place and imagine how you as a member of a minority would deal with the majority's month-long religious celebration sanctioned by businesses, schools, and the government. Would you experience any tensions? What compromises would you be willing to consider? Would you want to make any recommendations to remove religion from the public sphere? Why or why not?

3. Write an essay about what Christmas means to you personally. If you celebrate Christmas, reflect on how your family observes this holiday and on how the holiday enriches your life. If you do not celebrate Christmas, how do you and your family deal with what Chodos describes as the "December Dilemma" (paragraph 17)?

Connecting with Other Texts

1. Focus on a religious, racial, ethnic, or other minority group discussed in this book's readings, and show how the dominant culture makes assumptions about that group.

2. Research a celebration of a group other than your own. For example, if you do not practise a religion, find out about the Muslim holiday Ramadan. If your background is European, research the Indian Festival of Lights, Divali. Or, if you are an Anglophone, research Quebec's Saint-Jean Baptiste Day. You may want to research holidays that your friends celebrate that you do not.

The Business of Being Half and Half
Julia Nunes

1   My father set forth by ship from Karachi in 1953, a 30-year-old bachelor with a science degree, two suitcases and an immigration visa from the government of Canada.

2   My mother left England several years later, answering the call of an ad campaign that sold citizenships to a new, exciting country to the east.

3   They met in Montreal, two newcomers from separate continents whose paths coincided at a YMCA dance.

4   It was, for the times, an unlikely union: my father's skin a rich, deep brown, my mother's British white and sensitive to the sun.

5   My own skin is, well, somewhere in between—a genetic marker that has

at various stages of life brought grief, pride, dismay and much confusion.

6   Raised in the homogeneous suburbs of Ottawa in the 1970s, I was easily identified as "different," cast into a minority status of my own. To be different is to be derided, as many a schoolground could attest, with taunts, and teases and creative name-calling: "Fudgesicle," "chocolate bar," "Paki."

7   One confused young neighbour, having heard my father was "Indian," would greet me after school with mock war cries, batting a hand to his lips in imitation of the cowboys-and-Indians movies he'd no doubt seen on TV.

8   At such times I would, with bowed head, quietly curse my own bad luck. With a child's dichotomous thinking, I loved my father, respected my Indian relatives and fervently wished that I had somehow managed to look like everyone else.

9   I wanted, I am now ashamed to say, to be white. As a preteen who coveted the blond good looks of Marcia Brady, I stood before the bathroom mirror, blow dryer in hand, willing my wild, dark hair to straighten. In summer, as my friends baked their skins in the sun, I considered the possibility that for a brief few months our colouring might be the same.

10   The paradox is that, looks aside, I was the same. My father—part of India's tiny Catholic minority from the once-Portuguese colony of Goa— was English-speaking, British-educated and had, by the time I was born, completely adapted to Canadian ways of life.

11   My own exposure to Indian ways was limited to weekend visits with relatives in Toronto who cooked curries that scorched my uninitiated tongue, and spoke on occasion of a home country I knew nothing about.

12   Within the narrow confines of Ottawa's uniformly white society I was "different" only because my skin colour and my unusual last name had defined me as so.

13   The stakes began to change when I left for university in the far more cosmopolitan city of Montreal. Brown skin was suddenly not only acceptable but also desirable. Being "different" had become akin to being "exotic."

14   "Where do you come from?" I was often asked.

15   "What kind of last name is that?"

16   "Does your father wear a turban?"

17   These eager inquiries were received with a pleasure tinged with guilt, flattered as I was for the very features that had once inspired self-deprecation.

18   Those who know me now express surprise at all that I have encountered. In the multicultural Toronto of 1995, my childhood wish has been granted. I blend in. I fit in. I am no longer seen as "different" in anybody's eyes.

19   Old feelings of exclusion surface only when I meet with Indo-

Canadians who are shocked to hear my father is one of them.

20   "You mean he's a *real* Indian?" I am sometimes asked—a polite way of inquiring if his skin is really brown.

21   It is a strange hybrid, this business of being half and half; not quite white and not quite brown. And in this mix, the search for self-identity is complex.

22   I recently found myself side by side in an airport lounge with a five-year-old who is himself part-Asian.

23   Swinging his legs under his chair, he asked a simple question.

24   "Is your face white or is your face brown?" he said, with the same impartial curiosity he had displayed in asking if our plane would be big or small.

25   What struck me first was that to this small boy either answer would be equally acceptable; brown or white carried no weight of moral judgment.

26   What struck me next was that I had no idea how to answer.

27   "I suppose," I said weakly, "it could be either."

28   "You mean you don't know?" was the astonished reply.

29   He studied me for a moment, grinned and offered this pronouncement—"I think your face is white"—before returning to his box of Lego.

30   And, as if to prove that I have come full circle, I found that I was disappointed with his choice. I wished that he had found in me something of himself; an element of something different, a piece of who we are and where we come from.

Thinking about the Text

1.   How did living in Ottawa affect the author's perception of herself? In what ways did her perception of herself change when she moved to Montreal?

2.   Nunes describes her struggle for self-identity at three different stages in her life. What are the three stages? Discuss the defining features of each stage. How do these features indicate that the author lives between cultures?

3.   Explain the significance of Nunes's contention that she has "come full circle" (paragraph 30).

4.   Discuss the effectiveness of Nunes's use of direct speech, rather than reported speech, at the end of the essay.

Writing from the Text

1.   Are there any ways you are "half and half"? Write an essay in which you explore and define two conflicting sides of your identity. Like Nunes, see if you can come to some self-awareness in the process of writing about this state of being in-between.

2.   Nunes's essay closes with a wish: "I wished that he had found in me

something of himself; an element of something different, a piece of who we are and where we come from." What does she want the little boy to find in her? Write an essay comparing his sense of her with her sense of herself.

Connecting with Other Texts

1. In her search for identity, Nunes seems to be struggling between two views of herself: an *either/or* identity, in which she must see herself as either Indian or white, versus a *both/and* identity, in which she is both Indian and white. Compare Nunes's *either/or* conflict with the similar problems of identity discussed in Carl Wilson's essay "Did You Ever Have to Make Up Your Mind?" (p. 123).

2. Nunes describes herself as having been "a preteen who coveted the blond good looks of Marcia Brady" (paragraph 9). What role does the media play in defining "good looks" for young people? Watch a number of sitcoms or dramas, popular movies, or music videos, and keep a record of the races of the main characters. Then write an essay arguing that whites are (or are not) the dominant models for defining what it means to be good-looking.

3. Using current periodical articles, find out about racially mixed marriages and the children who grow up in them. What is the success rate for racially mixed marriage? How do children from these marriages learn to live between two worlds? Write a research essay discussing your findings.

Discovering My Native Identity

Sean Kelly

1 There are times when my flesh feels picked completely from my bones, when the fire of my anger is at the height of its truth. These are the fragments of insight, compassion and need that inspire me. My memories force me to live with purpose. My emotions force me to write.

2 I am a Native who lives among whites. Growing up I believed government was wrong and that Indians were right. My mother fought for Native land claims and that influenced what I—and anyone around her—thought of Native issues.

3 Yet ironically, for most of my life my identity as an Indian wasn't clear to me. I saw no difference between myself and the people around me, and therefore took their identity as my own. If anything, I felt a benefit: My race meant I had a year-round tan.

4 But by junior high school, I noticed that there was one part of my maturing that was missing. I was the only one in my group who had never been

involved with a girl. I was a bit fat, so I lost weight, but that didn't help.

5   I came to realize that the problem was that I looked different from the white people around me. Once, standing before a mirror with a friend, I noticed how his wavy, blond hair hung loosely over his smooth, pinkish skin, while my hair was stiff, in thick, combed clumps above my tan skin. Around my deep black eyes was a darkness created by my high cheekbones that gave me an almost brooding look. If it were possible to symbolize our differences, my friend would have been warmth and brightness; I would have been anger and darkness. And not dark like James Dean, but more like a thug in an alley.

6   These revelations energized the parasite that continued to gnaw away at my confidence. It was an ache that possessed me. All my friends were, or had been, romantically involved. The only difference between us was my ethnicity. Being rejected by white girls is hardly a tragedy, but when that's all you're surrounded with, it can feel like one.

7   The sense of not belonging grew. Memories of failed job interviews and people's worried stares and pompous grins returned to me. At some level I had known that these rejections existed, but I had always thought, "Let people have their racist little shots of power. I have friends who don't care about that shit."

8   But now I began to wonder if I really did. I was at a party with about 40 people once and I was the only non-white. People discussed the contempt they had for the gangs of "Pakis," "Nips" and "Brothers" at our school. I realized that if people of my race formed into a group, my "friends" probably would have talked in a derogatory way about them too. The fact that I didn't have a group also made me realize that I was alone as an Indian.

9   My early assumption that because I lived among whites I could shed my race had proved painfully false. I realized I was ashamed of who I was because of the Indians I had been around. They had either been drunk in city streets or dying on the reserves. I remember an incident at a beer store where a truck full of Natives pulled up and I asked one of them to buy beer for me. When we stood face to face and I saw his missing teeth and drunken gaze, I couldn't see any correlation between us. Now I wished that I could have. I longed to live proudly among a group where I felt equal.

10   I wondered how other minorities survived, because it didn't seem possible that they could be as desperate as I was. When I looked around my school I saw that they had one another. When a group of East Indians hang out together, they can date each other and relate feelings without the burden of crossing any lines.

11   When one race dominates a population, there is going to be a boundary. That boundary in my life was around the white man's world. By some magic, whites accepted me at a sort of mascot level, but they did not understand or respect my race. My physical differences made the females around me wary, a fact at the core of my need to be with my own kind.

12   We human beings can't help thinking about our differences. I don't know why we dwell on the thickness of lips, the structure of cheekbones or the colour of skin, but when we separate and form into teams, I want to be on one. I want to have girls around me, with my thick black hair and wide jawline, to love and respect me without reservation or fear.

13   But that is unlikely. At my school I am the only Indian. The other Indians I see are in the poorer areas of the city. The only way we can be with our own kind is if we throw away our lives and move to the failed reserves.

14   I began to die inside when I saw my situation. Everywhere I went I felt like an outsider. Every little stare seemed to be someone's way of telling me that they were better than me, and that I didn't belong. When I went to dances and nightclubs, the girls around me were always white. I felt they were unobtainable. This depressed me so I usually got drunk.

15   Then one night I wandered into the bathroom of a nightclub after I'd been drinking. When I looked in the mirror I saw a "hard" Indian, like the ones I had seen at the beer store. I wasn't any better. Perhaps I deserved the stares and grins. I realized that I could not drink as my friends did because no matter how many drunk whites surrounded me, I would be seen as another pathetic Indian.

16   That night woke me up to how I'd given up on my life. My feelings of alienation and inferiority had paralysed my ambitions. I knew I needed help. So I began to involve myself deeply with other Natives. Not the hapless ones on reserves or in inner cities, but Indians who had overcome the challenge of white society and found success. I came to understand why our race is failing so badly, why one in seven Native teenagers commits suicide and why 70 percent of us are on welfare. It is because the feelings that had been destroying me were rabid in every other Indian as well.

17   I now believe that if the society I live in does not accept me, I must take away its reasons not to. I will not let people bump me down into the savage cage of alcoholics and brutes.

18   I can't make females shed their fear of my differences, nor can I blame them. But I have also realized I was a little bit sick. I had thought that none of the white girls would ever consider involving themselves with someone of my disrespected race. I was wrong. When alienation takes hold of someone it makes them see things worse than they are.

19   That is why our people have a chance. We have the ability to save our-selves if we only realize that our lives have potential. Once I saw that there were people different than me, that were willing to accept me, I was saved. I could see a reason for keeping my life intact.

20   I also stopped hanging out with many of my so-called friends. It both-ered me that out of all the people in our school I was their only non-white friend. One night at a party I waited for one of them to make a racist com-ment. When it happened and they laughed, I confronted them. They got defensive, claiming that they weren't racist. A few of them said they didn't know it bothered me and promised to stop. Most of them didn't change at all. After seeing the problems that my people have I would be a traitor and a fool to tolerate racism.

21   Many minority groups in my school release their anger through vio-lence. I've decided to release mine through writing. And when I say "anger," I don't mean that I want to shame anyone or make villains of anybody. I've always hated movies that show racists as one-dimensional beasts because no understanding is ever reached. And although most of my pain has been because of white society, I've never had contempt for white people.

22   Which leads me to my desire to become a screenwriter. I want to reveal a truth to society that most minorities already know. It is that racial harass-ment, whether brashly in the city streets or subtly in everyday situations, is a form of violence—one that leaves it victims unable to move freely in soci-ety. It imprisons us, and makes us want to give in or strike out. And for those so racist that they don't care about our feelings, I want to warn them that their forms of assault will return to haunt them. As our people die off, there will be those who cannot contain the desperation within themselves. Such was the case in Oka and during the Los Angeles riots.

23   Indians need to know that although we are physically alone, spiritu-ally we all struggle together. To stumble into a movie theatre and see our lives on the screen would, piece by piece, work to save our race. The Native individual must believe that there is a place for him in white soci-ety, a place that can only be found through determination and confidence. I know if there had been a story telling me this as I grew up, my life would have been easier and more successful.

24   I've wondered if there is a place for Native stories. We are, after all, a mere 0.5 percent of the U.S. population—which I have concluded makes our stories worthy of being told. One day in biology class we discussed how species of the frog had become extinct, and if that was Mother Nature's way of hinting to us our fate. It occurred to me that Natives are a much more prominent hint.

25   Natives have slowly been pushed out of their habitats by man and his technology. Our people die from tuberculosis and alcoholism, brought by the white man and his modern world. We used to survive with nature, taking from her what we needed and nothing more. We can no longer do this. Instead we are being assimilated into the modern world and dying because of it. Perhaps we are a sacrifice to warn civilization that it is greatly flawed and hurtling toward self-destruction.

26   As society becomes more immense and chaotic, our stories will become increasingly more valuable to others.

27   I went to a Native screenwriting workshop and met the first Native screenwriter. He was 28. He told me that there were only three other Native screenwriters in all of Canada. This is when I realized why there is so much ignorance of our people. I realized I had an obligation to try and change that. That is why I have chosen screenwriting as a career.

Thinking about the Text

1. How did Kelly's viewpoint about himself change as he was growing up? What personal conflicts did he experience? Give examples from the text.

2. How does the author perceive himself by the time he has decided on his career? Summarize what he hopes to accomplish as a screenwriter.

3. In what ways can movies change our perceptions of ourselves or each other? Support your answer with examples from the text.

Writing from the Text

1. Kelly says that racial harassment is a form of violence. Using examples from this essay and from your or your friends' experience, explain how this statement is true.

2. Have you ever been in a position like Kelly's, where emotions about how you have been treated force you to write? Write an essay like Kelly's in which you explore how events have led you to a realization about yourself, your relationships, and your place in the world.

Connecting with Other Texts

1. Look in periodicals written for Native audiences, such as *Aboriginal Voices*, for an indication of how other Native people are also discovering and celebrating their Native identity. Write an essay on your findings.

2. Robert Chodos, in "Being a Jew at Christmas" (p. 94), also writes about what it is like to be a member of a minority in Canada today. Compare Chodos's experience with Kelly's and write about the causes and effects of social alienation in minority groups.

I Lost My Talk

Rita Joe

I lost my talk
The talk you took away.
When I was a little girl
At Shubenacadie school.

5 You snatched it away:
I speak like you
I think like you
I create like you
The scrambled ballad, about my word.

10 Two ways I talk
Both ways I say,
Your way is more powerful.

So gently I offer my hand and ask,
Let me find my talk
15 So I can teach you about me.

Thinking about the Text

1. What words indicate how the speaker's loss was accomplished? What is the effect of the repetition in the second stanza?

2. Why does the speaker use the word "talk" rather than "language"? What does she mean by the word "word" (line 9)?

3. Discuss the possible meanings of the phrase "scrambled ballad" (line 9).

4. The speaker alludes to the power of one language over another language. Does the final stanza indicate defiance or acquiescence to people more powerful than herself? Use examples from the text to support your answer.

Writing from the Text

1. Is the speaker bilingual and therefore caught between two worlds, or is she divided? Or, is she both bilingual and divided? How has language determined this woman's identity? Analyse this poem and write an essay answering these questions.

2. Write a cause-and-effect essay discussing what happens when the right to speak is lost. You may want to focus on particular groups that have been silenced in the past, such as Natives, women, or Blacks. Or, you may prefer to consider censorship or propaganda as forms of silencing.

Connecting with Other Texts

1. In what ways do Sean Kelly, the author of "Discovering My Native Identity" (p. 101), and the speaker in this poem both live life as a "scrambled ballad"? Write an essay comparing their experiences.

2. Search for information about the effects of residential schools on Native children in Canada and write a research essay on your findings.

An Accent on Learning English

Sun-Kyung Yi

1 The words "No speak English" were essential to my survival for a long time as an immigrant in Canada. These three magic words made people feel sympathetic toward yet another newcomer, and to my relief, people also tended to shy away and leave me alone. Later on, the phrase even proved to be a good excuse to mutter if I didn't want to be bothered by door-to-door salesmen or telemarketers.

2 But those days are long gone. My English has improved greatly, but I have two major problems that don't seem to go away: my accent is evident as soon as I open my mouth and my use of grammar seems to fluctuate from bad to worse at the best of times.

3 At first I didn't worry too much about the thick accent that coated every syllable I pronounced with painstaking effort, because I assumed that it would eventually disappear with time and practice. Yet 17 years after I landed here at the age of 9, it still hangs around like a relative who has overstayed his welcome.

4 Since I went to school surrounded by kids and teachers who all sounded the same—white—I was under the illusion that I sounded like them. When I mispronounced words, teachers rarely acknowledged my mistakes or attempted to correct them. Once they got used to my way of communicating, they left me alone, leaving me convinced that the problem was solved.

5 Not true.

6 In university, I took a French class that was compulsory for my degree. Needless to say, it was mission impossible. The language demanded too much twisting and twirling of my tongue and called for unnatural, gurgling sounds to spill out from the back of my throat, distorting my features and leaving my jaw tired at the end of each class.

7   It just wasn't natural that someone like me should even try to learn a third language. The French words just got buried beneath my Korean and Canadian accents (a poor replica of the latter). It was cruel and unusual punishment for both the professor and me. I finally surrendered, giving up these torturous attempts to speak French.

8   But I didn't give up on my accent easily. I tried everything from private voice lessons from a radio announcer to singing lessons from an opera singer to poetry reading, with little success.

9   Over time, I grew complacent. With the continuing acceptance of friends and colleagues who were used to my accent, I had forgotten about the ongoing problem. However, I was forced to confront it again recently when I went into a CBC radio studio to read a documentary script I had written. My producer patiently coached me and corrected the mispronounced words.

10   For example, when he said "these" is pronounced "theez," not "this," and "women" was "wimmen," not "woman," I looked at him puzzled. Why didn't anybody tell me this before? When I tried to repeat after my producer, the sounds that came out of my mouth were foreign to my ears. After so many years of mispronouncing them, I had assumed that my way was the right way.

11   Playing back my own voice in the studio, I was horrified at the result. Not only did I sound terrible, I could hardly understand what I was saying.

12   My producer comforted me by saying that *he* understood everything I read. But people had often reassured me and told me not to worry about my accent and yet here I was unable to understand myself. I can hear in my head the way words are supposed to sound, but I'll be damned if I can make my mouth say them.

13   The mispronunciations of the th's and r's were legion throughout the reading, and the emphasis on the wrong syllables was too obvious.

14   As a consolation, the producer told me the script was well written. But what he didn't know was how long it took me to labour over the words on those pages, not for creativity necessarily but to catch those grammar mistakes that seem to pop up when least expected.

15   To this day, I still get confused and flustered when it comes to the use of determiners, "the" and "a" (which don't exist in Korean grammar). I know the basic rules, but there always seem to be some exceptions that make me second-guess and question my familiarity with the language all over again.

16   At least I have my prepositions under control. But I'm still not too clear

on the differences between "at the café" and "in the café." Is it "at the beach" or "on the beach"?

17   In the ESL class I took before I entered the school system, instructors didn't teach me about the subtle but very important usage of determiners, prepositions and adjectives. And they taught with antiquated elementary-school texts in which we read such useless singsong phrases as "Dick and Jane ran down the hill" and "Look Spot look! Look at Dick and Jane run!" instead of practical phrases such as "Where is the bus stop?" or "I am sick and need to see a doctor."

18   Once you get into the education system, teachers seem to give you an A in English if you have neat handwriting and if your homework is done on time. (I got an A in my high-school English classes, but was told by university professors that I needed remedial English study.)

19   I accept the fact that speaking and writing don't come naturally to me, and I don't think they ever will (as fate would have it, I write for a living), but I do wonder if I'm ever going to be free of these two particular problems.

20   I wouldn't be so anxious about them if I had a perfect grasp of the Korean language to compensate, but I stopped learning that as a child. I was too busy learning basic English to keep up with my Korean.

21   Now, I feel stranded between two languages neither of which I feel comfortable speaking or writing.

Thinking about the Text

1. In what ways is Yi caught between worlds?
2. Compare Yi's self-perception with the ways others perceive her.
3. Summarize Yi's criticism of the Canadian school system.
4. In your opinion, why are Canadians hesitant to correct the pronunciation errors that people like Yi make?

Writing from the Text

1. If you speak another language besides English, do you feel "stranded" as Yi describes it? Write an essay comparing your experience with hers.
2. Yi contends that high-school English teachers give A's for neat handwriting and homework done on time. Is this true of English or ESL instructors at your college? How should an instructor ensure that high grades reflect genuinely high achievement and not effort alone? Write a persuasive essay arguing that high grades must reflect the highest level of achievement.

Connecting with Other Texts

1. Compare and contrast Yi's experience with Julia Nunes's in "The Business of Being Half and Half" (p. 98). In what ways is Yi also "half and half"?

2. In an essay, compare Yi's experience with that of the narrator in Rita Joe's poem "I Lost My Talk" (p. 106).

3. Ask an ESL student in your class to talk to you about his or her experience learning a second language. Or go to a multicultural students' group and ask to interview an ESL student. What are his or her main problems learning English? What is easy and what is hard to learn? How can colleges help ESL students get the help they need? Write an essay on your findings.

Ajax Là-Bas

Yeshim Ternar

1 Saliha Samson sits on one of the empty washing machines in the basement and lights a cigarette. There are three loads of wash in the machines. The wash cycle takes 35 minutes; the drying cycle another 25. The French couple who employ her are very nice people. They leave for work early in the morning, as soon as she arrives at 8:30. They trust her with everything. They know she is a conscientious worker, that she doesn't slack off like some of the other cleaning women.

2 Madame Rivest tells Saliha to eat whatever she wants from the refrigerator. She always leaves some change in the ceramic vase on the telephone table just in case Saliha needs to get extra detergent, cigarettes, or whatever. Madame Rivest knows she likes to snack on strawberry and blueberry yoghurt, so she always makes sure there is some in the refrigerator for her. This morning she has told her she hasn't done her weekly shopping yet, so she is leaving some money for Saliha especially to buy fruit yoghurt.

3 Now that's a nice gesture! I wish everyone were like that, thinks Saliha as she takes a deep puff from her cigarette. The Rivests live a long ways off from where she lives. She has to take the 80 bus from Park Extension, then the metro at Place des Arts to Berri, and then change metros at Berri to go to Longueuil; afterwards she has to take yet another bus to come here. But the trip is worth it because some of the people she works for close to home treat her so badly that she'd rather lose an hour on the way and work for Madame and Monsieur Rivest. That's a lot easier than working for the two old spinsters on upper Querbes.

4   Saliha notices the unbalanced load signal flash on one of the washers, and gets off the machine she is sitting on to straighten things out. As she untangles the heavy blue cotton velour bedspread from the black rotor blades of the washing machine, she thinks it was lucky she decided to take this cigarette break in the basement because if she had gone straight upstairs to continue her vacuuming, she would have lost an extra 25 minutes by having to wait for this load after all the others were completed. That would have thrown her schedule off perhaps by an hour because she would have had to take the elevator up and down twice more and delay other tasks in the meantime. That's how cleaning jobs are. You have to plan what you're going to do and how, and in what order. Otherwise. . . . Well, the machine starts churning again and she jumps back on the machine she was sitting on before to finish her cigarette.

5   She has her period again. It's crazy, she thinks. Madame Rivest calls her every two weeks. And every other time she has to work for Madame Rivest, she gets her period. It's either the first day or the second day of her period when she has to make that long trip to come here. I've never had any luck with periods, thinks Saliha as she massages her back with her left hand. Saliha's dream is to be able to lie in bed the whole day when she gets her period. But it never works that way.

6   The first time she had her period when she was eleven, she was in Istanbul then, she ran up to her mom to announce it. Her mother slapped her. "Why did you do that?" Saliha asked. "So that you won't lose your wits." Saliha went to her room and cried less for the mess of blood than for the fact that she was getting too old to play hopscotch. That was fifteen years ago. Saliha cannot remember when she stopped playing hopscotch, but it was at least a year after she got her first period.

7   Some things in life are like that. First they come to you like big worries, and you spend days and nights worrying about them, but they have the life span and personality of a soap bubble. They grow and grow like a wart in one's heart and just when you're sure they are big and strong and will never go away, they pop out of your life not even leaving a rind, not even a speck of dust, but the dry flake of a single detergent grain.

8   Canadians are funny, thinks Saliha. They have detergents and lotions and soaps for everything. Everything has its own cleanser here. And every cleanser has its own name. Like Mr. Clean. But Mr. Clean is also M. Net. Wisk! What a strange way to call your laundry detergent. And Ajax. Particularly Ajax. George, the Greek *dépanneur* at Park Ex, told her Ajax was a Greek hero. Old heroes live on as detergents in Canada. Saliha smiles at her own joke. She thinks she should write this to her mom.

9   The wash is done in one of the machines. She opens a dryer and transfers the load there. Just as she starts the dryer, the other two machines go off. So she puts these loads in the dryers too, and feeds quarters to the machines. It's time to go up and vacuum the Rivests' bedroom, she decides.

10   She goes up on the elevator, happy that no one else is on it. She hates to be seen in her work clothes. She is wearing a pink cotton jumper, a navy blue shirt with the sleeves rolled up underneath that, and knee socks and her red moccasins. She had tied a Turkish scarf on her head with a knot in the back to keep her hair away from her face. Madame Rivest says she looks like a school girl like that. But Saliha feels uneasy in her work clothes. After all, it is hard to resign herself to being a cleaning woman on the sly in Canada.

11   As she is vacuuming the Rivests' bedroom, she remembers her friend Frederiki's warning. Frederiki told her to be careful most when she is vacuuming because when you have the vacuum on full blast, you can't hear if someone is approaching from the back. Frederiki said she knows a couple of cases of rape that happened when the cleaning woman was vacuuming and the old geezer tip-toed and caught the cleaning woman and forced her on the bed . . . Saliha shivers at the thought. She drops the vacuum cleaner and goes to check if she locked both locks on the door. Not that M. Rivest would do anything like that. He has two married daughters, but you never know who might have keys to the apartment.

12   On her way back from the door, walking through the living room, Saliha checks the time on the mantel clock that she guesses comes from Spain. The clock is set in a gold and black lacework metal fan that reminds one of the Spanish flamenco dancers. The Rivests appear to be well-travelled people. Scattered about the apartment there are several photographs of Madame and M. Rivest, in silver-rimmed frames, from various countries. The one on the side table next to the loveseat in the living room looks like it was taken in Spain. Madame Rivest, looking several years younger, is smiling in front of a white-washed Mediterranean-type house with red gardenias blooming in clay pots along the window sill. She is slightly tanned. It is a sunny photograph, making Madame Rivest whose face carries many wrinkles from cold Canadian winters look out of place in the country where Saliha assumes the true residents greet the sunshine with less suspicion and distress.

13   Nevertheless, Madame Rivest smiles in that photograph as all middle-aged tourists do on well-deserved holidays. A straw handbag hangs from her left shoulder, and in her right hand, she holds something like a camera lens cover.

14   Saliha notes that the dryers must have completed their cycle, so she goes back to the bedroom and quickly finishes off the corners of the room with the special attachment Madame Rivest has taught her to use.

15   She takes along the yellow plastic laundry basket to carry the wash. She gets unlucky going down. A young housewife and her son step into the elevator on the second floor and ride with her to the main floor. Saliha tries to act oblivious to the woman's presence, but she winks surreptitiously at the little boy. The boy responds with a blank face.

16   Saliha is relieved when they get out. In the basement she quickly piles all the wash together in the laundry basket and after turning the drums around and feeling around the ridges for a stray sock or handkerchief, she goes up to the Rivests' apartment to sort the clothes. She is folding the towels and the sheets neatly and mechanically when she looks up at the ceiling of the Rivests' bedroom for an instant and starts remembering.

17   She is back in fourth grade at her elementary school on the Asian side of Istanbul. It was late September, several weeks into the fall term when the school principal had given the all-important Monday morning speech to the whole elementary school population: rows of fidgety kids lined up in twos behind overweight maternal teachers.

18   They had all finished pledging allegiance to the Turkish nation and Turkish morality. In unison, they had proclaimed the following verses with pride:

19   "I am Turkish, I am honest, I am industrious. My motto is: to love my inferiors, to respect my superiors, to love my country and my people more than my own life. May my existence be a gift to the existence of the Turkish people."

20   It was after the whole schoolyard had fallen silent that the old principal had cleared his throat, adjusted his glasses with a nervous push of the index finger of his right hand, and straightened the arms of his worn navy blue jacket by pulling at the sleeves. He had then solemnly said, more like a poet than the disciplinarian that the Ministry of Education demanded him to be:

21   "My dear children, today I would like to tell you about your counterparts in America. Little boys and girls your age in America are very different from you in some very important respects. For one, they are often more industrious, and they are better behaved. I felt it was my duty to remind you of this after the very grave accidents your wild running about in the schoolyard during recesses last week has caused. Several of your friends are not at school today because they gashed their heads or sprained their ankles from all the savage games they have been playing.

The weather has been very nice. The school year has just begun. Your teachers and I understand that you are all happy to join your friends after the summer holidays, but school is not a place where you come to play unruly games of tag and hide-and-seek. School is a place where you come to learn about the vital skills that you will need for all your lives and where you receive the benefits of civilization. Your counterparts in America understand what school is all about. At recess, they don't run around like you, but make use of their time to practise the knowledge that they learn in the classroom. For example, when they go out into the schoolyard— and let me remind you that not all of them are blessed with a schoolyard such as ours—they examine their surroundings. Look at all the leaves on the ground about you. You have perhaps not noticed them during all your frenzied horseplay. An American child, however, would pick up a leaf, examine it, do research to identify it, and record his observations in his notebook. An American child would do the same for an ant, a worm, or a spider instead of madly crushing it. If you, as young Turks, the adults of the future, learn to do the same, you will help to build a better nation and honour this country that our great Ataturk had offered to you as your most cherished gift."

22   With this, the principal ended his speech. Saliha felt she was one of the few who had heard the true message of the principal's words. She looked about and saw, for the first time, the mounds of leaves in the schoolyard and the shady corners teeming with insects. After that day, every dry copper-coloured leaf, every quiet ant bespoke of her new task to pay attention to the world.

23   Saliha went on to finish her primary school education with distinctions despite some uncomfortable failures in the science class of her fifth year. Then she went to teacher's college to become a primary school teacher. After teaching in remote Anatolian villages where she gained the awe and respect of the peasants, she came to Canada to join her brother who is an auto mechanic in Montreal. She is presently enrolled at Plato College on Park Avenue to learn English and French.

24   Saliha folds all the towels and linen neatly. She separates Madame Rivest's lingerie from M. Rivest's underwear and pairs up his socks. She puts away all of the clean laundry on the appropriate shelves in the closet and the dresser. She does not neglect to arrange what was already there before she puts away the newly washed clothes. Everything looks fresh and clean! Only some light dusting remains to be done. Then she will clean the bathroom. First she'll throw away the dirty water in the pail from mopping the floors, then she'll rinse out the cleaning rags and put away

all the cleaning materials. Afterwards she'll take her shower and scrub the bathtub clean.

25   But before she finishes up the remaining tasks, Saliha decides to take a cigarette break on the blue floral patterned armchair in the living room. She makes some fresh coffee in the kitchen, brings her cup over to the living room and lights a cigarette. She unties her scarf and lets her wavy black hair down. As she sips her coffee in between puffs, Saliha goes over her cleaning appointments for the next two weeks. To remember the exact dates, she visualizes the Chrysler calendar in her kitchen with pictures of different kimono-clad Japanese geishas for each month.

26   She has to clean the two spinster sisters on Thursday. She certainly doesn't look forward to that one. They are very messy people. They are also very careful with their money.

27   Contrary to the Rivests, they always follow her around and check how much detergent and soap she uses. They never offer her much at lunchtime. Not that she would eat what they eat. They always eat some strange food that she is unaccustomed to, things like blood sausage and sauerkraut; topping it off with stale May West cakes they buy at Steinberg or Provigo. Saliha prefers to keep to herself when she works there.

28   On Friday afternoon, she will clean for the old Czech at Côte des Neiges. He is a kind and quiet man who doesn't demand much from Saliha. He is glad to have a woman clean up once every few weeks. When she is there, Saliha cooks a couple of light dishes for him. He is always grateful for that and gives her an extra two dollars.

29   Saliha hopes that Eleni will call her on the weekend to confirm a cleaning job next week. Eleni lives close to where Saliha lives in Park Extension. But the best part of working for Eleni is that at the end of the work day when she is done at her hairdressing salon downstairs, Eleni comes upstairs to have coffee with Saliha and trims her hair and manicures her nails as a gesture of appreciation. Eleni's house is large and demands all of Saliha's energy but the extra reward makes the effort worth it. Eleni expects the cleaning to be done well, but always offers refreshments like Kool-aid and Tang. Last time Saliha worked there, Eleni gave her some of her daughter's old clothes. Saliha hopes she might receive a reasonable sweater next time because she badly needs something a little fashionable for the end of the term party at Plato College.

30   Sipping the last of her coffee, Saliha rises from the armchair and looks around the living room to plan her dusting strategy. She will do just the outside panels of the display cabinet this time, leaving the silver goblets and British china for the next time. Then she will dust the buffet and the

little figurines on top of it, taking care to dust off the folds of the Chinese jade Buddha. She decides not to waste too much time polishing the wood this time as all the wooden surfaces are still sparkling from the last time she did it. The Rivests don't seem to have invited anyone over for dinner in the meantime because the guest sets remain as she last arranged them.

31   Saliha has just finished drying her hair and changing into her street clothes after her shower when Madame Rivest comes back from work. She greets Saliha in French, glances around the house and shows her approval with many "Oohs" and "Wonderfuls," stretching her words to make Saliha understand her heart-felt appreciation. Then she says in French that she will call Saliha again next week to confirm their next cleaning date. As she says this, Madame Rivest gestures as if she were dialling and holding on to the receiver of an imaginary telephone.

32   Of course Saliha can understand everything Madame Rivest is saying without the added gestures, but Madame Rivest is being so kind and helpful that Saliha decides not to use a couple of appropriate French phrases she has recently learned at Plato College.

33   Madame Rivest goes into her bedroom and comes back out with a sealed white envelope containing Saliha's thirty-five dollars. The Rivests are the only people that put Saliha's earnings in an envelope. They are considerate people.

34   As Saliha takes the envelope, she says, "Merci beaucoup, Madame Rivest." Stepping out the door, she switches the plastic bag containing her work clothes from her right hand to her left hand and extends her right hand to Madame Rivest and says, "Bonjour, Madame Rivest," and smiles. These are the first real words she has uttered since she woke up that morning.

35   In the elevator, going down, Saliha is alone. She checks the contents of the envelope and smiles with satisfaction. Before the elevator reaches the ground floor, Saliha has time to reflect on her day. She has earned enough for the week's food and cigarettes. Last week, she paid the last instalment for her tuition at Plato College. She is tired but life is under control. Her only regret is that she hasn't answered Madame Rivest in longer sentences. But she chases away her regrets with a light shrug and admits the reality.

36   We come here to speak like them, she thinks; but it will be a long time before they let us practise.

Thinking about the Text

1. What is the significance of the setting of "Ajax Là-Bas"? How does it relate to the theme of "between worlds"?

2. List the details of Saliha's flashbacks. What purpose do these flashbacks play in the story?

3. How and why does Saliha's principal compare her and her schoolmates unfavourably to American children?

4. All short stories have conflict; if there is no conflict, there is no story. But some stories do not have an obvious antagonist/protagonist conflict. What are the conflicts in Saliha Samson's life?

Writing from the Text

1. Write a comparison of Saliha's life in Canada and her life in Turkey.

2. Using examples from this story and your own experience, write an essay about how "outsiders" view Canadians and how Canadians views "outsiders."

3. Reread the story and look for references to time and timing. Write an essay discussing the role time and cycles play in Saliha's life.

Connecting with Other Texts

1. The story ends with the line "We come here to speak like them, she thinks; but it will be a long time before they let us practise." Using this story and "An Accent on Learning English" (p. 107), write an analysis of some of the problems immigrants to Canada face when learning to speak a second language.

2. Use Robert L. Heilbroner's "Don't Let Stereotypes Warp Your Judgments" (p. 128) to argue that Saliha's employers stereotype (or do not stereotype) her.

Quebec
Michael Ignatieff

The Frenchies

1 There were Frenchies hiding in the cemetery, we were sure of that. They were tough Catholic kids and they had slingshots. We all knew they were there, hiding behind the gravestones, waiting to get us. The cemetery was up on the hill above Juliana Road, where we lived, and I knew that I

shouldn't ever go up there on my bike alone. Everyone at school knew that they pulled kids off their bikes and rode away on their wheels. They were bad kids, it was common knowledge.

2   Once, we English kids on Juliana got up the courage to lead an expedition into the cemetery. We planned it like a military raid, like General Wolfe sneaking up on the French at Quebec in 1759. We armed ourselves— my pockets were full of the sharp stones the gravel truck dumped on our street—and we fanned out at the base of the cliff leading up to the cemetery, and we advanced from headstone to headstone, right up to the top, just as we had seen it done by the Indians in the U.S. Cavalry movies on television. They were bigger than us, that was all we knew, big ignorant boys who spoke nothing but French and used real ball bearings in their slingshots. You could tell they did, because the ball bearings left neat round indentations on the STOP signs at the crossings on the cemetery road.

3   I was eight at the time, and I was excited that the older kids on Juliana had let me join the raid. I made a point of how small I was, and how I could get ahead of them, hide behind the gravestones, and act like a scout. That was what I did. I was the first to reach the top of the cemetery hill. It was so quiet up there, hiding among the gravestones of the Camerons and Frasers, McDonalds and Robertsons, heaved up into crooked positions by the frost, and above my head, the sound of the autumn maples rustling in the wind. The others were some time making it to the top, so I waited for them, crouched behind a gravestone, keeping watch for the Frenchies, who were supposed to be preparing an ambush for us on the other side of the crematorium. I could hear the English boys sneaking up behind me, taking their positions, and I knew they would be asking me where we should move next, to get closer to the Frenchies. And I knew that I was going to have to say, as I felt the stillness and emptiness of the graveyard all around me, that there were no Frenchies there at all. It was obvious. I am not saying they didn't exist. They were there, all right. It is just that none of us could see them. And we never did.

Imagined Community

4 You can never know the strangers who make up a nation with you. So you imagine what it is that you have in common, and in this shared imagining, strangers become citizens, that is, people who share both the same rights and the same image of the place they live in. A nation, therefore, is an imagined community. Yet these imaginings never exactly overlap, are never exactly shared. As I look back now at the Canada I thought we had in common, it strikes me that English and French never did imagine it the

same way. The myth I grew up believing was that Canada was a partnership between two peoples, two languages, two histories, and two traditions. I believed this, yet I never actually met any Québécois when I was growing up, although Ottawa, where I lived, is just across the river from Quebec. When I went to Quebec, I went to the English-speaking Eastern Townships, to a house where my Russian grandparents lived.

5   The Canada I thought I belonged to was, believe it or not, an example to the rest of the world. We were a binational, bi-ethnic federal community, living proof that different races, different languages could live together within the framework of a single state. In my imaginings, I turned that dull but intricate contrivance, Canadian federalism, into a moral beacon to the whole benighted world. I had no idea, for example, that what for me was a family romance was, for the other partner, a loveless marriage. As for what came to be known as the First Nations, the Native peoples, they didn't figure in my equation of the country at all.

6   It seems extraordinary, in retrospect, that I should have supposed that we—the Québécois and I—actually knew each other well enough to constitute any kind of community at all. That childhood memory of the cemetery was actually closer to the truth. Yet is it a memory of mine or a fantasy? I had better confess that I didn't always remember it as I have told it now. For years, I thought I had actually fought the Frenchies. I believed I had seen the big rough French boys, storming down from the heights of the cemetery, chasing us back into Juliana Road with a hail of ball bearings. Now I am quite sure: we never even saw them. They were phantoms to me, as I was to them, and phantoms they have remained.

. . .

Hockey Night in Canada

7 Dennis Rousseau is in his late twenties and works for Wayagamack, a paper mill in Trois-Rivières, on the north shore of the Saint Lawrence. His wife works as a bookkeeper in town, and they live, with their baby girl, in a two-bedroom bungalow on a suburban street a few minutes' walk from the paper mill. Outside, it is about fifteen below zero and snow is falling through the light cast by the streetlamps. In Dennis's front yard, there is a gigantic snow fort, and half of the kids on the street are attacking it with snowballs and the other half are defending it. Snowballs are whizzing through the night air around me, splattering against the fort, against Dennis's front door. He pulls me inside and shuts the door with a laugh.

8   Dennis is wearing a hockey shirt and jeans, and his thin blond hair is down to his shoulders. His Québécois is fast, heavily accented, and sometimes too much for my French-French to understand. He apologizes that he doesn't speak English, and then points down to his three-year-old daughter, who is pushing a large plastic tractor across the living room. "She's going to be in English immersion." English immersion courses are in their first year in Trois-Rivières. "We don't want to be cut off," he says.

9   I was looking for someone who could talk to me about the economics of independence from a worker's point of view, and union organizers in Montreal gave me Dennis's name. Besides, Trois-Rivières is the heart of Quebec, a unilingual town that used to be the capital of its pulp and paper industry. There used to be twelve mills in the region, going twenty-four hours a day, making the paper for the phone books and newspapers of a whole continent. No more. Demand is down, due to the recession, and in Alabama and Georgia they have plants that can produce the paper for less. Only six mills are left, and at Dennis's factory they have lost one-third of the workforce in the last year.

10   "A lot of layoffs at my mill. Over two hundred. Same at the Belgo, Kruger, and worst of all is the PFCP, which used to have a thousand workers. Now it's closed. We've got 17 percent unemployment in Trois-Rivières. It's bad. I could lose my job anytime. When I go out to the rink to play hockey with the guys I never know who's going to be there."

11   Hardly the moment, I would have thought, for nationalist experiments. But that's not how Dennis sees it. "The government ought to do something. We need a jobs policy, but Quebec doesn't have the power. Employment is federal. We need to get our hands on the levers."

12   Dennis isn't a Parti Québécois militant, but he is a phenomenon—he represents the spread of Quebec nationalist doctrine from the cafés of Montreal intellectuals to the industrial heartland. Three years of recession have, paradoxically, turned him into a nationalist. "We've got the businessmen, we've got the skills, we could make this place work, I'm sure of it." The Canadian government, he thinks, takes care only of English Canada.

13   Why, I suggest, don't you make common cause with the workers in Ontario? They're having just as hard a time as you. Dennis won't budge. "Ontario won't give us the powers we need. They say we have too much already."

14   Dennis is a cheerful, openhearted man, diffident with strangers, but with convictions no amount of arguing on my part can shift. It doesn't make much impression when I tell him the Canadian government has been pouring money into the fight against unemployment in Quebec. It

doesn't matter that an independent Quebec might have just as much trouble keeping a tired old paper mill in business. He knows what he knows, and that is that a sovereign Quebec couldn't make a bigger mess of his life than Ottawa has already.

15   I can't help feeling that for Dennis, nationalism may just be a welcome flight from disagreeable economic realities. One reality is that his mill used to be owned by a Quebec company. They failed to put in the necessary investment and sold it off to an American company. The Americans are now investing, but it may be too late for the plant to compete against the company's own lower-cost plants in the United States. What, in other words, can Quebec ownership or Quebec sovereignty do in the face of the competitive economics in a continental market?

16   But, then again, if he thought the way I do, he would give up. Nationalism gives him hope, and in Trois-Rivières you need all the hope you can get. The curious thing, of course, is that it is such a Canadian style of hope. We Canadians believe in government. Social democratic interventionism is as much in my bones as it is in Dennis's. The sad thing is that this common faith is leading us into different countries.

17   Although Dennis feels strongly, there is little or no aggression in what he says toward English Canadians. He did visit Niagara Falls once, and while he had some trouble making himself understood, he liked it "down there." Had Dennis ever been in my hometown, Toronto? He shakes his head and grins. As for holidays, he and his wife would rather head south to the East Coast beaches in New Jersey and Massachusetts, or farther south, to Florida, where there are so many Québécois in the winter that they run a newspaper in French just for them. This is part of a pattern I observe throughout my visit in Quebec. When you ask people where they go when they have a little free time, they all say the States. They never say Canada.

18   After a couple of beers, it is time for Dennis to head down to the arena for his hockey game with the works team. It's one of those places from my Canadian childhood, a big, gloomy, vaulted place, bitterly cold, with a lozenge of white gleaming ice in the middle, and no glass to keep the pucks from flying into the rows of hard, gray-painted bleachers where I take my seat.

19   This isn't just any hockey arena. It's like the sandlots of Santo Domingo, where the world's best baseball shortstops grow up; or like the pitches in north London where Arsenal players learn how to curve a ball into the net. Trois-Rivières is one of those places where hockey is played best in all the world; it is from arenas like this one that the National Hockey League (NHL) draws its talent.

20   I have hockey in common with Dennis, as any Canadian does. I grew up listening to NHL games on the radio in the days before television. I have all the same names in my head that he does—Geoffrion, Beliveau, Richard—from the Canadiens' teams of the 1950s and 1960s. I used to play in arenas like this.

21   I sit in the stand and I watch the Wayagamack boys play. Dennis is good: low, fast, crafty, hardworking, darting in and out of the play, digging pucks out from under people's skates, hitting people when he has to, a big smile playing on his face. When he's on the bench, he pushes the helmet back off his face, sips on a Coke, and roars, *"Allez les boys! Allez les boys!* Look at that guy's acceleration! Tabarnak!"

22   I sit watching him, levering himself over the boards to join in a power play, wishing I still had my skating legs and wondering, finally, why I feel such fierce separation from a Canadian scene which is just as much mine as it is his. We share all these things, and yet we don't. Language falls between us, even though I am bilingual. His Québécois is not my French. We play the same game, in the same arenas, and we cannot quite connect. Class, perhaps? But it is much more than that: a question of language and old resentments and a history of bitterness, real and invented, which seems more robust and full of life than any of our understandings.

23   A scene like the hockey rink in Trois-Rivières sets you thinking about what exactly it is that people must share if they are to live together in a political community. Is it mere sentimentality to suppose that people ought to share the same rituals, the same cold nights under the bright lights of a hockey rink, in order to feel a common belonging? Nation-states, after all, can cohere even when the peoples who compose them share much less than I share with Dennis. The core of my separation from Dennis comes down to this: we cannot share a nation—we cannot share it, since I am English-speaking and he is French-speaking, and he was born in Quebec and I was not. Because we do not share the same nation, we cannot love the same state. I tell myself this might be just as well. Shared love for a nation-state might be a dangerous thing. Perhaps the gentleness, tolerance, and good-naturedness of so much of Canadian life depends, in fact, on the absence of a fiercely shared love. Yet one can sit in a hockey arena in Trois-Rivières on a Tuesday night, watching a young man skating his heart out, with a wild grin on his face, and wish, suddenly, that we did actually love the same nation and not merely cohabit the same state.

Thinking about the Text

1. What does Ignatieff mean when he says that the "Frenchies" were hiding in the cemetery but that none of his friends could see them (paragraph 3)?

2. Discuss the advantages of Ignatieff's use of hockey as a motif in the third section. How does such a motif connect Québécois and English-speaking Canadians of his generation?

3. Explain the irony of Dennis Rousseau's statement "'We don't want to be cut off'" (paragraph 8).

4. What are the major differences between Anglophones and Francophones that Ignatieff can see by the end of his visit to Trois-Rivières?

Writing from the Text

1. Summarize Ignatieff's definition of an "imagined community" (paragraph 4). What examples does he give to support his definition? How does his use of the word "myth" contribute to his definition?

2. Write an essay in which you discuss the proposition that all Canadians, whether they are Anglophone, Francophone, or allophone, are caught "between worlds."

Connecting with Other Texts

1. Write an essay comparing the ways Ignatieff's memories in this excerpt and Wallace Stegner's memories in "In Search of Whitemud" (p. 160) are at odds with the reality they see as adults.

2. The author writes that, when he was a young man, "the First Nations, the Native peoples, . . . didn't figure in [his] equation of the country at all" (paragraph 5). Write about how such a concept of Canada, *without* Native people, would have shaped the self-perception of people like Sean Kelly, the author of "Discovering My Native Identity" (p. 101). Use Ignatieff's essay for examples of the dominant culture's definition of what it means to be Canadian.

Did You Ever Have to Make Up Your Mind?

Carl Wilson

1 The hype level on that gritty-vacant Brit flick *Trainspotting* has scared my little bod away from the ticket stampede, but it also makes me feel like

I've already seen the movie. And guess what? I liked it.

2   Descriptions of the opening speech have stolen my second-hand heart. Here's smack-shooting hero Renton snarling a litany of reasons not to go straight: "Choose life, choose a job, choose a career, choose a family, choose a big fucking television, choose washing machines, cars, compact disc players, and electric tin openers. . . ."

3   The Quebec City police, who think taking rebel street kids to *Trainspotting* will help turn them into productive citizens, are in for a nasty surprise. But my delight isn't only in how the best-laid plans of pigs and punks may go awry. It's in the way Renton's vintage anti-consumerist rant puts the boots to a bigger myth of "choice."

4   Identity involves options; the more the better. But Renton says our choices don't tell the full story. You might partly be the sum of your birthright and the sequence of homes, jobs, and fashions you select, but there are elements your curriculum vitae can't capture.

5   How about the homeless youths in Berri Square, trying to decide between moving along to nowhere or being hauled off to jail? Some choice. For that matter, isn't there a difference between democracy and voting, or between "free abortion on demand" and the tamer "pro-choice"?

6   Sprinter Donovan Bailey was put through the "choice" wringer this week after his 100-metre win in Atlanta. He'd barely bitten down on his gold medal when reporters began asking whether he'd won it for his birthplace, Jamaica, or his current home, Canada. When he refused to choose, you could almost hear the Olympic whatzit blow an IBM chip.

7   Maybe living so intimately with computers is bamboozling us into thinking life is a series of ones and zeros. What makes computers inanimate, after all, is that they answer every question Yes or No—never Sorta, It Depends, Both, Neither, or, None of Your Business.

8   Donovan Bailey, by contrast, can be both Jamaican and Canadian—not hyphenated, but simultaneous. He can also be a runner, a businessman, a champion, a performing stud, a suburban dad, a proud Black man, even a smoker, a joker, and a midnight toker if he wants to be. He's large, in every sense, and he not only contains multitudes, he entertains them, too.

9   Still, everywhere he turns, Bailey finds another personal border crossing, with a social-customs official asking what he has to declare. This game is especially vexing for immigrants, who are routinely strip-searched for dualities. What language do you think in? Where is home?

10   But the inquisitors eventually stare each of us down. Are you gay, or are you a real man? Are you liberal, or moral? The national women's group

NAC is bogged down in whether it's feminist or anti-racist. They might as well pass resolutions on whether NAC's a good witch or a bad witch.

11   Then there are the Quebec zero-sum Olympics; life as a voice-mail menu. Press only one: Anglo-, Franco-, or allo-? Montrealer, Canadian, or Québécois(e)? Separatist or federalist? Minority or majority?

12   Université de Montréal professor Jane Jenson—whose new essay "Quebec: Which Minority?" appears in the U.S. journal *Dissent*—points out that Anglos are confused over whether to act like a Quebec minority or a Canadian majority, while Francophones are a majority here, but a minority in North America.

13   So which is which? Both are both, Jenson says, and I'd add that perhaps that's different from being either of the above. When we import ill-fitting terms, we end up in major feuds over minor red herrings.

14   A while ago, I had a long discussion with a woman of Haitian origin who grew up in French and identifies with Quebec nationalism but who is attracted to the vibrant Black scene in Toronto. Also partaking were an Eastern Townships Anglo now living in BC and an Ontario-born East European who calls herself an allophone here.

15   And then there was me, an English-speaking Canadian *arriviste*, but not an "Anglo," I suggested, because I don't share the special certainties and anxieties that go along with having English roots in Quebec.

16   We debated the divisions but allowed ourselves not to use them as limits. That way, we could go on exploring, instead of becoming a living punchline: "Two allos meet two Anglos at a party. . . ."

17   *Trainspotting*'s most-quoted joke comes when Renton, who's Scottish, riffs on Scottish nationalism, saying that the British are "wankers" and that the Scots "are colonized by wankers."

18   Well, mate, which side are you on? Renton's answer is neither. Donovan Bailey's is both. Through abstention or alloy, they each come up gold, and prove that *being* is not (yet) digital.

19   Personally, the longer I'm in Quebec, the more I hum, "Freedom's just another word for choosing not to choose."

Thinking about the Text

1. What statements encapsulate Wilson's thesis? Explain his thesis in your own words.

2. In his essay, the author recalls his discussion with a woman of Haitian origin (paragraph 14). How does this brief example support his thesis?

3. Explain Wilson's description of life in Quebec as a "voice-mail menu"

(paragraph 11). Why does Wilson believe the computer age is part of the problem?

Writing from the Text

1. The author uses a border-crossing metaphor in which people, especially immigrants, are asked what they have "to declare" (paragraph 9). In a short essay, explain this metaphor. Who or what do you think is forcing us to "choose" and what "choice" are we being asked to make?

2. What do you think Wilson means by the "myth of 'choice'" (paragraph 3)? How does this myth relate to his definition of freedom? Write an essay discussing the author's perspective on choice and freedom. Do you agree or disagree with his stance?

3. Is it possible to be many things at once, or must a person always choose between two options? Writing from your own experience and ethnic, cultural, religious, or racial background, discuss this question.

4. Wilson says: "Identity involves options" (paragraph 4). Write an essay arguing that people such as Donovan Bailey are the best role models for young people today because such public figures are not limited by social demands to choose one identity over another.

Connecting with Other Texts

1. Wilson decries the thinking that forces immigrants to choose between such dualities as "What language do you think in? Where is home?" In contrast, Sun-Kyung Yi writes in "An Accent on Learning English" (p. 107) that she feels uncomfortable caught between two languages, Korean and English. Write an essay in which you compare and contrast Wilson's and Yi's positions on what it means to be an immigrant between cultures. Does the fact that Wilson is Canadian by birth whereas Yi is Canadian by choice affect their different perceptions of identity?

2. Relate the ideas in Robert L. Heilbroner's "Don't Let Stereotypes Warp Your Judgments" (p. 128) to "Did You Ever Have to Make Up Your Mind?" Argue that just as stereotyped views others have of us are limiting, so are our choices, because they don't tell the full story about us as people.

3. Both Carl Wilson and Michael Ignatieff, in "Quebec" (p. 117), raise the issue of myth as a factor in our perceptions of ourselves and our neighbours. Write an essay in which you compare and contrast the authors' explanations of how myths shape our identities as Canadians.

CHAPTER 4
Between Perceptions

How we perceive ourselves is intrinsically related to our upbringing, sex, and ethnic roots. Our sense of self, however, goes beyond any definition of male or female, family background, or culture. Self-perception is often conditioned by the roles we assume—as students, workers, family members—but our self-image and how others see us may be distinct from the roles we play. You regard yourself as a college student, but when you are at home you might be the "baby" in the family, or the one diapering the baby. You know that your competence at work can gain you much-needed overtime pay, but your perception of yourself as an "A" student prompts you to cut back on hours instead. A woman who has a physical disability may not define herself as "handicapped," and a man who qualifies for affirmative action may not see himself as "disadvantaged." Perceiving ourselves beyond the labels others use to identify us and beyond beliefs that may limit our view of our own lives is an essential process, as the readings in this chapter indicate.

In the opening essay, Robert L. Heilbroner documents the pervasiveness of stereotypes in our culture. He explains some of the dangers inherent not only for others but also for ourselves when we resort to stereotypes, and offers solutions to the problem.

Other people's images and stereotypes of us can complicate and threaten our self-perceptions. Writing in defence of single parents, Joan Donaldson challenges current prejudices; Janice Giavedoni and Aspasia Kaplaneris fight to preserve the dignity of people with visible and invisible disabilities. These three essays express the frustrations of active individuals whose self-acceptance is threatened by others' delimiting views of them.

The language others use to describe us and our personal history can have a profound effect on our sense of self-identity. A recent news item accompanying M. Nourbese Philip's poem supplements her observation that names to describe her racial group fall in and out of fashion. Archibald J. Crail's short story demonstrates that naming a solution to a problem does not make that problem disappear. These readings raise questions about the individual's power to choose his or her own identity beyond social constraints and prejudices.

As you may realize, eating disorders often develop from our perception of what is attractive or our need to gain control of how we perceive ourselves. In "Adding Weight to an Image of Beauty," Catherine Pigott's experience with women in Gambia prompts us to reconsider our culture's definition of slimness and beauty. In "Bodily Harm," Pamela Erens chronicles the problems of many women who have eating disorders and who struggle toward self-understanding and acceptance rather than perpetuate destructive behaviour.

Wallace Stegner's closing essay leads us to wonder about how our own memories, not just our multiple roles or disparate self-images, can shape our perceptions of ourselves. Balancing how others see us with who we think we are is the condition of being between perceptions—and the basis of all of the writings in this chapter.

Don't Let Stereotypes Warp Your Judgments
Robert L. Heilbroner

1 Is a girl called Gloria apt to be better-looking than one called Bertha? Are criminals more likely to be dark than blond? Can you tell a good deal about someone's personality from hearing his voice briefly over the phone? Can a person's nationality be pretty accurately guessed from his photograph? Does the fact that someone wears glasses imply that he is intelligent?

2   The answer to all these questions is obviously, "No."

3   Yet, from all the evidence at hand, most of us believe these things. Ask any college boy if he'd rather take his chances with a Gloria or a Bertha, or ask a college girl if she'd rather blind-date a Richard or a Cuthbert. In fact, you don't have to ask: college students in questionnaires have revealed that names conjure up the same images in their minds as they do in yours—and for as little reason.

4   Look into the favorite suspects of persons who report "suspicious characters" and you will find a large percentage of them to be "swarthy" or "dark and foreign-looking"—despite the testimony of criminologists that

criminals do not tend to be dark, foreign or "wild-eyed." Delve into the main asset of a telephone stock swindler and you will find it to be a marvelously confidence-inspiring telephone "personality." And whereas we all think we know what an Italian or a Swede looks like, it is the sad fact that when a group of Nebraska students sought to match faces and nationalities of 15 European countries, they were scored wrong in 93 percent of their identifications. Finally, for all the fact that horn-rimmed glasses have now become the standard television sign of an "intellectual," optometrists know that the main thing that distinguishes people with glasses is just bad eyes.

5   Stereotypes are a kind of gossip about the world, a gossip that makes us prejudge people before we ever lay eyes on them. Hence it is not surprising that stereotypes have something to do with the dark world of prejudice. Explore most prejudices (note that the word means prejudgment) and you will find a cruel stereotype at the core of each one.

6   For it is the extraordinary fact that once we have type-cast the world, we tend to see people in terms of our standardized pictures. In another demonstration of the power of stereotypes to affect our vision, a number of Columbia and Barnard students were shown 30 photographs of pretty but unidentified girls, and asked to rate each in terms of "general liking," "intelligence," "beauty" and so on. Two months later, the same group were shown the same photographs, this time with fictitious Irish, Italian, Jewish and "American" names attached to the pictures. Right away the ratings changed. Faces which were now seen as representing a national group went down in looks and still farther down in likability, while the "American" girls suddenly looked decidedly prettier and nicer.

7   Why is it that we stereotype the world in such irrational and harmful fashion? In part, we begin to type-cast people in our childhood years. Early in life, as every parent whose child has watched a TV Western knows, we learn to spot the Good Guys from the Bad Guys. Some years ago, a social psychologist showed very clearly how powerful these stereotypes of childhood vision are. He secretly asked the most popular youngsters in an elementary school to make errors in their morning gym exercises. Afterwards, he asked the class if anyone had noticed any mistakes during gym period. Oh, yes, said the children. But it was the unpopular members of the class—the "bad guys"—they remembered as being out of step.

8   We not only grow up with standardized pictures forming inside of us, but as grown-ups we are constantly having them thrust upon us. Some of them, like the half-joking, half-serious stereotypes of mothers-in-law, or country yokels, or psychiatrists, are dinned into us by the stock jokes we

hear and repeat. In fact, without such stereotypes, there would be a lot fewer jokes. Still other stereotypes are perpetuated by the advertisements we read, the movies we see, the books we read.

9   And finally, we tend to stereotype because it helps us make sense out of a highly confusing world, a world which William James once described as "one great, blooming, buzzing confusion." It is a curious fact that if we don't know what we're looking at, we are often quite literally unable to see what we're looking at. People who recover their sight after a lifetime of blindness actually cannot at first tell a triangle from a square. A visitor to a factory sees only noisy chaos where the superintendent sees a perfectly synchronized flow of work. As Walter Lippmann has said, "For the most part we do not first see, and then define; we define first, and then we see."

10   Stereotypes are one way in which we "define" the world in order to see it. They classify the infinite variety of human beings into a convenient handful of "types" towards whom we learn to act in stereotyped fashion. Life would be a wearing process if we had to start from scratch with each and every human contact. Stereotypes economize on our mental effort by covering up the blooming, buzzing confusion with big recognizable cut-outs. They save us the "trouble" of finding out what the world is like—they give it its accustomed look.

11   Thus the trouble is that stereotypes make us mentally lazy. As S.I. Hayakawa, the authority on semantics, has written: "The danger of stereotypes lies not in their existence, but in the fact that they become for all people some of the time, and for some people all of the time, substitutes for observation." Worse yet, stereotypes get in the way of our judgment, even when we do observe the world. Someone who has formed rigid preconceptions of all Latins as "excitable," or all teenagers as "wild," doesn't alter his point of view when he meets a calm and deliberate Genoese, or a serious-minded high school student. He brushes them aside as "exceptions that prove the rule." And, of course, if he meets someone true to type, he stands triumphantly vindicated. "They're all like that," he proclaims, having encountered an excited Latin, an ill-behaved adolescent.

12   Hence, quite aside from the injustice which stereotypes do to others, they impoverish ourselves. A person who lumps the world into simple categories, who type-casts all labor leaders as "racketeers," all businessmen as "reactionaries," all Harvard men as "snobs," and all Frenchmen as "sexy," is in danger of becoming a stereotype himself. He loses his capacity to be himself—which is to say, to see the world in his own absolutely unique, inimitable and independent fashion.

13   Instead, he votes for the man who fits his standardized picture of what a candidate "should" look like or sound like, buys the goods that someone in his "situation" in life "should" own, lives the life that others define for him. The mark of the stereotyped person is that he never surprises us, that we do indeed have him "typed." And no one fits this strait-jacket so perfectly as someone whose opinions about other people are fixed and inflexible.

14   Impoverishing as they are, stereotypes are not easy to get rid of. The world we type-cast may be no better than a Grade B movie, but at least we know what to expect of our stock characters. When we let them act for themselves in the strangely unpredictable way that people do act, who knows but that many of our fondest convictions will be proved wrong?

15   Nor do we suddenly drop our standardized pictures for a blinding vision of the Truth. Sharp swings of ideas about people often just substitute one stereotype for another. The true process of change is a slow one that adds bits and pieces of reality to the pictures in our heads, until gradually they take on some of the blurriness of life itself. Little by little, we learn not that Jews and Negroes and Catholics and Puerto Ricans are "just like everybody else"—for that, too, is a stereotype—but that each and every one of them is unique, special, different and individual. Often we do not even know that we have let a stereotype lapse until we hear someone saying, "all so-and-so's are like such-and-such," and we hear ourselves saying, "Well—maybe."

16   Can we speed the process along? Of course we can.

17   First, we can become aware of the standardized pictures in our heads, in other people's heads, in the world around us.

18   Second, we can become suspicious of all judgments that we allow exceptions to "prove." There is no more chastening thought than that in the vast intellectual adventure of science, it takes but one tiny exception to topple a whole edifice of ideas.

19   Third, we can learn to be chary of generalizations about people. As F. Scott Fitzgerald once wrote: "Begin with an individual, and before you know it you have created a type; begin with a type, and you find you have created—nothing."

20   Most of the time, when we type-cast the world, we are not in fact generalizing about people at all. We are only revealing the embarrassing facts about the pictures that hang in the gallery of stereotypes in our own heads.

Thinking about the Text

1. Define the word "stereotype" in your own words. Are stereotypes different from generalizations? Why or why not? Can we classify without stereotyping?

2. What common stereotypes does Heilbroner cite to support his thesis that stereotypes warp our judgments? What additional stereotypes are you aware of that he did not mention?

3. According to Heilbroner, why do people depend on stereotypes?

4. What does Heilbroner mean when he writes that stereotypes "impoverish ourselves" (paragraph 12)? Explain the risk individuals who stereotype others take concerning their own identity. How is the result ironic?

Writing from the Text

1. Have you ever been stereotyped? Write an essay about how the experience affected you and your relationship with the person doing the stereotyping.

2. Heilbroner's essay concludes with three suggestions on how the problem of stereotyping can be solved. In a process essay, develop his three points further. Offer your readers concrete advice and examples from your own experience on how they can contribute to the solution.

Connecting with Other Texts

1. The connotation of a word is the range of secondary attitudes, feelings, and judgments associated with that word. What are the connotations of names such as "Bertha" and "Cuthbert"? What are the connotations of the different words to describe Blacks, as listed in M. Nourbese Philip's poem "What's in a Name?" and the news item "'Negro' Name Change Protested" (p. 143)? Write an essay entitled "What's in a Name?" in which you discuss the relationship between stereotyping and connotation in names.

2. Consult books in the psychology section of your library to get more information on stereotypes, prejudice, and discrimination. In what ways are these concepts related? Write a research essay reporting your findings.

3. Consider print and television advertisements for particular types of consumer goods, such as convenience foods, cleaning products, or cars. Is Heilbroner's contention that advertising perpetuates stereotypes valid today? Support your argument with concrete examples.

Singling Out Single Parents
Joan Donaldson

1 The last time I went to church in my suburban parish, the congregation prayed for single-parent families. I was so mad, it was all I could do not to jump out of my pew and yell at the whole sanctimonious lot. I know the prayers were offered with the best of intentions, but as a single parent, I felt that I was being stereotyped as part of a down-and-out group. My integrity as a parent was in question.

2 Before the divorce, I was assumed to be part of the good-enough parent group. Now I am expelled from that group, as if by virtue of the break-up, my parenting skills and love for my child went out with the trash. I am now presumed to be part of a group that does not provide well for its children.

3 The sloppy stereotyping goes something like this: A happy family breaks down and a divorce ensues. The children are irreparably damaged by the divorce and end up failing school, doing drugs and probably living a life of crime.

4 Well, here's a new flash: Happy marriages don't generally end in divorce. Why would they? Contrary to opinions I've been reading in newspapers lately, it's generally unhappy marriages—very unhappy—that end in divorce.

5 Divorce is not easy and the decision to divorce is a harrowing one. I don't know of anyone who has come to the decision to leave his or her marriage lightly. My divorce may have looked easy from the outside, but that's because I confided in only a few individuals. Why would I want to air my dirty laundry in public? People jumped to all sorts of conclusions about why I would leave and how foolish and selfish I must be. Without the gory details, though, their understanding of our marriage was very superficial.

6 During that difficult time, I wasn't about to try to battle for my reputation. My plate was full. As the French say, *Bien faire et laisser dire* (roughly translated: Do right and let 'em talk).

7 For reasonable people to choose to divorce, the marriage has to be very wrong. Think of what the couple is deciding to do: dividing all joint holdings (divorce can ruin you financially); splitting up the family (parents have to believe that the divorce will allow for a better future for their children or they wouldn't do it); and resuming lives as single adults (and facing guilt, dating, loneliness, the fear of being alone).

8   To me, divorce is like heart surgery. You'd be crazy to go through it if you didn't need it. Both heart surgery and divorce are last-resort treatments for serious conditions.

9   Divorce is a gruelling experience. It is not a rejection of responsibility, but a commitment to make a better future. To stay in a destructive marriage and sleepwalk through life is not heroic; it is weak. Divorce is a deliberate, active response to an intolerable situation. Divorce is not for the faint of heart, and it isn't for the lazy. It requires painful admissions and major re-evaluations to create a new order, and a better life. Maybe there are people who have divorced frivolously. Maybe there are good marriages that end in divorce. I have never seen either.

10   And what about the impact of divorce on the children? I won't argue that two, loving, active, well-functioning parents aren't preferable to one loving, active, well-functioning parent. But I would argue that one loving, well-functioning parent is better than one good one and one who makes life intolerable for the whole family. I would also argue that in the two-good-parents model, both parents don't always have to live in the same house to remain loving and active parents.

11   The difference is essentially this: Marriage is a contract between two adults. A contract that proves unbearable can be undone, broken. Parenthood is not a contract—it is a blood relationship, and unbreakable. It doesn't matter how well or how badly you perform the task, or even if you abandon your children entirely; once you become a parent you are always that person's parent.

12   So, while divorce changes the living arrangements, it can't alter the fact of parenthood and it doesn't necessarily have to affect the essential quality of the parent–child bond. It can stay good, it can stay bad, or it can be transformed. It exists irrespective of the marriage.

13   When I hear others saying that a child is suffering from the effects of a divorce that happened many years ago, I always find myself doubtful. I don't blame the divorce and I wonder about the quality of parenting that was provided along the way. Maybe that particular set of parents didn't know how to parent while they were married and maybe they still don't. If those same two parents had stayed together, would the situation have been better for that child?

14   And what of the thousands of children who have maintained good relationships with one or both parents after a divorce and who grow up just fine? No one studies or reports on these kids. They don't sell newspapers. Our society prefers to pity, scorn and scapegoat children of divorce.

15   How was my daughter supposed to feel when the congregation prayed for single-parent families? Proud? Part of a distinguished group? Satisfied? Content? I would have gladly joined in prayer for children in need, and children who are suffering. But these are not synonymous with single-parent families. I would also pray for parents who are struggling, and partners who need to learn to love each other, whether they are married or not.

Thinking about the Text

1. Describe the stereotypes of single parents that Donaldson wants to dispel.
2. What metaphor (a comparison of two things not usually associated with each other) does the author use to illustrate that divorce is not a course of action people enter into lightly?
3. How does Donaldson explain the difference between marriage and parenthood?
4. What does the author have to say about children of divorced parents? How do such children perceive themselves?

Writing from the Text

1. Argue that Donaldson's contention that North American "society prefers to pity, scorn and scapegoat children of divorce" (paragraph 14) is accurate or inaccurate. Use examples from Donaldson's essay and the experience of any family members or friends who have been affected by divorce.
2. Sometimes people have good intentions but their actions are based on stereotypes rather than reality. Write about a time when you have been misperceived by someone with good intentions. What steps did you take to correct that person's perception of you?

Connecting with Other Texts

1. Would Donaldson agree or disagree with Moira Farr's thesis in "Welcome to FamilyValuesWorld!" (p. 9)? Write a response to Farr's essay from a single parent's point of view.
2. Some writers are now calling single-parent families "binuclear" families, to remove the stigma associated with families who have experienced divorce. Look in current periodicals for articles on successful single-parent or binuclear families. Based on your findings, write an essay directed to the children of binuclear families in which you dispel their fears that their new family configuration might be damaging to their well-being.

Jerry Lewis and the MDA Telethon: Is It Really That Bad?

Janice Giavedoni

1 The Labour Day weekend marks the beginning of a new academic year for students everywhere. As a disabled student, however, [I find] this weekend has added significance for me: it is the time when the Jerry Lewis Telethon is broadcast across North America. The Telethon raises money for the Muscular Dystrophy Association (MDA) to find a cure for muscular dystrophy and related neuro-muscular disorders, one of which (Friedreich's Ataxia) has resulted in my disability. It raises millions of dollars annually, and has become a tradition since it began almost 30 years ago. In recent years, however, the Telethon has come under attack for its negative portrayal of disabled people.

2 Essentially, the criticism suggests that the Telethon reinforces the idea that people with a disability are pathetic cripples that one should feel sorry for. Its sporadic messages of support for things like disability rights and employment equity create confusion when seen alongside images of us as weak and ineffectual. In fact, the Telethon makes it difficult to view and still believe that a person with muscular dystrophy is not inferior to a nondisabled person. This "pity" approach is totally incompatible with our need for choices, rights and opportunities in our lives.

3 Long before I acquired a disability-rights consciousness, I remember feeling uncomfortable watching the Telethon. Now, however, I am able to analyse that discomfort. I see how telethons reinforce the stereotype that it is acceptable for disabled people to beg for money because we are desperately hoping for a "cure." I admit that research of this nature is important, and acknowledge that Jerry Lewis has devoted a lot of time to the MDA . . . but at what cost?

4 He's been raising money by "tugging at people's heartstrings," as he himself claims. At the same time, he's done it by destroying our self-images.

5 For example, on the September 3, 1992, episode of ABC's *Prime Time*, Lewis maintained that I/we are only "half a person" and justified this with "Well, they can't walk down the hall, can they?" Call me naïve, but I didn't realize that using a wheelchair automatically diminished my humanity!

6 Watching the 1992 Telethon reinforced the popular perception of disabled people as helpless and hopeless. A film clip of a "happy" young

immigrant couple described their "happiness" as "short-lived" upon discovering that their young child had muscular dystrophy. Another clip showed a young, intelligent woman about whom her parents worry. "We can't leave her alone—she can't answer the telephone, she can't answer the door!" I couldn't help but wonder why a handle-free phone was never mentioned; would MDA not purchase one for this woman?

7   During the 1993 Telethon, Jerry showed a film clip of a man whose daughter had muscular dystrophy (in fact, she used a motorized wheelchair similar to mine). He was lamenting that his daughter will never be able to go out for pizza on a Friday night and never be able to go to the beach with her friends. Why the hell not?! I wondered. Maybe there is no accessible transportation in their city, or daddy is overprotective and won't let her go out, or the girl has no friends. The message was clear. "Without a cure, we can't go anywhere or do anything. We are pathetic and pitiable." Dad's gloomy thoughts were never challenged by Jerry because the Telethon's viewers are supposed to believe that we are pathetic and pitiable.

8   At the end of the Telethon, Jerry promised to do everything he could to make a young family "perfect" (the family includes an active, handsome son who happens to use a wheelchair because he has muscular dystrophy). Perfect?

9   What effect does this kind of remark have on this child, on me, on all disabled people (whether or not we have muscular dystrophy)? Do we feel guilty for causing our families' alleged imperfections? Do we wish we were never born? But seeing as we were, do we desperately hope for a cure? Is this our goal in life? Without a cure, are we miserable?

10   Actually, disabled people do not inherently feel that way. These feelings have been projected onto us, when we hear the desperation in Jerry's voice, the apologies for not having located our defective gene earlier. It tears at my heart and tries to destroy my self-esteem.

11   I believe that our lives are certainly worth living. For myself, Friedreich's Ataxia is tightly interwoven with every part of me. I can't imagine being who I am without the values, insights and experiences that it has shown me. I'm glad I am who I am.

12   So you see, I'm happy my mother didn't abort me. If she had, you wouldn't be furrowing your brow right now. And I wouldn't be gritting my teeth.

Thinking about the Text

1. What is the thesis of this essay?

2. What reasons does the author cite for the Jerry Lewis Telethon coming under attack? What perceptions about people with disabilities does the Telethon promote? How do you think people with hidden disabilities react to this fund-raiser?

3. Is it possible for the Jerry Lewis Telethon to make families "perfect" (paragraph 8)? Why or why not?

4. What has Giavedoni gained as a result of her disability? Why does she make a point of mentioning these advantages?

Writing from the Text

1. Write an essay in which you define the ideal televised fund-raiser. Your thesis should assert what the important elements of your program would be. Reference to Giavedoni's points might be part of your support.

2. Write a letter to Giavedoni showing your support for her view or expressing concern that she has shocked a number of sensitive, charity-supporting people into scepticism about donating money to the Muscular Dystrophy Association.

3. If you are a person with a visible or hidden disability, write about your reaction to Giavedoni's essay. Does her viewpoint reflect your own?

Connecting with Other Texts

1. Interview an acquaintance who has a disability, or, if your college offers services for students with disabilities, arrange with the director to interview a student interested in discussing the issue of disabilities with you. Try to gain insight into the person's feelings about the best and worst features of his or her condition. You might begin by asking how your college could better meet the needs of students with disabilities.

2. Look at the ways different organizations for the disabled use print media and television in their fund-raising efforts. How do the media differ in the way they present people with disabilities? Which organizations show the greatest respect for the abilities of the people they serve? Write an essay on your findings.

3. Research what your community is doing to improve the lives of people with disabilities. Limit your essay to one feature of improvement: accessibility to public buildings, improved employment possibilities, increased visibility in advertising, film, and television, improved educational opportunities, or any other area that interests you. (See the model research paper on p. 368.)

Earthbound . . . for Now

Aspasia Kaplaneris

1 In hindsight, I realize that planning a life can be compared to the process of building a pair of wings.

2   This is how my theory works. As children, we have no idea what we want to do in the future. We are confused, as if trapped in an endless labyrinth. As we grow older, however, we realize that there is only one way to escape this confusion: by flying out of the maze. We begin to turn our attention to the sky, planning our flight path, our dreams. As well, we begin collecting our skills and experiences; these are our feathers. Most importantly, though, we need to gather our self-confidence; this is the wax needed to hold our feathers together. Once we have built our wings, we can strap them on and soar toward our goals.

3   Unfortunately, though, not everyone's life follows this pattern. I myself, for example, was not able to plan my escape from the labyrinth until very recently. As a student with an undiagnosed learning disability, I found it almost impossible to concentrate on wing-building. In fact, my experiences at school kept me earthbound.

4   Soon after I started going to school, I began to suspect that I was different from the other children. I noticed that simple tasks, such as putting on my shoes, were quite difficult for me. For one thing, I didn't know the difference between my left foot and my right foot, and if I did manage to put the correct shoe on each foot, I then had trouble tying the laces. My friends sometimes helped me tie my shoes so that I wouldn't break my neck on the staircase. Once we began learning how to write, I realized I also had problems with language that my friends didn't have. I didn't understand how to write a clear sentence or why spelling rules said that an "-ed" was added to the end of some words. My stomach used to churn so violently when I was trying to work on my writing that I would thankfully do my math homework immediately afterward. Apparently, numbers were the only antidote for my writing sickness. As I progressed through elementary school, other problems arose: the concept of paragraphing seemed as difficult as nuclear physics. Somehow I was still able to do well enough at school. My teachers never formally tested my understanding of grammar, and none of them paid much attention to my difficulties. They just dismissed me as an odd child.

5   But their dismissals had a negative effect on me. You see, I had sensed for a long time that I had some form of problem that the other children

didn't. When my teachers dismissed me, though, they made me question my own senses. I began to wonder, "Am I wrong? Am I beginning to lose my mind? Perhaps I am actually stupid and worthless." Once I began to doubt myself, I began to lose my ability to think of a future. After all, if I believed that I was stupid, that meant that I had no future anyway, except perhaps as a burger flipper. From that point on, I felt I was wandering around in a frightening and discouraging labyrinth, hopelessly looking for the exit.

6   Once I reached high school, I continued to feel that I was stupid. I wanted to do well in English, but my shortcomings became even more painfully obvious to me. I had trouble processing the questions that my English teacher asked me. Even if I did manage to come up with an answer, it would often sound garbled because my nervousness made my grammar errors worse when I spoke. Fellow students would snicker, "What the heck is she talking about? Was that in English?" As for my writing, I would write essays as one BIG paragraph. Of course, the sentences in this one BIG paragraph were also endless. Later in my high school career, I had many problems trying to come up with a thesis statement. No matter how many explanations I heard, the thesis statement remained a mysterious secret that I could not unravel. In a school where skilled essay writers were revered, I felt like a worthless misfit.

7   The incident that finally convinced me that I was utterly stupid, however, occurred in my Grade 11 history class. I took that course because I liked the course content (ancient and medieval European history). Unfortunately, though, I was overwhelmed by the required work. In addition to coping with my essay writing problems, I now had to be able to analyse complex questions in class. One time, for example, our class had a seminar based on articles written about Julius Caesar. Although I had managed to read the articles, I couldn't remember anything. To make matters worse, my history teacher's reputation as a brute was legendary. Whenever he was angry with a student's performance, he would ridicule that person in front of the class; in essence, he would try to rip the student's psyche to shreds. On that day, he asked many long, complex questions. My classmates were able to analyse and answer his questions with ease. When he asked me a question, though, I couldn't even understand it, let alone answer it. I felt so stupid that I just bowed my head and said, "I don't know."

8   He responded, "Oh, really? I suggest that you go get a lobotomy."

9   I felt completely humiliated. From that day on, I was 100 percent sure that I was a pathetic excuse for a human being. After all, I couldn't

handle tasks that everyone else could do effortlessly. I stopped thinking of any future for myself. I continued to feel I was walking around aimlessly in a maze, except now I was unable to see any skills that I had. For six long years I had to ask others for help with all of my schoolwork. I didn't trust my judgment or abilities; my experience in high school was telling me that I had none.

10   This despair ended in an unexpected way. I was talking to my family doctor one day, and happened to mention that I was always making reading errors. When she questioned me more and realized that this had been a life-long problem, she grew quite solemn and asked whether I had experienced any other difficulties with language. I began to rhyme them off as if they were on a shopping list: grammar trouble, thesis trouble, paragraph trouble, essay trouble and on and on. At that point, she suggested that I might have a learning disability. On that day, for the first time in my life, I was not told I was imagining my symptoms, and I was not treated as if I were stupid. She made no mention of lobotomies or other barbaric medical procedures. Instead, she told me she would book me an appointment with a neurologist. When I saw the sincere concern in her eyes, I no longer felt so lost and confused. I felt relieved, because I finally had some guidance.

11   Within a few months, a neurologist and a counsellor were conducting tests of my abilities. Like my doctor, both of them were kind, marvellous people. When they told me the diagnosis, that I indeed did have a learning disability, I was both relieved and sad. I was relieved because now I understood why I couldn't do some tasks at all but excelled at others. Also, I now knew that my instincts had been right all along. On the other hand, I was sad, because I knew that I had spent many years in limbo for nothing. I cried a lot the day the diagnosis was made, but at least I knew that I had a genuine, and manageable, problem. I was finally free of all my self-doubts and could turn my attention to handling my learning problems more constructively.

12   It has been a year since I heard the results of these tests. Of course, I am still trying to recover from the years that I wasted. The memory of my unhappy experiences in school are still very fresh in my mind, and I frequently have nightmares about school in general and writing in particular. A few months ago I had a series of nightmares about one specific essay assignment. Every time my mind aired another instalment of this nightmare series, the due date crept closer. I still experience anxiety when it comes to English. After one of my English essay tests, for instance, I was ill for four days. I felt like someone had used my head as a football and set a new record for the number of field goals kicked in one game.

13   Overall, however, things are different for me now. I have had some time to think more about my strengths and less about my weaknesses. Now that I'm in college and know what my needs are, I can get the right kind of help in my problem subjects. In fact, I am actually getting A+'s in my English course. (I'm so glad that I didn't have that lobotomy!) Most importantly, though, I no longer berate myself for every problem that I experience. Now that I know that I'm not stupid, I can focus on planning a future for myself.

14   Although I am still in the maze, I am no longer dashing around, frantically encountering dead ends. Instead, I have started to gather the feathers and wax that I need for my long-delayed pair of wings. I can now look at the sky and contemplate the various paths that I can follow. Best of all, though, I now know that I will soon be ready to strap on my wings and escape this labyrinth and its terrors once and for all. On that day, I will be earthbound no more.

Thinking about the Text

1. List the examples the author gives that indicate she was different from her classmates in both elementary school and high school.

2. What role did the author's teachers play in shaping her early perception of herself? How accurate (or inaccurate) was this self-perception? What are your feelings as you read about her experiences at school?

3. Why was the author both relieved and sad when she received the diagnosis of her problem?

Writing from the Text

1. Write an essay arguing that classroom humiliation is or is not an important learning experience. Use additional experiences of your own to support your thesis.

2. Metaphors are comparisons of two things we don't usually associate with each other. Kaplaneris uses an extended metaphor to explain her theory of personal growth. Identify this metaphor and trace the ways she weaves it through her essay.

Connecting with Other Texts

1. In Kaplaneris's essay and Janice Giavedoni's essay "Jerry Lewis and the MDA Telethon" (p. 136), the authors show how much power people who don't live with a disability have in shaping the public's perceptions of people who do. Write an essay discussing this problem and proposing a possible solution.

2. Sun-Kyung Yi also experienced difficulties learning about language, as she points out in her essay "An Accent on Learning English" (p. 107). In what ways do Yi's difficulties parallel Kaplaneris's? In what ways are they different? Using these two essays for your examples, write an essay comparing and contrasting the experiences of a learning-disabled person with those of a second-language learner.

What's in a Name?
M. Nourbese Philip

I always thought I was Negro
till I was Coloured,
West Indian, till I was told
that Columbus was wrong
5 In thinking he was west of India—
that made me Caribbean.
And throughout the '60s, '70s and '80s,
I was sure I was Black.
Now Black is passé,
10 African de rigueur,
and me, a chameleon of labels.

"Negro" Name Change Protested
Canadian Press

1 About 50 people travelled from Toronto to Holland Township, south of Owen Sound, on Saturday to protest the changing of the name Negro Creek Road.

2   Holland Township Council has renamed the road Moggie Road after George Moggie, a white settler.

3   A town official said he isn't comfortable using the name Negro in the 1990s.

4   But protesters said the contributions of Black pioneers should not be "wiped out."

Thinking about the Text

1. Although this poem was written before the accompanying news item, both discuss the same issue. Summarize the implied "thesis" of both works. In what other ways are the two connected?

2. What do "passé" and "de rigueur" mean? What does the speaker in this poem imply by using these French words in conjunction with "Black" and "African"? What connection might the French words have with the underlying idea of the news item?

3. According to the news item, how are places named? Compare this information to what is implied in the poem. Who attaches and later changes labels describing people?

4. Discuss the denotative and connotative meanings for the word "Negro." Is there a difference between the two? Does the difference change over time, or is it constant?

Writing from the Text

1. In what ways are people affirmed, limited, or forced to become "chameleons" to blend in with their surroundings by the language we use? Write a cause-and-effect essay on the way words and labels can shape a person's identity, using "What's in a Name?" as a starting point.

2. Do you agree with the protesters that changing the name "Negro Creek Road" to "Moggie Road" will erase the contributions Black settlers made? Can changing a few words shape history that much? Write a persuasive essay in which you argue that history depends (or does not depend) on the language we use to discuss it.

3. Describe events that contributed to your understanding the full implications or dynamics of a word or phrase used to describe you. You might think about an apparently innocuous word like "student" or "middle child," a potentially more volatile word like "tourist," "immigrant," or "foreign student," or a more inflammatory and insulting word that may have affected you in a negative way.

Connecting with Other Texts

1. How do we develop our perceptions of ourselves? Discuss some of the factors affecting development of our self-perceptions using examples from "What's in a Name?" as well as Aspasia Kaplaneris's essay "Earthbound . . . for Now" (p. 139) and Julia Nunes's essay "The Business of Being Half and Half" (p. 98).

2. In "Did You Ever Have to Make Up Your Mind?" (p. 123), Carl Wilson explores the issue of choosing one's identity. Would Philip agree with Wilson that "identity involves options; the more the better" (paragraph 4)? Write an essay comparing the two points of view.

Affirmative Action

Archibald J. Crail

1 One of the first things the woman at personnel had told him was that the corporation was now following a policy of affirmative action.

2 "Now what does that mean?" Marius had asked, his face beneath the bushy Afro, expressionless.

3 "Why, haven't you heard?" the woman answered. "It means that the search is now on for handicapped persons and visible minorities to fill positions they're qualified for."

4 "So, I'm just lucky to have applied when I did, hey!" he had exclaimed. However, she seemed in no mood for familiarity and had quickly showed him out of the office.

5 Finally after months of despair he had found himself a half-decent job. Even if it were just a job as accounting clerk, he'd work his way up and show them what he could do. That evening he celebrated by himself in front of the television set with a case of Molson Canadian.

6 The job of accounting clerk was relatively easy. Most of his work dealt with reports of absence. On these forms appeared the employee's name and the amount of time taken off for sick leave or vacation. On a card filing system he noted the time taken off from work and subtracted the hours from the outstanding holidays and sick-leave days. Sometimes he had come across employees who had used up all their allowed days of absence. His job was then to deduct the time taken off from the employee's fortnightly earnings. All this was not really accounting work. It belonged to the personnel department. However, Marius kept his opinions to himself.

7 The remainder of his day was spent increasing those employees' salaries who had attained a new level of seniority. This of course brought resultant increased deductions in income tax, unemployment insurance and company pension. He fed these into the computerized payroll system. Then he had to send out the paycheques every pay period.

8 He got quite a shock at the end of the first pay period when two paycheques went missing in the company mail system. After a week of frantic searching and phoning branch offices all over the province, they still couldn't be traced. Unable to provide an answer as to how the cheques got lost, he could only agree lamely with the supervisor that they were indeed lost. Although handwritten cheques were issued in the meantime, he still felt a cloud of responsibility hanging over him. This later grew into

a suspicion that perhaps, just maybe, there was a conspiracy to get rid of him.

9   Like all new brooms, Marius believed that he should do his work well and be seen to be diligent. Every morning he came to work half an hour early and started work right away. None of the chit-chat about last night's happenings could draw him into any of the women's conversations. A few times he'd let out a loud guffaw at something funny Christine related to Rhonda. Both girls had then looked at him strangely, but embarrassed with this sudden attention, he'd just continued working.

10   Unlike Christine, who was loud and physically aware of herself, Rhonda was the quiet mousy type. She rarely spoke unless spoken to, and on the whole was the sort of person who quietly and unobtrusively got things done her way. Perhaps she knew that her voice was not as melodious as Christine's and it always seemed as if she croaked with a cold.

11 Marius had gone for the twice-daily coffee breaks in the cafeteria. Usually all the people from the various accounting sections would push a few tables together where they would talk about the most recent game the Rough Riders had just lost or the difficulties in farming in this day and age. He knew very little about prairie farming and didn't particularly like football. Once he tried introducing a book he had recently read and another time a movie showing at the local Odeon. Some of those present stared at him as if this was the most unreal thing to discuss, while others just pointedly ignored him. He finally decided that it was best to avoid the coffee breaks since he couldn't contribute anything to the conversations, and instead of feeling difficult and uneasy, he just remained at his desk.

12   This latest batch of reports of absence didn't look any different from any previous ones. At the very top of the six-inch pile of paperwork, the first one read: "One and a half hours to see a chiropractor." He quickly found the employee's name in the card file and reduced her remaining sick leave by one and a half hours. He now turned to the next sheet. "A day to get married."

13   He turned to Christine: "What happens when somebody takes a day off to get married?"

14   "Don'tcha know?" she screeched. "Has it been signed by the head of the department?"

15   "Yes," he said.

16   "Well, fuck," she giggled, "then treat it accordingly."

17   "You mean I should deduct it from his holidays?" he asked in an almost begging tone. "The guy has got none left."

18   With a sneer Christine whispered (loud enough for him to hear) to Rhonda, "The guy's an absolute asshole. I don't know why they got these dumb niggers here. All this affirmative action is just a bunch of shit." In a louder voice, she continued, "This is supposed to be compassionate leave. Three weeks on the job and you still can't make out head or tail, hey!"

19   "Give him time," Rhonda croaked condescendingly. "Just give him time."

20   He was quiet for a minute. Jumping up from his chair he roared, "Hey! I don't want any of your bloody racist remarks! Why don't you guys bloody well give me a job description list? Every time something new comes up I have to ask you guys! I'm sick and tired of asking what the hell to do every time something new comes up!" He threw the pile of papers on the floor.

21   The girls were quietly ignoring him. He felt he could punch the life out of both of them. Stooping down, he tried gathering his wits while picking up the papers from the floor. But it was no use.

22   Suddenly he just got up and marched out of the office. He didn't expect such blatant racism in Canada. Least of all not here, where management had made such a hoo-ha about affirmative action.

23   Passing the supervisor's office, he wondered whether he should take this matter up with her. When he had got this job, she had told him there was no written job description for the accounting clerks—the reason being that accounting functions and company policy in the area had changed so much over the past year that anything formalized and adopted became invalid within six months. However, she had stressed that Christine and Rhonda as senior clerks would be most willing to be helpful whenever he needed information.

24   During the first week it was okay and the women seemed to fall over each other trying to be helpful. However, after the second week he could clearly see that they were getting tired of being bothered.

25   He decided not to talk to the supervisor. She always seemed so busy and angry. Instead he continued to the washroom.

26   Looking into the mirror, he saw his own agony staring back at him. Opening the cold-water tap wide, he bathed his face repeatedly. Consciously he reminded himself that he was a man and that this was life. Okay, so he did come to Canada with expectations. "Safety from legal racism" was what the immigration officer had told him. Suddenly a new thought struck him. Maybe he should try to be more friendly towards people here. Accept them for what they are. Show them that he also has some fine human qualities. That he's able to crack a joke and share a laugh.

Surely life isn't all seriousness and hard work. He might even get fired for that earlier outburst. This sudden fear made him wonder if there wasn't something about "incompatibility with fellow workers" in the union contract.

27   A sudden swish as the washroom door opened jarred him back to reality.

28   He was in no mood to talk to anybody now and opened the tap wider in order to make conversation impossible. He saw Bill, one of the junior clerks, staring over his shoulder. He didn't particularly like Bill and saw no reason to start his friendliness campaign with him.

29   "Hi, and how's things today?" Bill shouted above the rush of water.

30   "Okay, okay," Marius grunted, again bathing his face in cold water. Before Bill could join him at the washbasin, he shut off the tap, almost running to the paper towel dispenser. Drying his face hurriedly, he left. He didn't find that peace he was looking for in the washroom.

31   Back in the office he found everybody hard at work. What a relief. He didn't have to talk to them. He wasn't even going to apologize for his earlier outburst. They could all go to hell as far as he was concerned. He started working on the pile of reports of absence again. "Arnold Armbruster," the first one read, "two days vacation." Then there was Emma Emmanuel, who took a day off because she was feeling under the weather.

32   In Saskatoon there was a man named David Petrovski who took seven days off in order to take his six-year-old boy to Toronto for open-heart surgery. He checked the card file and found that the man had used up all his holidays and sick leave to take his child to various doctors in the province. Surely this should be treated as compassionate leave? He looked at the slip of paper again and saw the manager had added that the "seven days are to be deducted from the employee's wages as all holidays have been exhausted." This of course would mean that Petrovski was only going to get half his fortnightly earnings.

33   He wondered what had happened to the co-operative interdependence people from this province had spoke so much of. Was there no sense of compassion left in this society? Perhaps their compassion was only for the Third World.

34   After a moment of further musing he decided that this was not his battle. He was not employed as a human rights activist. His job was that of accounting clerk. Still, he felt a little guilty that he hadn't done anything on David's behalf (whomever he might be) and a slight sense of having betrayed somebody irked at his insides. He started working on the rest of the pile of papers.

35   After another month on the job, he felt confident and strong. Payroll sheets were submitted for computerization on time. No cheques had subsequently gone missing. Reports of absence were a piece of cake. A feeling of utter well-being took hold of him.

36   "So, missy," he said to Christine one day when the two of them were alone in the office, "how are things working out in your section?" She looked at him enquiringly. "I thought you might need a hand in getting something done," he continued carefully. "I've met my deadlines and see my desk is all clear."

37   "Why sure, Marius," she said, brushing a stray blonde curl out of the way. "If you feel so kindly, please post these figures in the ledger for me."

38   "Anytime, ma'am. Anytime. But what's in it for me, hey!" he asked, swinging the swivel chair sideways so he faced her directly. "Surely one good turn deserves another?"

39   "Come on, Marius. I thought we were supposed to help each other out," she said, unsure where the conversation was leading.

40   Getting up from the chair, he stretched his thin frame to its full height of six feet and walked towards her desk. "Well, how about coffee after work," he said, taking the sheet of figures before she changed her mind. He walked the two steps back to his own desk without once letting her out of his gaze.

41   Christine met his stare. "Can't you offer a lady anything better than that?" she parried.

42   "Let's say, a drink at your favourite place?"

43   "Well, I don't know. Maybe. When?"

44   "Tonight after work." There was a finality to his tone.

45   "Sure," she said, busying herself with papers.

46   Christine never turned up for the date. After spending half an hour waiting for her at the main entrance, he assumed she must have gotten cold feet and taken another exit out of the building. On second thought he felt that perhaps he shouldn't have sprung this date on her. Maybe he should have cultivated her friendship first before asking for a date. Perhaps that was the way things were done in this country. Since she didn't give him either an explanation or an apology the next day, he was left wondering for the rest of the week as to why she never turned up.

47 Going through the alphabetical listing of employees one day, he discovered two employees who shared exact same names and dates of birth. After he had checked their social insurance numbers, he found that except for the last two numerals, the numbers were the same. He quickly decided that this was merely coincidence. Besides, the two female employees worked in dif-

ferent departments.

48   What disturbed him, however, was that the incident was repeated twice subsequently. On a separate sheet of paper he noted down all the particulars and the following pattern emerged: there were three pairs of employees. Each pair shared the same first and last names as well as dates of birth. As for the social insurance numbers of each employee, only the last two numerals in each pair were different. Checking further, he found that out of each pair, there was one person working the claims department. The other three employees worked in the systems, microfilm and auto departments respectively.

49   Assuming that three of the six were legitimate employees, what does that make the others, he wondered. He glanced up from his notes and lit a cigarette. Exhaling the smoke slowly through his nostrils, he was at a loss as to what to do with this information. Should he show it to the supervisor? If he did and was proved wrong, he'd end up the laughingstock of the whole accounting department. On the other hand, who knows, perhaps the supervisor was in on the deal. But then, was this right keeping such information to himself when the company was probably losing hundreds of thousands of dollars through this scheme?

50   He finally decided to keep quiet about what he had detected. It was not his job to play company cop. Auditors were paid to keep a lookout for such fraudulent practices. Besides, he was not going to risk his position with such revelations.

51   Later in the morning everybody was called to the supervisor's office. In her foreboding manner the supervisor told the payroll clerks that, as from the following week, all reports of absence were going to be handled by the human resources department. Marius was acutely aware that this new arrangement was going to reduce his workload tremendously. He wondered which new duties he was going to be given. Nevertheless, he kept quiet as nothing was directly asked of him. But then in his naiveté he expected that management in their corporate wisdom would arrive at a decision which would meet everybody's needs and tasks. So he said nothing and left the supervisor's office quietly ahead of everybody else.

52   Back at his desk he found a fresh pile of reports of absence waiting for him. Halfway through the batch, he came upon David Petrovski again. He read that a week ago the man, who earlier had lost a week's pay taking his child to Toronto for open-heart surgery, had requested three days' unpaid vacation to bury his son. Marius felt himself getting very hot and suddenly very cold. Mixed emotions of anger at the bureaucracy of the company and empathy with the unknown man's suffering clouded his thoughts. He reached for his packet of cigarettes and suddenly stopped midway. The idea

just struck him that there would be something banal in smoking at a time like this. There was a certain holiness in the suffering of this man. Reaching into his desk, he got hold of a standard memorandum sheet. Writing in his best copperplate he informed David that he had seen his suffering and expressed his deepest sympathy. As an afterthought, he wrote a cheque and added that the man should please accept this gift of one hundred dollars from one human being to another. He sealed both cheque and note in an envelope and marked it for the Saskatoon office.

53   Looking up from his writing, he saw the supervisor standing in the door-way. "Marius, can I see you in my office for a minute, please?" Averting her eyes to the traffic outside the window, the supervisor led the way to her office.

54   "Marius," she began, standing behind her desk, "we don't want you to take this personally"—holding a large white envelope in her left hand—"but in view of the new arrangement, we have decided that instead of a month's notice, we'll give you a month's pay."

Thinking about the Text

1. What is affirmative action? In what ways is this title ironic, given the outcome of the story?

2. List examples illustrating how Marius's co-workers perceive him. Do his co-workers see beyond stereotypes? Why or why not? How do their perceptions of him compare to his perceptions of himself?

3. What moral dilemmas does Marius encounter in his job as accounting clerk?

Writing from the Text

1. Based on details from this story, write a character analysis of Marius.

2. If you have ever experienced discrimination because of your race, ethnic background, or religion, write about your experience as it relates to what Marius encountered.

Connecting with Other Texts

1. Research the origin of affirmative action and how it developed in the work-place. Is affirmative action proving to be a success or a failure?

2. Is Marius's experience representative of what other minority groups have experienced? Find periodical articles that feature stories of people from vis-ible minorities who have met with discrimination on the job. Analyse the problem using specific examples from the articles to support your thesis.

3. Write an essay using W.H. Auden's essay "Work, Labour, Play" (p. 170) as background to decide whether Marius is a "worker" or a "wage slave."

Adding Weight to an Image of Beauty

Catherine Pigott

1   The women of the household clucked disapprovingly when they saw me. It was the first time I had worn African clothes since my arrival in tiny, dusty Gambia, and evidently they were not impressed. They adjusted my head-tie and pulled my *lappa*, the ankle-length fabric I had wrapped around myself, even tighter. "You're too thin," one of them pronounced. "It's no good." They nicknamed me "Chicken-hips."

2   I marvelled at this accolade, for I had never been called thin in my life. It was something I longed for. I would have been flattered if those ample-bosomed women hadn't looked so distressed. It was obvious I fell far short of their ideal of beauty.

3   I had dressed up for a very special occasion—the baptism of a son. The women heaped rice into tin basins the size of laundry tubs, shaping it into mounds with their hands. Five of us sat around one basin, thrusting our fingers into the scalding food. These women ate with such relish, such joy. They pressed the rice into balls in their fists, squeezing until the bright-red palm oil ran down their forearms and dripped off their elbows.

4   I tried desperately, but I could not eat enough to please them. It was hard for me to explain that I come from a culture in which it is almost unseemly for a woman to eat too heartily. It's considered unattractive. It was even harder to explain that to me thin is beautiful, and in my country we deny ourselves food in our pursuit of perfect slenderness.

5   That night, everyone danced to welcome the baby. Women swivelled their broad hips and used their hands to emphasize the roundness of their bodies. One needed to be round and wide to make the dance beautiful. There was no place for thinness here. It made people sad. It reminded them of things they wanted to forget, such as poverty, drought and starvation. You never knew when the rice was going to run out.

6   I began to believe that Africa's image of the perfect female body was far more realistic than the long-legged leanness I had been conditioned to admire. There, it is beautiful—not shameful—to carry weight on the hips and thighs, to have a round stomach and heavy, swinging breasts. Women do not battle the bulge; they celebrate it. A body is not something to be tamed and moulded.

7   The friends who had christened me Chicken-hips made it their mission to fatten me up. It wasn't long before a diet of rice and rich, oily stew twice a day began to change me. Every month, the women would take a stick

and measure my backside, noting with pleasure its gradual expansion. "Oh Catherine, your buttocks are getting nice now!" they would say.

8   What was extraordinary was that I, too, believed I was becoming more beautiful. There was no sense of panic, no shame, no guilt-ridden resolves to go on the miracle grape-and-water diet. One day, I tied my *lappa* tight across my hips and went to the market to buy beer for a wedding. I carried the crate of bottles home on my head, swinging my hips slowly as I walked. I felt transformed.

9   In Gambia, people don't use words such as "cheating," "naughty," or "guilty" when they talk about eating. The language of sin is not applied to food. Fat is desirable. It holds beneficial meanings of abundance, fertility and health.

10   My perception of beauty altered as my body did. The European tourists on the beach began to look strange and skeletal rather than "slim." They had no hips. They seemed devoid of shape and substance. Women I once would have envied appeared fragile and even ugly. The ideal they represented no longer made sense.

11   After a year, I came home. I preached my new way of seeing to anyone who would listen. I wanted to cling to the liberating belief that losing weight had nothing to do with self-love.

12   Family members kindly suggested that I might look and feel better if I slimmed down a little. They encouraged me to join an exercise club. I wandered around the malls in a dislocated daze. I felt uncomfortable trying on clothes that hung so elegantly on the mannequins. I began hearing old voices inside my head: "Plaid makes you look fat. . . . You're too short for that style. . . . Vertical stripes are more slimming. . . . Wear black."

13   I joined the club. Just a few weeks after I had worn a *lappa* and scooped up rice with my hands, I was climbing into pink leotards and aerobics shoes. The instructor told me that I had to set fitness goals and "weigh in" after my workouts. There were mirrors on the walls and I could see women watching themselves. I sensed that even the loveliest among them felt they were somehow flawed. As the aerobics instructor barked out commands for arm lifts and leg lifts, I pictured Gambian women pounding millet and dancing in a circle with their arms raised high. I do not mean to romanticize their rock-hard lives, but we were hardly to be envied as we ran like fools between two walls to the tiresome beat of synthesized music.

14   We were a roomful of women striving to reshape ourselves into some kind of pubertal ideal. I reverted to my natural state: one of yearning to be slimmer and more fit than I was. My freedom had been temporary. I

was home, where fat is feared and despised. It was time to exert control over my body and my life. I dreaded the thought of people saying, "She's let herself go."

15   If I return to Africa, I am sure the women will shake their heads in bewildered dismay. Even now, I sometimes catch my reflection in a window and their voices come back to me. "Yo! Chicken-hips!"

Thinking about the Text

1. How does Pigott's perception of beauty change during her visit to Gambia?

2. What evidence of self-hatred does Pigott observe in the women in her exercise club on her return to Canada? Have you made similar observations?

3. In her comparison of Gambian and Canadian attitudes toward food and the body, the author says that in Gambia, "the language of sin is not applied to food" (paragraph 9). What specific words does she use throughout her essay to indicate the cultural differences in attitude she is describing?

Writing from the Text

1. Look in the text for evidence that Gambian and Canadian attitudes toward women's bodies are polar opposites. Then write a comparison-and-contrast essay discussing the different perceptions of beauty each culture has.

2. Pigott says: "It was time to exert control over my body and my life" (paragraph 14). Does she manage to take charge of her life once she is back in Canada? Use examples from the text to support your thesis that Pigott is successful (or unsuccessful) in taking charge of her life.

Connecting with Other Texts

1. All of us conform to cultural norms, even if we are not aware of it. Write an essay about the harm done when people fail to realize the damage that can arise from such conformity. Include examples from "Adding Weight to an Image of Beauty" and either "The Shackles of Everyday Lies" (p. 34), "The Beauty Myth" (p. 57), or Sean Kelly's "Discovering My Native Identity" (p. 101).

2. Write an essay in which you explore the relationship between love and food. Use examples from "Adding Weight to an Image of Beauty," Judith Timson's "Here's to Family Feasting" (p. 4), and Andrew Pyper's short story "Kiss Me" (p. 81) to support your position.

Bodily Harm
Pamela Erens

1 "Before I'd even heard of bulimia," said Gloria, "I happened to read an article in *People* magazine on Cherry Boone—how she'd used laxatives and vomiting to control her weight. I thought: Wow, what a great idea! I was sure that I would never lose control of my habit."

2 Recent media attention to the binge–purge and self-starvation disorders known as bulimia and anorexia—often detailing gruesome particulars of women's eating behavior—may have exacerbated this serious problem on college campuses. But why would a woman who reads an article on eating disorders want to copy what she reads? Ruth Striegel-Moore, Ph.D., director of Yale University's Eating Disorders Clinic, suggests that eating disorders may be a way to be like other "special" women and at the same time strive to outdo them. "The pursuit of thinness is a way for women to compete with each other, a way that avoids being threatening to men," says Striegel-Moore. Eating disorders as a perverse sort of rivalry? In Carol's freshman year at SUNY-Binghamton, a roommate showed her how to make herself throw up. "Barf buddies" are notorious on many college campuses, especially in sororities and among sports teams. Eating disorders as negative bonding? Even self-help groups on campus can degenerate into the kinds of competitiveness and negative reinforcement that are among the roots of eating disorders in the first place.

3 This is not another article on how women do it. It is an article on how and why some women stopped. The decision to get help is not always an easy one. The shame and secrecy surrounding most eating disorders and the fear of being labeled "sick" may keep a woman from admitting even to herself that her behavior is hurting her. "We're not weirdos," says Nancy Gengler, a recovered bulimic and number two U.S. squash champion, who asked that I use her real name because "so much of this illness has to do with secrecy and embarrassment." In the first stages of therapy, says Nancy, much of getting better was a result of building up the strength to (literally) "sweat out" the desire to binge and to endure the discomfort of having overeaten rather than throwing up. "I learned to accept such 'failures' and moreover, that they would not make me fat. . . ."

4 Secret shame or college fad, eating disorders among college women are growing at an alarming rate: in a recent study at Wellesley College, more than half the women on campus felt they needed help to correct destructive eating patterns. These included bingeing, chronic dieting, and

"aerobic nervosa," the excessive use of exercise to maintain one's body ideal—in most women, invariably five to ten pounds less than whatever she currently weighs.

5   Why now? Wasn't the Women's Movement supposed to free women to be any body size, to explore the full range of creative and emotional possibilities? Instead, women in epidemic numbers are developing symptoms that make them feel hopeless about the future, depleting the energy they have for schoolwork and other activities, and if serious enough, send them right back home or into the infantalizing condition of hospitalization. What has gone wrong?

6   For Brenda, college meant the freedom to question her mother's values about sex. But when she abandoned her mother's guidelines, "I went to the other extreme. I couldn't set limits about sex, food, or anything else." The pressure on college women to appear successful and in control, to know what they want among the myriad new choices they are offered, is severe. So much so that many choose internal havoc over external imperfection. Naomi, a bulimic student at Ohio State University, said she would rather be alcoholic like her father than overweight like her mother because "fat is something you can see."

7   One reason college women hesitate to enter therapy, says Stephen Zimmer, director of the Center for the Study of Anorexia and Bulimia in New York City, is that the eating disorder has become a coping mechanism. It allows the person to function when she feels rotten inside. "In the first session," says Zimmer, "I tell my patients: 'I'm not going to try to take your eating behavior away from you. Until you find something that works better, you get to keep it.' Their relief is immense."

8   Brenda at first did not even tell the counselor whom she was seeing that she was bulimic. She started therapy because of a series of affairs with abusive men. As Brenda developed the sense that she had a right to say no to harmful relationships and to make demands on others, her inability to say no to food also disappeared.

9   However, if a woman is vomiting three times a day, she may be unable to concentrate on long-term therapy. Behavioral therapy, which directly addresses the learned habit of bingeing and purging, is a more immediate alternative. For eight years, Marlene Boskind-White, Ph.D., and her husband, William White, Jr., Ph.D., ran weekend workshops for bulimic women at Cornell University, usually as an adjunct to other forms of therapy. The sessions included nutritional counseling, developing techniques of dealing with binge "triggers," feminist consciousness-raising, and examining the hidden "payoffs" that keep a woman from changing her eating

behavior. Boskind-White and White report that a follow-up of 300 women they had treated one to three years earlier showed that 70 percent had entirely stopped purging and drastically reduced their bingeing.

10   Group therapy (an increasingly popular resource on college campuses) may be the first time a woman realizes she is not alone with her problem. Rebecca Axelrod, who was bulimic throughout college, and now counsels bulimics herself, found that joining the Cornell workshop and meeting other bulimic women defused many of her fears about herself: "I saw ten other women who were not mentally ill, not unable to function," Axelrod says. She remembers the moment when she understood the meaning of her bingeing and purging. "Saturday afternoon, Marlene took the women off alone, and we discussed the 'superwoman syndrome'—that attempt to be the perfect friend, lover, hostess, student . . . and perfect-looking. And bingeing, I saw, was my form of *defiance*. But if you're living life as the perfect woman, you won't cuss, you won't get drunk or laid or drive too fast. No, in the privacy of your own room you'll eat yourself out of house and home. But how dare you be defiant? And so you punish yourself by throwing it up."

11   But "groups can fall into a cycle I call 'bigger and badder,'" says Axelrod. "It starts when one person comes in and says, 'I feel terrible, I binged yesterday.' Somebody else says: 'Oh, that's okay, so did I.' Then a third person says: 'That's nothing, did you know I. . . .' Pretty soon everyone is lending support to the binge instead of to the woman who needs ways of coping with it."

12   However, Axelrod feels that there is much potential for women to help one another. She encourages bulimics to ask for help from their friends, saying that while she herself was initially frightened that being open about her bulimia would alienate her friends, most were very supportive. "The important thing," says Axelrod, "is to be specific about what you need. Don't say: 'Be there for me.' Tell a friend exactly what she can do: for instance, not to urge you to go out for pizza if you tell her you're feeling vulnerable. And rely on three friends, not one."

13   One of the most important strategies in treating eating disorders, says Dr. Lee Combrinck-Graham of the newly opened Renfrew Center for anorectics and bulimics in Philadelphia, is breaking old patterns. Renfrew is a residential center that houses patients for between three weeks and two months, a period that can give women with eating disorders a respite from repetitive and destructive habits that are reinforced by the college environment. But Renfrew is not a "retreat"; its residents work hard. They participate in therapy workshops, take seminars in assertiveness-training

and women's issues, and even participate in "new attitude" cooking class-es. Dr. Combrinck-Graham stresses that therapy itself has often become a "pattern" for women who come to Renfrew. . . . Many of Renfrew's patients, says Dr. Combrinck-Graham, can say exactly what's "wrong" with them and why, yet are still unable to control their eating habits. Renfrew combines a philosophy that recovery is the patient's responsibility—she sets her own goals and contracts for as much supervision as she needs—with innovative art and movement therapy that may bypass some of the rationalizations that block the progress of "talking" therapies.

14   Women who live close to home and whose parents are not separated may want to try family therapy. Family therapy considers the family itself, not the daughter with an eating disorder, to be the "patient." Often, the daughter has taken on the role of diverting attention from unacknowl-edged conflicts within the family. Family therapists behave somewhat like manic stage managers, interrupting and quizzing various members of a family, orchestrating confrontations in an attempt to expose and demolish old, rigid patterns of relating. Ideally, family therapy benefits all the mem-bers of the family. Carol, the student at SUNY-Binghamton, said that fam-ily therapy revealed how unhappy her mother was as a homemaker in a traditional Italian family.

15   Situations like Carol's are at the heart of today's epidemic of eating dis-orders, argues Kim Chernin in her book *The Hungry Self: Women, Eating, and Identity.* Chernin claims that today's college woman is the heir of a particular cultural moment that turns her hunger for identity into an uncon-trollable urge for bodily nourishment. Young women of an earlier genera-tion were educated to have children and remain in the home, yet our cul-ture devalued the work they did there. Later, the Women's Movement opened up vast new emotional and career possibilities, and many daugh-ters, on the verge of achieving their mother's suppressed dreams, are struck by panic and guilt.

16   Carol agreed: "I would try to push my mother to take classes, but my father was always against it. I was a good student, but how could I keep on getting smarter than my mother? When I was young, we'd been like one person. I wanted to be a homemaker because she was one. But when I got older, I said to myself: 'This woman has no life. She never leaves the house except to get groceries. And she's miserable.' I wanted to stop grow-ing up, and then she would always be able to lead me and guide me." According to Chernin, an eating disorder may be a way to postpone or put an end to one's development, one's need to choose, the possibility of sur-passing one's mother. In a world hostile to the values of closeness and

nurturance women learn from and associate with the mother–daughter relationship, an eating disorder can disguise a desire to return to the "nourishment" of that early bond.

17   And why do the daughter's problems focus around food? As Chernin reminds us, originally with her milk, the mother *is* food. Femininity itself has historically been associated with food gathering and preparation. Food—eating it, throwing it up—can become a powerful means of expressing aspects of the mother's life or of traditionally defined femininity that the daughter is trying to ingest or reject. And relationships with other women later in life can replicate this early pattern: food mediates hostility and love.

18   Whatever forms of therapy prove most helpful for women with eating disorders, it is clear that therapy is only half the battle. The Stone Center for Developmental Services and Studies at Wellesley College recognizes the need for early prevention and is preparing a film for adolescents that will feature women and health professionals speaking about the uses and abuses of food in our culture. Janet Surrey, Ph.D., a research associate at the center, stresses the need to educate girls in the 10- to 15-year-old age bracket—66 percent of whom already diet—about the psychological, physical, and reproductive danger of dieting and excessive thinness. Nutritional counseling is another imperative. But to Kim Chernin, our first priority is outreach centers and school programs that will provide developmental counseling and feminist consciousness-raising for this crucial pre–high school group. If women could learn early on to confront their conflicts over their right to development, the use of power, and their place in a still male-dominated world, there might no longer be a need for the "silent language" of eating disorders.

Thinking about the Text

1. According to Erens, how has popular press coverage exacerbated the problem of eating disorders?

2. According to Rebecca Axelrod, who is quoted in Erens's review, how does the "superwoman syndrome" contribute to the problem of recognizing and treating eating disorders?

3. How can group therapy sessions, frequently joined by people with eating disorders, actually complicate the treatment?

4. What is Kim Chernin's perception of one cause of eating disorders?

5. What is proposed to stop the increasing number of young women with eating disorders?

Writing from the Text

1. Do you think that women compete with each other by pursuing thinness? Do you think women bond in an effort to achieve thinness? Write an essay in which you describe and analyse the eating patterns of women you know, including yourself, if you are female.

2. Argue that the cause of eating disorders is not based in the mother–daughter relationship but in the superthin images in advertising. Cite and *describe* specific examples of advertising to support your view.

3. Do men also suffer from eating disorders? Think about the men you know, or yourself, if you are male, and discuss this question in an essay.

Connecting with Other Texts

1. Pamela Erens and Naomi Wolf ("The Beauty Myth," p. 57) describe the kinds of harm that can be done to women who try to conform to a standardized concept of beauty. In an analysis essay, examine the problem by connecting the ideas expressed by these two writers.

2. This article, published in 1985, gives a good review of eating problems, but new information may provide increased or different insights. Use Erens's essay as a model but use more current material to analyse the problem of eating disorders.

3. Author Terry Poulton, in her book *No Fat Chicks*, gives a personal account of her participation in a weight-loss program monitored by and reported in a national women's magazine, as well as the discrimination she has faced as an "overweight" woman. Read the book and relate Poulton's experience to the issues discussed in "Bodily Harm."

In Search of Whitemud

Wallace Stegner

1 In the fall it was always a moment of pure excitement, after a whole day on the trail, to come to the rim of the South Bench. More likely than not I would be riding with my mother in the wagon while my father had my brother with him in the Ford. The horses would be plodding with their noses nearly to their knees, the colt would be dropping tiredly behind. We would be choked with dust, cranky and headachy with heat, our joints loosened with fifty miles of jolting. Then miraculously the land fell away below us, I would lift my head from my mother's lap and push aside the straw hat that had been protecting my face from the glare, and there

below, looped in its green coils of river, snug and protected in its sanctuary valley, lay town.

2   The land falls below me now, the suddenness of my childhood town is the old familiar surprise. But I stop, looking, for adult perception has in ten seconds clarified a childhood error. I have always thought of the Whitemud as running its whole course in a deeply sunken valley. Instead, I see that the river has cut deeply only through the uplift of the hills; that off to the southeast, out on the prairie, it crawls disconsolately flat across the land. It is a lesson in how peculiarly limited a child's sight is: he sees only what he can see. Only later does he learn to link what he sees with what he already knows, or has imagined or heard or read, and so come to make perception service inference. During my childhood I kept hearing about the Cypress Hills, and knew that they were somewhere nearby. Now I see that I grew up in them. Without destroying the intense familiarity, the flooding recognition of the moment, that grown-up understanding throws things a little out of line, and so it is with mixed feelings of intimacy and strangeness that I start down the dug-way grade. Things look the same, surprisingly the same, and yet obscurely different. I tick them off, easing watchfully back into the past.

3   There is the Frenchman's stone barn, westward up the river valley a couple of miles. It looks exactly as it did when we used to go through the farmyard in wagon or buckboard and see the startled kids disappearing around every corner, and peeking out at us from hayloft door and cowshed after we passed. Probably they were *métis*, halfbreeds; to us, who had never heard the word *métis*, they were simply Frenchmen, part of the vague and unknown past that had given our river one of its names. I bless them for their permanence, and creep on past the cemetery, somewhat larger and somewhat better kept than I remember it, but without disconcerting changes. Down below me is the dam, with its wide lake behind it. It takes me a minute to recollect that by the time we left Whitemud Pop Martin's dam had long since washed out. This is a new one, therefore, but in approximately the old place. So far, so good.

4   The road I bump along is still a dirt road, and it runs where it used to run, but the wildcat oil derrick that used to be visible from the turn at the foot of the grade is not there any longer. I note, coming in toward the edge of the town, that the river has changed its course somewhat, swinging closer to the southern hills and pinching the road space. I see a black iron bridge, new, that evidently leads some new road off into the willow bottoms westward, toward the old Carpenter ranch. I cannot see the river, masked in willows and alders, and anyway my attention is taken by the

town ahead of me, which all at once reveals one element of the obscure strangeness that has been making me watchful. Trees.

5   My town used to be as bare as a picked bone, with no tree anywhere around it larger than a ten-foot willow or alder. Now it is a grove. My memory gropes uneasily, trying to establish itself among fifty-foot cottonwoods, lilac and honeysuckle hedges, and flower gardens. Searched for, plenty of familiarities are there: the Pastime Theatre, identical with the one that sits across Main Street from the firehouse in my mind; the lumber yard where we used to get cloth caps advertising De Laval Cream Separators; two or three hardware stores (a prairie wheat town specializes in hardware stores), though each one now has a lot full of farm machinery next to it; the hotel, just as it was rebuilt after the fire; the bank, now remodelled into the post office; the Presbyterian church, now United, and the *Leader* office, and the square brick prison of the old school, now with three smaller prisons added to it. These are old acquaintances that I can check against their replicas in my head and take satisfaction from. But among them are the evidences of Progress—hospital, Masonic Lodge, at least one new elevator, a big quonset-like skating rink—and all tree-shaded, altered and distorted and made vaguely disturbing by greenery. In the old days we all used to try to grow trees, transplanting them from the Hills or getting them free with any two-dollar purchase from one of the stores, but they always dried up and died. To me, who came expecting a dusty hamlet, the change is charming, but memory has been fixed by time as photographs fix the faces of the dead, and this reality is dreamlike. I cannot find myself or my family or my companions in it.

6   My progress up Main Street, as wide and empty and dusty as I remember it, has taken me to another iron bridge across the eastern loop of the river, where the flume of Martin's irrigation ditch used to cross, and from the bridge I get a good view of the river. It is disappointing, a quiet creek twenty yards wide, the colour of strong tea, its banks a tangle of willow and wild rose. How could adventure ever have inhabited those willows, or wonder, or fear, or other remembered emotions? Was it along here I shot at the lynx with my brother's .25-.20? And out of what log (there is no possibility of a log in these brakes, but I distinctly remember a log) did my bullet knock chips just under the lynx's bobtail?

7   A muddy little stream, a village grown unfamiliar with time and trees. I turn around and retrace my way up Main Street and park and have a Coke in the confectionery store. It is run by a Greek, as it used to be, but whether the same Greek or another I would not know. He does not recognize me, nor I him. Only the smell of his place is familiar, syrupy with

old delights, as if the ghost of my first banana split had come close to breathe on me. Still in search of something or someone to make the town fully real to me, I get the telephone book off its nail by the wall telephone and run through it, sitting at the counter. There are no more than seventy or eighty names in the Whitemud section. I look for Huffman—none. Bickerton—none. Fetter—none. Orullian—none. Stenhouse—none. Young—one, but not by a first name I remember. There are a few names I do remember—Harold Jones and William Christenson and Nels Sieverud and Jules LaPlante. (That last one startles me. I always thought his name was Jewell.) But all of the names I recognize are those of old-timers, pioneers of the town. Not a name that I went to school with, not a single person who would have shared as a contemporary my own experience of this town in its earliest years, when the river still ran clear and beaver swam in it in the evenings. Who in town remembers Phil Lott, who used to run coyotes with wolfhounds out on the South Bench? Who remembers in the way I do the day he drove up before Leaf's store in his democrat wagon and unloaded from it two dead hounds and the lynx that had killed them when they caught him unwarily exposed out on the flats? Who remembers in *my* way the stiff, half-disemboweled bodies of the hounds and the bloody grin of the lynx? Who feels it or felt it, as I did and do, as a parable, a moral lesson for the pursuer to respect the pursued?

8 , Because it is not shared, the memory seems fictitious, and so do other memories: the blizzard of 1916 that marooned us in the schoolhouse for a night and a day, the time the ice went out and brought both Martin's dam and the CPR bridge in kindling to our doors, the games of fox-and-geese in the untracked snow of a field that is now a grove, the nights of skating with a great fire leaping from the river ice and reflecting red from the cutbanks. I have used those memories for years as if they really happened, have made stories and novels of them. Now they seem uncorroborated and delusive. Some of the pioneers still in the telephone book would remember, but pioneers' memories are no good to me. Pioneers would remember the making of the town; to me, it was made, complete, timeless. A pioneer's child is what I need now, and in this town the pioneers' children did not stay, but went on, generally to bigger places farther west, where there was more opportunity.

9   Sitting in the sticky-smelling, nostalgic air of the Greek's confectionery store, I am afflicted with the sense of how many whom I have known are dead, and how little evidence I have that I myself have lived what I remember. It is not quite the same feeling I imagined when I contemplated driving out to the homestead. That would have been absolute denial.

This, with its tantalizing glimpses, its hints and survivals, is not denial but only doubt. There is enough left to disturb me, but not to satisfy me. So I will go a little closer. I will walk on down into the west bend and take a look at our house.

10 .   In the strange forest of the school yard the boys are friendly, and their universal air of health, openness, and curiosity reassures me. This is still a good town to be a boy in. To see a couple of them on the prowl with air rifles (in my time we would have been carrying .22's or shotguns, but we would have been of the same tribe) forces me to readjust my disappointed estimate of the scrub growth. When one is four feet high, ten-foot willows are a sufficient cover, and ten acres are a wilderness.

11   By now, circling and more than half unwilling, I have come into the west end of town, have passed Corky Jones's house (put off till later that meeting) and the open field beside Downs's where we used to play run-sheep-run in the evenings, and I stand facing the four-gabled white frame house that my father built. It ought to be explosive with nostalgias and bright with recollections, for this is where we lived for five or six of my most impressionable years, where we all nearly died with the flu in 1918, where my grandmother "went crazy" and had to be taken away by a Mountie to the Provincial asylum because she took to standing silently in the door of the room where my brother and I slept—just hovered there for heaven knows how long before someone discovered her watching and listening in the dark. I try to remember my grandmother's face and cannot; only her stale old-woman's smell after she became incontinent. I can summon up other smells, too—it is the smells that seem to have stayed with me: painting paint and hot tin and lignite smoke behind the parlour heater; frying scrapple, which we called headcheese, on chilly fall mornings after the slaughtering was done; the rich thick odour of doughnuts frying in a kettle of boiling lard (I always got to eat the "holes"). With effort, I can bring back Christmases, birthdays, Sunday School parties in that house, and I have not forgotten the licking I got when, aged about six, I was caught playing with my father's loaded .30-.30 that hung above the mantel just under the Rosa Bonheur painting of three white horses in a storm. After that licking I lay out behind the chopping block all one afternoon watching my big dark heavy father as he worked at one thing and another, and all the time I lay there I kept aiming an empty cartridge case at him and dreaming murder.

12   Even the dreams of murder, which were bright enough at the time, have faded; he is long dead, and if not forgiven, at least propitiated. My mother, too, who saved me from him so many times, and once missed

saving me when he clouted me with a chunk of stove wood and knocked me over the wood box and broke my collarbone: she too has faded. Standing there looking at the house where our lives entangled themselves in one another, I am infuriated that of that episode I remember less her love and protection and anger than my father's inept contrition. And walking all around the house trying to pump up recollection, I notice principally that the old barn is gone. What I see, though less changed than the town in general, still has power to disturb me; it is all dreamlike, less real than memory, less convincing than the recollected odours.

13   Whoever lives in the house now is a tidy housekeeper; the yard is neat, the porch swept. The corner where I used to pasture my broken-legged colt is a bed of flowers, the yard where we hopefully watered our baby spruces is a lawn enclosed by a green hedge. The old well with the hand pump is still in the side yard. For an instant my teeth are on edge with the memory of the dry screech of that pump before a dipperful of priming water took hold, and an instant later I feel the old stitch in my side from an even earlier time, the time when we still carried water from the river, and I dipped a bucket down into the hole in the ice and toted it, staggering and with the other arm stuck stiffly out, up the dug-way to the kitchen door.

14   Those instants of memory are persuasive. I wonder if I should knock on the door and ask the housewife to let me look around, go upstairs to our old room in the west gable, examine the ceiling to see if the stains from the fire department's chemicals are still there. My brother and I used to lie in bed and imagine scenes and faces among the blotches, giving ourselves inadvertent Rorschach tests. I have a vivid memory, too, of the night the stains were made, when we came out into the hard cold from the Pastime Theatre and heard the firehouse bell going and saw the volunteer fire department already on the run, and followed them up the ditch toward the glow of the fire, wondering whose house, until we got close and it was ours.

15   It is there, and yet it does not flow as it should, it is all a pumping operation. I half suspect that I am remembering not what happened but something I have written. I find that I am as unwilling to go inside that house as I was to try to find the old homestead in its ocean of grass. All the people who once shared the house with me are dead; strangers who would have effaced or made doubtful the things that might restore them in my mind.

16   Behind our house there used to be a footbridge across the river, used by the Carpenters and others who lived in the bottoms, and by summer

swimmers from town. I pass by the opaque and troubling house to the cut-bank. The twin shanties that through all the town's life have served as men's and women's bath houses are still there. In winter we used to hang our frozen beef in one of them. I remember iron evenings when I went out with a lantern and sawed and haggled steaks from a rocklike hind quarter. But it is still an academic exercise; I only remember it, I do not feel the numb fingers and the fear that used to move just beyond the lantern's glow.

17   Then I walk to the cutbank edge and look down, and in one step the past comes closer than it has yet been. There is the grey curving cutbank, not much lower than I remember it when we dug cave holes in it or tun-nelled down its drifted cliff on our sleds. The bar is there at the inner curve of the bend, and kids are wallowing in a quicksandy mudhole and shriek-ing on an otter slide. They chase each other into the river and change mag-ically from black to white. The water has its old quiet, its whirlpools spin lazily into deep water. On the footbridge, nearly exactly where it used to be, two little girls lie staring down into the water a foot below their noses. Probably they are watching suckers that lie just as quietly against the bot-tom. In my time we used to snare them from the bridge with nooses of copper wire.

18   It is with me all at once, what I came hoping to re-establish, an ancient, unbearable recognition, and it comes partly from the children and the footbridge and the river's quiet curve, but much more from the smell. For here, pungent and pervasive, is the smell that has always meant my childhood. I have never smelled it anywhere else, and it is as evocative as Proust's madeleine and tea.

19   But what is it? Somehow I have always associated it with the bath house, with wet bathing suits and damp board benches, heaps of clothing, perhaps even the seldom rinsed corners where desperate boys had made water. I go into the men's bath house, and the smell is there, but it does not seem to come from any single thing. The whole air smells of it, out-side as well as in. Perhaps it is the river water, or the mud, or something about the float and footbridge. It is the way the old burlap-tipped diving board used to smell; it used to remain in the head after a sinus-flooding dive.

20   I pick up a handful of mud and sniff it. I step over the little girls and bend my nose to the wet rail of the bridge. I stand above the water and sniff. On the other side I strip leaves off wild rose and dogwood. Nothing doing. And yet all around me is that odour that I have not smelled since I was eleven, but have never forgotten—have *dreamed*, more than once.

Then I pull myself up the bank by a grey-leafed bush, and I have it. The tantalizing and ambiguous and wholly native smell is no more than the shrub we called wolf willow, now blooming with small yellow flowers.

21   It is wolf willow, and not the town or anyone in it, that brings me home. For a few minutes, with a handful of leaves to my nose, I look across at the clay bank and the hills beyond where the river loops back on itself, enclosing the old sports and picnic ground, and the present and all the years between are shed like a boy's clothes dumped on the bath house bench. The perspective is what it used to be, the dimensions are restored, the senses are as clear as if they had not been battered with sensation for forty alien years. And the queer adult compulsion to return to one's beginnings is assuaged. A contact has been made, a mystery touched. For the moment, reality is made exactly equivalent with memory, and a hunger is satisfied. The sensuous little savage that I once was is still intact inside me.

Thinking about the Text

1. What feelings does Stegner experience as he tours his home town? Find examples that illustrate those feelings.

2. Stegner writes that, on his return to Whitemud, "things look the same, surprisingly the same, and yet obscurely different" (paragraph 2). List details that indicate the contrast between Whitemud as he perceives it now and the Whitemud he remembers.

3. What role has memory played in Stegner's life?

4. What is Stegner looking for on this visit to Whitemud? Does he find what he is seeking? How?

Writing from the Text

1. Analyse the sensory components of Stegner's memories of Whitemud. What role do his five senses play in shaping his memory?

2. Think about a place that was important to you when you were a child. Which of the five senses predominate in your memory? Describe this place using as many sensory recollections as possible.

3. Stegner's essay describes a conflict between an outer reality, the Whitemud he sees on this trip, and an inner reality, the Whitemud he remembers from his childhood. In an analysis essay, discuss the conflict he experiences. Why is it difficult for him to reconcile the two realities?

Connecting with Other Texts

1. Compare and contrast the father–child relationships as they are described in "In Search of Whitemud" and Madeleine Gagnon's "Respect and Balance in Our 'Tribe'" (p. 6). How do the fathers interact with their children and how do the adult children perceive their fathers years later?

2. With the help of your librarian, find some books or articles discussing psychological research on human memory. You may want to explore how memory is affected by aging, what different types of memory have been identified, or the role the senses play in shaping memory. Write an essay on your findings.

CHAPTER 5
Between Values

This final chapter of readings is necessarily a culmination of the other chapters because our age, sex, roots, and self-perceptions all influence what we value. This chapter invites you to think about your own beliefs and values concerning work, materialism, leisure, activism, and conformity.

Your various work experiences may have prompted you to think about the advantages and disadvantages of different jobs. An essay by W.H. Auden makes an important distinction between working and labouring, and Tom Wayman's imaginative poem exemplifies one of Auden's definitions. Kate Braid contends that our humanity is suffering because our work is becoming more sedentary and less physical. Lisa Gregoire's new job leads her to ponder what she learned when she was unemployed and to speculate about her generation's future. These readings may prompt you to consider the importance of work in your life and ask you to think about whether your jobs will provide satisfaction and self-definition along with a paycheque.

Working and living in any society requires us to balance social pressures and individual needs. Willa Marcus contemplates the transformation in her attitudes toward spending as she becomes more prosperous, while Kenneth J. Harvey observes the improvements in his family relationships after he cancels his household's cable television service. June Callwood, in her essay, urges us to follow through on fleeting wishes to make our community a better place to live and advises us how to become social activists.

The final two readings discuss two potential consequences of group membership. Charlie Angus writes about the irreconcilable chasm between two opposing groups, rural and urban Canadians, on the issue of gun control. Shirley Jackson's disturbing short story "The Lottery" illustrates destructive conformity within a group.

You already have a strong sense of who you are and what you value. The authors in this chapter invite you to confirm your convictions while they ask you to examine the values of others.

Work, Labour, Play

W.H. Auden

1 So far as I know, Miss Hannah Arendt was the first person to define the essential difference between work and labour. To be happy, a man must feel, firstly, free and, secondly, important. He cannot be really happy if he is compelled by society to do what he does not enjoy doing, or if what he enjoys doing is ignored by society as of no value or importance. In a society where slavery in the strict sense has been abolished, the sign that what a man does is of social value is that he is paid money to do it, but a labourer today can rightly be called a wage slave. A man is a labourer if the job society offers him is of no interest to himself but he is compelled to take it by the necessity of earning a living and supporting his family.

2   The antithesis to labour is play. When we play a game, we enjoy what we are doing, otherwise we should not play it, but it is a purely private activity; society could not care less whether we play it or not.

3   Between labour and play stands work. A man is a worker if he is personally interested in the job which society pays him to do; what from the point of view of society is necessary labour is from his own point of view voluntary play. Whether a job is to be classified as labour or work depends, not on the job itself, but on the tastes of the individual who undertakes it. The difference does not, for example, coincide with the difference between a manual and a mental job; a gardener or a cobbler may be a worker, a bank clerk a labourer. Which a man is can be seen from his attitude toward leisure. To a worker, leisure means simply the hours he needs to relax and rest in order to work efficiently. He is therefore more likely to take too little leisure than too much; workers die of coronaries and forget their wives' birthdays. To the labourer, on the other hand, leisure means freedom from compulsion, so that it is natural for him to imagine that the fewer hours he has to spend labouring, and the more hours he is free to play, the better.

4   What percentage of the population in a modern technological society are, like myself, in the fortunate position of being workers? At a guess I would say 16 percent, and I do not think that figure is likely to get bigger in the future.

5   Technology and the division of labour have done two things: by eliminating in many fields the need for special strength or skill, they have made a very large number of paid occupations which formerly were enjoyable work into boring labour; and by increasing productivity they have reduced the number of necessary labouring hours. It is already possible to imagine

a society in which the majority of the population, that is to say, its labourers, will have almost as much leisure as in earlier times was enjoyed by the aristocracy. When one recalls how aristocracies in the past actually behaved, the prospect is not cheerful. Indeed, the problem of dealing with boredom may be even more difficult for such a future mass society than it was for aristocracies. The latter, for example, ritualized their time; there was a season to shoot grouse, a season to spend in town, etc. The masses are more likely to replace an unchanging ritual by fashion which it will be in the economic interest of certain people to change as often as possible. Again, the masses cannot go in for hunting, for very soon there would be no animals left to hunt. For other aristocratic amusements like gambling, duelling, and warfare, it may be only too easy to find equivalents in dangerous driving, drug-taking, and senseless acts of violence. Workers seldom commit acts of violence, because they can put their aggression into their work, be it physical like the work of a smith, or mental like the work of a scientist or an artist. The role of aggression in mental work is aptly expressed by the phrase "getting one's teeth into a problem."

Thinking about the Text

1. How does the "labourer" contrast with the "worker," according to Auden?
2. How does "play" figure in his contrast study? How much validity do you find in his prediction of how the unhappy masses will use their new leisure?
3. How reliable do you find Auden's figure of workers numbering only 16 percent of the work force? To what does Auden attribute the unhappiness in the workplace?

Writing from the Text

1. Write an essay in which you analyse happy workers, using your own experiences or your observations of family and friends for support. Organize your support around a thesis that asserts something about worker happiness and use a variety of supporting examples, as if to acknowledge Auden's view that satisfaction is unrelated to status or paycheque.
2. Write an analysis of unhappy workers, using your observations of family and friends for supporting examples. Proceed as in the above topic.

Connecting with Other Texts

1. Use Lisa Gregoire's essay "On Jobs and Humility" (p. 182) to argue that the issue facing people today is not Auden's view of work but whether or not jobs are available.

2. Research your future occupation, and interview people who work in the field. Write a paper in which you argue that it will be possible to be a "worker" in this field.

Factory Time

Tom Wayman

The day divides neatly into four parts
marked off by the breaks. The first quarter
is a full two hours, 7:30 to 9:30, but that's okay
in theory, because I'm supposed to be fresh, but in fact
5 after some evenings it's a long first two hours.
Then, a ten-minute break. Which is good
another way, too: the second quarter
thus has ten minutes knocked off, 9:40 to 11:30
which is only 110 minutes, or
10 to put it another way, if I look at my watch
and it says 11:10
I can cheer up because if I had still been in the first quarter
and had worked for 90 minutes there would be
30 minutes to go, but now there is only
15 20. If it had been the first quarter, I could expect
the same feeling at 9 o'clock as here I have
when it is already ten minutes after 11.

Then it's lunch: a stretch, and maybe a little walk around.
And at 12 sharp the endless quarter begins:
20 a full two afternoon hours. And it's only the start
of the afternoon. Nothing to hope for the whole time.
Come to think of it, today
is probably only Tuesday. Or worse, Monday,
with the week barely begun and the day
25 only just half over, four hours down
and 36 to go this week
(if the foreman doesn't come padding by about 3
some afternoon and ask us all to work overtime).

Now while I'm trying to get through this early Tuesday afternoon
30 maybe this is a good place to say
Wednesday, Thursday and Friday have their personalities too.
As a matter of fact, Wednesday after lunch
I could be almost happy
because when that 12 noon hooter blast goes
35 the week is precisely and officially half over.
All downhill from here: Thursday, as you know
is the day before Friday
which means a little celebrating Thursday night
—perhaps a few rounds in the pub after supper—
40 won't do me any harm. If I don't get much sleep
Thursday night, so what? I can sleep in Saturday.
And Friday right after lunch Mike the foreman appears
with the long cheques dripping out of his hands
and he is so polite to each of us as he passes them over
45 just like they taught him in foreman school.
After that, not too much gets done.
People go away into a corner and add and subtract like crazy
trying to catch the Company in a mistake
or figuring out what incredible percentage the government
50 has taken this week, or what the money will actually mean
in terms of savings or payments—and me, too.

But wait. It's still Tuesday afternoon.
And only the first half of that: all the minutes
until 2—which comes at last
55 and everyone drops what they are doing
if they hadn't already begun drifting toward
their lunchboxes, or edging between the parts-racks
in the direction of the caterer's carts
which always appear a few minutes before the hooter
60 and may be taken on good authority as incontrovertible proof
that 2 o'clock is actually going to arrive.

And this last ten minute break of the day
is when I finally empty my lunchbox and the thermos inside
and put the now lightweight container back on its shelf
65 and dive into the day's fourth quarter: only 110 minutes.
Also, 20 to 30 minutes before the end I stop

and push a broom around, or just fiddle with something
or maybe fill up various parts-trays with washers
and bolts, or talk to the partsman, climb out of my
70 coveralls, and generally slack off.
Until the 4 p.m. hooter of hooters
when I dash to the timeclock, a little shoving and pushing
in line, and I'm done. Whew.

But even when I quit
75 the numbers of the minutes and hours from this shift
stick with me: I can look at a clock some morning
months afterwards, and see it is 20 minutes to 9
—that is, if I'm ever out of bed that early—
and the automatic computer in my head
80 starts to type out: *20 minutes to 9, that means*
30 minutes to work after 9: you are
50 minutes from the break; 50 minutes
of work, and it is only morning, and it is only
Monday, you poor dumb bastard . . .

85 And that's how it goes, round the clock, until a new time
from another job bores its way into my brain.

Thinking about the Text

1. Consider the tone of this poem. How does the poem's language reflect the speaker's attitude toward his factory job?

2. Is it clear what the speaker's job is at the factory? Does it matter whether we know this detail? Why or why not?

3. What is the significance of the poem's title?

Writing from the Text

1. Write about a job that you have disliked. Start from a thesis that asserts why you did not like the job, and support your thesis with specific examples.

2. Write about a job that you have enjoyed. Start from a thesis that asserts what you found good about the job, and support your thesis with specific and vivid examples.

3. Write an essay in which you argue that we should develop a definition of ideal work to satisfy workers at all levels of employment. Set up the "ideals" in your thesis.

Connecting with Other Texts

1. Compare the speaker's preoccupation with time in "Factory Time" to Saliha Samson's in Yeshim Ternar's short story "Ajax Là-Bas" (p. 110). Write an essay in which you discuss how these references to time reveal something about the characters and their relationship to their work.

2. Write an analysis of "Factory Time" to show that the speaker is a "wage slave," not a "worker." Refer to W.H. Auden's essay "Work, Labour, Play" (p. 170) in your essay.

A Plea for the Physical
Kate Braid

1 In North America, we are losing touch with the physical. We drive rather than walk, use computers or telephones rather than visit, would rather work in a nice clean office than get "dirty" using our bodies at blue-collar work. Only slowly have I learned how vital it is to be in touch with the physical.

2 Perhaps it has something to do with our North American aversion to dirt. I will never forget once dropping into a small café in Mexico City for a drink with a friend on a hot day. The owner had just taken an earlier patron's glass off the counter and was casually flicking it under a stream of cold water. When I asked for an orange soda, the man whipped the wet glass onto the counter without so much as a pass of his dirty tea towel, and, after swishing the flies from its mouth, he began to pour orange soda from a half-empty litre container. Then, in a single motion and with great elan, he reached behind him to take a second glass from among the dozen that rested, open-side up, on a once-white towel. Absently, he again swung his hand through a jungle of flies, swatting them aside to fill a second glass for my friend.

3 I hesitated only a second before drinking the orange mixture down. Cavalier as I was on the surface, I was sufficiently a child of North America to monitor every ache and pain during the next 24 hours to determine whether I had, as I fully expected, imbibed botulism with my orange.

4 An amazing thing happened: I didn't get sick. All my life, my aunts had spent routine hours scrubbing every tiny dark mark off gleaming pots. My mother, with six children, made sure her wooden floors were a miracle of wax and polish. "Good enough to eat off!" she used to brag about

those floors, and they were certainly cleaner than the café owner's counter. I was the obedient daughter in a good Christian house where cleanliness was next to godliness, but in that tiny Mexican café I realized with a shock (and some small delight) that the frenzied cleaning of the women in my family was now something to be questioned rather than emulated. A little dirt, I now knew, wouldn't kill me.

5   Even Europeans, I later learned, laugh at what they see as a North American obsession with hygiene and a desire to enclose everything in HandiWrap. My aunts still do not let any meat touch their lips that has not been fried, baked or boiled until it is grey in colour, cardboard in consistency and devoid of even a single germ.

6   North Americans are loathe even to touch each other. In most other cultures of the world, men and women shake hands, embrace, even kiss, upon meeting or leaving each other. Not North Americans. Too many germs. Too physical. When we touch each other accidentally in public, we apologize.

7 Perhaps this purism is one reason why I eventually chose to work in the trades doing physical work. As a construction carpenter, I began to see what I had been missing. North American distaste for the physical is reflected in the fact that, when it comes to manual work, most Canadians don't even know what a trade is—except that "vocational" in high school is where the "dumb" guys go.

8   The word "trade" was first recorded in 1546 to distinguish a "skilled handicraft" from a profession, business or unskilled occupation. In Europe, there is a centuries-long tradition of tradespeople as vital, highly respected members of the community. First there was farming, then crafts or trades. Until recently, many British tradesmen went to work in a shirt and tie. There is a legend that the masters didn't even bother to change, so careful were they, so good at their craft that not even a small splash of mud could escape their skilled hand.

9   But above all, painting, carpentry and plumbing are physical. The apprentice who has tried to match a colour or cut a straight line—so easy in the journeyperson's hands—is shocked to find how difficult it is when she tries it herself. The apprentice spends one month of the year learning theory, in school. During the other eleven, she learns how to move her body and her hands. The body must know.

10   Consider the advantages of a tradesperson. Here is someone who never has to pay for a gym. "Workout" is a part of her daily routine. Tradespeople have more bad backs but fewer heart attacks than the general population. Although most of them will deny any physical awareness

of the job, for me there is a physical exhilaration, a feeling of being intensely alive that comes from working outside every day, under the sun and in the wind and rain, in a rhythm of bend and nail and lift. As a tradesperson, I developed a relationship with my body that was never demanded by more traditional "women's" work in an office or school.

11   An awareness of pain and physical resistance, though a routine part of being a physical worker, was a revelation to me. As a girl, I was taught that if something hurt or was difficult, I should run to Mummy, who would "fix it." Even if someone "hurt" my feelings, she would advise me to "go play with someone else," avoid pain.

12   But as a construction worker, I learned that the need to push past resistance—even if it hurts—is part of the job. A favourite saying in carpentry is, "If it doesn't fit, hit harder." The only reason you would stop work was in case of a wound that offered significant amounts of blood. Pain was a new physical sensation that could be pushed through. Pain, I learned, would not kill me any more than dirt would. It was not uncommon to come home and notice, for example, deep purple bruises on my legs that I had no memory of receiving. I had learned how to accept certain knocks and strains as part of the physicalness of doing a job. My mind had learned to drown out the incidental pain of physical labour, the pain that didn't present immediate danger. This was a liberation. I was no longer kept busy servicing my body with bandages and "rest." I felt stronger, more confident, less vulnerable to hurt in the world at large.

13   Often we call such behaviour "macho" and attach it to certain less-than-intelligent males. It's only a little embarrassing to say that I have learned to enjoy this macho. I recognized it in my second year when I worked on a high-rise building with an older, heavy-set journeyman. We were on the fourth floor when it became obvious that one of us was going to have to put on the safety belt and swing out over space to finish nailing columns.

14   This man—perhaps because of his age, perhaps because of his Old European background—had been desperately trying to "protect" me by not letting me do many of the more difficult jobs that go with heavy construction. But as we stood contemplating the columns, we both knew that, according to the rules of apprenticeship, I, as the younger, fitter apprentice, should go out on the columns, while he, as journeyman, had the right to stay behind and "supervise," passing tools and material. When I saw that he did not want to go, in spite of his determination to protect me, I volunteered. Reluctantly, he agreed. Quivering with eagerness, I buckled on the safety belt made for someone several sizes larger, filled my pockets

with nails, anchored the belt and swung out over 40 feet of space.

15   After the headiness settled down, I thought, "This is what bodies can do. They can push things, pull things, build things, and they can throw themselves out over clear air to hang suspended while arms and hands do the work that is called for. Why would anybody avoid this?" There was a fierceness of concentration that day, an *I'm alive here!* feeling that popped champagne bubbles all up and down my veins—like rock-climbing but getting paid for it. I had discovered the crushed-ice taste of fear and exhilaration and physical strength and when I swung back to the solid concrete of the deck, I had changed. Suddenly I understood the puffed-out chest, the swagger of macho. I had danced the fine footwork of danger, pushed past fear, and survived. Now I, too, was entitled to boast. This is why carpenters and mountaineers and farmers walk with a certain confidence. We push to the physical limits and survive. But more. As tradespeople, we do what has to be done—building things, fixing things, keeping electricity, water and power moving. These are things physical, unquestionably creations, things of value. And so the unshakable calm of tradespeople—we do this thing. It is useful.

16   There is sanity and connection in the physical. It is literally "knowing where you are," being "rooted." This struck me most clearly after I lived two years in a rural area without a telephone. My friends and I regularly connected by dropping in on each other or going out to have a coffee at the café when we felt like company, staying home when we did not. But eventually, for reasons of work, I had to have a telephone. When I got my first call, I found myself white-knuckled, clutching the receiver, saying over and over to the caller, "Where are you? Where are you?"

17   "Here," he replied, puzzled. "I'm here, at home."

18   Two minutes later I'd have to ask again, "But where are you?" Intellectually, of course, I knew where he was, but like a child who nods at the voice on the telephone, I had physically and emotionally forgotten within two years that technology allows a voice without a body.

19 Sharon Butala, author of *Perfection of the Morning*, spent years wandering alone, on foot, through the grassy hills near her ranch in the Palliser triangle in southwestern Saskatchewan, where she had inexplicable and powerful experiences. She was moved to follow certain courses, and at the end she found Native paths and spiritual sites, as if the land itself could instruct all people if only they listened carefully enough.

20   Butala thinks that our habit of living a life increasingly detached from the earth—of riding in cars, living in cities, of "paving Paradise," as Joni Mitchell puts it—is steadily cutting us off from one of the most powerful

physical influences we have, the land. People's resulting spiritual desolation and feelings of abandonment (even when it is we who are abandoning the land and not vice versa) are reflected in a general sense of fear and a lashing out in violence.

21   I wrestled for a while with the contradiction that I, as a construction worker, was one of those people "paving Paradise"—and enjoying it. Then I recognized the truth of what Butala wrote, and I phoned her to thank her for her book. Butala said she now thinks this is why we, as a civilization, are increasingly fascinated by space. We send men and women to the moon, we create movies like *Star Wars* that become objects of semi-religious reverence, we see a steady increase in the popularity of science fiction as a literary genre. We are using technology as a way to increase our separation from nature and the physical. Perhaps this is not entirely voluntary, I suggested. Perhaps the technology—e-mail, telephones, fax machines—makes us run to catch up, but running means we have less time to touch down, to be in touch with our own selves, until finally we don't dare slow down for fear of what pent-up demons will pour forth when we do.

22   "Perhaps," Butala said. "At any rate, we are getting further and further away from the earth, to the point that our feet have almost left the ground and we are floating up toward the stars, in danger of becoming completely out of touch." We are becoming a nation of space people.

23   This increasing sense of being "out of touch" with our bodies, of not having our feet on the ground, is reflected in our fascination with computers. Within 10 years we have gone from a culture that was impressed by an electric typewriter to a culture where more than one in four of all households have at least one personal computer on which adults and kids spend hours "surfing the net," playing games, doing homework, not looking at each other, not touching each other. People make up whole personas for themselves, change genders, "meet" and "date" without ever setting eyes on a living human being. Of course, this is one way to overcome many of the assumptions and stereotypes of racism, sexism and homophobia, but it comes at a price. Our e-mail addresses have become a vital part of our identity, along with fax numbers and telephones.

24   Many people are uncomfortable with computers because, they say, there is no body language to a computer, no facial expression or voice, no physical cues, only the word. Perhaps the Bible got it all wrong. In the beginning was not the Word. In the beginning was the Body and we have been moving away from it, at our own cost, ever since.

25   Computer networks are not without benefits. They do offer invaluable

sources of information where up-to-the-minute international events can be transferred by grassroots channels, not controlled by the small number of wealthy elites who own the press and TV. I was recently on a network where messages came directly from Commander Marcos of the rebel Indian forces in Chiapas, Mexico, telling us what happened in the field that day from the Native perspective. Occasionally we would see this same information, from a very different viewpoint, in the next day's newspaper. Our "net" source helped us know more of the truth.

26   "Good night," Commander Marcos would sign off. "I hear the military planes flying overhead, and I must extinguish my candle, but I wish you all God speed and I will be back tomorrow." Even the Internet can't help but deliver some of the poetry of drama.

27   But a computer can't deliver a touch. There is no crinkling of paper, no sharp smell of ink, no tight neatness of a newspaper freshly laid on your table, no satisfying weight of a good, thick book. Computers offer only the crackle of keys, the strain of arms and neck in a single position for as long as you can hold it. This is not physical connection. This is torture.

28   Maybe this explains the profound but simple pleasure people take in gardening. When you ask what they like about gardening, these folk answer vaguely, "I don't know. I just like to get my hands in the dirt." One First Nations woman told me her people believe that burying a personal amulet in the earth for three days cleanses it, as only Mother Earth is large enough to take away all our negative energies and replace them with positive.

29 William Gibson has been recognized with numerous awards for his work on science fiction novels that portray a possible computer future just over the horizon. His fantasies are so realistic, so consistent with the present course of events, that inventors have developed some of the concepts and machines he describes because they make such sense as consistent moves "forward" from where we now stand with technology. Gibson describes a world far from Butala's, where the population spend much of their lives artificially stimulated by drugs and "sim-stims," virtual realities so real that people see no need to go to the trouble of immersing themselves in the real, messy, physical world itself.

30   People travel, work and communicate in "cyberspace" (a word Gibson invented), which is nothing more than an accumulation of all known technical data, a non-place. Artificial intelligences meet and "mate" and exercise awesome political and economic authority. Simulation has reached such refined heights that the rich can even survive and interact (by TV screen and simulation) without any physical body whatsoever. The physical

remnants float in heavily guarded tanks that hold elabourate mixes of chemical and electronic impulses. In other words, according to Gibson, we are on our way to no bodies at all.

31   This would be a tragedy. A sensitivity to the physical creates a still place in ourselves, a place of calm, reason and perspective, a place of reconnection. This is the value of the physical and all that accompanies and promotes it—be it physical work like construction, a beautiful sunset, one's hands in the dirt of the garden or simply a willingness to reach out and shake a neighbour's hand—grounds us. They allow us to take a deep breath and think, "Yes, it's OK. I am here."

Thinking about the Text

1. Using Braid's examples, compare North American attitudes toward hygiene with those of other cultures. How does this comparison relate to Braid's thesis?

2. According to the author, what are the advantages of working in a trade?

3. Why does Braid contend that physical pain is liberating?

4. Do you agree that North Americans are losing touch with the physical? Why or why not?

Writing from the Text

1. Classify the advantages and disadvantages of computers, according to Braid. Is Braid a technophobe, a person afraid of technology? Why or why not?

2. Compare and contrast Sharon Butala's affinity for the land with William Gibson's affinity for technology, as described by Braid.

Connecting with Other Texts

1. Braid writes that "most Canadians don't even know what a trade is—except that 'vocational' in high school is where the 'dumb' guys go" (paragraph 7). Is this assertion correct? Using library resources and interviews, research current attitudes toward trades as a career path in North America.

2. Both Braid and Brenda Austin-Smith in "The Internet and Gender" (p. 66) discuss gender and technology, but in different ways. Compare and contrast these two authors' arguments about gender and technology.

3. Write an analysis of "A Plea for the Physical" to show that the speaker is a "worker," not a "wage slave." Refer to W.H. Auden's essay "Work, Labour, Play" (p. 170) in your essay.

On Jobs and Humility

Lisa Gregoire

1 Prolonged joblessness is like sitting in a Montreal no-smoking section: it's empty and the service is bad.

2 It's like looking through an expensive camera and knowing you have assembled all the right equipment, that you've cleaned the lenses with that special cleaner, that you've set your F-stops correctly and turned your shutter speed to the lowest it can go, but for some reason you just can't focus.

3 My world has recently come into focus and I've found a good job, which puts me in a category of one among my well-educated colleagues who struggle from one contract to another. They don't plan on buying a house any time soon. They don't plan on buying cars. In fact, they don't plan on going out for dinner for the next 10 years while they pay off their debt to society for allowing them to become educated and more employable.

4 What a joke. And the joke's on them, unfortunately. They don't aspire to be rich. They don't pine for a house in the country. They haven't even been able to afford a vacation in years, save for the odd weekend trip to the Maritimes for a wedding and a harried 10-hour journey home late on a Sunday night to make it to work or school on Monday.

5 Savings accounts? Retirement savings plans? GICs? A decent down payment? Come on. Speak in a language I can understand, like clipping coupons, cheap draft and socks that come three to a bushel. We 20-somethings, we between-the-boomers-and-their-children generation of overeducated and underemployed sods could be heading for disaster. We pray to the credit-card gods to bestow upon us just one more thousand dollars of credit so we can give them our grocery money in interest. We fill our résumés with valedictory honours, awesome volunteer records and flawless academic performances. We are not slackers. We are not asking for something for nothing. And we are no longer young.

6 What we are is approaching 30 with nothing but second-hand cars and the will to drive just about anywhere for a decent living and a chance to pay off our debts.

7 Being unemployed for seven months was enlightening. I like to use the phrase "character-building." And if I heard one more middle-aged yuppie in a comfy suit and job say, "Gosh, it's really tough out there for you young people," I may just have acquired me a firearm.

8 There is a revolution afoot. Mark my words (that's something my mom used to say). There are too many of us frustrated 20- and 30-somethings

who tire easily of the perfect imperfection of *Friends* episodes and who've grown beyond cappuccino and magazines in trendy coffee shops. We want to live in places where we can make our own coffee and look around and see our own stuff on the shelves.

9   My every waking hour was spent thinking about work, trying to find work, working for work. Jobs became like tiny birds on the edge of a lake sipping water: so beautiful and so natural, but as soon as I took a step toward them, they took flight in a flurry of feathers and I was left saying, "Come on, I'm not going to hurt you."

10   I used to get a lump in my throat when I went into shopping malls. I became obsessed with price tags; I could spot a sale tag at 50 paces. Some shops I avoided altogether, feeling financially inadequate next to the sales help, knowing they'd look at me and, barely concealing soap-opera sighs, ask whether they could help me with something to thwart my clumsy fingers from touching their perfectly folded merchandise. Or they'd peg me a non-buyer and ignore me completely. Sometimes I wonder which is worse.

11   Actually, I know which is worse: my mother taking me out to buy me something nice. It wasn't her selfless generosity and good will I despised. It was the way I felt standing with her at the cash when she drew money from her wallet and turned to me and smiled and I'd be thinking to myself, if there was any kind of justice in the world the roles would be reversed and I could start—just start—giving back a fraction of what she'd given me for nearly three decades. Instead, I'd smile back and swallow a golf ball of humiliation, knowing I could really use that sweater. It was then I realized that pride in the needy is like lint: you just pick it off and flick it away and then everything looks fine.

12   That's how it is to be part of a generation that, generally speaking, will be the first in this century not to achieve a better standard of living than its parents.

13   I don't want to be rich. I don't want a fancy car or a cellphone. I don't want to buy a house (owning a house seems about as likely as a February thaw in Iqaluit). Designer clothes? Please. I had more disposable income when I was 16 and working at McDonald's. I just [want] to be able to take a friend to the movies or buy a bottle of good wine for a change.

14   I learned a few things sitting in that lonely section. I learned how to cook potatoes 10 different ways. I learned how to mend clothes. And I learned how to appreciate small wonders. Elders who've lived through lean times might say it was good for me. And you know, they're right. I learned we're all one paycheque from poverty. And I accept my newfound job as a blessing. And I am humbled.

Thinking about the Text

1. What is Gregoire's thesis? How does her camera metaphor in the second paragraph relate to her thesis?

2. What are the things the author says that people of her generation will *not* be able to have that their parents had? Do you agree with her?

3. What kind of revolution do you think Gregoire is predicting?

Writing from the Text

1. Have you (or a friend or family member) experienced prolonged unemployment? In what ways did your experience parallel Gregoire's? In what ways did it differ?

2. Finding a job can take patience and creativity. Write a process essay suggesting creative ways for people your age to find work.

Connecting with Other Texts

1. Gregoire's essay suggests that there is a connection between self-esteem, employment, and purchasing power. Compare and contrast Gregoire's position with Willa Marcus's in "Need, Want, Deserve" (below). Do the authors agree or disagree on this issue?

2. Much has been written about baby boomers, yuppies, and Generation X. Research the differences among these demographic groups and write a comparison-and-contrast essay on the two that are the most different.

3. What solutions have been proposed by current writers to ease unemployment in Canada? Research the issue of unemployment versus full employment and report your findings in a research essay.

Need, Want, Deserve
Willa Marcus

1 I didn't realize I had honoured Earth Day by buying a car until, on my first jaunt, I almost sideswiped cyclists heading to a park with spades and infant trees.

2   My husband and I did not own a car for many years. In the eyes of some who knew us, it was a sign of our communion with the environment. This type of moral superiority is not to be abandoned lightly. But several months ago, almost in unison, we looked at each other and said: "Let's buy a car."

3   To our friends, we emphasized our need. In fact, our need was no greater than ever. We had taken public transit because we held both a heavy Toronto mortgage and the quaintly Dickensian view that increased indebtedness, even "debt-load" at levels acceptable to the bank, was inappropriate. Now that we could properly afford it, we deftly turned want into need. So when the man on the car radio spoke solemnly about reducing pollution, we self-righteously told ourselves we had done our turn by doing without for eight years.

4   Never in my life have I been so prosperous. Never has the list of objects I lack been so long and so close at hand. Simply put, the more I have, the more I want.

5   *Need, want* and *deserve* have become intermingled ideas in my mind. I only picked up the last in this trio recently, on a sightseeing afternoon with an out-of-town cousin and a friend. We started at a museum, but soon we were charging through clothes racks at Toronto's most expensive stores. Inevitably window shopping degenerated into the real thing. As I stood back in horror, calculating prices as a percentage of mortgage payments, my cousin Janet, less well off than I, fell in love with the most expensive suede jacket in sight.

6   You could see the battle before you: the smartly dressed woman in the mirror versus the more realistic woman in the flesh. As Janet struggled, my friend Bonnie adjudicated: "Oh buy it, you deserve it."

7   "But you've never met her before," I almost blurted out. Then I grasped that this was the shopper's credo: if you want it, you have a right to it.

8   I have since used this line on myself. At first it did not fit comfortably. So I refashioned it in my own image: if I want it and *I can afford it*, I deserve it. Now it fits as well as Janet's suede jacket.

9 I spent the seventies in east-end Montreal, active in community groups. Such a life provided little basis for preoccupying material cravings. I lived frugally and rightly considered myself rich in relation to those around me. A lot of people my age have similar histories. How my generation has changed!

10   I like to blame all the change on forces beyond my control. I say that whatever moral rectitude in the past led me (and my peers) to eschew material possessions is still intact. It is merely repressed.

11   One of my favourite targets is Toronto. Since moving there, I have made a profession out of pinpointing its fiendish materialism as a corrupting factor. In my recounting, nothing better typifies the contrast between Montreal and Toronto than neighbourhood street parties. In Montreal, a late August *fête de quartier* meant that the roadway was turned

into a playground, blocked to cars. Magically, as the sun set and fiddlers played, a vat of fresh corn on the cob would appear, fifty cents an ear.

12   In Toronto, I explain, a neighbourhood party means a tour of houses for sale, followed by canapés catered by real-estate agents. My story conveniently overlooks the Montreal of today, where the old street, once filled with tenants, has gone condo.

13   The truth is that the major factor in my changed behaviour is increased prosperity. More is possible; hence more has become desirable. Moreover, I spend no time agonizing over the moral dynamics of this new materialism. On the contrary. What concerns me is my backwardness. Shopping, I realize, is a social activity, and like a person who learns to drive late in life, I fret that I will never fully master it.

14 Having now accepted that shopping is a basic social skill, I still like to blame external forces. Indeed, I have seen these forces in action. In stories I have covered in my work as a journalist, I have observed the shopping-centre business up close. Almost like a spy, I have watched North American consultants in London explain the lure of shopping centres to potential British investors.

15   The first slide in the presentation by one of these missionaries for the mall was a single phrase projected overhead and magnified many times: "Shopping is retail therapy." His message has public-health overtones: if you're depressed, don't drink, don't take drugs, don't eat a pound of chocolates. Instead, do something good for you. *Go shopping.*

16   But shopping is supposed to provide more than emotional balm. It holds out the promise of economic cure as well. In northern England, people are hoping that regions forsaken by the industrial revolution will be saved by the "retail revolution."

17   Consider Gateshead. It's the biggest suburban shopping mall in Europe, and it comes complete with a kiddy-rides area à la West Edmonton Mall. Inside, you could be in New York or New Westminster. In fact, you're in Newcastle-on-Tyne. Gateshead, the vanguard of the retail revolution, is literally built atop the dustbin of history; it sits on an abandoned coal mine.

18   Norwegians anxious to escape their country's very onerous goods and services tax come on packaged tours. Leaving home Friday morning, they sail for twenty-four hours and arrive in time to catch the entire Saturday shopping day. At closing time, they head right back to their ferry and another twenty-four-hour trip.

19   Buying is only one part of the day. The shopping activity also includes greed, envy and worry about paying the rent. In short, it runs the gamut of major human emotions.

20   Gateshead is based on the proposition that the Norwegians and others who come will bring cash to Newcastle, which is the opposite of bringing coal: there has been little cash in this depressed area for a long time. Nevertheless, the mall is packed on Saturday; you can circle for forty-five minutes until you find a parking spot.

21   Most of the people there are locals, or at least people from the surrounding region. If Gateshead is to be the economic salvation of Newcastle, it will be at the expense of High Street shops in smaller towns where people could once go on foot. It is not only the shopping mall that has reached Britain; it is also the notion that a private car is central to modern life.

22 When my husband and I bought our new car, the process was swift. We first made an informed decision on what precisely we wanted. We chose a colour so standard we usually can't distinguish it in a parking lot with more than three other cars. And we bought it at the second dealer we visited, interrupting the salesman in mid-pitch. Flustered, he said, "Don't you want to hear about the features?" We already knew.

23   As we left the lot with the car, he was shaking his head. He had his commission, but we had denied him any joy in clinching the sale. We have joined our rightful place on the road with that car. But I can't shake the nagging, anxious feeling that we're still behind the times.

Thinking about the Text

1. Marcus's essay contains several ironic observations about her own life as a consumer. List these ironies using examples from the text.

2. How do people tend to use the word "deserve" as it pertains to shopping?

3. Can our love of shopping change the economy for the better or for the worse? Use Marcus's examples to illustrate.

4. Is Marcus comfortable as a consumer of material goods? Why or why not?

Writing from the Text

1. Is the author concerned about the morality of materialism or consumerism? Use examples from the text to support your position.

2. In a persuasive essay, argue that shopping is a valid form of therapy.

3. Do you agree that prosperity encourages people to reinterpret their wants as needs? What other, more positive, changes does prosperity bring to an individual's life? Write an essay comparing and contrasting the positive and negative implications of prosperity.

Connecting with Other Texts

1. Marcus mentions the Gateshead shopping mall in England and the West Edmonton Mall. What effect have these and other shopping malls had on people's buying habits and on regional economies? Write a research essay on the development of shopping malls and the social and economic changes they have brought.

2. Are any Canadians reversing the trend to consumerism and becoming *less* materialistic? Ask your librarian to suggest sources and research the issue to find out. Write an essay on your findings.

Life After Cable

Kenneth J. Harvey

1 We are surviving. Six months ago our cable company disconnected the electronic life-support box. Immediately, upon disconnection, my family began sputtering and gasping for breath. Was it possible to survive without being plugged in?

2   The sales manager at Regional Cable had ignored my earlier calls. I had left several messages asking that he contact me to discuss the possibility of better programming. They had just added a second country-and-western channel to the roster (Whoopee and Yee-Haw!) without having so much as a single arts-related channel. No Bravo. No A&E. What's a thinking person to do?

3   I had also been calling about the company's substandard service. The audio levels on certain channels varied, the reds on a couple of stations sparkled, and channels occasionally offered nothing but dead air. Regional Cable had no monitoring station and so the client was expected to perform this task for the cable company, and call their offices whenever anything went wrong. When one of their operators suggested this course of action I suggested that they send along my first paycheque and I would gladly carry out the service for them.

4   Anyway, the sales manager continued to ignore my calls. In retaliation

for the staff's ignorance, I responded with my best volley of financial ignorance: I refused to pay my bill. In reply to my outrageous negligence, they pulled the plug, without so much as a warning. Returning home one day, we found the tag on the door: "We were here today for the purpose of . . ." The blank square in front of the word "disconnection" had been ticked. We all gasped. We all went weak in the knees. All those glamorous televised lives, those surreal music videos, those urban laugh-track sitcoms had been hauled away with the length of cable. The cable company had won the war. Or had they?

5   My family grumbled for a while. They challenged my firm stand, my claims that television corrupts, with the stock accusations so often directed at fathers: "It's always what *you* want. We have to do what you want." This went on for a while, but then—like all arguments—the words soon lost their freshness, their power. The argument became stale and the family settled into the idea of life without other people's imagined lives plugged directly into our mental veins.

6   Contrary to what I expected, the bored proclamation, "There's nothing to do," was never sounded by my children (and the disconnection was perpetrated in *winter*, of all seasons!). We played games together: Snakes & Ladders, Don't Wake Daddy, Senet, Hangman. . . . We listened to each other's stories, and we actually paid attention. We watched each other's faces, our eyes not tempted by the pulse of the television screen flickering off along the periphery. We asked questions, and were actually answered. We read more books.

7   Sitting around the living room—without the constant, "Just wait till this is over" or "You're blocking the screen" or "Shhhhhhh"—I watched my children play. One day, my son anxiously stood before me and joyfully explained the specifics of what he had been reading as his eyes shifted toward the walls. As he imagined what he had read, he envisioned his own *personal* imaginings, not those already packaged and preselected for the masses, which require no mental collabouration from the viewer, and thus inspire little mental resonance.

8   Over the past six months I have noticed the subtle changes in my three children. I have noticed the minor gestures they have added to their repertoires. I have taken my time to study my glorious children with wonder, to enjoy and cherish them. I have noticed their growth, the minute shiftings in facial features and body language, with undistracted clarity. And I have realized that watching television truly does distract a person from real life, from the movements and variances that connect one to the present. When [we are] watching television, the workings of our own lives become distractions. Real life becomes a *distraction*.

9   I have to admit that we did not entirely shed our electronic tunics; we did not become complete monastic purists. The television did—indeed—continue to flicker. Movie videos were selected from the store, played and savoured. But this viewing spectacle became something that was finite. The movie did not continue to flicker eternally, tempting the watcher away from other interests. When it was over, it was over and the viewer moved on.

10   However, two weeks ago, my three-year-old poked a marble into the video machine, slid in a tape and pressed the play button. That was the end of that. So now we are totally without visuals, totally on our own: without the ability to laugh at a perfect stranger's stumblings and fumblings, without the means to fall in love with the body of a person who we will never meet or know, without the televised emotional promptings that beckon us to cry for the sorrows of someone who has absolutely nothing to do with us. The television's peculiar hypnotic power defeated.

11   Now, the television sits blankly on its pedestal, like a statue honouring a silenced dictator. Since its fall, since we have come out from under its tyrannical rule, our freedom restored, our lives have faded back into full focus. Our own lives have become more important than the televised ones we had been idolizing.

Thinking about the Text

1. What is Harvey's purpose in comparing the television to a dictator?
2. Harvey writes that television distracts people from real life, and real life becomes a distraction from television viewing. What evidence does he give to support this assertion?
3. Do you agree that television seduces viewers into developing relationships with "other people's imagined lives" rather than with each other? Why or why not?

Writing from the Text

1. Write a persuasive essay in which you argue that the computer poses a bigger threat to family relationships than television does.
2. Write a narrative about a change imposed on your life that you initially resisted but later came to appreciate.
3. Harvey's essay presents a humorous recounting of poor customer service. Write a similar humorous narrative about a time you were on the receiving end when service to the customer was ignored.

Connecting with Other Texts

1. Analyse ways technology is changing our values. Use examples from "Life After Cable" and Kate Braid's "A Plea for the Physical" (p. 175) to support your position.

2. Moira Farr's "Welcome to FamilyValuesWorld!" (p. 9) suggests that the media perpetuate views of family life that are unlike most families. Using ideas from Farr's essay and "Life Without Cable," write a cause-and-effect essay about television's impact on the ways families perceive themselves.

Making a Difference
June Callwood

1 About a year ago, newspapers were full of a story about a woman, new to Canada, who had been beaten by her husband. Many people who read about it felt sympathy for the friendless stranger hiding in a women's shelter, facing an uncertain future.

2 A widow of small means, a woman with grown children, called some friends. "We should do something about this," she said.

3 "You're right," one of her friends replied. "You should."

4 "Oh dear," she replied. "Me?"

5 "Why not?" the friend said.

6 The next day, news stories about the case included a few lines about a new fund that had been established. The public was informed that donations to help the battered woman could be sent to a bank, and an address was given. The widow had done three things: after consulting her bank manager, she opened an account in the woman's name with a donation of her own; then she called the media to tell of the existence of the fund; and then she contacted the police officer in charge of the case and asked him to give the woman her name and telephone number.

7 The assaulted woman gratefully called and they met for coffee. Over the next few weeks her benefactor raised enough money to help the woman get resettled and became the newcomer's companion, assisting her to find her way around the city.

8 "I feel very good about this," she told everyone. "I've learned a lot."

9 What she meant by that was her visits to a women's shelter where she talked to women fleeing from violence, and her indignant discoveries about how the welfare system works. Her experiences had changed her

comfortable view of society and she was telling her friends about it, her opinions given weight because she was the only one among them with first-hand knowledge. She didn't seem to notice that she had changed greatly. She had been a warm, sympathetic woman who believed herself to be hopelessly ineffective; she had discovered instead that she was a warm, sympathetic woman who was capable and resourceful. The difference in her was pronounced; there was a new firmness in her voice and bounce in her walk.

10   Hannah Arendt, philosopher and writer, was absorbed much of her life with an effort to understand the nature of good and evil. In her book, *Eichmann in Jerusalem* (Penguin, 1977), a study of the trial of Adolf Eichmann, the Nazi who bore a major responsibility in the Holocaust, she directed her considerable intellect to an analysis of evil. Her conclusion was that evil thrives on apathy and cannot exist without it; hence, apathy *is* evil.

11   When injustice encounters inertia, it uses that passivity exactly as if it were approval. In the absence of protest, evil is nourished and can flourish. The nature of goodness, therefore, bears a keen relationship to intervention. Individuals who seek to save their souls, or serve their consciences, or find meaning in their lives, or who wish to attain the quiet splendor of moral growth, are obliged to participate in their society.

12   The American feminist Gloria Steinem advises women, for the sake of their health, to do something outrageous every day. For instance, today a woman might write to the president of her favourite supermarket and ask him (certainly it will be a man) to list all the branches in her area with a woman manager because she wishes to shop where a woman is in charge. Tomorrow she might write to her bank president with the same reasonable request. By the third day she'll be combustible with plenty of ideas of her own.

13   Nietzsche said that people wait all their lives for an opportunity to do good in their own way. Such patience is rarely rewarded. Moments when a useful contribution can be made by taking action almost never wear a name tag. Instead, they always look like "someone else's responsibility—not my business."

14   In moments when they are dissatisfied with themselves, most people yearn for a chance to do a redemptive good deed. They fantasize about taking leadership to get a much-needed crosswalk for the neighbourhood, or throwing themselves into good works. The problem is: how to start.

15   First, no one should shrink from the healthy element of selfishness that nourishes selflessness. While seeking to better their society, it is reasonable

for people also, and not incidentally, to hope to improve their self-worth. It is a motive not to be derided or denied. Elevating self-esteem by behaving admirably has an ancient and honourable tradition, so long as self-liking is not so abysmally low that beneficiaries are obliged to be eternally grateful and respectful.

16   Altruism is the expression of the individual's best self, the god in the machinery. Instead of waiting shyly to be asked, some people simply seize an opportunity. One woman who visited a geriatric facility seven years ago noted that some of the aged were too weak to lift a spoon. Since then, twice a day she feeds a meal and chats to lonely people. Another woman read about children on ventilators who live in a hospital. She enrolled as a volunteer and goes twice a week to see a little girl she takes for walks in the corridor, reads to, and for whom she entertainingly describes the caprices of her cat. Another woman dropped in at Nellie's, a Toronto hostel for women, and asked what she could do. The staff person was dealing with an emergency at the time and asked her to get herself a cup of coffee and wait. Later, when she went in search of the volunteer, she found her scrubbing the stairs.

17   Another woman, a welfare recipient, was incensed that a developer had his eye on some green space where children played. She went to City Hall and persevered through polite evasions and pointed snubs until she found a civil servant and an alderman who listened. What she began snowballed into a noisy community meeting that resulted in saving the playground.

18   Making a difference starts with having a spunky attitude. The first thing to get out of the way is expectation that virtue always triumphs: in truth, most attempts to confront and defeat misdeeds are only partially successful or else seem to be outright failures. It doesn't matter; nothing is wasted in the universe. Even an effort that apparently goes nowhere will influence the future. Though the system looks untouched, it has a fatal crack in it. The next assault, or the one after that, will bring it down. At the very least, someone, somewhere, has learned a lesson and will be more thoughtful.

19   Victory, though highly desirable, is the second-best outcome of wading into a controversy on behalf of others. The real triumph is the act of making a stand and taking on the battle. It matters when someone makes an attempt to improve the quality of life for the neighbourhood, the society, the world. Even if contaminated soil continues to be dumped in the nearby lake, or the school board still won't accept a child in a wheelchair, or better street lighting is denied, something has been achieved; someone

cared enough to fight.

20   Real defeat isn't failure to attain the objective: it's not trying. Most people, as theatre critic Walter Kerr once put it, live half-lives half-heartedly. They cast themselves in the role of spectator, whatever the provocation to take action. The excuses are that no effort of theirs would succeed, or that in any case they don't know what to do, or they might look foolish, or what they do might make matters worse. "Innocent bystander" is an oxymoron. People who do not intervene when something is amiss give tacit permission for injustice to continue.

21   Becoming an activist takes practice, which can start on a small scale— like a beginner's slope for skiers-to-be. People can rehearse by responding to minor acts of tyranny: a racial insult, for instance; a clerk being high-handed with someone too intimidated to protest. The very young are powerless to challenge wrongdoing and therefore must tolerate it, but futile hand-wringing is unsuitable and unbecoming in an adult.

22   In recent years, so many people have taken up slingshots against corporate and government Goliaths that the paths are blazed for newcomers. Expertise abounds in where and how to apply pressure. Umbrella groups have been established in such fields as environment and disarmament; libraries list them in catalogues. Many communities have information centres that provide the location of such specialized services as daycare advocacy specialists or ratepayers groups. The National Action Committee on the Status of Women knows the field of women's issues and Tools for Peace or Oxfam Canada can give the latest information about what's happening in Nicaragua.

23   A critical step, in short, is information-gathering. It makes no sense to waste enthusiasm and indignation by plunging blindly into a fight. Do as the 19th-century Prussian military strategist Carl von Clausewitz always advised: secure your base, gather informed cohorts, study the terrain: knowledge is power.

24   A few years ago a group of young mothers decided their neighbourhood would benefit from a parent–child drop-in centre. A friendly lawyer helped them incorporate and then they applied for tax-deductible status in order to launch a fund-raising campaign. A year later, when they were negotiating a lease for storefront space, they approached the government for help—and discovered that there was an underused parent–child drop-in centre only two blocks from their own site.

25   Duplication is an inexcusable waste in a country that sorely needs the energy and acumen of people who hold ideals of conduct. No effort to achieve social improvement should be launched without research of

regulations and the historical background, analysis of the need, consultation with experts, collection of statistical data where appropriate.

26   Before launching Nellie's 15 years ago, for instance, the founders counted the number of beds available in Toronto for homeless men (approximately 800), and the number available for homeless women (approximately 20). They enlisted the support of the police, who acknowledged that there was no place for women who needed to escape family violence. The municipality had no choice but to give support.

27   Similarly, Jessie's, a Toronto centre established seven years ago for pregnant teenagers and teenaged parents, was the work of a task force that included some 25 representatives from every agency dealing with teenaged mothers—children's aid societies, public health, maternity homes, the YWCA, hostels, community centres, clinics, parent–child drop-in centres. By the time the task force presented the provincial government with a proposal that had been almost three years in the making, the authority behind the recommendations was too persuasive to fail. Jessie's now is backed by the Ministry of Community and Social Services, the Ministry of Health and the Toronto Board of Education, plus a host of foundations, corporations and private donors.

28   Success is no fluke. When the government changes its mind about allowing a logging road through a park, when officials do an about-face concerning schooling for learning-disabled children, those desirable outcomes are the consequence of a hundred meetings, most of them tiring and frustrating, where people with good information plan strategy and put together briefs. Often the catalytic force is one event or one person whose life has been touched by loss, but the movement that results depends for its power on attracting the most creditable expertise the community can provide.

29   A well-informed team, making thought-out moves, is invincible. Often the opposition is frayed and fragmented in comparison. It whines, obfuscates, denies. Positive-minded, fair-speaking citizenry, equipped with clear, well-researched proposals, has a distinct advantage.

30   When Bruce Porter, a Toronto activist in the field of housing, was battling adults-only apartment buildings in Ontario, he assembled a group of low-income mothers and took them to the legislative hearings. One after another, they told stories of being homeless with their children. The media, adjusted to ho-hum reports read by executive directors, leapt into life and interviewed the mothers for television, radio and newspaper headlines. It was no coincidence that restrictions on adults-only buildings soon afterwards passed into Ontario law.

31   Such ingenuity is often rewarded. A handful of people who wanted to start a women's hostel in a small community were frustrated for four years by a town council that maintained that the area had no battered women. Someone had a bright idea. She contacted the *wives* of councillors and asked them to the next meeting. Enough of them came, and were impressed enough by the police reports and other statistics, to shake up a smug council.

32   People fear being ridiculous more than they fear disaster. It takes courage to go against the stream. Never mind. If the path has heart in it, it's the right one and you're right to be on it. Moreover, you'll enjoy yourself.

Thinking about the Text

1. What is Callwood's thesis? How does her opening narrative contribute to her thesis?

2. What are the values Callwood is urging her readers to develop in themselves?

3. What example does Callwood use to illustrate the importance of advance information-gathering? How useful are the examples Callwood uses throughout the essay?

Writing from the Text

1. If you have been involved in a social action project, write a process essay on how you overcame any reservations you had about getting started, how you tackled the problems you encountered, and how you handled the outcomes.

2. Do you believe your generation is interested in social action? Why or why not? Write an essay discussing the factors that encourage people your age to "make a difference" or discourage them from doing so.

Connecting with Other Texts

1. Research a charitable organization such as Amnesty International, the Canadian Save the Children Fund, or a local women's shelter. Write an essay on the origin, goals, and successes of this organization.

2. Write a persuasive essay in which you urge readers to volunteer for your favourite charity. Suggest concrete ways they can "make a difference."

3. What do you think Callwood would say to Lisa Gregoire, the author of "On Jobs and Humility" (p. 182)? Write an essay weighing the relative merits of volunteering versus full-time employment.

The Battle over Gun Control: Marking the Divide Between Rural and Urban Canada

Charlie Angus

1 Go to a party in Northern Ontario and mention guns. Chances are it will engage a lively discussion, not on what to do about them, but on what kind of brand you have. Men, women, young and old, can talk about the merits of the 410, the 30-30, and the 30 odd six. Go to a party in the city and tell someone you own a gun. You might as well be saying you collect child pornography.

2 Gun control has become a marker of the great divide between rural and urban Canada. There is probably no other issue that is so divided along regional lines as the issue of guns.

3 In the North, guns are part of the landscape. Gun owners include people who hunt and people who don't. Many who live in the country keep a gun handy for protection against pesky and sometimes ominous critters. Some have guns to shoot pop cans and clay pigeons.

4 Northerners who do hunt know very well that their way of life isn't articulated or listened to in the power centres. They believe that people in the cities tend to equate a gun rack with red necks, big beer bellies and a white sheet. The values, respect and traditions of the hunt are tossed off as so much chaff by people who look upon it as barbarism.

5 This sense of being ignored and misunderstood has fuelled the surprisingly vocal response of gun owners against the new gun laws proposed by Justice Minister Allan Rock. A line seems to once again have been drawn in the sand dividing rural Canada from urban.

6 In this latest debate, the division has been made worse by the rhetoric coming from the Gun Rights Lobby. At the much publicized pro-gun rallies, Canadians have been exposed to a lot of propaganda that looks like it was lifted right out of the media arsenals of the National Rifle Association across the border.

7 In the United States the right to bear uzis and grenade launchers has been cloaked in the holy garment of participatory democracy. Being able to buy an assault rifle without any restrictions is painted as being more important than being able to vote.

8 People in Canada don't want the free-for-all chaos that goes on in the United States. Looking over the border we can see the destabilizing

influence that easy access to assault rifles and hand guns has had. Taking a stand against this chaos doesn't infringe on the legitimate rights of responsible gun owners in Canada. But unfortunately, the Canadian gun lobby has set out to blur this distinction. Not only are they against tightening the laws, they want many of them rescinded.

9   The gun lobby is telling Canadians that by registering guns, Canadians are somehow giving the upper hand to criminals who wouldn't register them anyways. "Bad guys will always be able to get guns" is the common argument that is imported from the United States. But few Canadians believe that arming everyone is somehow a remedy.

10   Whether the gun registry will be able to do much is up for debate. But the fact is, pretty much everything in our culture is registered. What's the big deal? Marriages are registered. Cars are registered. Even poodles and cats are registered.

11   Because the issue is really about two different cultures and realities, some common-sense thinking is needed. In the North, people want to be able to hunt and to shoot recreationally. In the cities, people want to cut back on the access of weapons and to bring some order to the streets. One thing that both sides could admit to is that there is no easy solution to this dilemma.

12   In the end, the question of guns as a cultural issue is going to have to be addressed by a better dialogue between rural and urban areas. It is part of the need for southern people in the cities and folks in the North to start talking and listening to each other. It is important that the needs of the two Canadian realities—urban and rural—be understood clearly and efforts made to come to some kind of consensus.

Thinking about the Text

1. Describe Northern Ontario gun culture as Angus portrays it. In contrast, what is the city-dweller's stereotype of the Northern gun owner?

2. In what ways has the Canadian gun rights lobby borrowed from American gun culture to inflame the debate on gun control?

Writing from the Text

1. Propose a course of action that will help urban and rural Canadians acknowledge and reconcile their different realities and cultures.

2. If you are a city-dweller, do you agree with Angus's contention that gun ownership is equal in your friends' minds to collecting child pornography? Analyse your own reaction to his statement and write a response to Angus showing how his assessment is correct (or incorrect).

Connecting with Other Texts

1. Research methods of conflict resolution. What can be done to get opposing parties "talking and listening to each other" to find consensus? Discuss your findings in a research essay.

2. What other differences in perceptions and culture divide urban and rural Canada? Use Joe's comment about "city boys" in Lauren Griffin's essay "Making Big Deals out of Little Deals" (p. 72) as a starting point. Add any other observations of your own to write a comparison-and-contrast essay.

3. Write a research essay on what countries outside North America have done about gun ownership and use.

4. Find two articles on gun control, one for and one against. Evaluate the articles and analyse them for logical fallacies.

The Lottery

Shirley Jackson

1 The morning of June 27th was clear and sunny, with the fresh warmth of a full-summer day; the flowers were blossoming profusely and the grass was richly green. The people of the village began to gather in the square, between the post office and the bank, around ten o'clock; in some towns there were so many people that the lottery took two days and had to be started on June 26th, but in this village, where there were only about three hundred people, the whole lottery took less than two hours, so it could begin at ten o'clock in the morning and still be through in time to allow the villagers to get home for noon dinner.

2   The children assembled first, of course. School was recently over for the summer, and the feeling of liberty sat uneasily on most of them; they tended to gather together quietly for a while before they broke into boisterous play, and their talk was still of the classroom and the teacher, of books and reprimands. Bobby Martin had already stuffed his pockets full of stones, and the other boys soon followed his example, selecting the smoothest and roundest stones; Bobby and Harry Jones and Dickie Delacroix—the villagers pronounced this name "Dellacroy"—eventually made a great pile of stones in one corner of the square and guarded it against the raids of the other boys. The girls stood aside, talking among themselves, looking over their shoulders at the boys, and the very small children rolled in the dust or clung to the hands of their older brothers or sisters.

3   Soon the men began to gather, surveying their own children, speaking of planting and rain, tractors and taxes. They stood together, away from the pile of stones in the corner, and their jokes were quiet and they smiled rather than laughed. The women, wearing faded house dresses and sweaters, came shortly after their menfolk. They greeted one another and exchanged bits of gossip as they went to join their husbands. Soon the women, standing by their husbands, began to call to their children, and the children came reluctantly, having to be called four or five times. Bobby Martin ducked under his mother's grasping hand and ran, laughing, back to the pile of stones. His father spoke up sharply, and Bobby came quickly and took his place between his father and his oldest brother.

4   The lottery was conducted—as were the square dances, the teen-age club, the Halloween program—by Mr. Summers, who had time and energy to devote to civic activities. He was a round-faced, jovial man and he ran the coal business, and people were sorry for him, because he had no children and his wife was a scold. When he arrived in the square, carrying the black wooden box, there was a murmur of conversation among the villagers, and he waved and called, "Little late today, folks." The postmaster, Mr. Graves, followed him, carrying a three-legged stool, and the stool was put in the center of the square and Mr. Summers set the black box down on it. The villagers kept their distance, leaving a space between themselves and the stool, and when Mr. Summers said, "Some of you fellows want to give me a hand?" there was a hesitation before two men, Mr. Martin and his oldest son, Baxter, came forward to hold the box steady on the stool while Mr. Summers stirred up the papers inside it.

5   The original paraphernalia for the lottery had been lost long ago, and the black box now resting on the stool had been put into use even before Old Man Warner, the oldest man in town, was born. Mr. Summers spoke frequently to the villagers about making a new box, but no one liked to upset even as much tradition as was represented by the black box. There was a story that the present box had been made with some pieces of the box that had preceded it, the one that had been constructed when the first people settled down to make a village here. Every year, after the lottery, Mr. Summers began talking again about a new box, but every year the subject was allowed to fade off without anything's being done. The black box grew shabbier each year; by now it was no longer completely black but splintered badly along one side to show the original wood color, and in some places faded or stained.

6   Mr. Martin and his oldest son, Baxter, held the black box securely on the stool until Mr. Summers had stirred the papers thoroughly with his

hand. Because so much of the ritual had been forgotten or discarded, Mr. Summers had been successful in having slips of paper substituted for the chips of wood that had been used for generations. Chips of wood, Mr. Summers had argued, had been all very well when the village was tiny, but now that the population was more than three hundred and likely to keep on growing, it was necessary to use something that would fit more easily into the black box. The night before the lottery, Mr. Summers and Mr. Graves made up the slips of paper and put them in the box, and it was then taken to the safe of Mr. Summers' coal company and locked up until Mr. Summers was ready to take it to the square next morning. The rest of the year, the box was put away, sometimes one place, sometimes another; it had spent one year in Mr. Graves's barn and another year underfoot in the post office, and sometimes it was set on a shelf in the Martin grocery and left there.

7   There was a great deal of fussing to be done before Mr. Summers declared the lottery open. There were the lists to make up—of heads of families, heads of households in each family, members of each household in each family. There was the proper swearing-in of Mr. Summers by the postmaster, as the official of the lottery; at one time, some people remembered, there had been a recital of some sort, performed by the official of the lottery, a perfunctory, tuneless chant that had been rattled off duly each year; some people believed that the official of the lottery used to stand just so when he said or sang it, others believed that he was supposed to walk among the people, but years and years ago this part of the ritual had been allowed to lapse. There had been, also, a ritual salute, which the official of the lottery had had to use in addressing each person who came up to draw from the box, but this also had changed with time, until now it was felt necessary only for the official to speak to each person approaching. Mr. Summers was very good at all this; in his clean white shirt and blue jeans, with one hand resting carelessly on the black box, he seemed very proper and important as he talked interminably to Mr. Graves and the Martins.

8   Just as Mr. Summers finally left off talking and turned to the assembled villagers, Mrs. Hutchinson came hurriedly along the path to the square, her sweater thrown over her shoulders, and slid into place in the back of the crowd. "Clean forgot what day it was," she said to Mrs. Delacroix, who stood next to her, and they both laughed softly. "Thought my old man was out back stacking wood," Mrs. Hutchinson went on, "and then I looked out the window and the kids was gone, and then I remembered it was the twenty-seventh and came a-running." She dried her hands on her apron,

and Mrs. Delacroix said, "You're in time, though. They're still talking away up there."

9   Mrs. Hutchinson craned her neck to see through the crowd and found her husband and children standing near the front. She tapped Mrs. Delacroix on the arm as a farewell and began to make her way through the crowd. The people separated good-humoredly to let her through; two or three people said, in voices just loud enough to be heard across the crowd, "Here comes your Missus, Hutchinson," and "Bill, she made it after all." Mrs. Hutchinson reached her husband, and Mr. Summers, who had been waiting, said cheerfully, "Thought we were going to have to get on without you, Tessie." Mrs. Hutchinson said, grinning, "Wouldn't have me leave m'dishes in the sink, now, would you, Joe?," and soft laughter ran through the crowd as the people stirred back into position after Mrs. Hutchinson's arrival.

10   "Well, now," Mr. Summers said soberly, "guess we better get started, get this over with, so's we can go back to work. Anybody ain't here?"

11   "Dunbar," several people said. "Dunbar, Dunbar."

12   Mr. Summers consulted his list. "Clyde Dunbar," he said. "That's right. He's broke his leg, hasn't he? Who's drawing for him?"

13   "Me, I guess," a woman said, and Mr. Summers turned to look at her. "Wife draws for her husband," Mr. Summers said. "Don't you have a grown boy to do it for you, Janey?" Although Mr. Summers and everyone else in the village knew the answer perfectly well, it was the business of the official of the lottery to ask such questions formally. Mr. Summers waited with an expression of polite interest while Mrs. Dunbar answered.

14   "Horace's not but sixteen yet," Mrs. Dunbar said regretfully. "Guess I gotta fill in for the old man this year."

15   "Right," Mr. Summers said. He made a note on the list he was holding. Then he asked, "Watson boy drawing this year?"

16   A tall boy in the crowd raised his hand. "Here," he said. "I'm drawing for m'mother and me." He blinked his eyes nervously and ducked his head as several voices in the crowd said things like "Good fellow, Jack," and "Glad to see your mother's got a man to do it."

17   "Well," Mr. Summers said, "guess that's everyone. Old Man Warner make it?"

18   "Here," a voice said, and Mr. Summers nodded.

19   A sudden hush fell on the crowd as Mr. Summers cleared his throat and looked at the list. "All ready?" he called. "Now, I'll read the names—heads of families first—and the men come up and take a paper out of the box. Keep the paper folded in your hand without looking at it until everyone

has had a turn. Everything clear?"

20 The people had done it so many times that they only half listened to the directions; most of them were quiet, wetting their lips, not looking around. Then Mr. Summers raised one hand high and said, "Adams." A man disengaged himself from the crowd and came forward. "Hi, Steve," Mr. Summers said, and Mr. Adams said, "Hi, Joe." They grinned at one another humorlessly and nervously. Then Mr. Adams reached into the black box and took out a folded paper. He held it firmly by one corner as he turned and went hastily back to his place in the crowd, where he stood a little apart from his family, not looking down at his hand.

21 "Allen," Mr. Summers said. "Anderson. . . . Bentham."

22 "Seems like there's no time at all between lotteries any more," Mrs. Delacroix said to Mrs. Graves in the back row. "Seems like we got through with the last one only last week."

23 "Time sure goes fast," Mrs. Graves said.

24 "Clark. . . . Delacroix."

25 "There goes my old man," Mrs. Delacroix said. She held her breath while her husband went forward.

26 "Dunbar," Mr. Summers said, and Mrs. Dunbar went steadily to the box while one of the women said, "Go on, Janey," and another said, "There she goes."

27 "We're next," Mrs. Graves said. She watched while Mr. Graves came around from the side of the box, greeted Mr. Summers gravely, and selected a slip of paper from the box. By now, all through the crowd there were men holding the small folded papers in their large hands, turning them over and over nervously. Mrs. Dunbar and her two sons stood together, Mrs. Dunbar holding the slip of paper.

28 "Harburt. . . . Hutchinson."

29 "Get up there, Bill," Mrs. Hutchinson said, and the people near her laughed.

30 "Jones."

31 "They do say," Mr. Adams said to Old Man Warner, who stood next to him, "that over in the north village they're talking of giving up the lottery."

32 Old Man Warner snorted. "Pack of crazy fools," he said. "Listening to the young folks, nothing's good enough for *them*. Next thing you know, they'll be wanting to go back to living in caves, nobody work any more, live *that* way for a while. Used to be a saying about 'Lottery in June, corn be heavy soon.' First thing you know, we'd all be eating stewed chickweed and acorns. There's *always* been a lottery," he added petulantly. "Bad enough to see young Joe Summers up there joking with everybody."

33   "Some places have already quit lotteries," Mrs. Adams said.

34   "Nothing but trouble in *that,*" Old Man Warner said stoutly. "Pack of young fools."

35   "Martin." And Bobby Martin watched his father go forward. "Overdyke. . . . Percy."

36   "I wish they'd hurry," Mrs. Dunbar said to her older son. "I wish they'd hurry."

37   "They're almost through," her son said.

38   "You get ready to run tell Dad," Mrs. Dunbar said.

39   Mr. Summers called his own name and then stepped forward precisely and selected a slip from the box. Then he called, "Warner."

40   "Seventy-seventh year I been in the lottery," Old Man Warner said as he went through the crowd. "Seventy-seventh time."

41   "Watson." The tall boy came awkwardly through the crowd. Someone said, "Don't be nervous, Jack," and Mr. Summers said, "Take your time, son."

42   "Zanini."

43   After that, there was a long pause, a breathless pause, until Mr. Summers, holding his slip of paper in the air, said, "All right, fellows." For a minute, no one moved, and then all the slips of paper were opened. Suddenly, all the women began to speak at once, saying, "Who is it?," "Who's got it?," "Is it the Dunbars?," "Is it the Watsons?" Then the voices began to say, "It's Hutchinson. It's Bill," "Bill Hutchinson's got it."

44   "Go tell your father," Mrs. Dunbar said to her older son.

45   People began to look around to see the Hutchinsons. Bill Hutchinson was standing quiet, staring down at the paper in his hand. Suddenly, Tessie Hutchinson shouted to Mr. Summers, "You didn't give him time enough to take any paper he wanted. I saw you. It wasn't fair!"

46   "Be a good sport, Tessie," Mrs. Delacroix called, and Mrs. Graves said, "All of us took the same chance."

47   "Shut up, Tessie," Bill Hutchinson said.

48   "Well, everyone," Mr. Summers said, "that was done pretty fast, and now we've got to be hurrying a little more to get done in time." He consulted his next list. "Bill," he said, "you draw for the Hutchinson family. You got any other households in the Hutchinsons?"

49   "There's Don and Eva," Mrs. Hutchinson yelled. "Make *them* take their chance!"

50   "Daughters draw with their husbands' families, Tessie," Mr. Summers said gently. "You know that as well as anyone else."

51   "It wasn't *fair,*" Tessie said.

52   "I guess not, Joe," Bill Hutchinson said regretfully. "My daughter draws with her husband's family, that's only fair. And I've got no other family except the kids."

53   "Then, as far as drawing for families is concerned, it's you," Mr. Summers said in explanation, "and as far as drawing for households is concerned, that's you, too. Right?"

54   "Right," Bill Hutchinson said.

55   "How many kids, Bill?" Mr. Summers asked formally.

56   "Three," Bill Hutchinson said. "There's Bill, Jr., and Nancy, and little Dave. And Tessie and me."

57   "All right, then," Mr. Summers said. "Harry, you got their tickets back?"

58   Mr. Graves nodded and held up the slips of paper. "Put them in the box, then," Mr. Summers directed. "Take Bill's and put it in."

59   "I think we ought to start over," Mrs. Hutchinson said, as quietly as she could. "I tell you it wasn't *fair.* You didn't give him time enough to choose. *Every*body saw that."

60   Mr. Graves had selected the five slips and put them in the box, and he dropped all the papers but those onto the ground, where the breeze caught them and lifted them off.

61   "Listen, everybody," Mrs. Hutchinson was saying to the people around her.

62   "Ready, Bill?" Mr. Summers asked, and Bill Hutchinson, with one quick glance around at his wife and children, nodded.

63   "Remember," Mr. Summers said, "take the slips and keep them folded until each person has taken one. Harry, you help little Dave." Mr. Graves took the hand of the little boy, who came willingly with him up to the box. "Take a paper out of the box, Davy," Mr. Summers said. Davy put his hand into the box and laughed. "Take just *one* paper," Mr. Summers said. "Harry, you hold it for him." Mr. Graves took the child's hand and removed the folded paper from the tight fist and held it while little Dave stood next to him and looked at him wonderingly.

64   "Nancy next," Mr. Summers said. Nancy was twelve, and her school friends breathed heavily as she went forward, switching her skirt, and took a slip daintily from the box. "Bill, Jr.," Mr. Summers said, and Billy, his face red and his feet overlarge, nearly knocked the box over as he got a paper out. "Tessie," Mr. Summers said. She hesitated for a minute, looking around defiantly, and then set her lips and went up to the box. She snatched a paper out and held it behind her.

65   "Bill," Mr. Summers said, and Bill Hutchinson reached into the box and felt around, bringing his hand out at last with the slip of paper in it.

66   The crowd was quiet. A girl whispered, "I hope it's not Nancy," and the sound of the whisper reached the edges of the crowd.

67   "It's not the way it used to be," Old Man Warner said clearly. "People ain't the way they used to be."

68   "All right," Mr. Summers said. "Open the papers. Harry, you open little Dave's."

69   Mr. Graves opened the slip of paper and there was a general sigh through the crowd as he held it up and everyone could see that it was blank. Nancy and Bill, Jr., opened theirs at the same time, and both beamed and laughed, turning around to the crowd and holding their slips of paper above their heads.

70   "Tessie," Mr. Summers said. There was a pause, and then Mr. Summers looked at Bill Hutchinson, and Bill unfolded his paper and showed it. It was blank.

71   "It's Tessie," Mr. Summers said, and his voice was hushed. "Show us her paper, Bill."

72   Bill Hutchinson went over to his wife and forced the slip of paper out of her hand. It had a black spot on it, the black spot Mr. Summers had made the night before with the heavy pencil in the coal-company office. Bill Hutchinson held it up, and there was a stir in the crowd.

73   "All right, folks," Mr. Summers said. "Let's finish quickly."

74   Although the villagers had forgotten the ritual and lost the original black box, they still remembered to use stones. The pile of stones the boys had made earlier was ready; there were stones on the ground with the blowing scraps of paper that had come out of the box. Mrs. Delacroix selected a stone so large she had to pick it up with both hands and turned to Mrs. Dunbar. "Come on," she said. "Hurry up."

75   Mrs. Dunbar had small stones in both hands, and she said, gasping for breath, "I can't run at all. You'll have to go ahead and I'll catch up with you."

76   The children had stones already, and someone gave little Davy Hutchinson a few pebbles.

77   Tessie Hutchinson was in the center of a cleared space by now, and she held her hands out desperately as the villagers moved in on her. "It isn't fair," she said. A stone hit her on the side of the head.

78   Old Man Warner was saying, "Come on, come on, everyone." Steve Adams was in the front of the crowd of villagers, with Mrs. Graves beside him.

79   "It isn't fair, it isn't right," Mrs. Hutchinson screamed, and then they were upon her.

Thinking about the Text

1. To understand Jackson's use of understatement (a weaker description than the circumstances warrant), cite all of the details in the opening paragraphs that seem contrary to the real nature of this lottery.

2. Describe Mr. Summers. Discuss the significance of Mr. Summers and Mr. Graves conducting this lottery. In what ways are their names significant?

3. What are the earliest signs that people are anxious about this lottery?

4. How does Old Man Warner defend the lottery tradition?

5. What is Tessie Hutchinson's initial attitude toward the lottery? How does each of the Hutchinsons react to Tessie "winning" the lottery? Use these details and others to demonstrate that this lottery seems to be perverting more noble human instincts even before the actual stoning.

6. The story is narrated objectively, or dramatically, without revealing the thoughts or feelings of the characters. Why does Jackson choose this point of view?

Writing from the Text

1. Using details from the story as well as from your own experience, explore why close-knit societies are not always as safe as they seem.

2. Adding to your answers for Question 1 above, list all examples of understatement and of irony (a discrepancy between appearance and reality) in this story. Then write a paper analysing Jackson's use of irony in "The Lottery."

Connecting with Other Texts

1. Compare and contrast the ways Shirley Jackson and Judith Timson ("Here's to Family Feasting," p. 4) approach the concept of tradition.

2. List insights that "The Lottery" and the essay "The Shackles of Everyday Lies" (p. 34) suggest about conservatism and the place of the individual in a conservative society. Then write an essay about how the issue of conformity is treated in both works.

PART II
The Rhetoric

This Rhetoric is designed for you to use easily and constantly, not only in class with your instructor but also at home when you are on your own. We begin by demonstrating many prewriting techniques to help you move quickly beyond the blank page or computer screen. Students learn to write better by actually writing, and our prewriting exercises prompt you to do just that. We guide you through the entire process, from discovering a topic and writing a draft to supporting a thesis and revising the essay.

In order to demonstrate the stages of an actual writing assignment, we trace one student's progress from prewriting and information gathering through organizing, outlining, drafting, revising, documenting, and editing the essay. This assignment typifies the writing that you could be asked to do in college; it begins with responses to readings and shows you how to relate your experience to other writers' ideas. The sample essay will also teach you how to paraphrase, quote, and document material responsibly.

Throughout this Rhetoric, then, you will gain skills to craft the varied types of papers that you will need to write. We provide instruction, examples, and discussions of particular methods for developing essays, and we show you how to draft these essays, too. We make suggestions for note taking and interviewing, and we offer opportunities for you to practise active reading and incorporating quotations—all important skills to help you write successful papers. We show how important it is to consider purpose, audience, and style. In addition to the many shorter assignments, we provide instruction for all stages of a longer research paper, with guides to both MLA and APA documentation forms.

CHAPTER 6
Prewriting as Discovery

Because writing involves discovery, this section will help you find ways to explore the ideas, experiences, and information that you bring to the composition class. We want you to understand the discovery process because that process has so much to do with your finished product

Let's think for a few moments about how you will begin your assignments—about strategies that will encourage you to become involved in your subject and discover what you want to write about it.

It seems paradoxical to suggest that you will discover what you want to write by writing, but students frequently tell us—and our own writing habits confirm—that the very act of working with words, ideas, or feelings on a page or computer screen will help you learn what you want to express about a topic.

Conversations with friends, too, can help you mull over your ideas. Sometimes a spirited exchange with a classmate or roommate will help you "get going" on a writing topic because you start to reconsider and refine your ideas as you discuss them, and you start to care if your ideas have been communicated or accepted. If your perceptions are questioned, you may want to present your point more convincingly in written form. In fact, the best thing you can do when you are assigned a writing task is immediately to jot down any responses and ideas. Consider this initial, quick writing as a conversation with yourself, because that is what it is. It is also like the stretching exercises or warm-ups that runners, dancers, and musicians do.

To help you get moving, here are some prewriting exercises on freewriting, journal writing, clustering, listing, active reading, and group brainstorming that come from the reading and writing topics in this book. Try these different methods; you may find a few that help you get beyond the blank page or screen.

FREEWRITING

As the term implies, **freewriting** involves jotting down uncensored thoughts as quickly as you can. Don't concern yourself with form or correctness. Write whatever comes into your mind without rejecting ideas because they may seem silly or irrelevant. In freewriting, one thought might trigger a more intriguing or significant one, so anything that comes into your head may be valuable. Here is one student's unedited freewriting response to the topic of stereotyping:

> Stereotyping? I don't think I stereotype--maybe I do. But I sure have had it done to me. When people see my tatoo they seem to think I'm in Hell's Angels or a skinhead. Talk about prejudgements! It's as if the snake coiling up my arm is going to get them, the way they look at it and pull back from me. I remember once, in a campground in northern B.C., a bunch of us campers were stranded when the road washed out. As food and supplies dwindled, people started borrowing from each other. In the john one morning I asked this guy if I could borrow a razor blade and he jumped back. Not till he looked away from my arm and into my eyes did he relax. He gave me a blade, we talked, later shared some campfires together. . . . I could write about that experience, a good story. I wonder if people with tatooes have always been connected with trouble--pirates maybe, sailors and gang members today anyhow. It could be interesting to find out if the negative stereotypes about tatooes have always been there. Now that's some research I could get into.

Ryan's response to the topic of stereotyping starts with his personal feeling that the subject doesn't really relate to him, but then he thinks about the fact that he has been stereotyped by others. As he considers how people react to his tattoo, he recalls an incident he thinks he could write about as a narrative. As he thinks more about the nature of tattoos, he finds an aspect of stereotyping that concerns him and that he might like to research. If he had not written down his feelings about stereotyping, he might have settled for a more predictable response to the assignment.

Notice that Ryan's freewriting starts with a question that he asks himself about the topic—a perfect way to get himself warmed up and moving. He's not worried about checking his spelling. He can consult a dictionary when he is drafting his paper to learn that *tattoos* is the correct spelling and *prejudgments* is the common Canadian spelling. Ryan also uses language in his prewriting that is likely inappropriate in his essays: "guy," "bunch," "john," "anyhow," and "get into." Most important is that Ryan got started on his assignment without procrastinating and that he explored his own unique thoughts and feelings. He found a personal experience he might relate and discovered research that he would like to do.

Practising Freewriting

To help you see how freewriting can lead to discovery, write for 15 minutes, without stopping, on one of the topics below. Do not worry about form and do not censor any idea, fact, picture, or feeling that comes to you. Freewrite about one of the following:

a. one of your parents or one of your children

b. a time spent with a grandparent or favourite aunt or uncle

c. a particular family occasion when you learned something

d. your response to "Here's to Family Feasting" (p. 4)

e. your response to "The Phone Call" (p. 31)

Your freewriting may be written on a sheet of paper, composed at a computer, or jotted down in your journal.

JOURNAL WRITING

Journals may be used to record your feelings or respond to others' ideas, including material that you have read. As a conversation with yourself, journal writing may also help you warm up before writing a paper. It will give you another way to discover your ideas; in fact, many professional writers rely on journals to store ideas for future stories, articles, editorials, and poems.

Your instructor may ask you to keep a journal just so that you will have additional writing practice while you are in a composition course. Nearly all of the "Thinking About the Text" questions and many of the "Writing from the Text" assignments in the Reader make ideal topics for a journal. If you use your journal to write responses to assigned readings, you will

• be better prepared for class discussions
• retain more material from the readings
• gain more writing practice

For your journal, you can use a notebook of any size. Some writers prefer ones that are thin enough to fit into a purse or a full backpack. That way, they can pull out their journals whenever the inspiration strikes them, such as on a bus or while waiting for someone. Others prefer binders so that they can add or delete loose-leaf pages as needed. It helps to date each entry so that you can trace the development of your thoughts and your writing.

Using a Journal for Active Reading

One type of assigned active reading is a **dialectical journal**. In this journal you write down specific phrases from your readings and then record thoughts that are evoked by these phrases—in effect, having a conversation with your reading material. You may find yourself jotting down questions you would like to ask the writer or words and terms you looked up in a dictionary. Include specific details that you want to interpret or analyse. You will find yourself discovering feelings about particular topics related to the reading.

Imagine Ryan, the student who did freewriting about stereotypes, responding specifically to the essay "Don't Let Stereotypes Warp Your Judgments" (p. 128). His journal response to the essay might look like this:

> "Are criminals more likely to be dark than blond?" That's a provocative question the author asks. It makes me think about all the bad guys in movies. Aren't they always dark? You never see Robert Redford playing a villain--or do you? I think some of our stereotyping comes from film, which is Heilbroner's point when he writes about "type-casts." Maybe only bad films use "types." I like what the author says about stereotypes making us "mentally lazy." I can see what he means when he says there are two people hurt in stereotyping--the person who is unjustly lumped into some category and the person who is "impoverished" by his laziness. Heilbroner says that a person can't "see the world in his own absolutely unique, inimitable and independent fashion." That makes sense about being independent. But I wonder what "inimitable" means?

Notice that Ryan begins his journal entry with a question from the essay itself; he also might have started with his own question about the work. Ryan jots down ideas that come to him as he responds to the assigned reading. It is important that he puts quotation marks around any words, phrases, or sentences from the text. Ryan wants to remember that the ideas and language belong to the author in case he uses these later. He will then be able to acknowledge Heilbroner accurately by including parenthetical references to his source. (For more on parenthetical references, see pp. 386–91 and 405–407.)

In addition to moving Ryan into his assigned topic, his journal writing lets him record his responses to parts of Heilbroner's essay. He is practising finding the essence of the essay, as well as parts that he might want to quote in his own work. Further, if Ryan reads "The Babysitters Club: No Boys Allowed" (p. 54) or "Discovering My Native Identity" (p. 101), he will have additional relevant material in his journal to connect to that essay, either for his own interest or for other writing assignments.

Practising Journal Writing

Respond to any of the following topics by conversing with yourself in an uncensored dialogue. Start with the question or topic, but permit your mind to wander in any direction your thoughts take you.

a. Sibling rivalry—does it relate to me?

b. How have my parents changed since I've been in college?

c. What kinds of generational conflicts have I experienced with members of my family?

d. Do I agree with Moira Farr when she writes in "Welcome to FamilyValuesWorld!" (p. 11), "whenever I hear the term 'family values' . . . I never feel as though they are talking about me, or about any other human beings I know"?

CLUSTERING

Clustering is a visual grouping of ideas on a page. It is the perfect prewriting exercise for students who tend to see ideas or concepts in spatial relationships. Many students use clustering for in-class writing assignments, including essay exams, where the object is not to discover a topic but to organize information that they already have. For these writers, clustering is the best way to see the assigned question in terms of main topics and subtopics.

One student used clustering in response to an assignment to discover some "between-worlds" topics in her own life. Rachel wrote the assignment as a question in the middle of the page. Then she drew lines from the topics to several subtopics, which she placed in boxes. As you can see on the next page, her subtopics are the chapter titles in the Reader portion of this text. She placed "perceptions" and "genders" in the same box because, for her, these areas are closely related. Next to each subtopic, she then wrote down a brief phrase or reference to experiences and concerns that related to it. By clustering her responses, Rachel discovered topics that are important to her.

She was also able to group related issues—an immediate advantage of clustering. You may want to read the paper (p. 262) that came from this prewriting discovery work, but first look at Rachel's clustering exercise, which is reproduced on the next page.

Notice that Rachel started with the assigned question of how she was "between worlds" and used that as a centre or starting point for her personal inquiry into specific areas where she felt "betweenness."

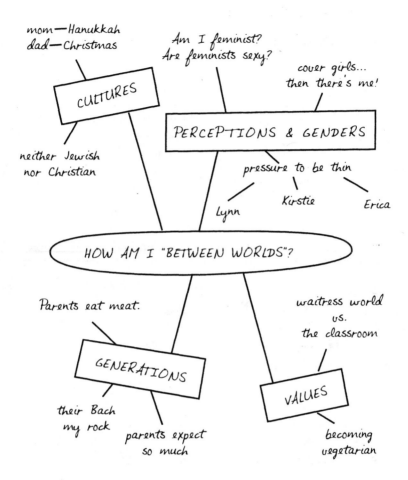

mom—Hanukkah
dad—Christmas

Am I feminist?
Are feminists sexy?

cover girls...
then there's me!

CULTURES

PERCEPTIONS & GENDERS

neither Jewish
nor Christian

pressure to be thin

Lynn   Kirstie   Erica

HOW AM I "BETWEEN WORLDS"?

Parents eat meat.

waitress world
vs.
the classroom

GENERATIONS

VALUES

their Bach
my rock

parents expect
so much

becoming
vegetarian

Practising Clustering

Respond graphically to the topics below by clustering:

1. Centre "self and family" in a box on a page. As you cluster, consider how you are "a part of" your family and how you are "apart from" your family.

2. Centre "incidents that united my family" in a box on a page. Draw lines to other boxes that will include specific outings, celebrations, crises, customs, and events that have united your family. Don't forget the surprising or unlikely incidents that no one expected would draw you together.

Clustering may help you discover topics that interest you, as well as find relationships between ideas that you have written on your page.

LISTING

You can use **listing** as a way of making a quick inventory of thoughts, ideas, feelings, or facts about a topic. The object is to list everything, again without censoring any notion that comes to you. In addition to clustering her "between-worlds" experiences (p. 215), Rachel listed her ideas after she discovered a topic for her paper. (You can see her listing on pp. 234–35.)

If you are answering a specific question or know what your topic is, you can also use listing to collect from your reading the information and ideas that will be useful in your paper. Listing will help you see ways to group and arrange the material that you have found.

For example, a student who is assigned a character analysis based on a particular reading may list details from the text that indicate the character's traits. In order to write a character analysis of Grandmama in the short story "The Jade Peony" (p. 17), student Victoria Hogan wrote a list that you can see on page 340. Notice how Victoria's list helps her find important details and then organize those details for her essay.

Practising Listing

1. Write a list of options or advantages your parents or grandparents had that you feel you do not have. List options or advantages you have that they did not.
2. List the tensions that occur between generations in your family.
3. List the customs, habits, and values in your family that are transmitted between generations.
4. List the behavioural traits of Saliha Samson in "Ajax Là-Bas" (p. 110).

ACTIVE READING

Active reading is an appropriate prewriting strategy when you are asked to write a specific response to something that you have read, or when you know that your own experience and knowledge provide insufficient information for a meaningful essay. A great deal of college writing—in every course—fits these circumstances, so it is important that you either learn active reading or perfect the skills that you already have.

Active reading involves reading with a pen in your hand. If you are using your own book, you can read and mark directly in the copy. If you are using a library book, you will need to photocopy the pages you intend to read actively. As you read your own text or the photocopied pages, make the following markings:

- *Underline* key points and supporting details.
- *Place check marks* and *asterisks* next to important lines.
- *Jot* brief summary or commentary *notes* in the margins.
- *Circle* unfamiliar words and references to look up later.
- *Ask questions* as you read.
- *Seek answers* to those questions.
- *Question* the writer's *assumptions* and assertions as well as your own.

Reading actively allows you to enter into a conversation with your authors in which you examine and challenge their ideas. Active reading will also help you find important lines more easily so that you don't have to reread the entire work each time that you refer to it during class discussions or in your essays. Don't underline or highlight *everything*, however, or you will defeat your purpose of finding just the important points.

If you have a writing assignment that requires you to summarize an entire essay or use information from readings in addition to your own experience, you will profit from learning how to read actively and how to incorporate information that you have read into your own work. Rachel, the student who used clustering to discover her concern about the pressure among her friends to be thin, decided to do some reading about eating disorders. The excerpt below, from "Bodily Harm" (p. 155), illustrates her active reading.

check specific definitions

Recent media attention to the binge–purge and self-starvation disorders known as <u>bulimia</u> and <u>anorexia</u>—often detailing gruesome particulars of women's eating behavior—may have exacerbated this serious problem on college campuses. But why would a woman who reads an article on eating disorders want to copy what she reads? Ruth Striegel-Moore, Ph.D., director of Yale University's Eating Disorders Clinic, suggests that <u>eating disorders</u> may be a way to be like other "<u>special</u>" <u>women</u> and at the same time strive to outdo them. "The pursuit of thinness is a way for women to compete with each other, a way that <u>avoids being threatening to men</u>," says Striegel-Moore. Eating disorders <u>as a perverse sort of rivalry?</u> In Carol's freshman year at SUNY-Binghamton, a roommate showed her how to make herself throw up. "Barf buddies" are notorious on many college campuses, especially in sororities and among sports teams. Eating disorders as <u>negative bonding?</u> Even self-help groups on campus can degenerate into the kinds of competitiveness and negative reinforcement that are among the roots of eating disorders in the first place.

"special" = how to be unique?

How ironic!

Media may exacerbate the problem

general term

thinness as competition — without threatening men.

Self-help groups as negative reinforcement

This is not another article on how women do it. It is an article on <u>how and why some women stopped</u>. The decision to get help is not always an easy one. The shame and secrecy surrounding most eating disorders and the fear of being labeled "sick" may keep a woman from admitting even to herself that her behavior is hurting her. "We're not weirdos," says Nancy Gengler, a recovered bulimic and number two U.S. squash champion, who asked that I use her real name because "so much of this illness has to do with <u>secrecy and embarrassment</u>." In the first stages of therapy, says Nancy, much of getting better was a result of building up the strength to (literally) "sweat out" the desire to binge and to <u>endure the discomfort of having overeaten</u> rather than throwing up. "I learned to accept such 'failures' and more-over, <u>that they would not make me fat</u>. . . ."

the focus:

labelled "sick"

secrecy is part of the problem

Need to accept our "failures"

Writing notes in the margins helped Rachel stay involved as she read and remember details from the essay. Like Rachel, you can better understand and retain what you read if you practise active reading.

Practising Active Reading

1. Practise the steps listed on page 217 and actively read the next work that you have been assigned in this course. Do you feel better prepared for class discussion? Did you find the central point or thesis of the essay as a result of your active reading? Was the author's organization scheme apparent to you?

2. Actively read "The Shackles of Everyday Lies" (p. 34), "As a Dad, Will I Do Right by My Daughter?" (p. 37), or "Here's to Family Feasting" (p. 4). After you have actively read one of these essays, join a small group of others who have read the same essay. Compare your active-reading notes with the markings of others in your group.

GROUP BRAINSTORMING— COLLABORATIVE LEARNING

Writing doesn't have to be a lonely activity, with the writer isolated from the world. In fact, much professional writing is a collaborative effort in which writers work together or consult editors. Corporations, educational institutes, and governmental organizations hold regular **brainstorming** sessions so that everyone can offer ideas, consider options, and exchange opinions. Reporters often work together on a story, business administrators pool ideas for a report, and public relations experts work as a team to draft a proposal. Many of your textbooks—including this one—are the result of extensive collaboration.

Your college writing classes may offer you opportunities to work together in small groups, brainstorm for paper topics or supporting details, and critique and edit your classmates' writing. Just as freewriting is a conversation with yourself, group brainstorming provides a conversation with others. These small groups can provide new thoughts, multiple perspectives, and critical questions. Small-group discussion can prompt you to consider others' ideas, as well as help free you from the fear that you have nothing to say. You may find you are more comfortable sharing ideas with a few classmates rather than the entire class.

In the classroom, groups of four or five work well, with each person recording the different comments and key ideas for an assigned question and then sharing these responses with the entire class. Students in your group can decide who will explain each response so that the burden for reporting the discussion does not fall on any one group member. Your instructor, however, may ask that someone from each group serve as "group secretary," recording responses and then reading them. Either way, the goal is to generate as many different responses as possible to a given topic or question. Your group may need to be reminded that everyone's ideas are welcome and needed and that even seemingly far-fetched comments can trigger very productive discussions. As in all of the prewriting activities, no idea or comment should be censored.

Let's assume you have been assigned a paper about growing up with or without siblings. Each group can choose a different subtopic:

- the advantages of growing up with siblings
- the advantages of growing up as an only child
- the ways that only children find "substitutes" for siblings
- the reasons for sibling rivalry and competition, and the solutions to these problems
- the unexpected bonds that develop among siblings
- the reasons that sibling friendships often outlast other friendships

After 10 to 15 minutes of discussion, you should each make sure your group has recorded the key points so they can be shared with the class as a whole. After each report by a group, all students should be invited to add comments or insights on that topic. Students who are listening to a group should take notes to supplement their own essay ideas.

Group brainstorming is an ideal way to discuss reading assignments, and most of the "Thinking About the Text" questions in the Reader are designed for collaborative work. Any of those questions may be used for this exercise. Below you will find brainstorming exercises for both general topics and specific readings.

Practising Brainstorming in Small Groups

1. Brainstorm about the forces threatening the family unit today, and consider ways of preventing or solving particular conflicts. (All groups can do this, since the responses will be so varied.)

2. Discuss the extent to which grandparents are or are not valued by families. Support the discussion with your own experience.

3. Discuss the various types of families currently portrayed on television. One group can analyse the impact of the media on the family. Other groups can compare sitcoms with family dramas or documentary films on the family. Another group can contrast portrayals of more conventional families with those of less conventional ones. A final group can suggest programs that could help or support the family.

4. Read "The Jade Peony" (p. 17) and discuss specific ways that the family's generations live in harmony and in discord. You may add your own experiences to this discussion.

Brainstorming lets you see others' perspectives and consider their views in relation to your own—an awareness you will need when you are writing for an audience. Collaborative work gets you away from the isolation of your own desk or computer screen and into a social context.

INCUBATION

After you have done one or more of the prewriting responses to an assignment, allow yourself time to think about your topic before you begin to draft the paper. Rather than being a way to avoid the writing assignment, the **incubation** period lets you subconsciously make connections and respond to your focus. Students often comment on experiencing flashes of insight about their papers while in the shower, falling asleep, or doing some physical activity.

You, too, will find that your brain will continue to "work" on your paper if you are preoccupied with it, and productive insights can occur during this incubation period. If you do some prewriting on your paper when it is first assigned, your early thoughts and ideas may develop during incubation. Clearly, though, if you have waited until the night before the assignment is due, you aren't going to enjoy much of an incubation period!

The need for incubation continues throughout the drafting process. While you are away from your desk or computer screen, you can still be thinking about ways to refine your topic, increase support of your points, discover links between ideas in your paper, and recall words that will sharpen your meaning. This is also an ideal time to remind yourself that you are writing for readers and to consider their expectations.

CONSIDERING AUDIENCE AND PURPOSE
Identifying Your Audience and Purpose

All writing is intended for an **audience**. Except for personal journal writers, who may be able to understand their own notes to themselves, writers have certain responsibilities to meet the needs and expectations of readers. However, an important question arises: who are the readers?

In some specific writing situations, you can easily define the audience and your purpose for writing; for example, your purpose in writing a letter may be to let a friend or family member know how you are settling in during your first semester at college. You are surely aware that your writing tone—the voice that affects your word choice and emphasis—will differ if you are writing to your lover, brother, elderly aunt, or mother, even if your purpose is the same for each reader.

You may be less able to define the audience for other writing situations. For example, you might assume that for papers assigned in your college classes, your typical reader is a classmate or an instructor, or any thoughtful person who may know something about the subject of your writing and who is very willing (indeed, eager) to learn more.

Your purpose for writing an essay about adjusting to college life, however, will be more complex than in the letter-writing situation. You may want readers to realize the kinds of challenges new students face over the first few weeks. Or you may want to do more than inform; you may want to convince readers to take action by supporting a college-wide mentoring system to ease students' entry into college life. In both cases, you will use details and examples to illustrate issues surrounding your topic, but your approach, informative versus persuasive, will vary according to your purpose.

In general, you should not assume that your only reader is your composition instructor, for that conclusion will prompt you to write for a very small audience. Further, your English instructor may be your easiest audience, because he or she is *required* to read what you have written, comment on your thinking and writing skills, and then perhaps place a grade on your work. In the real world, when you are writing for a boss, readers of a newspaper, or a community organization member, your easily distracted or unwilling readers may lack the empathy an academic instructor has for the effort you have put into your writing. The skills that you learn in your composition class, however, will prepare you to both define your audience and refine your purpose for your broader college and "real-world" writing requirements.

Academic Audiences

Academic readers (your instructors and classmates) will assume that you have carefully considered the assigned topic. They will expect you to show that you understand what is expected of you and that you are writing to satisfy that assignment. This may require finding out what other people know or believe, collecting specific data, or sorting through your own thoughts and information on the subject. Your audience will expect a certain depth of response, even for a short paper. Readers will expect to learn specific facts, find actual examples, discover important insights, or see particular relationships that they were not aware of prior to reading your paper. The paper's required length may define how many dimensions of the subject you can explore to satisfy these expectations.

An academic audience will also expect you to have worked with integrity if you incorporate the ideas, facts, or words of another writer. (See the discussions of plagiarism on pp. 248–49 and 361–63.) Your readers will assume that you have understood any material that you have brought in from another source, that you have not distorted the material in any way, and that you have given credit to the writer whose words or ideas you have used.

An academic audience will expect you to make some point and to support that point logically and with sufficient details (of description, fact, or example) to be convincing. Such readers will expect that you know what you are writing about and that your work has not just been assembled from other people's work—that your treatment or perspective is fresh.

Academic readers will expect your material to be presented in an orderly way, so that a lack of organization does not obscure the points you are making. They will expect your points to cohere. Finally, they will expect the language of your work to be appropriate: standard English (see "Voice" below) and well-chosen words, edited to remove errors in grammar, spelling, and mechanics.

Nonacademic Audiences

When writing outside the classroom—for example, a letter to the newspaper, a report for your boss, or an analysis for a community project—it is vital for you to engage an audience that is not required to read your writing. What are the expectations of this audience?

To start, your purpose will be to convince those readers that your subject and the way you have treated it are worth their time. Depending on the attention span of your readers, you may have to establish the value of your subject and the quality of your writing in the first few sentences! Developing an engaging style will help keep readers interested and encourage them to think more about your topic or take action. Paying attention to the way your

voice permeates your writing will also help you find the appropriate style for nonacademic audiences.

Voice

Most instructors will tell you to "write in your own voice." That means that they want you to write using the vocabulary, sentence structure, and style that you use for communicating as an adult.

Writing in your own voice requires more skill than you might think, because you need to find the balance between your own way of using language and **standard English**, the type of language readers expect to find in most written work. Standard English is what is used by journalists and taught in schools. In fact, this book is written to reflect the authors' voices as we use standard English.

Your voice also becomes apparent to readers through the **register** or level of language you choose, given your subject, purpose, and audience. For most written work, you do not want to use an overly formal register, with too many long, complex sentences and pretentious words. Such a register is usually too impersonal and artificial for most of your writing tasks and is not anything like your own voice. Similarly, you will want to be careful using a more informal or colloquial register. The shorter sentences and slang of the informal register may be more like your own voice, but they are more appropriate for talking with a friend than for writing. The best choice of register reflects what we call a general level of language: sentences will vary in length and vocabulary will be accessible to readers. Overall, the general register is intelligent, but not phony or overly chatty.

Some instructors may want a register that is slightly formal; others may want you to use a more informal register, especially if you are writing about a personal experience. Awareness of both standard English and register will certainly help you find the best version of "your own voice" for every writing task you encounter, whether it is for an academic or nonacademic audience.

Tone

Closely related to voice, **tone** indicates a writer's attitude to both the topic and the audience. In other words, tone is not only what a writer says, but how a writer says it. A writer's tone has the power to alienate an audience or encourage an audience to agree.

Tone comes across in the words you choose; it can be serious or humorous, sincere or ironic. Your tone will depend on your purpose for writing. For example, a humorous tone is appropriate in a narrative about a day when everything seemed to go wrong. A sincere tone could encourage readers to make donations to a local charity.

To engage your audience quickly and achieve your purpose, you should write in a tone that is positive and respectful for all readers, even those who are indifferent or hostile to the topic you are writing about. You may want to anticipate possible objections, doubts, or lack of interest by writing in a tone that does not put off any reader. Consider these openings from three students' drafts for an essay advocating licensed day care for preschoolers:

> Only someone ignorant of young children's social needs will force a child to stay home all day. Young children need day care so they can learn how to interact with each other.

> It seems that licensed day care might have a positive effect on young children's social skills. Perhaps licensed day care is a good idea.

> Many working parents feel guilty about placing their young children in day care. However, the social skills young children learn in licensed day-care centres give them an advantage that can help them thrive in elementary school.

Although the assertion of the first example is straightforward, the tone is insulting. Readers who are unsure about the value of licensed day care run the risk of being labelled "ignorant" if they do not agree with the writer. Such an opening may impress readers who already share the same opinion as the writer, and some readers may continue to read in spite of the brash tone, or even because of it. However, such aggressiveness will probably alienate the very readers whose minds the writer is trying to change. They may conclude that the tone is too hostile to tolerate, and will stop reading.

In contrast, the tone of the second example is cautious, but overly so. Words and phrases such as "it seems," "might have," and "perhaps" indicate a timid writer who, in trying not to offend, has lost confidence and may have become unsure about the importance of this topic. The tone here is overly apologetic and therefore ineffective.

In the third example, the writer's tone indicates respect and empathy for parents placing their children in day care. The writer counters parents' ambivalence by suggesting that the social skills their children learn can become an asset in later years. By using a reasonable and sincere tone, the writer may win sceptical readers who have always believed that children should only be raised at home by their parents. This writer has tried to create a reasonable and informing relationship between writer and reader, one that should attract readers and achieve the purpose of persuading them to agree that licensed day care has definite advantages.

You will need to choose the tone that you want to use for your particular writing assignment. The subject matter of your work and the audience for whom you are writing will help you determine whether a neutral tone will keep your audience engaged.

Style

Style is conscious use of language, and good style will help assure the attention of an audience. This means considering everything from your choice of words to your construction of sentences. Style includes the following elements:

- word choice—precisely chosen words, wordplay, and level of diction (formal, conversational, or slang); see also pp. 463–79
- sentence structure—different types of sentences, varying in length
- voice—a voice that sounds real, rather than artificial or pretentious
- tone—the attitude you show toward your readers and subject

Consider the opening lines below from "Did You Ever Have to Make Up Your Mind?" (p. 123), in which we are urged to explore the nature of "either/or" values and beliefs. Notice that the style of the author, Carl Wilson, indicates from the first sentence that this is not a typical formal essay.

> The hype level on that gritty-vacant Brit flick Trainspotting has scared my little bod away from the ticket stampede, but it also makes me feel like I've already seen the movie. And guess what? I liked it.

The most noticeable feature here is the way the author uses informal and even colloquial language ("hype," "my little bod") to appeal to his target readers, young adults. The complicated structure of the first sentence is offset by the more simply structured question and answer: "And guess what? I liked it." Wilson's tone, or attitude toward his readers and topic, is apparent in his reference to the unconventional film *Trainspotting*, popular with young adults (except him!) but possibly not their parents. Each of these stylistic decisions contributes to Wilson's fresh approach to an old cliché: that between the extreme positions of black and white are always shades of grey. Overall, Wilson's style is confident: it's clear that he is writing in his own voice.

Academic readers who are required to read your writing may not insist on lively style, wit, or exquisite word choice, and they may tolerate a brash tone (like Wilson's) or hostile stance. Nevertheless, ideas about engaging an audience are as applicable to writing done for academics as to the writing done for nonacademic readers.

Practising Style

1. Write two letters—one to your best friend and one to your parents or children— describing a party that you recently attended. (Your letters probably will vary in vocabulary, kinds of details, sentence structure, and tone.)
2. Write two memos—one to a co-worker who is a friend and one to your boss— arguing for a particular change at work.

Analysing Audience Awareness

Clearly, professional writers have an understanding of audience when they direct their texts for publication. We can profit from a study of the techniques that they use to engage and hold their particular audiences, and thus achieve their purpose for writing.

Robert Chodos

In his essay "Being a Jew at Christmas" (p. 94), Robert Chodos intends to present a view of Christmas that most readers might not be aware of or understand. Chodos first engages readers by contrasting the eleven months of the year when he feels he is a full participant in Canadian life with the one month when he does not. In December, he explains, most of Canadian society becomes preoccupied with Christmas, but complications arise for non-Christians like him because Christmas celebrates a Christian holiday based on Christian beliefs. And since the Christmas season dominates public life for a full month, it becomes something that people "cannot avoid passively absorbing" (p. 94). While most readers might consider the events leading up to December 25 as benign and all-inclusive, Chodos's description of his family's December trip to Washington, D.C., offers another, perhaps surprising, perspective: for many North American citizens, Christmas is a government-sanctioned holiday that makes them feel like "refugees."

The author anticipates his readers' protests that Christmas can be enjoyed by everyone. He recalls how much pleasure he took in attending his friends' Christmas celebrations years ago, and how appealing he finds the themes of the Christmas narrative and majesty of Christmas music. However, as he patiently explains, it is possible to enjoy another culture's finest points without adopting that culture as one's own.

Chodos shows audience awareness by acknowledging the deep and sometimes unconscious emotional attachment people have to Christmas. He offers as an example his Unitarian friend's acceptance of Christmas as a given, even though she had rejected other aspects of Christianity. He also demonstrates that he respects the right of people who celebrate Christmas to have that holiday included in December programming at school. The author's carefully reasoned request for similar understanding of other points of view mirrors the sentiments underlying the Christmas theme of "goodwill." By presenting an unfamiliar perspective on a familiar cultural event, Chodos asks readers to consider their tolerance for cultural differences, but without threatening them or questioning their beliefs.

In your own writing, you should consider the assumptions about audience that professional writers make and employ the techniques that they use to engage and keep their readers. You can do this by assuming a stance that will be attractive to your audience and maintaining a voice that will keep readers interested in your work.

Practising Audience Awareness

1. Read Pam Withers's essay "The Babysitters Club: No Boys Allowed" (p. 54), and analyse the ways the author shows awareness of her audience.

2. Write a short essay for a men's magazine, such as *Esquire* or *Playboy*, using some of the information and ideas in Naomi Wolf"s "The Beauty Myth" (p. 57) or Catherine Pigott's "Adding Weight to an Image of Beauty" (p. 152).

3. Write a short letter to the editor of a parents' magazine, such as *Today's Parent*, explaining the emotional turmoil gay and lesbian teens often face. Use the material in Joy C.'s essay "The Phone Call" (p. 31) for your letter.

Good style—achieved with deliberately chosen vocabulary, sentence structure, and tone—can engage readers immediately. With a realistic understanding of your audience in mind, you are ready to begin organizing and drafting your essay. You will gain an understanding of that stage of the writing process in the next chapter.

CHAPTER 7
Organizing and Drafting an Essay

DISCOVERING A THESIS
From Prewriting to Working Thesis

The prewriting experiences described in the previous chapter should have helped you discover focus points and different ways that you might respond to your writing assignment. You were also given some ideas about considering the audience and purpose for your writing. It is now important that you determine your specific approach for your paper. All essays require a focus— a controlling idea for both the writer and the readers. So after doing some prewriting activities, thinking about your topic, considering your audience and purpose, and writing an initial draft, you should be able to construct at least a tentative or working thesis that will help you direct your writing. That thesis may change a number of times as you draft and revise your paper. Let's think about how the controlling idea for your paper might be expressed.

Developing a Thesis

A **thesis** is an assertion about a limited subject that will be supported, proven, or described by the writer of the essay. Often, but not always, the view of the writer shows in the language of the thesis. Sometimes the writer constructs a thesis to forecast the plan or organization of the paper. The thesis will reflect the aim or intention of the paper.

Let's imagine that Ryan is deciding from his prewriting experiences (pp. 211 and 213) how to respond to his assignment on stereotyping. His particular interest has to do with his tattoo and how he is stereotyped because of it, an awareness he gained in freewriting. Ryan realized that he had a good focus for a story he could narrate. He also discovered that he was interested in doing some reading about the history of tattoos to learn whether they have always been regarded negatively.

If Ryan's assignment had been to write about a personal experience involving stereotyping, he probably would have written about the incident in the northern B.C. campground. Had he been asked to define stereotyping or show its consequences, Ryan might have recalled his dialectical journal prewriting (p. 213) on the essay "Don't Let Stereotypes Warp Your Judgments," and he may have developed his paper in a different way. Ryan may have used any of the following for a working thesis, depending on his purpose in writing the paper:

- An experience when I was camping showed me how uncomfortable stereotyping can be for the person stereotyped.
- Stereotyping, or prejudgments based on "standardized pictures" in our heads, can create unnecessary anxiety and deprive us of worthwhile experiences.
- Because tattoos have been worn by the lower classes and fringe members of various cultures throughout history, there has been prejudice against them.
- Because prominent citizens of the world have started to wear tattoos, earlier prejudice against tattoos has diminished.

Each of these assertions requires Ryan to develop his paper in a slightly different way. The first thesis can be supported with his own experience. The second statement requires some incorporation of definitive and appropriately documented material from Heilbroner's essay on stereotyping, as well as personal experience. The third and fourth thesis statements will require Ryan to research material in order to support his assertions. As in Ryan's case, your personal interests, as well as the aim of the assignment itself, will help you decide on a suitable thesis.

Recognizing a Thesis

If a thesis is a complete sentence that makes an assertion about a limited subject, which of the following are supportable thesis statements? Which are not? Which statements forecast a plan or direction for the paper?

1. Sexism in college courses.
2. Sexist language in college textbooks can be eliminated with the right attitude and language awareness.
3. I think the college cafeteria should post a nutritional analysis of every meal it offers.

4. When grandparents live with two younger generations, everyone learns flexibility and new reasons to laugh.
5. Should Canadians buy only Canadian-made products?
6. Siblings can remind us of our family's history and values, and can provide physical and emotional support as we age.

Example 1 may be a suitable subject or topic for an essay, but it is not a thesis. As the absence of a verb indicates, the example lacks an assertion that makes a claim about sexism. Example 2 does make a claim about sexist language and is a reasonable thesis. It has a limited subject (sexist language in college textbooks), and it forecasts that "attitude" and "language awareness" will be the subtopics discussed to support the thesis. Example 3 contains a clear assertion, but "I think" is unnecessary. The thesis should directly express this conviction: "The college cafeteria should post a nutritional analysis of every meal it offers." Example 4 is an effective thesis that forecasts two benefits of generations living together. A question like that in Example 5 may be a good way to engage readers in an introduction, but it is not an assertion, so it is not a suitable thesis. The question encourages an unfocused, disorganized response. Contrast the direction implicit in the statements of Examples 2, 4, or 6 with this question, and you will see why it is not effective. Example 6 is a very explicit thesis statement. It cites exactly the areas of support that will come in the paper: the "family's history and values" and "physical and emotional support." Writers who write from a strong thesis will know where they are going, and so will their readers.

Changing the Thesis

Before we discuss thesis statements any further, it is important to acknowledge some qualities of the thesis. For one thing, the thesis can undergo many changes in the course of drafting and rewriting a paper. We have all had the experience of finishing a draft only to discover that our feelings about the subject have changed. In order to reflect that new awareness in the paper, the writer will want to return to the thesis, revise it, and then reshape the points in the paper so they will adequately support the new assertion. Perhaps it is best to consider any thesis as only a working thesis until you are about to edit your final draft. (See Rachel Krell's work on developing a thesis, pp. 234–39.)

The "Missing" Thesis

When you read essays written by professional writers, you may have trouble finding an explicit thesis statement, but even if a thesis is implied rather than stated, in a well-structured essay, you as a reader should be able to articulate the writer's fundamental assertion.

Sometimes a student writer is tempted to omit a thesis statement, expecting readers to discover the essay's central point as they approach the essay's conclusion. In many cases, however, the omission of a thesis statement during the drafting stage results in a rambling or unfocused discussion. A successful student writer works from an explicit, clear, and unambiguous thesis that guides the discussion and keeps it on track. Once satisfied with the direction the discussion has taken, the student may then opt to revise the essay so the thesis is implied rather than stated.

However, from the readers' point of view, an explicit thesis statement is preferable in most cases. You as a writer are more likely to achieve your purpose if you are straightforward about your central point from the outset, rather than depending on the element of surprise at the end. A strong focus—whether stated in a thesis or implied—contributes to good writing, and you will want to perfect your ability to focus your work and to make your readers' task easier.

Positioning the Thesis

For many writers, and for many essays, placing the thesis at the conclusion of the introduction makes sense. The thesis follows logically from the introductory materials used to engage the audience, and the plan or direction of the paper is set forth so that readers know not only what is coming, but in what order the support will be presented. This forecasting also helps you, the writer of the essay, to stay organized and on target.

Certainly most writing instructors will require that you place your thesis at least within the first few paragraphs of your essay. Tired of wondering and writing "Where is all of this going?" in the margins of student papers, most instructors favour a clearly stated thesis in the introductory paragraphs.

Sample Thesis Statements

The following chart shows how writers work from a limited subject to write a thesis that their experience or information can support.

Limited Subject	Focus	Thesis
College students	Commuting students	College students who live at home know the problems of living between worlds.
Native people	Popular depictions	Native people are stereotyped and denigrated in North American popular culture.
TV for children	Improved programming	In contrast to ten years ago, television programs designed for elementary-age children today are multicultural and interracial.
The men's movement	Is it necessary?	The men's movement is needed to create a social connection among men. The movement can rectify divorce and paternity inequities.

Practising Thesis Writing

Although seeing other writers' thesis statements will help you gain awareness of the thesis, you need to practise writing your own assertions for your own papers. You also need to have readers critique the thesis statements that you have written.

1. Return to one of your prewriting exercises or freewrite here on the subject of a parent's ability or inability to be open to new and possibly controversial ideas. Freewrite for 15 minutes without censoring any thought that comes to you. Then reread what you have written. Find a feature of that material that interests you. Limit your focus and write two or three different thesis statements that you can support with the ideas in your freewriting. Type or write these assertions neatly on a sheet of paper and make three copies prior to your next class session.

2. In the first few minutes of class time, work in groups of four students to comment on each other's assertions. Let each student in the group make comments about one thesis statement before you go on to look at each person's second assertion. Determine which statements are true assertions that can be supported. Then predict the type of support that is necessary (narrative of personal experience, definition, or examples from research material) for each thesis. If you are having trouble seeing what is lacking in your thesis statements, talk with your fellow students, instructor, or writing assistant.

Critical Thinking and the "So What?" Response

After you have a tentative assertion around which to direct your support, ask yourself, "So what?" A sure way to realize that your assumed assertion isn't headed anywhere meaningful is to discover yourself shrugging indifferently at your own claim. As you jot down answers to this question, you will start to see what you are actually claiming. For example, imagine what would happen if you started with this assertion:

> **Thesis:** Many people in the world are victims of stereotyping.

> "So what?"
> Some people have preconceived ideas about others.
> "So what?"
> It's unfair. People see them as types, not individuals.
> "So what?"
> These prejudgments limit the people who are stereotyped *and* the people doing the stereotyping.

As you continue to answer the "So what?" questions, you may discover a way to state your assertion that makes your readers more eager to read your paper. Compare the following assertion with the first one above. In what way is it better?

> **Thesis:** Prejudgments limit the lives of the stereotyped individual and the person doing the stereotyping.

Notice how this statement conforms to the requirements of a thesis. It is a complete sentence, not a question or a phrase, and it articulates a definite opinion or assertion. Unlike the first attempt at a thesis, this statement establishes a definite focus on prejudgments (they "limit . . . lives"), and it suggests an order for the analysis ("the stereotyped individual" and "the person doing the stereotyping").

By asking yourself "So what?" throughout your writing, you will not only sharpen your thesis but also help yourself discover points and insights worth sharing with readers. If you continue to ask this question, you will prompt yourself to think more critically about each claim as you make it. You also will ensure that you are writing from a worthwhile assertion and that you are explaining your points to your readers.

SUPPORTING A THESIS
Drafting

Once you have done some prewriting, you are ready to begin the **drafting** process. No two writers draft the same way; in fact, there are as many methods (and "nonmethods") for drafting as there are writers. There are countless strategies and approaches that help writers organize, develop, and support their ideas and assertions.

In the next pages, we will trace how one student, Rachel Krell, drafted her paper. Look back to page 215 to see Rachel's clustering exercise, in which she discovered a topic related to living "between worlds." From this initial prewriting, she perceived that recurrent topics of interest were related to food: her vegetarianism, her friends' preoccupation with slimness, her awareness that her body does not fit the cover-girl mould, and even her job as a waitress.

Developing Support

Reviewing all of these food-related topics, Rachel realized she was most interested in her friends' eating problems. She decided to pursue the topic; since her instructor had required her to incorporate readings in her paper, she started by actively reading "Adding Weight to an Image of Beauty" (p. 152), "The Beauty Myth" (p. 57), and "Bodily Harm" (p. 155). You can read an excerpt from Rachel's prewriting exercise on pages 217–18. This active reading helped stimulate Rachel's thinking and helped her understand her friends' experiences.

Listing

After her prewriting activities, Rachel started to list more specific ideas and experiences that related to eating disorders:

- The "beauty myth" continues to imprison women, especially when it comes to weight.
- My own insecurity about weight.
- My friend Lynn, hospitalized for anorexia, nearly died.
- Another friend, Kirstie, was proud she could vomit automatically every time she ate.
- My friend Erica, in a treatment program, was shocked by the number of women over thirty still plagued by eating disorders.
- Binge-and-purge syndrome.
- Ads depict tall models in size 3 bikinis.

- "Bodily Harm" examines psychological motives, "barf buddies," and "aerobic nervosa."
- "Adding Weight to an Image of Beauty" shows how Gambian women can celebrate being big, but Canadians want to be slim and perfect.
- Jane Fonda, once bulimic, hooked so many on her "Work Out" videos.
- Princess Di disclosed her bulimia--the "beauty myth" collapses.
- My cousin spent weeks in a hospital program for anorexics.
- Weight loss--the ultimate "control" mechanism?
- Women's movement trying to free women from such images.
- Young women torn between being feminist or sexy--why either/or?
- Sexy women are always pictured as thin.
- Women competing without threatening men.

Working Thesis

From this list, Rachel linked certain topics: friends' experiences, celebrities with serious eating disorders, advertising images of women, cultural differences, psychological motives, the women's movement, and dieting as a control mechanism. These groupings helped her draft a working thesis so she could start planning her paper.

Working Thesis: Many women suffer from eating disorders.

Using this preliminary thesis as a guide, Rachel started to write.

Example: First Draft

In this day and age many women suffer from eating disorders. Influenced by television commercials and movies, most women have been conditioned to believe they must be thin to be beautiful. Who wouldn't want to hear friends whisper, "What a body! She really knows how to stay in shape!" or "Don't you hate someone who looks that good?" Either way, the sense of envy is clear. A thin girl has something that others don't-- and this gives her power and control. She can make herself in the image of the cover girls. "The pursuit of thinness is a way for women to compete with each other, a way that avoids being threatening to men" (Erens 155).

Unfortunately, this competition keeps women from seeking or obtaining the help they might otherwise get from close friends. Many bulimics keep their secret as guarded as they can. For example, my friend Kirstie did this. She waited for years before she told friends (and later, her family) that she was bulimic. At first, only her "barf buddy" (from Erens?) knew.

Kirstie seemed to have a good life with her family and friends. But years later, she revealed to me that her greatest pride was when she discovered that she was now vomiting automatically after eating, without needing to use a finger or spoon.

Erica was another friend who needed help. In fact, her situation was so bad that she needed to go into a hospital. And my friend Lynn would have died had she not entered the hospital when she did. She had to drop out of college immediately and get prolonged therapy for herself and her family. As Erens notes, "Family therapy considers the family itself, not the daughter with the eating disorder, to be the 'patient.' Often, the daughter has taken on the role of diverting attention from unacknowledged conflicts within the family."

One problem Lynn had was conforming to her parents' expectations. Lynn decided to major in art even though her parents wanted her to get a degree in computer science so she would have a job when she graduated. There was so much stress in that house every time Lynn enrolled in another art class. Maybe she felt that the only thing she could control in her life was how thin she could get.

The message to be thin comes from popular role models. Actress Jane Fonda has sold many on the value of her "Work Out" and has helped spawn "aerobic nervosa" (Erens 156). Many women who admire her shape may not know that Fonda was once bulimic. And no one watching the televised spectacle of Prince Charles and Princess Diana's wedding could have predicted that years later, even after her death, the media would be discussing "Di's bulimia."

Not just the superstars but all models seem incredibly thin today. Wolf contends: "the weight of fashion models plummeted to 23 percent below that of ordinary women, eating disorders rose exponentially, and a mass neurosis was promoted that used food and weight to strip women of that sense of control" (58). It seems that many women--celebrities, models, and my friends-- have not escaped this curse.

Evaluating the First Draft

As Rachel was writing this draft she found herself crossing out occasional words and adding phrases, but her main concern was getting her ideas down on the page. She remembered relevant ideas from some assigned readings in *Between Worlds*, and she put some of the quoted material in her draft. She didn't worry about the form of her quotes, but she was careful to copy the page numbers correctly so she wouldn't have to waste time searching for them later. Once she had written this rough draft, she reread it with a pen in hand, spotting weak areas and making quick notes to herself. Her critique of her first draft is shown below.

Example: Draft with Author's Comments

cliché?   *dull!*

(In this day and age) many women suffer from eating disorders. Influenced by television commercials and movies, most women have been conditioned to believe they must be thin to be beautiful. Who wouldn't want to hear friends whisper, "What a body! She really knows how to stay in shape!" or "Don't you hate someone who looks that good?" Either way, the sense of

maybe   envy is clear. A thin girl has something that others don't--
re...   and this gives her power and control. She can make herself in
t   the image of the cover girls. "The pursuit of thinness is a
sis   way for women to compete with each other, a way that avoids
re?   being threatening to men" (Erens 155).

Unfortunately, this competition keeps women from seeking or obtaining the help they might otherwise get from close friends. Many bulimics keep their secret as guarded as they can. For example, my friend Kirstie did this. She waited for years before she told friends (and later, her family) that she was
page?
bulimic. At first, only her "barf buddy" (from Erens?) knew.

Kirstie seemed to have a good life with her family and
develop friends. [illustrate] But years later, she revealed to me that her greatest
too pride was when she discovered that she was now vomiting auto-
gross? matically after eating, without needing to use a finger or spoon. > *bet*
or *link*
OK? Erica was another friend who needed help. In fact, her sit- *her*
uation was so bad that she needed to go into a hospital. And
develop my friend Lynn would have died had she not entered the hospital when she did. She had to drop out of college immediately
and get prolonged therapy for herself and her family. As Erens
notes, "Family therapy considers the family itself, not the
daughter with the eating disorder, to be the 'patient.' Often,
the daughter has taken on the role of diverting attention from
unacknowledged conflicts within the family."

discuss & One problem Lynn had was conforming to her parents' expec-
link tations. Lynn decided to major in art even though her parents
better wanted her to get a degree in computer science so she would
have a job when she graduated. There was so much stress in that
house every time Lynn enrolled in another art class. Maybe she
felt that the only thing she could control in her life was how
thin she could get. > *link?*

The message to be thin comes from popular role models.
Actress Jane Fonda has sold many on the value of her "Work Out"
and has helped spawn "aerobic nervosa" (Erens 156). Many women
Put who admire her shape may not know that Fonda was once bulim-
earlier ic. And no one watching the televised spectacle of Prince
Charles and Princess Diana's wedding could have predicted that
years later, even after her death, the media would be discussing "Di's bulimia."

Not just the superstars but all models seem incredibly thin
lead in?
today. Wolf contends: "the weight of fashion models plummeted
to 23 percent below that of ordinary women, eating disorders
rose exponentially, and a mass neurosis was promoted that used
food and weight to strip women of that sense of control" (58).
It seems that many women--celebrities, models, and my friends--
have not escaped this curse. *OK for thesis?*

Revising the Thesis

Writing the draft helped Rachel realize the link between her friends' experiences and the influence of the media. She decided to revise her thesis to reflect this connection between the media and eating disorders.

> **New Working Thesis:** Magazine ads and commercials influence how women see themselves and how they behave.

Rachel felt that her material—both her personal experiences and readings—would support her new thesis. She also realized that this thesis helped her link the influence of the media to women's actions and behaviour. Rachel showed her thesis to her instructor, who suggested she apply the "So what?" response to this assertion:

> Ads and commercials influence women's self-perceptions.
> "So what?"
> Women try to look like the skinny models.
> "So what?"
> It's dangerous! Women are starving themselves.
> "So what?"
> The media has to change—they are responsible for programming women this way.

After thinking about this conversation with herself, Rachel revised her working thesis again:

> **Revised Working Thesis:** The media must be forced to stop programming young women to believe skeletal models are the ideal.

Rachel's revised thesis more accurately reflected her view that the media must change what they are doing to women. Her reference to the "skeletal models" would permit her to discuss her friends' experiences. A friend in her English class who knew her topic recommended she look at a book, *The Obsession: Reflections on the Tyranny of Slenderness* by Kim Chernin. Rachel found a page with pertinent information supporting her criticism of the media; she photocopied the page in case she wanted to use it later.

WRITING AN OUTLINE
Organizing to Highlight Key Points

Excellent ideas and interesting information can get lost or buried in a paper that is not carefully arranged and organized. After collecting your thoughts and materials during the prewriting exercises, you need to present these materials in a logical and effective order. You may decide to arrange your thesis to reflect your organization scheme and help you draft your essay.

Notice how Rachel's thesis forecasts her essay's key points:

> **Thesis:** The media must be forced to stop programming young women to believe skeletal models are the ideal.

Rachel's thesis suggests that she will first look at how the media is "programming" women, and then she will show how specific women become "skeletal" victims of the advertising that they see. Further, her assertion that the media "must be forced to stop" this practice invites her to propose a solution. Although Rachel devised a general scheme for organizing her paper, she knew she needed a more detailed outline.

To Outline or Not to Outline

By helping arrange your materials effectively, an **outline** can save you time and frustration. It can keep you from going around in circles and never arriving at your destination. Just as most drivers need a map to direct them through unfamiliar territory, most writers need outlines in order to draft their papers.

However, you probably have had the experience of being in a car without a map, when someone could intuit the right direction and get you where you needed to be. Some writers have that intuition and therefore find detailed outlines unnecessary, but these writers will still craft a strong thesis and rely on their intrinsic sense of organization to guide them as they write.

Most of us also have been in cars with drivers who were convinced they could manage without a map, but couldn't. All that aimless driving and backtracking should prove the value of maps and directions! Such indirection or "backtracking" in papers prompts instructors to note in the margins: "Order?" "Repetitious," "Organization needs work," "Relevant?" "Transition needed," or "Where is this going?" If you see these indicators on your papers, you know your intuition is failing you. Use an outline as an informal "map" of key points and ideas to present your ideas in a logical and effective order.

Ordering Ideas

You have a number of options for effective organization, and your purpose in writing will help you determine your arrangement. For example, Rachel's purpose was to convince readers that the media must stop promoting thinness as an ideal. Because this was the most important part of her argument, she saved it until the end, building support for it as she wrote. Rachel thus chose an emphatic arrangement scheme.

In an **emphatic** or **dramatic** organization, you arrange your material so that the most important, significant, worthy, or interesting material (for which you generally have the most information) is at the end of the paper. The virtue of this type of organization is that it permits you to end your paper in a dramatic way, using the most vital material or the bulk of your support for a concluding impression; a disadvantage you should keep in mind, though, is that readers may lose interest and give up reading before they have reached the end.

Some papers, in contrast, invite a **spatial** arrangement. Often used in description, this kind of arrangement permits you to present your points in a systematic movement through space. Wallace Stegner's essay "In Search of Whitemud" (p. 160) follows a route through his home town to the house he grew up in and the river behind it. An essay describing the obstacles disabled students may face as they tour your college would also lend itself to spatial arrangement. The essay could follow a disabled student's path from the bus stop or parking lot to the registrar's office, library, cafeteria, classrooms, and washrooms, noting the accessibility or inaccessibility of each space.

Because Stegner is describing a single event—his visit to the town—he also uses a **chronological** arrangement, describing the places he saw as a sequence of events in chronological order. Like Stegner, you may use a chronological arrangement to narrate a story, tell historical detail, or contrast past and present, but variations in the chronology of a story add interest, especially when you can incorporate the values of emphatic ordering as Stegner does.

After you have chosen a particular pattern of organization, you are ready to order your points further. Outlining can help.

An Informal Outline

Because Rachel found it was difficult to focus her initial draft and order her supporting details, she decided to write an **informal outline**: a list of points, written in a logical order, that she planned to cover in her essay. She knew this outline would simply be a personal guide to help her stay focused and to make sure she included all relevant materials. Therefore she didn't spend hours on the outline or concern herself with its wording.

Rachel wrote her working thesis first and then listed her key points in the order she planned to cover them. She knew that she might add other points or modify this order as she wrote the paper, but at least she would have a map to help keep her on track.

Thesis: The media must be forced to stop programming young women to believe skeletal models are the ideal.

Introduction
- Typical ad described: model in bikini
- Models as unhealthy and obsessed with being thin
- The horror: skinny models seem "right"
- Thesis

Anorexia and bulimia as epidemics
- Jane Fonda and her "Work Out"
- Princess Di, reputedly bulimic
- Women competing with each other (use Erens)

My friend Kirstie, bulimic
- Kept this secret; only her "barf buddy" and I knew
- Obsessed with food
- Out-patient counselling didn't really work
- I didn't know how to help her

My friend Erica, anorexic
- Enrolled in in-hospital program
- Shocked by number of older women in program
- Received nutritional and emotional help

My friend Lynn, anorexic, almost died
- Dropped out of college, enrolled in hospital
- Family received treatment too (use Erens)
- These friends felt programmed by the media to be thin
- Child models made to look like women (use Chernin)
- Model Christine Olman is only 12 (use Chernin)
- Ad photographer finds this deception disgusting
- Diet industry undermines women's control (use Wolf)

Conclusion
- A time for shock and action
- Refuse to support products that promote these images

In an informal outline like this, the ideas that you loosely group as "information blocks" may become paragraphs. In some cases, your grouping or block may end up being split into two or more paragraphs. This outline includes supporting details, but the topic sentences are not written out; therefore the outline is still rather sketchy. In Rachel's case, she didn't feel she needed more elaboration because she had already done some prewriting and initial drafting. Like Rachel, you may find that an outline will help you write stronger, more focused essays and ultimately save you time by organizing your ideas.

A Sentence Outline

Some instructors prefer that students write from a full-sentence outline. In a **sentence outline**, all the subtopics are complete sentences, so that the outline includes not only the topics the essay will cover, but the points that will be made about each topic.

The following sentence outline pertains to Rachel's final draft (p. 262). Notice how the various divisions (Roman numerals, capital letters, and Arabic numerals) are organized. Whenever you divide a point (A, B, and so on) into subpoints (1, 2, and so on), you must have more than one subpoint. For example, for every "1" you must have at least a "2" for support. If you lack material for a "2," you probably need to re-examine your material and either develop more support or incorporate this solitary subpoint into your initial heading.

As in an informal outline, the thesis belongs at the top. In the actual essay, however, it is usually integrated into the essay, often at the end of the introduction.

Thesis: The media must be forced to stop programming young women to believe skeletal models are the ideal.

I. <u>Introduction</u>: A typical ad is described and critiqued.
   A. Ads bombard us with images of bikini-clad models.
      1. Models sip diet drinks--only thin is in.
      2. Models are always surrounded by adoring males.
      3. Models stand 5'10" and wear a size 3.
   B. Ads don't reveal the dark reality of this image.
      1. Bony ribs and hunger pangs aren't so visible.
      2. Models pop "diet pills."
      3. Models may vomit their food to stay thin.
   C. Such models don't seem skinny; they seem "right."

II. <u>The problem</u>: Anorexia and bulimia plague college women.
   A. Anorexia and bulimia remain severe problems.
      1. Anorexia and bulimia are serious epidemics.
      2. Media attention has not helped.
      3. Women remain in bondage to their bodies.
   B. Even celebrities are victimized by eating disorders.
      1. Jane Fonda, once bulimic, pushes her "Work Out" videos.
      2. Erens describes "aerobic nervosa."
      3. Princess Di was once bulimic.

III. <u>The reasons</u>: Thin women have advantages.
   A. Lean shapes gain admiration and affirmation.
      1. Thin girls get all the compliments.
      2. They feel they have power over others.
   B. Women can compete without threatening men (Erens).

IV. <u>The illustrations</u>: Female friends seem obsessed with eating.
    A. Kirstie has a secret life with her "barf buddy."
       1. She had it all: boyfriend, looks, grades.
       2. Out-patient counselling didn't help.
    B. Erica met women over 30 who were still anorexic.
       1. She entered an in-hospital program during her break.
       2. She learned to handle emotions and food.
    C. Lynn nearly died before she got help.
       1. She left college for an in-hospital program.
       2. Her family joined in her therapy, too.

V. <u>The blame</u>: Advertisers program women to be thin.
    A. The ideal model today is the woman-child (Chernin).
       1. Christine Olman is only 12 but made to look sexy.
       2. Even photographers find this "disgusting."
    B. The message of our culture is girls must starve (Wolf).
       1. Anorexia is political damage done to women.
       2. Emaciated models were once shocking; now they're the norm.

VI. <u>The proposal</u>: We must pressure the media to stop perpetrating these deadly images of women.
    A. Send letters to producers and sponsors protesting ads.
       1. One letter represents many; 10 letters mean power.
       2. Models must reflect the diversity among women.
    B. Boycott products and shows that perpetrate "bodily harm."

Although a sentence outline takes more time and effort than an informal outline, the effort is seldom wasted because many of the sentences can be transferred into the essay itself. By ensuring an ordered presentation of material, outlining often strengthens an essay and ultimately saves you time.

WRITING A PARAGRAPH
Focusing the Paragraph

Once you have done some prewriting and have written a working thesis, you are ready to draft your essay. Your thesis has made an assertion you need to support, and the body of your essay consists of paragraphs that build this support. Each of those paragraphs may include a **topic sentence**—a sentence that expresses the central idea of that paragraph. The topic sentences emerge naturally from the groupings discovered in prewriting and from the subtopics of the outline.

Not all paragraphs in an essay will have a topic sentence, but all paragraphs must have a focus. The value of a topic sentence is analogous to the value of a thesis: both keep the writer and readers on track. Again, like the thesis, the topic sentence should be deliberately placed to help readers understand the focus of the paragraph.

Let's look at some short paragraphs that lack topic sentences.

Practising Writing Topic Sentences

The following paragraphs lack topic sentences. Practise writing your own topic sentence (the central idea) for each.

1. Registration lines extend beyond the walls of the gymnasium. Students wait in long lines to have their photographs taken for their student identification cards. The financial aid office assigns appointment times, but invariably lines form there, too. At the bookstore, students wait 20 minutes at a register, and since I don't have a bank account here yet, I need to go to a separate line to have a supervisor verify my out-of-province cheque. Even before classes begin, I'm exhausted.

2. A great amount of corn is used as feed for cattle, poultry, and hogs. Corn is also distilled into ethanol—a fuel for cars and a component in bourbon. Corn is made into a sweetener used in snacks and soft drinks and a thickener for foods and industrial products. A small amount of corn is consumed at dining tables in kernel or processed form.

Although each paragraph is clearly focused, each would profit from an explicit assertion. Compare your topic sentences with your classmates' assertions before reading the possibilities below. Although topic sentences may be placed anywhere in the paragraph, the topic sentences here seem to be most effective as the first or last sentence in these paragraphs.

Some possibilities for the first example include the following:

- Going back to school means going back to lines.
- Lines are an inevitability at my college.
- Lines are the worst aspect of returning to school.

Some possibilities for the second example are as follows:

- Corn is used for extraordinarily diverse purposes.
- Humans, animals, and machines profit from products made of corn.
- Corn is a remarkably useful grain.

In addition to evaluating your classmates' topic sentences, it may be worthwhile to evaluate the relative strengths of the sentences above. Which are stronger, and why?

Analysing an Effective Paragraph

In the following paragraph, notice how Rachel includes very good supporting details but lacks a topic sentence that expresses the central idea of the paragraph:

> During Kirstie's last year in high school, she was passing
> all her courses with honours and seeing one of the school's
> most popular guys. She jogged religiously every morning and
> every evening, and loved to ski with her family and beat
> her brothers down the slope. She seemed to crave the com-
> pliments she received from her brothers and their friends
> because of her good looks, and she received plenty! But
> years later, she revealed to me that her greatest pride at
> that time was when she discovered that she could vomit
> automatically after eating, without needing to use a fin-
> ger or spoon.

Rachel realized that she had not articulated the focus of her paragraph. She went back to clarify her point—that "Kirstie had it all." But Rachel also realized that her perception of her friend was an illusion. Rachel brought the two ideas together to form a topic sentence:

> Few of us ever suspected that Kirstie was in trouble,
> because she seemed to have it all.

Rachel asserts that Kirstie "seemed to have it all," but was really "in trouble." First Rachel shows specific examples of Kirstie's seemingly happy life: "passing all her courses with honours," "seeing one of the school's most popular guys," jogging "religiously," and skiing with her family. Then Rachel supports the fact that Kirstie was really a troubled young woman.

It is important that you use very specific examples to support your topic sentence. It would not have been enough for Rachel to claim that Kirstie had "everything" without showing specifically what that meant. She doesn't just mention that Kirstie had a boyfriend, but that he was a "one of the school's most popular guys." Kirstie doesn't simply have a close family; they go skiing together, and she spends time with her brothers' friends. Rachel's support is vivid, visual, and specific. Her shocking last sentence is graphic and unforgettable because it is so detailed in its description.

Unifying the Paragraph

This last sentence also contributes to paragraph coherence and unity. Rachel's opening sentence suggests Kirstie was in trouble, even though she did not appear to be. Subtle references to this trouble appear in the paragraph: Kirstie seems obsessed with exercise, and she craves compliments. Finally, after

enumerating Kirstie's apparent successes—what she *should* be proud of—
Rachel stuns readers with the irony of Kirstie's "greatest pride": her ability to
vomit automatically. Thus the concept of pride unites the paragraph. The key
word in the topic sentence, "seemed," predicts the illusions that permeate and
unite the paragraph. (For more on paragraph unity and coherence, see
pp. 268–76.)

Developing the Paragraph

When you have a topic sentence or controlling idea for a paragraph, it is
essential to support it with examples and any necessary explanation. Try to
anticipate questions or objections your readers may have; you can use the "So
what?" response here to make sure the significance of your idea is clear.
Support for your topic sentences can be drawn from your own ideas, experiences, and observations, as well as from your readings. If you are using
material that does not belong to you, you may find it easier to photocopy
pages so that you can mark comments directly on the source.

Practising Reading for Examples

One way to learn how to incorporate examples successfully into your own writing is
to read works by professional writers and pay close attention to how they use examples as support. Read one of the following essays and find the examples the author
offers to elaborate on the thesis or supplement a topic sentence:

a. "Here's to Family Feasting," p. 4

b. "The Shackles of Everyday Lies," p. 34

c. "The Beauty Myth," p. 57

d. "Love and Fear in the Age of AIDS," p. 75

e. "Being a Jew at Christmas," p. 94

USING SOURCES FOR SUPPORT
Using Photocopied Pages

Although in a formal research paper you may be required (or prefer) to use
note cards for recording data, for a short paper with few sources you may
choose to work from books or periodicals photocopied at the library. Here is
Rachel's photocopied excerpt from *The Obsession* by Kim Chernin. Notice the
quick notes she made as she read the photocopy:

Consider then the case of (Christine Olman,) one of the leading fashion models of our time. Her picture can be seen in *Vogue*, in *Bazaar*, in all the leading fashion magazines; she is photographed by the leading photographers, posing in the traditional seductive postures that sell consumer goods in our culture. Nothing unusual about all this we say? But then we look further. A newspaper article appears and then a television program, both talking about a new wave of young models. Suddenly, we are given a look behind the scenes, before the spotlights and cameras have begun to work. We are shown a room filled with people at work on the model, combing her, clothing her, making her up. But this time the labor of these illusion-makers is expended to its uttermost. For the model they are preparing is modeling clothes intended for mature women and she is twelve years old. This roomful of people is at work to transform a little girl into the illusion of a woman.

media →

12!

But what sort of figure in fact emerges when this labor of transformation has been accomplished? Is it a precociously full-bodied girl who actually looks like a mature woman? Not at all. What emerges is a preadolescent girl, with slender arms and shoulders, undeveloped breasts and hips and thighs, whose body has been covered in sexy clothes, whose face has been painted with a false allure and whose eyes imitate a sexuality she has, by her own confession, never experienced. And this, says fashion, is what a mature woman should attempt to look like.

anorexic

"It's disgusting," says the photographer who makes his livelihood recording the ideal form of a woman in this land. "It's not necessary," he says, "to have a twelve-year-old look. But that's the look that's selling right now. And Christine is one of the hottest young models around."

✳ *use!*

It might be redundant to spell out the implicit message in all this, but it can't hurt to state, with all the literalness possible in language, the lesson we are meant to learn as women studying the fashions deemed appropriate for us. According to fashion, large size, maturity, voluptuousness, massiveness, strength, and power are not permitted if we wish to conform to our culture's ideal. Our bodies, which have knowledge of life, must undo this fullness of knowing and make themselves look like the body of a precocious child if we wish to win the approval of our culture.

from The Obsession p. 94

Giving Credit and Avoiding Plagiarism

No matter what method you use to record supporting material from readings—note cards or photocopies—you must give proper credit for borrowed ideas and put quotation marks around the quoted words that you use in your paper. By including the author's name and a page number after every idea or quotation that she used, Rachel avoided **plagiarism**: using someone else's words or ideas without giving them credit.

Even if she paraphrased the material—put the ideas in her own words—Rachel knew she had to give the author credit for the idea or concept. Had she neglected to do this, for either a paraphrase from, or summary of, an author's work, she would have inadvertently plagiarized those ideas. (For more discussion of inadvertent plagiarism, see pp. 361–63.)

Rachel's instructor required her to use MLA documentation form. Therefore she gave credit either by citing the author's name before the material and then giving the source's page number in parentheses afterward, or by including both the author and page citations in parentheses immediately following the quotation. Two popularly used documentation forms (MLA and APA) are described in detail on pages 386–412.

Remember, giving credit means the following:

- using quotation marks around borrowed words or phrases
- acknowledging the source and page number of any borrowed words or paraphrased ideas immediately afterward
- including the complete source—author, title, and publishing information—in the list of works at the end of the paper.

Incorporating Quoted Material

Quoted material may support your ideas and may be a vital component of your paper. If the original material is particularly well written or precise, or if the material is bold or controversial, it makes sense to quote the author's words so you can examine them in detail.

All quoted material needs to be introduced in some way. It is a mistake to think that quoted material can stand on its own, no matter how incisive it is. Often, in fact, it is vital to introduce and also to comment on the quoted material. Let's look at an example from Rachel's final paper:

> Lynn's family became involved in her therapy, too. Erens emphasizes the importance of the family in any treatment plan: "Often, the daughter has taken on the role of diverting attention from unacknowledged conflicts within the family" (158). In therapy Lynn and her family gradually learned that her parents' "unacknowledged conflicts" over Lynn's choice of art as a major instead of computer science contributed to her stress. Therapy involved

acknowledging these internalized conflicts as well as seeing a relationship between her eating disorder and that stress.

In this passage, Rachel uses Lynn's experience to lead into the quoted material. The quotation provides an explanation of family dynamics that reflects Lynn's situation. Rather than letting the quotation stand by itself, Rachel uses it by discussing the connection between the quoted material and her friend's specific experience.

The "Sandwich"

Just as bread holds the contents of a sandwich together, Rachel uses the introduction and the discussion of the quotation to hold the quoted material together. The introduction, the top slice of bread, gives readers enough of a context for the quoted material to make sense. The quotation itself—the "meat" of the sandwich—comes next. Finally the sandwich needs that bottom slice of bread—a line or two of clarification or interpretation after the quotation. Rachel integrated key words from the quotation into her discussion. Depending on the quotation and the purpose of your paper, you may need to discuss, clarify, analyse, or interpret the quoted material. In all cases, your commentary after the quotation will demonstrate the importance of that quotation.

It may help you to visualize that the sandwich consists of the following:

- lead-in
- quotation
- analysis

The lead-in needs to be informative without duplicating the material in the quotation. In the following example from the page Rachel photocopied (p. 248), notice how she leads in to her quotation and then comments on it afterward without being redundant:

> In The Obsession, Kim Chernin claims that today's ideal model excludes many women: "According to fashion, large size, maturity, voluptuousness, massiveness, strength, and power are not permitted if we wish to conform to our culture's ideal" (94). Such conformity spells self-destruction and is threatening to reduce women to mere skeletons.

Practising Incorporating Quoted Material

1. Using the essay assigned for your next class, find a memorable line that you deem worthy of use in a paper. Write a lead-in to that line, quote it exactly, and

then analyse or comment on it so that readers would see the quotation's importance to the work as a whole.

2. Compare the following two uses of quoted material. Which one is better? In what specific ways? Rewrite the weaker example to make the quotation more effective.

    a. How can one see the world for what it really is, if one's vision is obscured by prejudgment? Heilbroner quotes Walter Lippmann as saying "'For the most part we do not first see, and then define; we define first, and then we see'" (130). Prejudging is a bad idea.

    b. In "The Battle over Gun Control: Marking the Divide Between Urban and Rural Canada," Charlie Angus compares the attitudes of Northerners toward guns with the attitudes of city-dwellers. Whereas a Northerner at a party might discuss with friends the relative merits of different types of guns, "Go to a party in the city and tell someone you own a gun. You might as well be saying you collect child pornography" (197). Angus suggests that part of the problem stems from urban dwellers' misunderstanding of the role of hunting in the lives of Northerners, whose "way of life isn't articulated or listened to in the power centres." Without better communication on both sides, the divisions will remain.

Paraphrasing

A **paraphrase** is an alternative to a direct quotation. When you paraphrase, you maintain the overall meaning of the original passage from another writer's work, but you restate the ideas in your own words. A paraphrase is an appropriate option for you to consider when the author's idea relates to your essay, but you want to use fewer direct quotations, or if the original material has complex wording or jargon that could be simplified for your readers. Like a quotation, a paraphrase requires that you credit the original author for the idea.

Choose a passage that is relevant to your essay and its thesis. When you are writing your paraphrase, emphasize the original passage's main points and avoid adding your own opinion or commentary. As well, remember to reword the original passage completely; otherwise, you will be plagiarizing. Even if it is unintentional, plagiarism is a serious academic offence. (For more on plagiarism, see pp. 361–63.)

Paraphrasing can be more challenging than it looks. It requires careful reading so you include all important information from the original passage. It also requires confidence on your part; you must be willing and able to convey the original meaning in your own words without depending on the original wording and sentence structure, and without inaccurate synonyms from a thesaurus.

Although both a paraphrase and a summary restate another's text in your own words, there is one important difference. A paraphrase is about the same length as the original passage; a summary condenses the main points of a longer passage or work into a considerably shorter version. (For more on how to write a summary, see pp. 347–51.)

Analysing Paraphrasing

Student Mario Silva was asked to write an essay responding to Moira Farr's "Welcome to FamilyValuesWorld!" (p. 9) by comparing or contrasting Farr's observations with experiences of his own. To begin, he wanted to paraphrase the main point of Farr's essay. Active reading led him to the following section of Farr's essay, where part of her focus is located:

> Yet it would be a shame if the only voices heard during the International Year of the Family were those of a vocal few who seek to deal with the apparent chaos by appropriating moral virtue and freeze-framing the family into desiccated stereotypes. There are good families and bad families, and sometimes the good ones look like nothing the planet's ever seen before and the bad ones live in lovely homes and have lots of RRSPs. (12)

Mario's paraphrase looked like this:

```
Despite the idealized stereotypes of family that a moral
minority insists are the norm, it's important to remember
that appearances can be deceiving; an unconventional fami-
ly might actually be "good," and an apparently "good" fam-
ily could be dysfunctional (Farr 12).
```

The primary meaning of Farr's original point has been retained: that stereotyped images of family can mislead us to believe that the quality of a family's life is indicated by its external appearance. Notice that some key words, such as "stereotype," "family," "moral," and "good" are necessarily repeated in the paraphrase. However, Mario changed other words and phrases, such as "few" to "minority," "bad" to "dysfunctional," and "like nothing the planet's ever known" to "unconventional." He also replaced the description of families who "live in lovely homes and have lots of RRSPs" with a more general phrase "apparently 'good.'"

You'll notice that Mario omitted references to the International Year of the Family and "the apparent chaos" here because they are not directly related to the meaning of this paraphrase. However, he decided that the ideas could be included in a sentence introducing the paraphrase:

Writing about the Canadian government's confusion over how to accurately define "family" during the Inter-national Year of the Family, author Moira Farr makes a claim that some people might find contentious (12).

This introductory sentence leads Mario's readers into the paraphrase and prepares them for the response to Farr's essay that is to follow.

Combining Paraphrase and Quotation

Most often, the material you use to support your points will be a blend of paraphrase and direct quotation. You can capture the essence of an author's idea by paraphrasing it, but there will be well-crafted phrases and key ideas that need to be quoted to convey the flavour of the original work. When you combine paraphrase and direct quotation, you still need to be careful to give credit for both.

Rachel decided to paraphrase most of the material that she photocopied at the library (see p. 248), but then she found a choice quotation that succinctly expressed what she wanted to say. Here is how Rachel used the material from her photocopied page:

In <u>The Obsession</u> Kim Chernin refers to the ideal model today as a "woman-child." She notes that one of the current top models, featured in <u>Vogue</u> and <u>Bazaar</u>, is twelve-year-old Christine Olman and that even professionals in the advertising industry are appalled by this: "'It's disgusting,' says the photographer who makes his livelihood recording the ideal form of a woman in this land. 'It's not necessary,' he says, 'to have a twelve-year-old look. But that's the look that's selling right now'" (Chernin 94).

Rachel introduces her quotation by referring to the title and author of this important study of women's eating habits. Rachel thus gains credibility by showing that she has consulted a respected writer on this subject. After identifying the source of her material, Rachel uses a key term from Chernin, "woman-child." This term must be quoted because it is from Chernin's book.

Rachel first summarizes Chernin's point about the current top models being children and then narrows her focus to the photographer, one of the "professionals" who is "appalled" by this practice. This serves as her lead-in to the specific quotation from the photographer in Chernin's text.

Practising Combining Paraphrase and Quotation

Practise incorporating choice quotations into your paraphrased versions of the following passages. In your lead-in, you may want to include the author's name and the source of the material. Compare your paraphrases with those written by your classmates. The page numbers given are from the essays as they appear in this textbook.

1. From "Men as Success Objects" (p. 50): "Because divorces led to a change in the pressures on women (should she *become* a doctor, marry a doctor, or have a career and marry a doctor?), that change became "news" and her new juggling act got attention in the media. Because the underlying pressures on men did not change (women still married men who earned more than they did), the pressure on men to succeed did not change, and, therefore, received no attention. With all the focus on discrimination against women, few understood the sexism directed against men."

2. From "The Beauty Myth" (p. 57): "And the unconscious hallucination grows ever more influential and pervasive because of what is now conscious market manipulation: powerful industries—the $33-billion-a-year diet industry, the $20-billion cosmetics industry, the $300-million cosmetic surgery industry, and the $7-billion pornography industry—have arisen from the capital made out of unconscious anxieties, and are in turn able, through their influence on mass culture, to use, stimulate, and reinforce the hallucination in a rising economic spiral."

3. From "Quebec" (p. 117): "The Canada I thought I belonged to was, believe it or not, an example to the rest of the world. We were a binational, bi-ethnic federal community, living proof that different races, different languages could live together within the framework of a single state. In my imaginings, I turned that dull but intricate contrivance, Canadian federalism, into a moral beacon to the whole benighted world. I had no idea, for example, that what for me was a family romance was, for the other partner, a loveless marriage. As for what came to be known as the First Nations, the native peoples, they didn't figure into my equation of the country at all."

4. From "Being a Jew at Christmas" (p. 94): "In one school, the music program last December consisted of learning carols and preparing to sing them in a church; there was no sense that this curriculum might be inappropriate for a Jewish child. It is more common, however, for there to be some effort at accommodation. Some teachers and principals limit Christmas observance to its secular aspects, but as we have seen this robs Christmas of most of its beauty and meaning without really solving the problem. An especially uncreative and insecure principal might take Christmas out of the school entirely, but this only makes people who do celebrate Christmas angry and deprives them of the legitimate right to have an important event in their lives recognized in the school."

As you work on refining your incorporation of paraphrased and quoted material, you also will be revising your essay. Rewriting is such a critical activity in preparing an essay that we have devoted the entire next chapter to various aspects of revision.

CHAPTER 8
Revising an Essay

REWRITING AND REWRITING

As we have already noted, rewriting may occur during all stages of the writing process, but it is essential that you give yourself time to reconsider your rough draft and make some necessary changes. Usually these changes involve sharpening the thesis, reorganizing ideas, developing sketchy points, adding new material for support, removing irrelevant material, improving transitions between ideas, strengthening the introduction and conclusion, and editing for word choice, mechanics, and spelling.

Thinking Critically for an Audience

Every phase of the writing process involves thinking critically—reasoning, analysing, and assessing so that your points are clear and your audience understands your points. The act of revision depends on good critical thinking.

Even during prewriting, which invites creativity and experimentation, you are evaluating your topic in relationship to your readers. For example, when you use clustering or listing techniques to generate ideas, you also discover ways to sort out your uncensored thoughts. It takes critical thinking on your part to group compatible ideas so your readers will understand the connections between them. In collaborative brainstorming, you have an opportunity to assess your ideas in light of your peers' views and to question others' assumptions as well as your own.

You use critical thinking to impose order on your material, and you assess your organizational plan to ascertain if your readers can follow your logic. Both logic and aesthetic considerations govern your judgment on which section of support belongs before another. Your decision to remove irrelevant details reflects your awareness that irrelevant points not only weaken your support but also confuse your readers.

The need for clarity and precision continues throughout drafting and revision. Even while you are revising, you continue to determine whether your depth of analysis has been sufficient and whether you have fully supported your assertions. You reconsider your focus, the logic of your organization, and the strength of your conclusion. As you edit, you scrutinize your word choice, sentence structure, grammar, and mechanics so that surface flaws do not frustrate your readers.

Thinking critically mandates that you recognize that your audience does not necessarily share your views. Thus the writing process forces you to challenge your own assertions and consider the readers' perspectives. Although it may appear that these stages of writing a paper involve a step-by-step process, all of these writing activities occur concurrently.

Revision may occur while you are drafting your paper, and editing may occur from the early drafts until the moment you hand the paper to your instructor. As noted in the last chapter, Rachel started revising her draft as soon as she had a printout from her computer. Thinking critically about her aim in writing this essay—to persuade readers of the media's role in fostering eating disorders—Rachel made substantial changes as she revised her rough draft.

Revising a Rough Draft

Working from her own evaluation of her rough draft (see pp. 237–38), Rachel rewrote her draft and, as required by the assignment, showed it to her instructor for comments. Rachel's paper had started out very rough, as most first drafts do, but she continued to develop her ideas and rearrange them. She felt that her second draft was stronger than the first but still could be improved. Her instructor helped her by identifying weak areas and suggesting improvements.

Example: Draft with Instructor's Comments

more striking or suggestive title?

Eating Disorders and the Media

except for?

[Bare, with the exception of] a bikini, the deep-
tanned model poses at a beach. <u>She is</u> surrounded by
five adoring guys. <u>She is</u> sipping a frothy drink
and inviting all of us to do the same . . . if we
want to get the guys . . . if we want to be the
envy of our friends. <u>She is</u> thin but tall. Viewers
don't notice the bony ribs, [how hungry she is,] and
all the "diet pills" she popped to stay that thin.

Tighten—
avoid repeating "she is"
How thin?
How tall?
not //

A picture doesn't reveal the vomit on her breath or ✔ *very graphic*
the spearmint gum used to mask it. In fact, our mag-
stronger verb?
azines and TV commercials <u>present</u> us with these ads
until such girls don't seem skinny any more--they
seem right. ✔ *clear point*

It doesn't seem to matter that, for some years
now, the media have been reporting the epidemic
diction (old-fashioned?)
among college girls of eating disorders, <u>anorexia</u>
briefly distinguish and <u>bulimia.</u> It doesn't seem to matter that the
Women's Movement has tried to free women from being
so caught up on the way they look. Despite the varied opportunities now available to women, "thirty-
three thousand American women told researchers that
they would rather lose ten to fifteen pounds than
achieve any other goal" (Wolf 57). In recent years,
actress Jane Fonda has sold many on the value of
her "Work Out" and has helped spawn "<u>aerobic ner-</u> *What is?*
<u>vosa</u>" (Erens 156). Many women who admire Jane
Fonda's shape may not know that Fonda was once
bulimic. And no one watching the televised spectacle of Prince Charles and Princess Diana's wedding
could have predicted that years later, even after
her death, the media would be discussing "Di's
bulimia." ⟩ *transition?*

necessary? Who wouldn't want to hear friends whisper, "What
a body! She really knows how to stay in shape!" or
"Don't you hate someone who looks that good?"
Either way, the sense of admiration and affirmation
specify what is wrong with this is clear. A thin girl has something that others
don't--and this gives her power and control. She *You need*
can make herself in the image of the cover girls. *Erens's name here or*
In "Bodily Harm," the author quotes Ruth Striegel- *in your () at end of*
Moore: "'The pursuit of thinness is a way for women *this line.*
to compete with each other, a way that avoids being
threatening to men'" (155).

Unfortunately, this competition keeps women from seeking or obtaining the help they might otherwise get from close friends. Many bulimics keep their secret as guarded as their mothers might have kept their sex life. My friend Kirstie ~~did this.~~ *tighten* ~~She~~ waited for years before she told friends (and later, her family) that she was bulimic. At first, only her "barf buddy" (Erens 155)--a cousin who had initially introduced her to this "great diet plan"-- knew. Gradually, their friendship revolved exclusively around this dark secret and was eroded by their unacknowledged rivalry. *awk* *split* *of* *subj/verb*

develop Few of us ever suspected Kirstie was in trouble: she seemed to have it all. ∧ But years later, *illustrate* she revealed to me that her greatest pride at that time was when she discovered that she was now vomiting automatically after eating, without needing to use a finger or spoon.

Even when Kirstie received out-patient counselling and her family thought she was "cured," she wasn't. ∧ *How could you tell?* For her it was either fasting or bingeing-- there was no in-between. As her friend, I often felt trapped between either respecting her confidence or letting some adult know so she might get the help she needed. While encouraging her to find other interests and to be open with her therapist, I felt quite helpless. I didn't want to betray her confidence and tell her parents, but I worried that my silence was betraying our friendship.) *transition?*

According to another friend, many young women continue to have obsessions with food for years afterwards. My friend Erica was shocked by the number of women over thirty ~~who were~~ in her hospital treatment program for anorexics. She admitted that *?* (this) is what made her decide she needed help while she was still in college. Unlike Kirstie, Erica decided she needed an in-hospital treatment program that cut her off from her old habits and helped her deal with her emotions and learn better nutritional habits. Erica managed to enter the program as soon as her finals were over and therefore she didn't jeopardize her schooling.) *good transition*

But some don't have that choice. My friend Lynn would have died had she not entered the hospital when she did. She had to drop out of college immediately and get prolonged therapy before she could be released to her parents and begin her recovery. Her family became involved in her therapy too. As Erens notes, "Family therapy considers the family itself, not the daughter with an eating disorder, to be the 'patient.' Often, the daughter has taken on the role of diverting attention from unacknowledged conflicts within the family" (158). In ther- *tighten this* apy, Lynn and her family gradually learned that her *discussion?* parents' "unacknowledged conflicts" over her mother's return to work and over Lynn's choice of art instead of computer science as a major contributed to Lynn's stress. Therapy involved acknowledging these internalized conflicts as well as examining the pressure to be thin.

effective link between personal experience & reading In addition to absorbing family conflicts, each of these friends felt that they were programmed by advertisers to accept and seek a lean look as the ideal. In <u>The Obsession</u> Kim Chernin refers to the ideal model today as a "woman-child." She points out that one of the current top models, featured in <u>Vogue</u> and <u>Bazaar</u>, is twelve-year-old Christine Olman and that even professionals in the advertising industry are appalled by this: "'It's disgusting,' says the photographer who makes his liveli- *ideal support for your thesis!*

hood recording the ideal form of a woman in this land. 'It's not necessary,' he says, 'to have a twelve-year-old look. But that's the look that's *better lead-in?* selling right now'" (Chernin 94). Chernin adds:

review "sandwich" "According to fashion, large size, maturity, voluptuousness, massiveness, strength, and power are not permitted if we wish to conform to our culture's ideal" (94). *comment or expand* → *Be specific. How?*

Such conformity threatens women today. It is ironic that this should happen at a time when women have more freedom to control their lives and their bodies. In "The Beauty Myth" Naomi Wolf notes that "the $33-billion-a-year diet industry" has undermined women's control over their bodies (63).

shorten quote or indent 10 spaces & delete " marks "Reproductive rights gave Western women control over our own bodies; the weight of fashion models plummeted to 23 percent below that of ordinary women, eating disorders rose exponentially, and a mass neurosis was promoted that used food and weight to strip women of that sense of control" (58).

It is time to let ourselves become shocked again. And then we need to move beyond shock and take action. Those who make the images will only change when those of us who support them stop buying products and tuning in on shows that continue to impose "bodily harm" on us. *Return to your opening image, if you can, and sharpen your thesis. Don't forget "Works Cited"*

Seeking Help for Revision

Every piece of writing can benefit from careful revision and editing. In fact, most professional writers ask at least one knowledgeable reader to comment on their work before they revise.

Unlike Rachel, however, many students do not have the opportunity to get their instructors' comments on their drafts. Some students therefore seek help from trained tutors who will provide feedback and make suggestions. Others ask a willing friend to comment on their essays. Some instructors show their students how to serve as "peer editors" who can critique each other's papers.

Whether trained or not, a good peer editor need not excel at grammar or be an excellent writer. An effective peer editor needs to be a careful reader, one who is sensitive to the writer's main point and supporting details. The resulting comments may not be a thorough as those Rachel received, but they can help the writer see the essay from another perspective.

A Checklist for Revising and Editing Papers

Whether you are revising your own essay or commenting on a classmate's, the following checklist should help:

- *Focus:* Is the thesis clear? Provocative? Convincing?
- *Support:* Are all points illustrated and supported?
- *Organization:* Is the order logical? Are there smooth transitions?
- *Paragraphs:* Is each paragraph well focused? Well developed?
- *Sentences:* Are all sentences coherent? Are the sentences varied in type?
- *Wording:* Are there any unnecessary or confusing words? Diction problems?
- *Introduction:* Is it captivating? Developed? Does it set the right tone?
- *Conclusion:* Is there a sense of resolution? Does it return to the thesis?
- *Style:* Does the essay read well? Are there any stumbling blocks?
- *Mechanics:* Correct punctuation? Grammar? Spelling?

These questions will help you determine the strengths of the essay, as well as any areas that need improvement. If you are editing a classmate's essay, you do not have to be able to correct the errors. A peer editor only needs to point out areas that seem flawed or confusing; it is then the writer's responsibility to use a handbook (like the one in this book) and correct the errors.

After studying the instructor's comments and corrections, Rachel continued modifying her draft. She rewrote certain phrases and paragraphs a number of times, shifted words and sentences, and found ways to "tighten" her prose by eliminating unnecessary words. Most of all, she tried to replace sluggish words with more precise and specific details. Notice below how her title gained more punch and how the opening is tighter and less repetitive. She also took the time to develop certain thoughts and paragraphs and to clarify her points. The following version is her final essay.

Example: Final Essay

Dieting Daze: No In-Between

Bare, except for a bikini, the deep-tanned model poses at a beach surrounded by five adoring and adorable guys. She is sipping a frothy diet drink and inviting us to do the same, if we want to get the guys and be the envy of our friends. She stands 5'10" and wears a size 3. Viewers don't notice the bony ribs, the hunger pangs, and the "diet pills" she popped to stay that thin. A picture doesn't reveal the vomit on her breath or the spearmint gum used to mask it. In fact, our magazines and TV commercials bombard us with these ads until such girls don't seem skinny any more--they seem right.

It doesn't seem to matter that, for years now, the media have been reporting the epidemic among young women of eating disorders, anorexia (self-starvation) and bulimia (binge and purge). It doesn't seem to matter that the women's movement has tried to free women from bondage to their bodies. Despite the varied opportunities now available to women, "thirty-three thousand American women told researchers that they would rather lose ten to fifteen pounds than achieve any other goal" (Wolf 57). In recent years, actress Jane Fonda has sold many on the value of her "Work Out" and has helped spawn "aerobic nervosa"--the excessive use of exercise to maintain an ideal weight (Erens 156). Many women who admire Jane Fonda's shape may not know that

Fonda was once bulimic. Certainly no one watching the televised spectacle of Prince Charles and Princess Diana's wedding could have predicted that years later, even after her death, the media would be discussing "Di's bulimia."

Such celebrities, and those females in the ads, are held up as models for all of us to mirror. A thin girl has something that others don't-- and this gives her power and control. She can make her body resemble a cover girl's. In "Bodily Harm," Pamela Erens quotes Ruth Striegel-Moore, Ph.D., director of Yale University's Eating Disorders Clinic: "'The pursuit of thinness is a way for women to compete with each other, a way that avoids being threatening to men'" (155). This competition threatens and endangers the women's well-being because it keeps women from seeking the help they might otherwise get from close friends.

In fact, many bulimics keep their secret as guarded as their mothers might have kept their sex lives. My friend Kirstie waited for years before she told friends (and later, her family) that she was bulimic. At first the only one who knew about her bulimia was her cousin who had initially introduced her to "this great diet plan." This cousin became Kirstie's "barf buddy" (Erens 155). Gradually, their friendship revolved exclusively around this dark secret and was eroded by their unacknowledged rivalry.

Few of us ever suspected Kirstie was in trouble, because she seemed to have it all. During her last year in high school, she was passing all her courses with honours and seeing one of the school's most popular guys. She jogged religiously every morning and every evening, and loved to ski with her family and beat her brothers down the slope. She seemed to crave the compliments she received from her brothers and their friends because of her good looks--and she received plenty! Years later, she revealed to me that her greatest pride at that time was when she discovered she could vomit automatically after eating, without needing to use a finger or spoon.

Even when Kirstie received out-patient counselling and her family thought she was "cured," she would still binge and purge at will. Every conversation with Kirstie inevitably returned to the subject of food--fasting or bingeing--there was no in-between. As her close friend, I often felt helpless, trapped between either respecting her confidence and keeping her dark secret or letting an adult know and perhaps getting her more help. I didn't want to betray her confidence and tell her parents, but I worried that my silence was betraying our friendship. Even though she moved out west and we gradually lost touch, I find myself wondering if Kirstie ever got the help she needed.

According to another friend, even mature women continue to have obsessions with food. My friend Erica was shocked by the number of women over thirty in her hospital treatment program for anorexics. She admitted that seeing these older women is what convinced her she needed help sooner rather than later. Unlike Kirstie, Erica decided she needed an in-hospital treatment program that cut her off from her old habits and helped her deal with her emotions and learn better nutritional habits. Erica managed to enter the program as soon as her final exams were over, and therefore she didn't jeopardize her schooling.

But some don't have that choice. My friend Lynn would have died had she not entered the hospital when she did. She had to drop out of college immediately and get prolonged therapy before she could be released to her parents and begin her recovery. Lynn's family became involved in her therapy, too. Erens emphasizes the importance of the family in any treatment plan: "Often, the daughter has taken on the role of diverting attention from unacknowledged conflicts within the family" (158). In therapy Lynn and her family gradually learned that her parents' "unacknowledged conflicts" over Lynn's choice of art as a major instead of computer science contributed to her stress. Therapy involved acknowledging these internalized conflicts as well as seeing a relationship between her eating disorder and that stress.

In addition to absorbing family conflicts, each of these friends felt that she was programmed by advertisers to accept a lean look as the ideal. In The Obsession Kim Chernin refers to the ideal model today as a "woman-child." She notes that one of the current top models, featured in Vogue and

Bazaar, is twelve-year-old Christine Olman and that
even professionals in the advertising industry are
appalled by this:

> 'It's disgusting,' says the photographer
> who makes his livelihood recording the
> ideal form of a woman in this land. 'It's
> not necessary,' he says, 'to have a
> twelve-year-old look. But that's the look
> that's selling right now.' (Chernin 94)

Chernin adds that this ideal excludes many women:
"According to fashion, large size, maturity, voluptuousness, massiveness, strength, and power are
not permitted if we wish to conform to our culture's ideal" (94). Such conformity spells self-
destruction and is threatening to reduce women to
mere skeletons.

It is ironic that this should happen at a time
when women have more freedom to control their lives
and their bodies. In "The Beauty Myth," Naomi Wolf
notes that the "$33-billion-a-year diet industry"
has undermined women's control over their bodies
(63). Within a generation,

> the weight of fashion models plummeted to
> 23 percent below that of ordinary women,
> eating disorders rose exponentially, and a
> mass neurosis was promoted that used food
> and weight to strip women of that sense of
> control." (58)

Stripped of control, many women feel compelled to
diet constantly; images of emaciated models that
were once so shocking have now become commonplace.

It is time to let ourselves become shocked
again--shocked by an epidemic that is destroying
women's lives. Then we need to move beyond shock
and take action. Insisting that our television
sponsors, magazines, and video artists stop perpetrating such deadly images of women is something we
can all do. A letter from one viewer carries clout
because stations often assume that each letter represents many who didn't take the time to write. Ten
letters from ten viewers wield even more power. It
is time to protest the images of bikini-clad models parading before us and demand images that
reflect the emotional and intellectual scope and
diversity among women in our society. With some of
our best and brightest dying among us, there is no
in-between position any more. Those who make the
images will only change when those of us who support them stop buying products and stop tuning in
on programs that continue to impose "bodily harm"
on us.

Works Cited

Bachmann, Susan, Melinda Barth, and Karen Golets Pancer. <u>Between Worlds: A Reader, Rhetoric, and Handbook</u>. Don Mills: Addison Wesley Longman, 1998.

Chernin, Kim. <u>The Obsession: Reflections on the Tyranny of Slenderness</u>. New York: Harper and Row, 1981.

Erens, Pamela. "Bodily Harm." Bachmann, Barth, and Golets Pancer 155-59.

Wolf, Naomi. "The Beauty Myth." Bachmann, Barth, and Golets Pancer 57-65.

REWRITING FOR COHERENCE

As you may have noticed, Rachel devoted considerable attention to the way she linked information and ideas within and between her paragraphs. The goal, of course, is to ensure that all parts of the paper cohere (that is, hold together).

To sustain your readers' interest and ensure their comprehension of your work, you will want to examine the drafts of your essays to see if your ideas hold together. Each idea should follow logically from the one before, and all of your points must support your focus. That logical connection must be clear to readers—not just to you, the writer of the essay, who may gloss over a link that is not obvious. All readers value clear connections between phrases, sentences, and paragraphs.

A Paragraph That Lacks Coherence

If the writing is carefully organized, readers will not stumble over irrelevant chunks of material or hesitate at unbridged gaps. Let's examine an incoherent paragraph:

> Students who drive to the college suffer indignities that
> students who live in residence can't imagine. Parking is
> expensive and lots are jammed. It is embarrassing to walk
> into class late. Often it takes over a half hour to find a
> spot. Commuters feel cut off from students who can return
> to their residence to eat or rest. Commuters seldom have a
> telephone number to get missed lecture notes. Study groups
> readily form in residence. Students living on campus have
> a sense of independence and freedom. Commuters who still
> live at home need to conform to old family rules and sched-
> ules, to say nothing of the need to baby-sit or cook for
> younger siblings and drive grandparents to the bank.

Although this paragraph has a clear focus and the ideas all belong, its coherence needs to be improved. You may sense that the information is out of order, the logic of the writer is not always obvious to readers, sentences do not flow together, words are repeated, and emphasis is lost.

In the pages that follow, you will learn how to correct paragraphs like the one above and to avoid these problems in your own writing. You will also have the opportunity to correct this paragraph.

Using Transitions

Even when material is carefully organized, well-chosen **transition** words and devices will help you connect sentences and paragraphs and will help your points cohere. You are familiar with most of these words and expressions. But if you have been trying for more than five minutes to find a specific word to connect two ideas or sentences in your essay, the list of particular terms shown below may be useful. The principal organizational or developmental method of your essay often will suggest the specific transition terms that will be useful to you for gaining unity in that essay. All will be useful at some time or another to help readers see the connections that you intend.

Transition Terms

- *time relationship:* first, second, before, then, next, in the meantime, meanwhile, finally, at last, eventually, later, afterwards, frequently, often, sometimes, occasionally, during, now, subsequently, concurrently
- *spatial relationship:* above, below, inside, outside, across, along, in front of, behind, beyond, there, here, in the distance, alongside, near, next to, close to, within
- *to contrast:* in contrast, on the contrary, on the other hand, still, however, yet, but, nevertheless, despite, even so, even though, whereas

- *to compare:* similarly, in the same way
- *to give examples or illustrations:* for example, for instance, to illustrate, to show, in particular, specifically, that is, in addition, moreover
- *to show a cause or an effect:* as a result, accordingly, therefore, then, because, so, thus, consequently, hence, since
- *to conclude or to summarize:* in conclusion, finally, in summary, evidently, clearly, of course, to sum up, therefore

Noticing Transitions

If you are writing a narrative, some part of your essay—if not the entire work—probably will be arranged chronologically. See if you can spot the **time signals** in the following excerpt from Bruce Halling's narrative "A Bully's Unjust Deserts" (p. 293).

> One day as I crossed the street, I heard something hit the ground near me. Then I felt the sting of a dirt clod hitting me in the head. I stopped and looked in the direction of Ricky's house, but I couldn't see where he was hiding. I brushed most of the dirt out of my hair and kept walking, trying to ignore being hit several more times before I made it home.

Can you see how "one day," "then," and "before" are transitions used to help readers connect the actions in the narrative?

With three or four of your classmates, read the next two paragraphs of this narrative (which appears in complete form on pp. 293–94) and note the transition words that have to do with the essay's chronological connections.

Chronological concepts need not be restricted to narratives. Look at this passage from "Earthbound . . . for Now" (p. 139) to see if you can identify the time concept around which this paragraph is structured:

> A few months ago I had a series of nightmares about one specific essay assignment. Every time my mind aired another instalment of this nightmare series, the due date crept closer. I still experience anxiety when it comes to English. After one of my English essay tests, for instance, I was ill for four days. I felt like someone had used my head as a football and set a new record for the number of field goals kicked in one game.

You may rightly perceive that "a few months ago," "every time," "still," and "after" are four terms that denote time within this paragraph. Read the rest of the essay to observe how Aspasia Kaplaneris uses time-relationship transitions to combine her narrative with the insights she gained after her learning disability was diagnosed.

Essays that include description often require terms that connect sentences or paragraphs in **spatial relationship**. Notice the spatial concepts that connect the descriptions in this passage from "In Search of Whitemud" (p. 160):

> My town used to be as bare as a picked bone, with no tree anywhere around it larger than a ten-foot willow or alder. Now it is a grove. My memory gropes uneasily, trying to establish itself among fifty-foot cottonwoods, lilac and honeysuckle hedges, and flower gardens. Searched for, plenty of familiarities are there: the Pastime Theatre, identical with the one that sits across Main Street from the firehouse in my mind; the lumber yard where we used to get cloth caps advertising De Laval Cream Separators; two or three hardware stores (a prairie wheat town specializes in hardware stores), though each one now has a lot full of farm machinery next to it; the hotel, just as it was rebuilt after the fire; the bank, now remodelled into the post office; the Presbyterian church, now United, and the *Leader* office, and the square brick prison of the old school, now with three smaller prisons added to it.

Author Wallace Stegner begins this passage with an overview of the town as a lush grove full of trees, and ends it with a more detailed description of the main street. The description of the place, as he sees it, is overlaid with the place as he remembers it. Buildings and spaces are presented to us in turn, as if our viewpoint is moving in tandem with his, some described in terms of their relationship to others: the theatre across from the firehall and hardware stores next to lots displaying farm machinery.

Using Transitions Effectively

Read some of the essays in Part 1 and look for the ways the authors use transition words. When revising your own essays, however, remember that the placement of the transition words listed on pages 269–70 will seem contrived if you use them too often in any one essay, or if you use the same ones in every essay you write. You also have other, more subtle ways to gain connections between sentences and paragraphs in your essays.

Parallel Constructions

If you pay attention to the way you use grammatically similar forms, called **parallel constructions**, in your sentences, you can increase coherence in your writing. (For more on parallel constructions and faulty parallelism, see pp. 442–43.)

In the essay "On Jobs and Humility" (p. 182), describing what it feels like to be unemployed, Lisa Gregoire uses many parallel constructions to connect her ideas. Consider this excerpt from her essay:

> We fill our résumés with valedictory honours, awesome volunteer records and flawless academic performances. We are not slackers. We are not asking for something for nothing. And we are no longer young.

The parallel constructions here include the phrases "valedictory honours," "awesome volunteer records," and "flawless academic performances," and the repetition of "we" followed by negative verb forms: "We are not slackers," "We are not asking for something for nothing," and "we are no longer young."

Key Word Repetition

In some cases you may want to repeat an important word, one that emphasizes the point that you are making. Judicious repetition of this word will reinforce the focus point of your paragraph and essay.

In the concluding paragraph of her essay, Gregoire emphasizes what seven months of joblessness taught her by repeating the word "learned":

> I learned a few things sitting in that lonely section. I learned how to cook potatoes 10 different ways. I learned how to mend clothes. And I learned how to appreciate small wonders. Elders who've lived through lean times might say it was good for me. And you know, they're right. I learned that we're all one paycheque from poverty. And I accept my newfound job as a blessing. And I am humbled.

Notice that the repetition of "learned" is very deliberate and strategic, so that readers will come away from the essay with the idea of learning from adversity resonating in their minds.

Look for other examples of both parallelism and key word repetition in Gregoire's essay.

Synonyms or Key Word Substitutions

Synonyms are words that have the same or similar meanings, and you can connect ideas or concepts within your paragraphs and throughout your essay by skilfully using synonyms—or key word substitutions—to emphasize your focus. For example, notice how Sean Kelly in "Discovering My Native

Identity" (p. 101) uses words with similar meanings to describe his white friend, and other synonyms to describe himself in contrast to his friend:

> I came to realize that the problem was that I looked different from the white people around me. Once, standing before a mirror with a friend, I noticed how his wavy, blond hair hung loosely over his smooth, pinkish skin, while my hair was stiff, in thick, combed clumps above my tan skin. Around my deep black eyes was a darkness created by my high cheekbones that gave me an almost brooding look. If it were possible to symbolize our differences, my friend would have been warmth and brightness; I would have been anger and darkness. And not dark like James Dean, but more like a thug in an alley.

Rather than saying his eyes are "dark," Kelly uses the synonym "black" to describe their colour; as well, he chooses the synonym "brooding" as a substitute for the "darkness" of his look, and later "anger" as a replacement word to indicate a possible source of his "brooding" appearance. These variations on the meaning of the "darkness" of his looks combine to create an image of a person darker in both physical appearance than his fair-haired, fair-skinned friend. Furthermore, Kelly is saying, his darker physical appearance could well contribute to the perception of whites that he is somehow a threatening presence of "anger and darkness," who is "like a thug in an alley." This perception is all the more pronounced given the contrasting presence of his white friend radiating "warmth and brightness."

Pronouns

Pronouns, words substituting for nouns that clearly precede or follow them, can effectively connect parts of a paragraph. By prompting readers to mentally supply the missing noun or see the relationship the pronouns imply, the writer also has a way to engage readers. To emphasize the contrast in attitudes between Gambian women and Canadian women, Catherine Pigott, in "Adding Weight to an Image of Beauty" (p. 152), uses pronoun substitutions in this passage about her fitness regime after she returns home from Africa:

> I joined the club. Just a few weeks after I had worn a *lappa* and scooped up rice with my hands, I was climbing into pink leotards and aerobics shoes. The instructor told me that I had to set fitness goals and "weigh in" after my workouts. There were mirrors on the walls and I could see women watching themselves. I sensed that even the loveliest among them felt they were somehow flawed. As the aerobics instructor barked out commands for arm lifts and leg

lifts, I pictured Gambian women pounding millet and dancing in a circle with their arms raised high. I do not mean to romanticize their rock-hard lives, but we were hardly to be envied as we ran like fools between two walls to the tiresome beat of synthesized music.

In the paragraph above, the pronouns *I, me,* and *my* contrast the author with the pronouns *themselves, them,* and *they* to emphasize the initial separation the author feels between herself and the other women in the fitness class. When Pigott's focus moves to the Gambian women, however, the pronoun *their* reflects this change; "they" are the Gambian women, whereas Pigott and her Canadian counterparts become "we." With this final move to the pronoun *we,* Pigott indicates that she is now more closely aligned with the Canadian women and their quest to keep in shape. Her presence in the gym means she has returned to the Canadian way of seeing beauty.

Transitions Between Paragraphs

Key word repetition is also one important way to achieve the important goal of connection between paragraphs. While your readers may be able to follow your movement and sustain your ideas within a paragraph, coherence within your essay as a whole requires transition sentences and, in longer essays, entire paragraphs of transition.

One device that works well is to pick up a key concept or word from the end of the earlier paragraph and use it toward the beginning of the new paragraph. Read the following excerpt from Aspasia Kaplaneris's essay (pp. 139–40). What moves readers between paragraphs?

> Somehow I was still able to do well enough at school. My teachers never formally tested my understanding of grammar, and none of them paid much attention to my difficulties. They just dismissed me as an odd child.
>
> But their dismissals had a negative effect on me. You see, I had sensed for a long time that I had some form of problem that the other children didn't. When my teachers dismissed me, though, they made me question my own senses. I began to wonder, "Am I wrong? Am I beginning to lose my mind? Perhaps I am actually stupid and worthless."

By repeating the key word "dismissed" and the concept of "dismissal," the author is able to connect the ideas in the earlier paragraph (the way she was rejected by her teachers) to her new material in the next paragraph (the terrible effect this rejection had on her self-esteem).

Although all paragraphs in your essay should hold together, the device of repeating key words should not be overused or strained. If your "technique" is perceived as a formula, that awareness can irritate your readers. For example, let's imagine you have written a paragraph that ended with the sentence "These are rationalizations, not reasons." Avoid merely repeating the exact phrasing, like "Although these are rationalizations, not reasons," at the start of your next paragraph. Instead, you might want to begin with something like this: "Such rationalizations are understandable if one considers...." With conscious practice of the technique, you'll improve your skills.

Avoiding Gaps

Transition terms and devices will help you achieve coherence in your work, but they can't fill in for gaps in logic—sentences or paragraphs that just don't go together, or that are out of order. You can't expect your readers to move from one point to another if you have failed to write into your work the sense that you perceive. For example, in the incoherent paragraph on page 269, the writer places the following two sentences together:

```
Parking is expensive and lots are jammed. It is embarrass-
ing to walk into class late.
```

In the writer's mind, there is a logical connection between these two thoughts. That link is not at all apparent to readers, and a transition term like *and* or *therefore* will not bridge that gap. The writer must express the connection between the two sentences so there is no gap and no need for readers to invent their own bridge.

Practising Coherence

In small groups, return to the incoherent paragraph on page 269 and discuss its problems. As a group, rewrite the paragraph so that all information is included, but also so that the ideas are logically linked. As you fill in the gaps in logic, practise using the transition terms and devices that will ensure coherence in this paragraph. Here is one solution to improve the coherence of the paragraph.

> Students who drive to the college suffer indignities that residence students can't imagine. Even before students who commute by car get to classes, they have a problem. Parking on campus is expensive and hard to find because the lots are jammed. Often it takes over half an hour to find a spot. By then class has started, and it is embarrassing to walk into class late. Commuters also feel

cut off from those students who can return to the residence to eat or rest. While study groups readily form in residence, commuting students seldom have even a telephone number to get missed lecture notes. Students living on campus have a sense of independence and freedom from their families, but if student commuters are still living at home, they need to conform to old family rules and schedules. Often the indignities of living at home include doing those tasks the students did through high school, like baby-sitting or cooking for younger siblings, or driving grandparents to the bank.

In addition to considering the links between ideas in the body of your essay, you will want to refine your introduction and conclusion to frame your essay and to achieve coherence.

WRITING INTRODUCTIONS
Introductions and Audience

Typically, a strong **introduction** "hooks" readers and then expands on the hook while building to the thesis statement, which often concludes the introduction. The introduction to an essay has two obligations: to attract readers to the subject of the essay and to establish for readers the particular focus of the writer. The focus of the writer—the assertion he or she is making about a limited subject—is contained in the thesis statement. The thesis statement does not have to be at the end of the introduction, but that is often a natural place for it because both the writer and readers are then immediately aware of the key assertion that will be supported in the essay. The concept of the thesis is discussed in more detail on pages 228–39.

If you have not discovered in your prewriting activities a useful way to lead to your thesis, you may find the ideas below helpful. Some subjects will seem best introduced by one type of introduction rather than another, and it's a good idea to keep your audience and purpose in mind as you draft possible "hooks" for your topic. Clearly, readers would be confused by, and find inappropriate, an amusing anecdote used as an introduction to a study of AIDS, unemployment, or infant mortality in Third World countries. Your introduction should anticipate the intention and tone of the paper that will follow.

Often you will have a working thesis before you write your first draft, but the idea for your introduction—the first words in the essay—will not come until you have worked extensively with your material. You may find that if you deliberately vary your introductions, perhaps trying each of the methods suggested here, you will not be intimidated by that blank sheet of paper or empty computer screen each time you start to write.

Types of Introductions

Reference or Direct Quotation

An essay that begins with the words of another person, especially a well-known person, should help convince your readers that you are a prepared writer who has researched others' views on the subject and found relevance in their words. In "Work, Labour, Play" (p. 170), W.H. Auden credits the twentieth-century philosopher Hannah Arendt with being the first person to distinguish between work and labour. The author of "Bodily Harm" (p. 155), Pamela Erens, begins with a direct quotation indicating how the media influenced one young woman to take up bulimia as a form of weight control:

> "Before I'd even heard of bulimia," said Gloria, "I happened to read an article in *People* magazine on Cherry Boone—how she'd used laxatives and vomiting to control her weight. I thought: Wow, what a great idea! I was sure that I would never lose control of my habit."

Description

Whether it presents a vivid picture of nature or of a person, an introduction using description can appeal to the imagination and the senses simultaneously. Wallace Stegner's introduction to "In Search of Whitemud" (p. 160) describes a cinematic overview of the approach to his home town. In the following paragraph from "Making Big Deals out of Little Deals" (p. 72), notice how Lauren Griffin's description of Joe also conveys her less than complimentary first impression of him:

> Joe is a flirt. The first time I met him he was driving a truck as big and loud as he was, with his reflector sunglasses, imposing frame and baseball cap emblazoned with the logo of a heavy diesel equipment company. If I had had any qualms about moving up north, it was because I had imagined I would end up meeting men like Joe.

Question

In most cases, your job as a writer is to answer your readers' questions about your topic, rather than to ask writer-imposed questions—such as "What is capital punishment?"—and expect your readers to furnish the answers. Using a simple question like this one may help you, the writer, focus and develop your topic during the prewriting and drafting stages; nevertheless, you should remove it from your draft as you revise. Readers find such questions irritating because they seem uninspired or contrived.

However, a thought-provoking question that may never have occurred to your readers until now can be a very effective hook. Notice your own interest as you read the questions in the introduction to Robert L. Heilbroner's essay "Don't Let Stereotypes Warp Your Judgments" (p. 128):

> Is a girl called Gloria apt to be better-looking than one called Bertha? Are criminals more likely to be dark than blond? Can you tell a good deal about someone's personality from hearing his voice briefly over the phone? Can a person's nationality be pretty accurately guessed from his photograph? Does the fact that someone wears glasses imply that he is intelligent?

Anecdote or Illustration

Just as listeners look up attentively when a speaker begins a speech with a story, all readers are engaged by an anecdote. Judith Timson opens "Here's to Family Feasting" (p. 4) with brief story about one of her family's most satisfying gatherings. Sometimes, if the story opens dramatically, the involvement of readers is assured. In Michael Ignatieff's anecdote about participating in a childhood raid against Francophone kids, in "Quebec" (p. 117), the author initially misleads his readers into thinking he actually fought against aggressive French bullies. Ignatieff later revokes this memory when, as an adult, he realizes that he had never even met any Québécois when he was growing up in Ottawa. The anecdote becomes all the more powerful when we see how his belief in fictitious raids had shaped his perceptions:

> There were Frenchies hiding in the cemetery, we were sure of that. They were tough Catholic kids and they had slingshots. We all knew they were there, hiding behind the gravestones, waiting to get us. The cemetery was up on the hill above Juliana Road, where we lived, and I knew that I shouldn't ever go up there on my bike alone. Everyone at school knew that they pulled kids off their bikes and rode away on their wheels. They were bad kids, it was common knowledge.

Definition

Often the definition of a term is a necessary element of an essay, and a definition may interest readers in the subject (if the writer does not resort to that boring and clichéd opener, "According to *Webster's Dictionary...*"). Brenda Austin-Smith opens her essay "The Internet and Gender" with her definition of what the Internet is (p. 67), using the metaphor of a "forum" instead of its more common definition, the information highway, for readers who may be familiar with the term:

> Considered as a social arena or forum rather than a highway, the Internet is an electronic space in which people using computers gather to send and receive information as varied as recipes, articles, virtual movies, erotica, and Seinfeld trivia.

Deliberate Contradiction

Sometimes the writer can start a paper with a view or statement that will be contradicted or contrasted with the subject matter of the essay. Madeleine Gagnon, in her essay "Respect and Balance in Our 'Tribe'" (p. 6), does just that in her introductory paragraph:

> According to a sociological theory long current in Quebec and Canada, traditional French-Canadian society was—and to a large extent is—a matriarchy. The tenets of this theory are taken to be self-evident: the men of my people were weak and absent from the family unit, dominated by women, even subjugated under their rule, which was no less implacable for being insidious.

Statistic or Startling Fact or Idea

An essay that starts with a dramatic statistic or idea engages readers at once. Notice how the following introduction from Charlie Angus's "The Battle over Gun Control" (p. 197) uses a dramatic comparison to child pornography to draw readers into his discussion of gun control:

> Go to a party in Northern Ontario and mention guns. Chances are it will engage a lively discussion, not on what to do about them, but on what kind of brand you have. Men, women, young and old, can talk about the merits of the 410, the 30-30, and the 30 odd six. Go to a party in the city and tell someone you own a gun. You might as well be saying you collect child pornography.

Mixture of Methods

Many enticing introductions will combine the approaches described above. For example, Brenda Austin-Smith asks questions about the nature of power and the Internet at the end of her introductory paragraph in "The Internet and Gender" mentioned above. Like many other articles written for magazines, "Love and Fear in the Age of AIDS" (p. 75) combines introduction strategies with facts to create an introduction that both presents background information and captures readers' attention. Writer John DeMont begins with description, moves to a direct quotation from Trudy Parsons, presents an anecdote about how she felt when she returned to her old high school to give a talk on AIDS, and concludes with a pair of potentially surprising facts: she is HIV-positive, and she worries that her family will be judged by her neighbours because of her:

> The car speeds west along the Trans-Canada Highway as snowflakes swirl from an aluminum-coloured sky. "The worst thing is going home," Trudy Parsons says, huddled in the front passenger's seat, wearing a baggy men's overcoat. As the car nears Bay Roberts, the Newfoundland outport 100 kilometres west of St. John's where she spent her teen years, Parsons, now 22, recalls the wave of panic she felt when she returned to her old high school a year ago. There, in a crowded classroom, her voice quavered as she warned teenagers about the danger of HIV, which is believed to cause acquired immune deficiency syndrome (AIDS); Parsons tested positive for the virus in November, 1991. Now, with another room full of students waiting at her old school, her anxiety again deepens. "I grew up with these people," says Parsons, who works full time for the Newfoundland AIDS Committee. "My family lives out there—and I fear that they will be judged because of a mistake that I made."

A Few Final Words on Introductions

In your prewriting activities, if you have not found a way to lead your readers into your paper, try one of the types of introductions defined and exemplified here. Those first few words can attract readers, set the tone for your essay, and predict the focus of your study. Ideally, the introduction will also anticipate your conclusion.

WRITING CONCLUSIONS

The **conclusion** of an essay should bring closure for readers, a feeling of completion or satisfaction. Ideally, the conclusion will fit like the lid on a box. You might return to your introduction and thesis, select key images or phrases that you used, and reflect them in your conclusion. This return to the start of the paper assures your readers that all aspects of your assertion have been discussed in the essay. An effective conclusion is one that echoes the tone of the introduction without merely repeating the exact words of the thesis (a type of closure that is contrived and dull). Although your conclusion may be weakened by "tacking on" a new topic or concept without sufficient explanation and development, you may want to suggest that there is some broader issue to think about, or some additional goal that might be achieved if the situation you have discussed were satisfied.

For his conclusion to the essay "Don't Let Stereotypes Warp Your Judgments" (p. 131), Robert L. Heilbroner returns to the images of the pictures in our mind, the ideas stirred by the questions he uses in his introduction:

> Most of the time, when we type-cast the world, we are not in fact generalizing about people at all. We are only revealing the embarrassing facts about the pictures that hang in the gallery of stereotypes in our own heads.

Another effective conclusion appears in Kerry Banks's essay, "As a Dad, Will I Do Right by My Daughter?" (p. 41). In the essay, Banks explores the impact fathering can have on a daughter's self-image and wonders about what kind of father he will be to his infant daughter. His concluding paragraph begins with a light-hearted prediction of what might be in store for him, an affirmation that he is willing to learn, and a description of the pleasures of fatherhood to come. Finally, he brings readers full-circle by repeating his daughter's first word, the focus of the anecdote he used in the essay's introduction:

> I don't know yet how I will deal with the familiar crises of fatherhood, such as when Riley begins dating boys with green hair and nose rings. But there is time to learn, and I will need to trust my instincts. For now, I am content simply to share the extraordinary discoveries of Riley's young life—her awe at seeing the night stars for the first time, the giddy tingle of walking barefoot on a freshly mown lawn, the magical spell of a street musician's guitar. For now, just being Da-Da is enough.

The student papers in this book also show effective techniques in their conclusions. Rachel Krell, who wrote the essay on eating disorders (p. 262), was advised by her instructor to strengthen the conclusion of her rough draft (p. 260) by returning to the images and key words of her introduction. Rachel did this in her final paper. She also was able to echo the title of a source that she used in her essay. The part of her conclusion that mirrors her introduction looks like this:

It is time to protest the images of bikini-clad models parading before us and demand images that reflect the emotional and intellectual scope and diversity among women in our society. With some of our best and brightest dying among us, there is no in-between position any more. Those who make the images will only change when those of us who support them stop buying products and stop tuning in on programs that continue to impose "bodily harm" on us.

Final Tips for Writing Conclusions

To draft a good conclusion, try the following:

- Return to your thesis and restate it in different words. Incorporate that restatement into your conclusion.
- Examine your introduction and try to incorporate the key words, images, description, anecdote, or response to the question into your conclusion.
- Consider your readers: have you brought a sense of significant closure to your topic?

You have been considering your readers and the purpose of your paper throughout as you have rewritten your rough drafts, verified the logic of your organization, strengthened the introduction and conclusion, and edited for surface errors. These essential revision strategies can help you with any paper that you write.

In the next chapter of the Rhetoric, we will show you ways to develop essays using specific methods or modes. Whether you are assigned a particular type of essay or you choose to use these methods of development within your papers, you will find the instructions, illustrations, and exercises pertinent to a variety of writing assignments.

CHAPTER 9
Methods for Developing Essays

Y our instructor may ask you to write a paper using a particular method of development for presenting your support. For example, he or she may ask you to write a narrative, or a comparison and contrast study. In this chapter, we isolate and discuss the most common strategies for developing essays, also known as **rhetorical modes**, to help you understand how to use these strategies effectively. However, we do not mean to suggest that all paper topics will fit precisely into one of these categories. In fact, most essay writers, including those whose works are included in the Reader, combine strategies to achieve their purpose.

Consider student writer Rachel Krell's essay "Dieting Daze," which we discussed in Chapters 7 and 8. Rachel incorporates several strategies in order to argue her point and defend her thesis—that we must stop the media from perpetuating images of skeletal models as the ideal. Since most essays are developed with combined modes, we will begin this chapter with an analysis of Rachel's multiple strategies. Please review her essay "Dieting Daze" (p. 262) before you read the commentary below.

COMBINING MULTIPLE STRATEGIES

If you read "Dieting Daze" to determine what kinds of support Rachel used, you may have noticed that she combines narration, definition, description, comparison–contrast, and research in a paper that analyses a problem and argues for a change. Such multiple approaches are effective complements, and together they help the writer thoroughly address the topic.

Analysing Mixed Methods

Introducing the Topic with Description and Contrast

A writer's first obligation is to attract readers' attention. Rachel begins by **describing** the familiar media image of a skinny model in a bikini surrounded by attractive men, the very image Rachel wants her readers to question. She **contrasts** this image with what may not be so apparent in the picture: "the bony ribs, the hunger pangs, and the 'diet pills,'" and "the vomit on her breath." The opening paragraph sets out the problem to be analysed: the fact that, for women, a skeletal body shape is coming to be perceived as the ideal.

Audience Awareness: Definition and Research

In our discussion of audience (pp. 221–27), we noted that the writer must be aware of readers' responses to the text. Rachel recognizes that her readers may be unfamiliar with certain terms, so she includes brief **definitions** of *anorexia, bulimia,* and *aerobic nervosa.* On the other hand, her audience is possibly very familiar with two celebrities who struggled with bulimia; by using Jane Fonda and Diana, the Princess of Wales, Rachel gives concrete **examples** of women in the public eye who had succumbed to the pressure of being thin, and reinforces the fact that eating disorders are often hidden.

Rachel also includes a **statistic** that may surprise some readers: despite the many opportunities open to women today, the primary goal for many is a fifteen-pound weight loss. In addition, Rachel **cites** one expert on eating disorders, who suggests that weight has become an area of competition for many women that does not threaten men, a thought-provoking feature of the issue that Rachel's readers may want to consider.

Analysing the Problem with Narration, Comparison, and Research

Rachel's development depends on three **narratives**, one for each of her three friends who have struggled to overcome eating disorders. Notice how Rachel supplements the stories, such as Lynn's family's involvement in her therapy, with related **citations** from other writers. Notice too how Rachel's description of Kirstie as someone who "seemed to have it all" invites a **comparison** with the image of the model presented in the introduction. The narratives illustrate the destructiveness of eating disorders and lend support to Rachel's thesis that the media contribute to the problem because "each of these friends felt that she was programmed by advertisers to accept a lean look as the ideal."

Using Sources to Help an Argument

To further convince her readers of the media's role in creating and idealizing thinness, Rachel turns to writer Kim Chernin's example of a twelve-year-old working as a popular model for high-fashion magazines. Rachel also refers to Naomi Wolf's contention that, over only a few years, "the weight of fashion models plummeted to 23 percent below that of ordinary women, eating disorders rose exponentially, and a mass neurosis was promoted that used food and weight to strip women of that sense of control."

Concluding the Argument: More Audience Awareness

Having analysed the possible causes of eating disorders and the problems they create, Rachel concludes with an explicit call to action. She advises readers who are outraged at the "epidemic that is destroying women's lives" to write a letter of protest to the creators of the images that are dictating the lives of too many women. Finally, Rachel reminds her readers that refusing to buy products or view programs that perpetuate the skeletal as the ideal can send a powerful message to the source of the problem.

Why This Analysis?

The purpose of this analysis of "Dieting Daze" is to encourage you to recognize the multiple modes and devices that writers can use to engage and persuade their readers. This recognition can have a positive effect on your own writing. By practising the single-development assignments given in the writing topics and described in the Rhetoric—description, narration, definition, classification, cause and effect, comparison and contrast, argument, analysis, and summary—you will learn to employ multiple methods confidently to write an engaging and convincing paper.

DESCRIPTION

Although **description** is often considered to be a synonym for *explaining*, description as a method of development in an essay uses words to construct a "sensory picture" for readers to imagine. Descriptive writing depends on visual images to shape readers' perceptions, but can also include the sounds, scents, tastes, and tactile qualities associated with a person, event, place, or object. While fiction writers depend on description to ensure that readers will see in their mind's eye the setting or characters of a story or novel, essay writers often use description as well.

When to Use Description

Use description if your purpose requires your readers to visualize a person, event, place, or object. A description can be as objective as a snapshot, or as subjective as a painting, depending on your purpose and audience. A police report of a minor car-accident scene must be objective, listing the make, model, and colour of the cars involved, the time of day and weather conditions at the time of the accident, the intersection where the accident occurred, the extent and type of damage to each car, and the fact that neither driver was injured. On the other hand, in an essay in which you are exploring the closeness your family feels at your old but beloved summer cottage, you can be more subjective and impressionistic in your description of the building and its surroundings. You can certainly describe the sloping floors, faded curtains, and leaky roof objectively. However, your readers will see your cottage the way you see it if the words you choose for your description convey not only the details but some of your warm feelings for the place. Writing about the sloping linoleum floors that you and your dad loved to use for toy car races, the faded blue curtains that your mother let you sew as your first grown-up sewing project, and the leaky roof in the bedrooms that forced your family to stage an impromptu camp-out in the kitchen one stormy night will show your readers why the place holds so many happy memories.

How to Write a Description

Once you have established your purpose for the description, brainstorm to list as many details as you can as a basis for the final draft, a word-picture your readers can easily imagine. Don't feel you must limit yourself to images alone, though. We have been explaining description as a verbal picture, but you can include any detail that is experienced through the five senses: sight, hearing, touch, taste, and smell. Using sensory details will help you *show* rather than *tell* readers what the thing you are describing is like.

Example: Description

Student Kenneth Chan's response to "Practising Writing Description," Exercise 2 (p. 288) follows the instructions in the assignment: write a neutral statement describing a familiar place, write a description of that place using sensory details, and finally write another, more subjective description containing details that reveal the speaker's attitude toward the place.

Dance Club

Neutral Statement: The popular dance club is always full of activity.

See: flashing bright lights, room is dark, crowds of people at bar and on the dance floor, bodies moving in all directions, dance floor has levels, stairs, reflections on shiny pillars, walls have mirrors with marble pattern, blue lighting around the bar

Hear: dance music, rhythms, pounding bass, lots of talk, laughter

Feel: bar is smooth, air feels heavy, room is hotter than usual

Taste: shooters are sweet and strong

Smell: cigarettes, perfume on men and women, sweaty bodies

Objective Description: White lights flash on and off in the semi-darkness, their reflections bouncing off the polished steel pillars into the electric blue lighting in the bar area. The multilevel dance floor is crowded with waves of men and women moving their bodies to the pounding rhythms of the latest dance mix. The air is heavy with perfume, sweat, and cigarette smoke.

Subjective Description: Blinding white lights flash on and off in the darkness, their reflections bouncing off the cold steel pillars into the piercing electric blue lighting in the bar area. The multilevel dance floor is crowded with waves of men and women trying to move their bodies to the deafening rhythms of the latest dance mix. The acrid air is heavy with perfume, sweat, and cigarette smoke.

Analysing the Description Example

The neutral sentence this exercise begins with states a general fact, but does little to create a picture for readers; in other words, it tells, rather than shows, the scene.

For his objective description, Kenneth chooses the most important sensory details and uses the most precise language possible to *show* his readers more vividly what the club is like. The details help determine the picture his readers imagine. Notice how he begins with the visual images of light and dark—"White lights flash," "semi-darkness," and "reflections"—and then describes the contrasting "electric blue lighting" at the bar.

The next visual images focus on the "multilevel dance floor" and "waves" of bodies dancing there. Kenneth completes his description with references to sound, "pounding rhythms," and smells, "perfume, sweat, and cigarette smoke."

In contrast, the words used in the second version suggest how the speaker thinks about the place and how readers should interpret this description. Since he wanted more of a challenge, Kenneth decided to imagine how his parents might see the place. To convey a parent's less favourable attitude toward the dance club, Kenneth adds or changes some words. The lights are now "blinding" or "piercing," and the steel pillars are "cold." On the crowded dance floor, people are "trying to move" to "deafening" music, and the air is heavy and "acrid." The overall impression to readers is considerably more negative than in the first version, a parent's-eye view of a favourite place for many young people.

Wallace Stegner's "In Search of Whitemud" (p. 160) is an outstanding example of an essay that depends on sensory details to show readers what the experience of returning to his boyhood hometown was like for the author. Read the essay, paying particular attention to the way Stegner incorporates details into his description. You will find the essay full of descriptions that show rather than tell.

Practising Writing Description

1. Think about an interesting person who you know. Write a description of that person, including at least ten visual details that distinguish him or her from anyone else.

2. Go to a familiar place and record what you see, hear, touch, taste, and smell there. Some possible places include the food court in a shopping mall, a children's playground, your college pub, a weight room in a fitness facility, or a video arcade. Write a neutral one-sentence description of the place. Then, write a three- or four-sentence paragraph, using details from your list of sensory details, to describe as objectively as possible. Then revise the piece so it becomes more subjective. Recall the feelings and reactions you experienced as you were recording the sensory details and choose words that will show readers whether you had a positive or negative experience in that place, without explicitly telling readers your feelings.

3. Using the same techniques listed in Exercise 2, describe an event from memory, such as a basketball game, a rock concert, a wedding, or a snowstorm. Focus on the sensory details at one moment in time rather than on what happened over a period of time.

4. Choose an object that is important to you. Write a paragraph describing that object. Use words that show readers your attachment to the object, without telling them outright why it is so important.

Readings That Use Description

The readings in this book that use description to help readers visualize people or places include the following:

Final Tips for Descriptions

- Establish your purpose for the description. Do you need to create a verbal "snapshot" of the object, or do you need an extended description that will dominate the essay?
- Decide whether your description must be as objective as possible, or if readers will benefit from a more subjective description.
- Brainstorm to list as many sensory details as possible about the object of your description. Consider the object through the five senses: sight, hearing, touch, taste, and smell.
- Choose precise descriptive words to show readers the object, rather than telling them about your feelings for the object.

NARRATION

Everyone loves a good story, and most people enjoy telling one. **Narration** is telling a single story or several related ones. It is often associated with fiction—with myths, fairy tales, short stories, and novels—but writers of all types of essays use narrative strategies. Description and narration are closely related and often overlap in writing. Where description focuses on the physical details of a person, event, place, or object at one point in time, narration describes events that happen over a period of time.

When to Use Narration

Narration can be used to argue a point, define a concept, or reveal a truth. Writers in all disciplines have discovered the power of the narrative. Journalists, historians, sociologists, and essayists often "hook" their readers by opening with a personal anecdote or a human interest story to capture readers and illustrate points. In fact, many writers use narration to persuade their audiences to a course of action. For example, George Orwell's famous narrative "Shooting an Elephant" is a compelling indictment of imperialism.

Personal narratives can be powerful if they focus on a provocative insight and if the details are carefully selected and shaped. Therefore, narratives are more than mere diary entries, because certain details may be omitted while others may be altered. Narratives may help the writer better understand the significance of an experience, and they help readers "see for themselves." Typically narratives require no library research (our lives are rich with resources for this type of essay), but often writers may choose to supplement personal narration with research and outside sources to move beyond their own experience.

How to Write a Narrative

Narratives typically focus on an incident involving a conflict, whether it is between opposing people, values, or perceptions. This incident is then dramatized so readers can picture what happened and can hear what was said. Such incidents often involve some aspect of change—a contrast between "before" and "after"—even though the change may be internal (a change in awareness) rather than external or physical.

Narratives do not have to feature life-shattering incidents; in fact, many of the best narratives involve profound realizations that are not always obvious to others. In "An Accent on Learning English" (p. 107), for example, Sun-Kyung Yi's insight comes after a relatively small incident, hearing her own voice played back to her after reading a script she had written for a radio broadcast.

Brainstorming for a Topic

Writers usually need to dig deeply to find those buried experiences that have changed their attitudes and views. To help generate ideas, you will find specific narrative assignments at the end of many poems and essays in the "Writing from the Text" sections of the Reader. If your assignment is more general—to write about any significant moment or change in your life—consider the following questions:

What are my most vivid memories of . . .
- kindergarten? Grade 2? Grade 6? Grade 8?
- junior high? high school? college?
- team sports? living in another culture?
- staying with friends or relatives?
- getting a job or working?

When did I first . . .
- feel ashamed (or proud) of myself?
- stand up to my parents?
- realize that teachers make mistakes?
- give in to peer pressure?
- pressure another to go against authority?
- wish I had different parents?
- wish someone would disappear from my life?

What one incident showed me . . .
- what living between two worlds really means?
- how it feels to be alone?
- why conformity isn't always best?
- how stereotyping has affected me?
- how different I am from my sister/brother/friend?
- why we have a certain law?
- how it feels to live with a physical disability?

If you prefer a visual strategy, you might try clustering or mapping your ideas. One method is to write your topic—for example, "significant changes"—in a circle in the centre of your page and then draw spokes outward from it. At the end of each spoke, write down a specific incident that triggered important changes in your life. Draw a box around each incident and then use more spokes, radiating from the boxes, to specify all the changes that resulted. (For an illustration of clustering, see p. 215.)

After you have brainstormed about all possible changes, choose the incident that seems most vivid and worth narrating. Make a list of all the details that relate to it. Once you have finished brainstorming for details, you are ready to focus these thoughts and draft your paper.

Drafting a Paper

In a narrative essay, the thesis may not be articulated at the beginning of the essay, or may only be implied rather than stated outright, to maintain the sense of discovery often associated with the course of a narrative. In some cases, an explicit thesis can slow the momentum of the story or spoil the ending. Whether it is articulated or implied, however, a thesis is still essential during the drafting stages in order to keep you focused and to ensure that the story has a point or insight to share.

For example, in the student essay that follows, Bruce Halling focuses on a time when he was intimidated by a bully, Ricky. His idea of writing about being intimidated is not yet a thesis because the insight, focus, or assertion is not at first clear. At the start of his writing, Halling had only a topic, but after he clustered or listed his details, he probably wrote a *working thesis*—a preliminary assertion that could be changed and refined as the narrative took shape.

> **Working Thesis:** Being plagued by a bully can make one yearn for revenge.

Most writers aren't lucky enough to identify the thesis immediately. Often, particularly in a narrative, it takes considerable writing before the best thesis is discovered. Therefore, writers typically continue sharpening their thesis throughout the writing process as they, too, discover the point of their story. As Bruce narrated this experience, it developed as a genuine "between worlds" experience.

> **Discovered Thesis:** As a child, I found myself caught between an intense wish for revenge and extreme guilt when this wish came true.

Once the thesis becomes clear to the writer, the rough draft needs to be revised so that all the details relate to this new thesis. Notice, however, that the thesis statement does not need to be specified in the actual essay.

Example: Narrative

The following essay by student Bruce Halling demonstrates a narrative focusing on a significant change in the narrator's life.

A Bully's Unjust Deserts
Bruce Halling

A young boy sits alone, admiring his father's gun. Ricky
knows he's not supposed to play with the gun, but his father
never keeps it loaded, so Ricky isn't afraid. Perhaps he imagines he hears a strange noise in his house and wants to investigate. Perhaps he imagines he's a private detective or a crim-
inal. He might have pointed the gun at himself as if he were
captured by the enemy. Or he might have been looking down the
barrel at the darkness inside. But we'll never know what Ricky
was imagining.

Ricky was in my Grade 6 class, and almost every day after
lunch we would have to wait by the door to our room until the
teacher returned. And almost every day Ricky would find some
way to amuse himself, at my expense.

"Oops! Sorry, Bruce," Ricky lied after he bumped into me
from behind. I turned and looked at him. Couldn't he see I wasn't
going to be any fun? He slapped me in the face and then stuck
his bottom lip out in an exaggerated pout. "Is Brucie gonna
cry?"

"No," I said as I turned my back on him and walked a few
steps away. I wanted so badly to knock him down on the ground
and have the other kids laugh at him as they were laughing at
me. Not all of the kids were laughing, though. My friends
weren't laughing. They were admiring their shoes. I walked away
from my friends to make it easier for them to ignore me. I didn't
need their help, and I was glad they didn't offer it. I was
prepared to take anything Ricky could give me, but no matter
how much I wanted to, I could never bring myself to hit him.
I always felt it was wrong to fight.

Ricky's house was on my street, and I had to pass it on my
way home from school. Walking home from school should have been
a nice stroll for a ten-year-old. I know that was what I had
always wished my walks home would be. It wasn't a long walk--
just three blocks, and that fall the weather was warmer than
usual. But even in those few blocks, I had an obstacle, and it
presented itself in the form of a young boy.

Some days I would stay after school to practise in the
choir or to help the teacher. For my reward on those days,
Ricky would be waiting for me on my way home. My house was on
the other side of the street, and I always made sure to cross
before I came to his house.

One day as I crossed the street, I heard something hit the
ground near me. Then I felt the sting of a dirt clod hitting
me in the head. I stopped and looked in the direction of
Ricky's house, but I couldn't see where he was hiding. I
brushed most of the dirt out of my hair and kept walking, trying to ignore being hit several more times before I made it
home.

I stood in the shower, holding the valves to the hot and cold water as the dirt was washed out of my hair. Every time I thought about Ricky, I turned down the cold water until it was uncomfortably hot. As my skin turned red from the heat, I closed my eyes and wished for his death. I imagined it. Sometimes I would kill him. Other times he died in an accident. But always I was a witness. Always I would be free from his torment.

Unfortunately, later that year, my wish came true. I remember when I heard about Ricky's death. I was in an elevator with two of my friends who had also known Ricky. After I stepped into the elevator, I pushed the button for the third floor.

"Did you hear what happened to Ricky Liverpool?" one friend asked.

"Yeah," sighed the other friend as the door started closing.

"What happened?" I asked, feigning moderate interest.

"He shot himself in the head," one friend replied. The elevator gave a slight jerk upward. I saw it in the way my friends bounced slightly, but I didn't feel it. I only felt the rigid walls of the elevator as my friends' polite lamentations seemed to punctuate my silence. The doors finally opened, and I followed my friends into the dim hallway.

I wasn't glad my wish came true. I wanted to feel happy. I wanted to feel freed. I could only feel sad. I felt sad because Ricky had died . . . and I had wanted it to happen. All of the hate I had built up inside for Ricky only brought me a tremendous amount of guilt. I realized then I had to be careful of what I wished for in the future. Because sometimes wishes do come true.

Analysing the Narrative Essay: Show Rather Than Tell

In our discussion of description, we introduced ways writers try to show, rather than tell, what an object or person is like. Similarly, when writers narrate a story, they try to recreate scenes so that their readers can experience the moment as they did. Rather than simply telling us what they felt, they try to *show* us. For example, in the student model, Bruce could have simply told us that Ricky would often deliberately ridicule him. Instead, he lets us hear this, see it, and feel it with him as Ricky bumped him from behind:

> I turned and looked at him. Couldn't he see I wasn't going to be any fun? He slapped me in the face and then stuck his bottom lip out in an exaggerated pout. "Is Brucie gonna cry?"

Such a scene draws in readers, because each of us can empathize with this moment of humiliation. Bruce doesn't need to write, "I felt humiliated," because he has *shown* this more vividly than any claim he could make. His use of dialogue, action, and vivid details (the exaggerated pout) makes Ricky seem real to readers.

Selecting Telling Details

The key to describing scenes and characters is to make sure each detail is revealing. It is not important to know the narrator's hair colour or height, so such details would not be relevant or "telling." The fact that he is in the choir and stays after school to help the teacher reveals that he is not a trouble-maker, not one who would typically want to kill a classmate. Such details help us to understand better the narrator's character as well as the extent of his hatred of Ricky.

Similarly, the setting can be revealing. Although the weather is not always important in a story, here an afternoon stroll on a warm fall day becomes darkened by the bully's attacks. In this scene, the pleasant weather is juxtaposed against the narrator's pain as the clods of dirt strike his head. The choice of setting itself can automatically reveal qualities about both character and conflict.

Practising Writing Narration

Many of the topics in the "Writing from the Text" sections of the Reader invite you to relate your own experience to the particular readings and to respond with a narrative. Here are some additional assignments:

1. Write an essay describing one school experience that taught you an unexpected lesson. Show the incident as it happened, and describe what you learned and why it was unexpected.

2. Write an essay focusing on a time when you bullied or were bullied by someone else. Let your readers see what happened and what you discovered about yourself and others.

3. Write about a time when one of your peers, parents, or children embarrassed you. Was the situation funny or painful, or a little of both? Recreate the moment of embarrassment so that your readers see and hear what happened.

4. Write about an incident when you felt that your cultural or family background was incorrectly prejudged. Describe what happened so that your readers can understand the event and your response to it. Did you make any discoveries as a result of this experience?

5. Write about an event that revealed that something you once believed or thought was important had lost its validity or importance. Dramatize the revelation as vividly as you can.

Readings That Use Narration

Examples of works in this text that depend on narration for at least part of their development include the following:

Final Tips for Narratives

- Focus on a provocative insight so that your story reflects some real thought.
- Continue sharpening your thesis as your narrative develops. Decide whether the essay needs an explicit or implied thesis.
- Dramatize a scene or two, using action and dialogue. Don't just tell readers; show the scene.
- Include telling details that reveal relevant character traits. Have your characters interact with each other.

- Rewrite sentences and revise paragraphs to eliminate wordiness and generalizations.
- Study other narratives in the text, looking for techniques and strategies. Experiment!

DEFINITION

If you've ever had difficulty understanding a piece of writing because of specialized terminology the writer used, you know first-hand how important **definition** can be. Readers appreciate explanation and clarification of unfamiliar terms. Whether an entire essay is an extended definition or the essay incorporates a shorter definition, explaining what a term or concept means is an integral part of writing.

When to Use Definition

Knowing your intended audience will help you determine which words or concepts you need to define. For example, in a paper for an information technology class, you would not need to define terms generally used in that field. But when you write on the same topic for general readers and use language unfamiliar to most people—a technical or foreign term, or a word peculiar to an academic discipline—you will need to define the term so your readers can understand it. Even if you are using a familiar word, you need to explain its meaning if you or an author you are quoting uses it in a unique way.

For some courses, you may be asked to write a "definition essay," a paper that develops with the primary intention of increasing readers' understanding of a term or an abstract idea. This type of paper topic might be assigned in a psychology, sociology, history, philosophy, or English course.

Finally, your purpose in writing a definition may be to convince your readers to consider the explained term in a positive light, or to compare it—even to prefer it—to something else. Sometimes the persuasive aspect of the essay relies on readers understanding the definition of a word.

How to Write a Definition

Sometimes a brief definition is all that you need. In that case, a few words of clarification, or even a synonym, may be incorporated into your text quite easily:

Québec me tue, or "Quebec Is Killing Me," is the title of Hélène Jutras's book.

Achondroplasia—a type of dwarfism—may affect overall bone structure and cause arms and legs to be disproportionately smaller than the rest of the body.

Whenever possible, incorporate into your text the necessary clarification of a term. As the above examples show, such incorporation is unobtrusive and therefore superior to writing a separate sentence to define the term.

A formal definition may be required for some writing situations. In that case, you will need to follow the dictionary model of establishing the term in a *class* and then distinguishing the term from its class by citing its *difference*:

Haiku is a form of poetry composed of seventeen syllables in a 5-7-5 pattern of three lines.

A paring chisel is a woodworking tool with a knife-sharp edge, pushed by hand and used to finish a rough cut of wood.

Always use your own explanation to define the term. A definition quoted directly from a dictionary will not focus on the aspects of the term relevant to your purpose.

Strategies for Incorporating Definitions

When an assignment calls for an extended definition of a concept or term, the following methods may be used alone or in combination:

- *Comparison–contrast:* You may want to contrast your definition of the word with the way it is typically used, or with a more conventional definition of the term. If the term is unfamiliar, you might show how it is similar to another concept.
- *Description:* You can define a term by describing its characteristics: size, shape, texture, colour, noise, and other telling traits.
- *Exemplification:* Giving examples and illustrations of a concept can help your readers understand it better, but examples are rather specific and therefore should help supplement a definition rather than be used by themselves.
- *Negation:* Understanding what something is *not* can help limit the definition and eliminate misconceptions, especially if you can combine your negation with a concrete description of the term's defining characteristics.

Example: Definition

Student Tony Perciasepe read Sonnet L'Abbé's essay "Hello, We're Not American!" (p. 91) and was asked to respond to with an extended definition. Here is the definition he wrote.

Defining a "Canadian"
Tony Perciasepe

The conclusion of Sonnet L'Abbé's essay "Hello, We're Not American!" raises an important question. She asks, "Do we really want to identify ourselves by a negation, by stating loudly what we are not?"

We Canadians have a hard time defining who we are and so we need to rely on Americans as a point of comparison. Americans support the right to carry a gun, and Canadians do not. Americans openly celebrate their patriotism, and Canadians do not, except perhaps on Canada Day. Americans think of their country as a "melting pot" for immigrants, a term that describes the way immigrants give up their native habits to become as American as other American citizens. Canadians initiated a multicultural policy to support and even encourage immigrants to keep part of their original nationality intact. In fact, when my grandparents came to Canada from Italy, they settled in the Italian area of Toronto, where they could adjust to Canada without having to learn English right away.

If I try to define what a Canadian is without using Americans as a comparison, the first characteristic I think of is tolerance; a Canadian strives to be tolerant of other people's differences. A Canadian tries to see both sides of an issue, and tries to make a decision based on compromise, because compromise lets both parties be winners in a dispute. Since balance and fairness are important, a Canadian is not locked into a "my way or the highway" mentality. That's why immigrants feel so comfortable here.

Overall, though, I feel most comfortable defining a Canadian in comparison to Americans. Since we share the same continent and language (except for Quebec), I think we can't escape seeing ourselves in relationship to our neighbours. And I agree with L'Abbé that, in the eyes of the rest of the world, we are very much like Americans. Still, I want to think of my Canadian identity as worth keeping separate, because the things that make Canadians different from Americans, although they may appear inconsequential to some, are important enough to preserve.

Analysing the Definition Essay

Tony's essay begins by picking up where L'Abbé's question leaves off. He states his belief that defining a Canadian by negation, as being "not American," is unavoidable. He then gives three examples-by-negation that compare and contrast two nationalities on the issues of guns, patriotism, and multiculturalism. Notice how Tony shows audience awareness by defining the term "melting-pot" for readers who may be unfamiliar with the term. Then he adds a personal example to illustrate what coming to a multicultural society meant to his grandparents.

Tony does try to move away from negation and comparison when he describes the term "Canadian" in terms of a key defining characteristic, tolerance. He explains how compromise, balance, and fairness contribute to a Canadian's tolerance. Nevertheless, he is compelled to return to the Canadian–American dichotomy, partly because other nationalities see the two as sharing more similarities than differences. In his conclusion, he justifies his wish to preserve the "differentness" of the Canadian identity.

Practising Writing Definitions

1. In your college papers, you will most frequently incorporate short definitions to clarify terms. Using your dictionary as a starting point for terms you may not be familiar with, practise writing single sentences in your own words that define the following terms:

    a. schizophrenia
    b. satire
    c. Marxist
    d. World Wide Web
    e. Cubist
    f. osmosis

2. Although you will use definition most often as a component of your papers, it is useful to practise writing short definition essays. In small groups, collaborate with your classmates to write a short essay that defines one of the following:

    a. power
    b. "between worlds"
    c. maturity
    d. witty
    e. unconditional love
    f. disabled

3. Read one of the following essays and consider what terms or concepts are central to that essay. Then write an extended definition of one term or concept:

    a. "Respect and Balance in Our 'Tribe,'" (p. 6)
    b. "Men as Success Objects," (p. 50)
    c. "Being a Jew at Christmas," (p. 94)
    d. "The Beauty Myth," (p. 57)
    e. "On Jobs and Humility," (p. 182)

Readings That Use Definition

Each of the following works incorporates definition to achieve its goal:

Final Tips for Definitions

- Consider your audience and define any terms that your readers cannot be expected to know.
- Whenever possible, incorporate into your text the necessary clarification of a term. Avoid writing a separate sentence to define the term.
- For a formal definition, first establish the term in a class and then distinguish it from this class by citing its differences.
- Remember that definitions can also be developed by comparing and contrasting that word with other terms, by describing the characteristics of a term, by presenting examples, and by illustrating what the term is not.

CLASSIFICATION

Classification, the grouping together of similar items, is a natural activity we all use to arrange information. Preschoolers learn to sort blocks according to colour; music lovers organize their CD collection by separating their classical, jazz, and rock sections; biologists categorize animals and plants according to family, genus, and species. As we mentioned in the previous section of this chapter, classification can be an important part of a definition. A formal definition first explains the larger category a term belongs to and then distinguishes that term from others by explaining how it is different. Classification, then, is closely related to definition, and is just as useful a technique for organizing information in an essay.

When to Use Classification

Many research assignments require you to discover interrelated facts or ideas about a subject and present your findings in essay form. If you are writing about a complex body of information, classification may be the best way to organize that information for your readers. For example, a journalism course could require students to research the kinds of periodicals that publish the work of freelance writers. In this case, classifying the publications into groups, such as news, arts, sports, business, and fashion magazines, will be an effective way of presenting your findings. This arrangement will show readers how these items are related (they are all parts of a larger class of magazines) and how they are different (each category of magazine has a different focus).

Classification can also be combined with other development methods, such as cause and effect (see pp. 306–13) and comparison and contrast (see pp. 313–20).

How to Write Using Classification

Before you begin, check that your topic is appropriate for classification by asking yourself if it can be divided into a minimum of three distinct subtopics. Then decide which dimension you will use as the basis for the classification. For example, if you want to write an essay on housing, you could subdivide the topic into different kinds of buildings—detached homes, duplexes, townhouses, and high-rise apartments. Such a classification is relevant for people looking at housing options, so you should include this rationale for the classification in your thesis statement.

It is possible, however, to subdivide this topic on other dimensions. If you want to draw finer distinctions between types of housing, you could choose to look at kinds of housing where occupants share facilities, such as rental townhouses, condominiums, and co-operative housing units. Residences in each subcategory must have some characteristics in common (the shared facilities), yet they are also distinct from each other (each is financed and operated in a different way).

Whatever subcategories or classes you choose for your classification, it is important that they have some characteristics in common, because your examples fall under the same general category; yet they must also be distinct enough from each other to form subcategories. As well, each subcategory should be of equal importance, and therefore worthy of the same amount of discussion. Labelling your categories using parallel construction can ensure balance and clarity in your discussion. (For more on parallel construction, see p. 442–43.) Finally, arrange the subcategories in your essay in a logical order, including the necessary transition words to show the connections between the categories.

Example: Classification

The following essay was written by student Cheri Castell as an in-class assignment. Cheri read Moira Farr's "Welcome to FamilyValuesWorld!" (p. 9) and was asked to write a classification essay based on her own experience and the ideas Farr raises about parenting.

Kinds of Parents
Cheri Castell

Unlike most jobs, parenting is lifelong work that has no training period. Most parents end up getting "on-the-job" training instead, so most raise their children the way they were raised.

Overprotective parents focus their lives on their children and worry about their children more than they need to. They often set high standards for their children, and if their children can't meet those standards, their parents want to rush in to fix the problems so the children don't suffer. The children often end up living for their mom and dad rather than living for themselves because they depend so much on their parents' approval.

Indulgent parents are afraid of frustrating their children. They buy their children anything they want and don't set many limits on their behaviour. Since their children have few restrictions, indulgent parents end up having little control as the children grow up. The children can become independent, but they can also become manipulative because they are so used to getting what they want.

Neglectful parents also avoid setting rules for their children, but out of a lack of concern or knowledge. The children are often left on their own, and so they get into trouble because their parents are not around to guide them. These children may show little self-control and may become aggressive as a way of getting the attention that they lack. Children whose parents are neglectful are often very unhappy.

Finally, democratic parents are supportive. These parents try to teach their children limits and the rules they need to know, but they also allow the children to discuss the rules and learn from their own mistakes. They give their children just enough control over their own lives to learn, but not so much that the children are overwhelmed and forced to grow up earlier than they should. Democratic parents achieve the most success, in my opinion. My parents raised me this way, and I hope that, whatever on-the-job training I go through, I will raise my children the same way.

Analysing the Classification Essay

Cheri's essay classifies her general topic into four categories. She identifies each group of parents with an adjective (overprotective, indulgent, neglectful, and democratic) to maintain parallel form, and defines each group according to the ways the parents deal with their children. Her thesis statement expresses the rationale for her classification: since parents receive little or no training for their task, they often repeat the behaviour of their own parents, but with different results. As the support for each category shows, each "class" of parents is distinct. Cheri clearly explains the different qualities of each of the four parenting styles she has observed. Yet even if two categories of parents are somewhat similar in that they avoid setting limits, Cheri is careful to point out that indulgent and neglectful parents are motivated to do so for very different reasons.

However, her discussion incorporates more than just defining qualities. It also implies that these qualities have an effect on the children's behaviour and the way they grow up. Cheri's introduction forecasts that parenting styles are a cause that have an effect on children, so she is wise to include a discussion of the effects of each style in her body paragraphs. Notice, too, how Cheri gives each category equal coverage in her discussion. Each is of equal importance in her overall classification scheme and so worthy of equal space in her essay.

By the end of her essay, Cheri reaches the conclusion that one of the parenting styles she has examined is preferable to the others. She ends her essay with an endorsement of the democratic way she was raised, and she ties this idea to the statement in her introduction that parents often use the same methods to raise their children that they themselves experienced growing up. Not every classification assignment will lead you to choose one category as preferable to the others, nor will you necessarily see causes and effects as crucial to your classification strategy. In this case, though, Cheri's essay demonstrates how classification as an organizing principle can make information more accessible for readers.

A Note About Classification and Stereotyping

Although classification is a normal human activity, if we classify people irresponsibly we run the risk of **stereotyping**. Broad generalizations about others can be useful if they give us insights that lead us to understand our differences, but such generalizations can be dangerous if they lead us to form inaccurate and destructive opinions that limit our perceptions of people. Cheri's essay is sensitive to this fact. She uses classification to explore some of the differences between parenting styles and is diplomatic and respectful in her classification of parents. Her approach indicates that she is trying to follow the advice Robert Heilbroner gives in "Don't Let Stereotypes Warp Your Judgments" (p. 128): she tries to be careful about making harmful generalizations.

Practising Writing Essays with Classification

Use some of the prewriting techniques suggested in Chapter 6 to discover categories into which you could divide the following topics. Then choose one topic and write an essay that uses a classification format for arranging your material:

a.	computer software	h.	movies
b.	Web sites	i.	fashions
c.	vacations	j.	family celebrations
d.	summer jobs	k.	self-help books
e.	investments	l.	emotions
f.	country music	m.	addictions
g.	soap operas	n.	crimes

Readings That Use Classification

The authors of the following two essays use classification in different ways to present their ideas:

"As a Dad, Will I Do Right by My Daughter?" p. 37
"Work, Labour, Play," p. 170

As our titles for the sections in the Reader indicate, we have used classification to organize the readings according to theme.

Final Tips for Classification

- Divide your information into at least three subcategories and check that each is different from the others, yet related to the overall topic.
- Write a thesis statement that explains the relevance of the classification.
- List each category using parallel form and discuss each category fully.
- If you are writing about people, avoid stereotyping.

CAUSE AND EFFECT

All your life you have been made aware of the consequences of your behaviour: not getting your allowance because you didn't keep your room clean; being elected to the student council because you ran a strong campaign; getting a C on an exam because you didn't review all of the material; earning a friend's trust because you kept a confidence. In all of these cases, a particular behaviour seemed to cause or result in a certain effect.

However, causes are not always so easy to identify, for there may be a number of indirect causes of an action or inaction. For example, you may have won an election because of your reputation as a leader, your popularity, your opponent's inadequacies, your vigorous campaign, or even a cause that you may not have known about or been able to control. Effects usually are more evident: homeless families, few jobs for college graduates, small businesses failing, and houses remaining on the market for years are all obvious effects of a recession. What has caused the recession typically is more difficult to discern, but good critical thinking involves speculating about possible causes and their effects. Good writing can come from such cause-and-effect thinking.

When to Use Cause and Effect

Cause-and-effect development can be used in diverse writing situations. For example, you will use this strategy when you trace the reasons for a historical event, such as the causes of World War II and the results of that conflict on the postwar map of Europe. You perceive cause-and-effect relationships when you analyse and write about broad social problems (like runaway teens) or more personal concerns (such as why you and your siblings are risk takers). You may rely on cause-and-effect description to discuss a small town's abandoned shopping district, or to compare the aspirations of college graduates in 1968 and those today. All of these thinking and writing tasks invite you to examine the apparent effects and to question what has caused them. This questioning inevitably involves speculation about causes rather than absolute answers, but this speculation can lead to fruitful analysis and provocative papers.

How to Write About Causes and Effects
Brainstorming for Causes and Effects

To produce a paper that goes beyond predictable or obvious discussion, take time to think about diverse causes for an effect you have observed and to contemplate plausible effects of situations that you perceive. You will want to brainstorm freely and let all of your hunches emerge. In fact, a lively prewriting session is the key to a lively cause-and-effect paper. However, be sure to differentiate clearly between causes and effects once you have completed your brainstorming.

For example, you may have noticed that your downtown area is no longer attracting people as it once did. Instead of stopping at the family-owned clothing store or the doughnut shop next to the downtown movie theatre, you and your family and friends go out to suburban malls for shopping, dining, and movies. Consider the causes for this phenomenon.

You can brainstorm this perceived problem by writing a list of every possible cause that comes to you. After you have written your own list, you might look at this one:

Why We Aren't Going Downtown Anymore

Stores
1. Limited stock—embarrassing, never have my size
2. Only carry expensive brands
3. Prices higher than at the mall, too few sales
4. Old-fashioned, dull window displays, ugly mannequins
5. Clerks are old ladies who've been around forever

Restaurants
6. Have boring menus: vegetable soup and bacon and eggs
7. Decorating is still very 1960s—pink and grey
8. Plastic plants
9. My favourite doughnut shop has closed
10. No inexpensive quick foods or snacks
11. Slow-moving waitresses

Movie Theatres

12. Seats have broken springs and torn upholstery
13. Warped screen, bad sound system
14. Musty smell, no air conditioning
- 15. Same features play for weeks

Overall Downtown

16. Only old people shop downtown
17. I never meet any of my friends down there
18. Lots of homeless people, gangs
19. Dusty window-fronts of abandoned shops are demoralizing
20. Need to pay to park in city lots or need to feed meters

If you give some energy to the prewriting, you will undoubtedly come up with more causes than we have, and the paper that you write will have interesting explanations for a problem threatening many communities. You might not have the sophistication of a city planner or the statistics and research of your city hall, but your insights are bound to create a provocative paper worth reading. And we think you will find that creative speculation is useful for any cause-and-effect brainstorming that you do.

Practising Finding Causes and Effects

1. In small groups or individually, list multiple causes for the following effects:
   a. prevalence of two-income families
   b. increased number of comic-book and sports-card stores
   c. trend toward instructors assigning collaborative projects
   d. popularity of high-risk sports
   e. resurgence of rock music from the late 1950s and the 1960s
2. Now list the effects of these realities:
   a. prevalence of single-parent families
   b. increase in multicultural materials in education
   c. more women in the professions
   d. more people from all economic classes attending college
   e. city-sponsored recycling projects

Any one of these brainstorming exercises could lead to a paper based on cause-and-effect development.

Drafting a Paper

After you have listed causes and/or effects, your next drafting step is to discover ideas that logically connect. As you link points, evaluate them to make sure your reasoning is clear and that your points are plausible and logical.

For example, the fact that the doughnut shop has closed is not why you have stopped shopping for clothing in the downtown area. That point would seem illogical to your readers without your developing a connection—perhaps that empty shops are disheartening reminders of the economic recession, or that a particular cruller the shop made provided a tasty, quick, and inexpensive snack during a shopping trip. Or you might see, as you draft, that some "causes" on your list are not worth developing.

In addition to developing plausible explanations for the points you do want to use, you need to consider organization. In your brainstorming, you may have perceived a natural grouping that worked well to get ideas down on paper. We answered our question about what was wrong with the downtown area by listing what was wrong with the stores, restaurants, movie theatres, and general atmosphere there. Suppose we realized that we could provide a better answer to the question if we organized our ideas according to issues rather than grouped examples. Here is the revised list that might result:

Why We Aren't Going Downtown Anymore

Economic issues: points 2, 3, 10, 20
Aesthetic issues: points 4, 6, 7, 8, 9, 12, 13, 14, 19
Social issues: points 1, 5, 11, 15, 16, 17, 18

You will also need to decide the order of the grouped points that you will include in your paper. In the student paper that follows, Elizabeth McMahon decided that the social causes of not going downtown were more significant than the aesthetic or economic issues, so she decided to conclude her paper by discussing social issues. (For more about ordering ideas, see pp. 240–41.)

Throughout your drafting, continue evaluating your points. Remove any points that are implausible or cannot be supported by the information you have, or do some research to find more convincing data. Continue to apply the "So what?" standard to ensure that you are developing a worthwhile paper. By this time in your drafting, it would help you to formulate a working thesis—in this case, an assertion that establishes the cause-and-effect relationship you perceive.

Example: Cause and Effect

In this essay, mature student Elizabeth McMahon discusses the reasons why the downtown area in her home town is less attractive to shoppers than it once was. As a member of a newly formed citizens' committee looking at this issue, she has a personal interest in this topic.

Why We Aren't Going Downtown Anymore
Elizabeth McMahon

When I was a child, a trip downtown was a special event. I remember the streets being busy with shoppers at all times of the year, but especially at Christmas time, or when stores were having their annual back-to-school sales. Nowadays, though, downtown is much quieter and many stores have "For Rent" signs in the window instead of enticing displays of the latest merchandise. If my children want to go shopping, they plead to go to the mall out near the highway. They don't share the fond memories of downtown that I have, probably because downtown is not what it once was. Economic, aesthetic, and social issues have combined to transform downtown, and the end result is, sadly, an unsatisfactory shopping experience for many people.

The downturn in the economy has had a serious effect in many areas, my home town included. These days, most consumers are careful about how they spend their earnings, and many like to comparison-shop for the best buys. In my home town, however, there are fewer value-oriented stores downtown for budget-conscious shoppers than there used to be. One department store closed over ten years ago and has sat empty since. The other department store closed last summer because the company has been in financial difficulty. The discount fabric store shut its doors recently when the owner retired and couldn't find a buyer for his business; people who want to sew their own clothes can't shop for patterns or fabrics downtown anymore. The stores that are still open tend to have higher-priced goods than those in the mall, because their owners need to make a living with fewer customers passing through their doors. All in all, shopping downtown is too costly for most people.

Aesthetically, most of the downtown area is not as attractive as it once was. The atmosphere is best described as forlorn, because so many stores have closed. I feel wistful for the downtown of my childhood whenever I walk past dusty storefront windows with empty display areas, or windows papered over so passersby can't look inside. Too many of the stores that are still in business look rather shabby and run-down. Their awnings are faded, or their entryways need a coat of paint. Some of the remaining stores have tried to spruce up with flower pots out front in the summer, an effort that, admittedly, improves the attractiveness of the area. As well, the downtown business association still decorates the street for Christmas. At most other times of the year, however, the relative emptiness of the streets makes the tired appearance of the overall area more noticeable than it might otherwise be.

Finally, social factors have affected the downtown area. For example, two competing video arcades attract teenagers, but in so doing they keep other people away. My neighbour, who is a senior citizen, says she is uncomfortable shopping downtown because she feels intimidated. In her day, young people showed more respect for the elderly. She can't help feeling vulnerable when she encounters groups of teens hanging out, skateboarding, or rollerblading in front of the arcades. Furthermore, families tend not to shop downtown because the stores don't cater to them. Our main children's wear retailer moved to the mall when it first opened, and no other store geared to children took its place. More recently, the toy store I loved when I was a girl closed its doors, and the place has been converted to a law office. This kind of transformation, while keeping the location in use, doesn't increase the amount of pedestrian traffic going by.

I joined the Citizens' Committee to Revitalize Downtown because it saddens me to see what was once a bustling area go to waste. Rather than replacing the mall, a renewed downtown can complement our entire town's retail sector and give consumers more, rather than less, choice. My hope is that the committee will examine these and other reasons why people aren't shopping downtown anymore, and will use the information to devise a plan to "restore" the economic benefits, aesthetic features, and social life to our downtown area.

Small-Group Discussion About the Cause-and-Effect Essay

Read Elizabeth's essay and meet in small groups to complete the following exercises:

1. Develop a list of the causes and a list of the effects that Elizabeth includes in her discussion of the changes in her downtown. Compare your list with those of other groups to check that you agree on which are the causes and which are the effects.

2. What additional causes and effects does Elizabeth refer to in her conclusion? Are they an effective addition?

3. To structure her ideas, Elizabeth chose to follow a five-paragraph format. Write an informal outline of this essay's five paragraphs. (For more on outlines, see pp. 239–44.)

4. As a group, brainstorm for a cause-and-effect essay explaining why people shop in malls. Then write an outline for a five-paragraph essay that would be a companion piece to Elizabeth's.

Practising Writing Cause-and-Effect Essays

Write an essay that focuses on the causes and/or effects of one of the following:

a. your family getting together for a holiday occasion, as Judith Timson describes (p. 4)

b. your having revealed an important truth about yourself to a member of your family, as Joy C. did (p. 31)

c. a friend or family member abusing alcohol or using drugs

d. your sense of standards of weight and beauty, as discussed by Catherine Pigott (p. 152)

e. your sense of being caught living between two languages, as Sun-Kyung Yi is (p. 107)

f, your sense of being caught between two cultures, as Julia Nunes (p. 98) and Sean Kelly (p. 101) depict

g. your need to conform to gender roles, as discussed by Warren Farrell (p. 50) and Naomi Wolf (p. 57)

Readings That Use Cause and Effect

You may be interested in reading some of the following essays to see the different ways their authors develop causes and effects:

"Respect and Balance in Our 'Tribe,'" p. 6

"Welcome to FamilyValuesWorld!" p. 9

"Fathers, Sons and Hockey," p. 26

"What Do Men Want?" p. 44

"Men as Success Objects," p. 50

"The Babysitters Club: No Boys Allowed," p. 54

"The Beauty Myth," p. 57

"Love and Fear in the Age of AIDS," p. 75

"The Business of Being Half and Half," p. 98

"Discovering My Native Identity," p. 101

"Don't Let Stereotypes Warp Your Judgments," p. 128

"Singling Out Single Parents," p. 133

"Jerry Lewis and the MDA Telethon," p. 136

"Earthbound . . . for Now," p. 139

"Adding Weight to an Image of Beauty," p. 152

"On Jobs and Humility," p. 182

"Need, Want, Deserve," p. 184

"Life After Cable," p. 188

"The Battle over Gun Control," p. 197

Final Tips for Cause-and-Effect Development

• Brainstorm in order to come up with every possible cause and/or effect for your particular topic.

- Go over your list of causes and effects to make sure you have listed them under the correct heading and then to determine that each point is reasonable and supportable. Eliminate any which are illogical or for which you lack data. Do research if additional evidence is needed.
- Apply the "So what?" standard. Will this cause or effect analysis make worthwhile reading?
- Group ideas that belong together and order your evidence to conclude with your most emphatic and well-developed support.
- Develop your explanations fully so that your readers don't have to guess your assumptions or suppose your connection between points.
- Check that the thesis of your paper is both clear and worth supporting.
- Listen to the voice you have used throughout your essay. If your purpose in writing is to consider possible cause-and-effect relationships, don't feign a voice that purports to know all the answers.

COMPARISON AND CONTRAST

Whether you are examining your own experiences or responding to texts, you will inevitably rely on **comparison-and-contrast** thinking. To realize how two people, places, works of art, films, economic plans, laboratory procedures, or aspects of literature—or anything else—may be alike or different is to perceive important distinctions between them.

While we may believe initially that two subjects are remarkably different (how they *contrast*), after thoughtful scrutiny we may see that there are important similarities between them. Conversely, although we may have detected clear similarities in two subjects (how they *compare*), the complete analysis may reveal surprising differences. Therefore, while comparison implies similarity and contrast implies difference, these two thinking processes work together to enhance perception.

When to Use Comparison and Contrast

Subtle comparison–contrast cues are embedded in writing assignments, both in-class exams and out-of-class papers. For example, an economics instructor may ask for a study of prewar and postwar inflation; a philosophy instructor may want the student to show how one philosophical system departs from another; a psychology instructor may require an explanation of how two different psychologists interpret dreams; or a literature instructor may assign an analysis of how a character changes within a certain novel.

The prevalence of such assignments in all disciplines underscores the importance of comparison–contrast in many experiences and learning situations. Assignments that ask writers to explain the unfamiliar, evaluate certain choices, analyse how someone or something has changed, establish distinction, discover similarities, or propose a compromise all require some degree of comparison and contrast.

How to Write Comparison and Contrast

If you have read the readings on gender issues in the Reader, you might have observed that women and men have quite different complaints about their lives. To write a comparison-and-contrast essay on this topic, you need to begin by making a parallel list of the complaints of each sex. For example, you might notice that women feel that they need to be physically attractive; they feel limited in their choices of careers; and they feel obligated to be domestic (good mothers, cooks, and housekeepers). Men feel they need to be successful at work to be attractive to women; they feel burdened to select high-status, high-paying jobs and to work continuously; and they feel left out of domestic life—cut off from their children and home life.

At first, the complaints of each sex appear to be quite different, but if you examine these complaints further, you may perceive that they have something in common: that women and men suffer from "an invisible curriculum," a series of social expectations that deprive human beings of choice. A thesis for this study might look like this:

> **Thesis:** Although women and men seem to have different problems, both sexes feel hampered by an "invisible curriculum" that affects their self-esteem and limits their choices at work and in their families.

There are two basic methods for organizing data to compare or contrast. In the **block method**, you would organize the material for a study of conflicts affecting gender like this:

Block A: Women
1. need to feel physically attractive to be successful
2. feel limited in workplace choices
3. feel obligated to be mothers, domestic successes

Block B: Men
1. need to feel successful at work to feel attractive

2. feel burdened to achieve high position, to work continuously
3. feel cut off from children and domestic choices

A **point-by-point** organizational pattern for the material would look like this:

Point 1: Factors that govern self-esteem
a. Women need to feel physically attractive.
b. Men need to feel successful at work.

Point 2: Relationship to work
a. Women feel restricted in choice.
b. Men feel burdened to achieve high position, to work continuously.

Point 3: Relationship to family
a. Women feel obligated to be mothers, domestic successes.
b. Men feel cut off from children and domestic choices.

Notice that in the block method, each point in the second block appears in the same order as the points in the first block. In the point-by-point method of arrangement, the first subject (in this case, women) will precede the second in each point of comparative analysis.

The first two paragraphs of Judith Timson's essay "Here's to Family Feasting" (p. 4) use the block method to compare and contrast two different family celebrations. The following essay illustrates the point-by-point method of organizing material.

Example: Comparison and Contrast

A disagreement with his girlfriend coupled with his interest in psychology prompted student Brian Brubacher to compare the ways men and women approach shopping. Brian conducted an informal research study to generate some facts about his male and female friends and their shopping habits.

Men, Women, and Shopping
Brian Brubacher

Conflicts are inevitable in any relationship, and if we have an open mind, it's possible to learn from them. My girlfriend has been complaining that I don't spend enough time with her. Wanting to avoid an argument, I offered to spend the next Saturday with her, but I cringed when she suggested we go shopping. My negative reaction surprised me, and since I was studying gender issues in my psychology course, I decided to conduct an informal survey (in other words, I asked my friends) to see if my attitude toward shopping is common in men, and how it compared to that of women. The results of my very unscientific research show that there are some differences, at least in my circle, in how much time women and men are willing to devote to shopping, where they like to shop, and how they go about it.

The most obvious difference I found was the amount of time each group is willing to spend shopping. Most of the women said that they love to shop; for them, looking in every store in the mall for the perfect "find" is a great way to spend a day, and they can easily go shopping two or three times a week. If they're fashion-conscious, they are more than willing to devote hours to visiting every clothing store around to find the latest styles and colours. One woman, who doesn't care for clothes-shopping as much as my other female friends, goes to the mall only two or three times a year, but she spends as long as necessary, even if it's a whole day, to finish finding the items she needs. All the women agreed that enjoying coffee in the food court or lunch in the restaurant makes a pleasant break in a long shopping trip and rejuvenates them for the next portion of their shopping day. In contrast, my buddies said they try to keep away from shopping as much as possible because feel they have better things to do with their time. They're in and they're out; there's no need to dawdle when there are more important things to do, like watching a video or televised basketball game. All but one of my male friends said the latest men's fashions don't interest them much, and two out of five said they'd rather grab a quick lunch at the drive-through of a fast-food restaurant and go home to relax than hang around a mall.

As for preferred shopping location, my female friends said they choose the mall first because of the variety it offers. They can find the latest in their favourite products, from make-up to shoes, from books to household items, and at a range of prices. As well, shopping at the mall means they don't have to worry about the weather or finding a parking spot. On the other hand, the men don't care if they shop in a mall or at a single store, because variety is not that important. The main criterion is that their store of choice has what they need. One friend said if he has to go to the mall, he parks at the entrance closest to the store he knows will carry the item he's looking for, and doesn't bother going anywhere else in the mall. Another, whose hobby is working on cars, joked that if only his favourite automotive supply store sold clothes, food, and beer, he would never have to shop anywhere else. Oddly enough, it would then offer one-stop shopping, exactly what the women like about the mall.

The participants in my informal study also have different

methods of shopping. For the women, a trip to the mall means they can comparison-shop. They compare everything: the quality of the merchandise, the level of service, and most of all, the price. Some like to visit the more expensive retailers first and then search for comparable styles in the value-priced stores. For all the women, getting a good deal brings them immense satisfaction. The men, however, said they don't care that much about comparisons between vast numbers of products. To them, the choice is obvious: just buy what you need. The price of a product is something the men said they don't usually worry about. Since they can't be bothered to shop around, they'll pay the price, so to speak. Most are in and out of the store so quickly, they are hardly aware of the salespeople. The cashier is the only employee they want to deal with. Since the men prefer the "dash-in-and-buy" method, they don't waste much time comparing items between stores, either.

Next time you're in a mall, keep a close eye on the shopping tendencies of the people there and judge for yourself if men and women have different attitudes toward shopping. As for me, my research has got me thinking that maybe the women are right, at least as far as getting a good price is concerned. So rather than engage in another skirmish in the battle of the sexes, I'm off to the mall--my girlfriend and I are going shopping. Who knows? I might even start to enjoy it as much as she does.

Analysing the Comparison-and-Contrast Essay

Brian opens by explaining how a difference between him and his girlfriend prompted him to compare women's and men's attitudes toward shopping. He cheerfully acknowledges that his survey is far from scientific, unlike the research he would be studying in his psychology course, and qualifies his "results" as being applicable to his circle of friends. Clearly, he wishes to avoid stereotyping here.

Brian previews his main points at the end of the introduction and uses the point-by-point method, in the same order, to concentrate on one focal point per paragraph. For example, he states that the amount of time each group is willing to spend is the most obvious difference he found. The first half of this paragraph discusses how much time his female friends spend on shopping and includes details to support this point: they say they "love to shop"; they can spend a whole day shopping and would not find two or three shopping trips a week excessive. Brian is careful to include an exception, yet she too is willing to spend an entire day at the mall and, like the others, also enjoys taking a coffee or lunch break in the mall.

The second half of this paragraph uses the transition term "in contrast" to shift the discussion from women to men, and proceeds to show how the men begrudge spending time shopping. Brian tries to balance his comments about the men by following the same order of discussion he used for the women: how little the men like shopping, the short length of time they want to spend, other things the men would rather do, their lack of interest in fashion, and the preference of two who would rather eat lunch away from the mall. Notice how Brian's shorter sentences describing the men's attitudes reflect their lack of interest in shopping, while the sentences about how much time the women want to spend are correspondingly longer.

Next Brian contrasts his friends' favourite place to shop. He again begins his discussion with the women, who like the variety of items, the prices, and the convenience of the mall. The transition term "on the other hand" connects discussion of the men's attitude with the first part of the paragraph. Compared on the same dimension, the men prefer to shop where they can locate the item they want. Apparently, convenience matters only to the men insofar as they can easily get to the store of their choice. However, the car-lover's joke at the end of the paragraph does more than just continue the essay's good-natured tone; ironically, this man's fantasy of convenience is the women's reality: one-stop shopping.

Then Brian gives specific examples to support his third point, the different ways women and men approach the shopping task itself. Here the transition term "however" marks the change in focus from women to men. The time women spend comparison-shopping for better quality, service, and price has a positive outcome: women get a better deal than men.

In his conclusion, Brian indicates how impressed he is by the women's success at shopping, and he begins to form an opinion about which sex's shopping habits offer more advantages. As is so often the case when a writer compares two options the way Brian has, one option starts to look more attractive than the other. Brian elaborates on how he learned from the conflict he had with his girlfriend, bringing his readers back to his opening remarks.

Which Method to Use: Block or Point-by-Point?

Student writer Brian Brubacher used a point-by-point method to compare and contrast his two subjects, whereas Judith Timson used the block method. The block method works best if you are making a brief comparison within a longer essay, as Timson does. In this case, the comparison or contrast comprises part of the support for the essay's thesis, rather than constituting the purpose of the essay.

The point-by-point method of development is most effective if the purpose of the entire essay is to discuss the similarities and differences between two related subjects. Although the block method may seem easier, it could encourage the writer to ramble vaguely about each subject without concentrating on specific points of comparison and contrast. The resulting essay may resemble two separate discussions that could be cut apart with scissors. Since many academic writing assignments require comparison and contrast of two related subjects, mastery of the point-by-point method is particularly useful for most students. Whenever it seems reasonable, use the point-by-point method to arrange your comparison and contrast material.

Practising Writing Comparison-and-Contrast Essays

Select one topic below to write an essay that compares or contrasts

a. a family member's response to an important decision with how you expected that person to respond

b. a perception of a family member that you held in your youth with a view of that person that you have today

c. your understanding or interpretation of a particular movie, song, or event with a friend's view

d. your concept of ideal employment with a job you have held or hold now

e. your understanding of how people of any age conform to the norms of their group with what happens in "The Lottery" (p. 199)

f. the narrator's and Leah's attitudes toward disfigurement in "Kiss Me" (p. 81)

g. your thoughts on the different attitudes men and women have toward technology after you have read "The Internet and Gender" (p. 66)

Readings That Use Comparison and Contrast

Works in this text that use comparison–contrast strategies for development include the following:

"Here's to Family Feasting," p. 4
"Welcome to FamilyValuesWorld!" p. 9
"Fathers, Sons and Hockey," p. 26
"Men as Success Objects," p. 50
"Hello, We're Not American!" p. 91
"Adding Weight to an Image of Beauty," p. 152
"A Plea for the Physical," p. 175

Final Tips for Comparison and Contrast

- Brainstorm by writing a parallel list of dimensions that the two subjects under discussion have in common.
- Make sure that your thesis includes both subjects that are being compared and contrasted, and that the wording is specific. Avoid a thesis that simply claims they are both alike and different.
- Use the block method for a paragraph-long comparison within a longer essay.
- Use the point-by-point method for an essay focusing on the comparison and contrast between two subjects, or for a more emphatic delivery of information.
- Continue interrelating the two subjects so that you never make a point about one without showing how it relates to the other.
- Search for subtle links and distinctions as well as for the obvious ones. Then analyse the reasons for those differences.

ARGUMENT

Convincing others that your beliefs and perspectives are worth understanding, and perhaps even supporting, can be a definite challenge. Sometimes one must counter both preconceptions and convictions in order to get readers to modify their beliefs or change their behaviour. In fact, persuasion is a part of many writing situations, and to convince readers that a certain assertion or opinion is supportable is the heart of argument.

Arguments and Proposals

A distinction can be made between two types of writing that attempt to convince readers to reconsider their views and beliefs:

- An **argument** employs logic to *reason* a point and get readers to *think*.
- A **proposal** employs logic to *influence* others and get readers to *think and act*.

Although these types of writing often overlap, some assignments seem to fit more in one category than the other. If you are asked to analyse an essay and argue for or against the writer's views, your essay will involve *argumentation*. You will be expected to focus on a thesis that can provoke readers' thoughts and to use supporting evidence that is logically presented and carefully analysed.

If you are asked to offer a solution to a problem or to persuade others to modify or change their behaviour, your essay will need to include a *proposal* in addition to argumentation. You will be expected to focus on a thesis that provokes a response. Therefore, you will also need to suggest a reasonable plan of action or activities for your readers.

Presenting a logical argument or proposal does not exclude appealing to your readers' emotions. For example, an essay may propose that the local school board establish more English-as-a-Second-Language programs in elementary schools to help immigrant children adjust to life in Canada. To appeal to readers emotionally, a Portuguese-Canadian writer may decide to begin by illustrating the isolation she felt when she was enrolled in an English-speaking kindergarten class but spoke no English. Another writer may start with research that demonstrates how bright students who have recently immigrated risk failing and dropping out before they finish high school. Both introductions would be designed to arouse an emotional response, yet both would need to be supported by logical evidence and analysis.

When to Use Argument

Argument strategies may be used in all types of essays. Whenever you are attempting to convince readers that one course of action is superior to another (comparison–contrast), that a particular behaviour caused a certain consequence (cause and effect), or that one interpretation of a reading has validity (analysis), you will need to employ argument strategies. Because you are attempting to convince readers of a view that may be different from their own, it often helps to begin by illustrating what is wrong with the current thinking or practice on this issue.

For example, if you are arguing that female students in the early grades need greater encouragement to succeed in math and science classes, then it would make sense to establish the need first. The introduction and part of the body of the essay might demonstrate how females are discouraged from enrolling in post-secondary math and science programs and how few women today excel in these fields, even though studies indicate females are no less capable of succeeding in science and math than males are.

How to Write an Argument

Like any other essay, an argument needs a clear thesis and strong support in order to convince readers that they should agree. In an argument, you should be willing to acknowledge other points of view, yet show why your argument is stronger. You should also be careful to avoid logical fallacies, which can damage your credibility.

Audience and Argument

It is critical to identify your *audience* and to find an approach that will best appeal to them. Identification of the audience may include asking these questions:

- Are readers aware that the problem exists?
- Will readers find the problem sufficiently important?
- Are readers affected by the problem?
- Do any readers have special interests or biases that will cause them to resist the information? The proposal? The essay?

If you are arguing for increased English-as-a-Second-Language programs in elementary schools, you may design your paper differently if your audience is comprised of immigrants as opposed to native speakers, or if it is predominantly educators as opposed to parents. If you can determine whether the audience is likely to be sympathetic, neutral, or hostile, you can design your approach with this in mind.

Organizing an Argument

In order to keep the argument focused and organized, an outline can be critical. Often this involves an informal list of points that you plan to cover, written in a logical order. The outline functions as a map to keep you on track. It may also help your instructor follow the argument and detect any flaws or gaps before the essay is actually written. In such cases, a more formal outline may be required. (For an illustration of an informal outline for an essay, see p. 242.)

Avoiding Logical Fallacies

Just as the argument must be presented in logical order, the thinking and analysis must be logical, too. Name-calling and personal attacks only weaken an argument because they suggest that the writer is desperate and has no other support or logical reasoning to defend the argument. Moreover, such devices are **logical fallacies**, having no basis or foundation in reason. These tactics discredit the argument and erode readers' trust.

Illogical claims, whether intentional or not, are often associated with advertisers and politicians, whose careers may depend on their power to manipulate and mislead the public. Calling someone a "liberal" or a "redneck" is intended to get the audience to respond emotionally to a prejudice rather than to think rationally about an issue. Often these attacks are designed to divert attention from the issue to the opponent's personal traits or associates, in order to cast doubt on his or her character or expertise.

Besides smearing or ridiculing the opponent, the following logical fallacies may involve manipulating the argument itself:

- A **circular argument** does not prove anything because it simply restates the assertion: "Writing instructors are the best teachers in college because the best teachers teach writing." This argument can be summarized as "The best teachers are the best teachers," illustrating the repetitive nature and consequent logical fallacy in the statement.
- An **either/or argument** sets up a false black-and-white dilemma, assuming that a particular viewpoint or course of action can only have two diametrically opposed outcomes: "If my parents don't pay for my education, I won't be able to go to college." The writer assumes there are no other possible financial alternatives available, such as a job or a student loan.
- A **hasty generalization** consists of drawing a broad conclusion from one or a few unrepresentative generalizations: "My roommate at college studies constantly and never goes to parties; therefore, college students are not interested in having a social life." The conclusion is based on only one piece of evidence, one roommate's habits, that does not represent all college students.
- A **false analogy** compares two things that are not really comparable and therefore results in a false conclusion: "Since developmental math classes can be taught effectively in a large lecture hall, developmental English classes can be, too." This argument assumes that the two subjects are so similar that they can be taught effectively in the same type of setting.
- A **bandwagon appeal** suggests that "everyone is doing this—why don't you?" This pressures readers to conform whether or not the view or action seems logical or right: "Most students buy essays these days rather than writing their own, so you should too." The writer argues that since most students cheat, readers should join the crowd.

These are only some of the many logical fallacies that can weaken an argument. Instead of relying on illogical attacks and charges, you must seek logical support for your positions and seek legitimate flaws in your opponent's argument.

Conceding and Refuting

Rather than twisting facts or attacking the person, it is best to anticipate the opponent's objections and refute them, logically and directly, before readers can even utter "But. . . ." Overlooking or ignoring potential holes in an argument can render your argument vulnerable to attack. It doesn't necessarily weaken your argument to recognize what may appear to be a weakness in your plan, provided you can refute it and show that it doesn't really undermine your argument.

Another effective strategy is to acknowledge conflicting viewpoints and perhaps even admit they have merit, but then show how your solution or viewpoint is still superior. Such a strategy suggests that you are informed, open-minded, and reasonable—qualities that will make readers more receptive to your argument.

Evaluating an Argument

Arguments and proposals written by students can be more than mere classroom exercises. They can be sent to newspapers, television stations, Web sites, corporations, and government agencies. Several of the argument assignments in the "Writing from the Text" and "Connecting with Other Texts" sections of the Reader involve college-related issues and may be appropriate for the editorial or opinion page of your campus or local newspaper.

Consider these questions in order to evaluate the effectiveness of an argument:

- Who is the targeted audience, and how does the writer appeal to this audience?
- What is the problem? What is the thesis?
- What are the supporting points?
- What are the strengths of the argument?
- What are the weaknesses? Are there any logical fallacies?
- How does the ending bring satisfying closure to the essay?

Example: Argument

The following essay was written by student Richard Evans. Think about the questions listed above as you read his argument.

Accepting Refugees for What They Are
Richard Evans

Last summer, newspapers and newscasts were full of stories about the arrival of Gypsies (or Roma, as they prefer to be called) from Czechoslovakia, seeking refugee status. During that time, many callers to radio talk shows expressed not sympathy for them, but outrage: here was a group that had circumvented the law, they said, that had avoided normal immigration procedures to enter Canada. Worse, the callers maintained, the Roma are known criminals in their home countries and are therefore undesirable as immigrants, even if they were to enter via the normal procedures. "Send them back to where they came from" was the cry of these angry Canadians, intent on maintaining a respect for law and order above all.

The sentiments expressed in these calls disturbed me, partly because I once held the same attitude. Life in Canada is comfortable, so it's hard to believe that it could be different anywhere else. Yet I have had the honour of getting to know some refugees personally and of hearing their stories; my opinion has now changed radically. In response to those angry callers, I say, accept refugees for who they are. Canadians need to understand that refugees are people in need of a haven from persecution, and that we should be helping them, not rejecting them.

Several years ago, because of its good location and low rents, my neighbourhood began to attract refugees as a place to live. As I got to know my new neighbours, I realized to my shame that I had formed my impressions based on stereotypes, well before I ever had met a single refugee. Too many people are influenced by negative stereotypes of refugees, as I was. I learned that my neighbours are not terrorists. They do not carry weapons. They are not lazy. They are not opportunists, trying to beat the system. If they are on welfare here, the reason is that the government forbids them to work until their immigration status is clarified. Those who work pay taxes without complaints. All live frugally so they can support their families here and help any loved ones they have left behind. All are grateful to live in Canada, in safety, despite the upheaval of leaving home and adjusting to a new culture. They want to raise their children to be good citizens, just as any Canadian does.

In my experience, it doesn't matter where the refugees come from; they have suffered in one way or another. One of my neighbours was arrested and tortured in his home country because he was a member of a union. Another watched helplessly as his son was gunned down by a sniper in the street outside his home. A third lost her parents and brothers when the restaurant they were celebrating her mother's birthday in was bombed by a terrorist faction. Unbelievable as these occurrences would be in Canada, these are the everyday occurrences for many refugees that prompt them to come to Canada. If the Roma or other groups say they are fleeing to avoid persecution, immigration officials should be the people to decide the validity of the claims, not the court of public opinion. Every group, even Canadian-born, has members of questionable character, and we should leave weeding out of undesirable immigrants to the immigration process. In the meantime, we should do what we can to help the newcomers adjust to life here.

Some people argue that refugees want to take jobs that belong to Canadians away from us. From what I have seen in my neighbours, even if they were professionals in their home country, they take the jobs that most Canadians don't want: noisy factory jobs, or work as night cleaners or cab drivers. Nor do refugees want social assistance; they prefer honourable work, at minimum wage, if necessary.

Some people believe that we need to be protected from refugees rather than the contrary, that refugees are in need of our protection. Refugees are not enemy invaders, landing in Canada with artillery, ready to confiscate our property, murder our families, or subjugate us to their political systems. Many refugees have lived through just such ordeals and wish to escape such torment, not bring it here. Most come with little more than an intense desire to build a new life in a safe country.

Canadians should have the same compassion for refugees as they have for the world's famine and flood victims. Refugees have suffered enough by the time they get to Canada; they have been victimized and deserve refuge, not harassment. They ask only for safety for themselves and their families, a chance to learn English, and an opportunity build a new life. It was no easier for them to escape their homelands, often at great risk, to a country where they must relearn almost everything, than it would be for you or me to leave Canada with nothing and start a new life somewhere else. I wonder how many Canadians, under the same circumstances, would show as much courage.

The undisguised racism I heard on the radio sickened me. I've seen bumper stickers on some cars that says "Hate hurts," and I used to think they meant that hate hurts the person it's directed to. I realize now that hate also hurts the person who perpetrates it, and by extension, the whole country. Hate diminishes us all. More people need to speak out against racism against immigrants in general, and racism against refugees in particular.

Analysing Argument Strategy

Richard's introduction begins with an account of events that prompted him to write this essay. This background establishes the rationale for his argument: hearing angry callers to phone-in shows reminds him of stereotyped views he once shared with them but came to change, based on experiences with his refugee neighbours. He is able to admit to his discomfort at hearing in the callers' arguments what once was his own prejudiced viewpoint, an openness that establishes common ground with his audience. If readers are against refugees' entry into Canada, they may wonder how someone who once held the same view came to change his mind and may be intrigued enough to read further. His thesis is clearly stated at the end of the second paragraph: "Canadians need to understand that refugees are people in need of a haven from persecution, and that we should be helping them, not rejecting them."

Richard goes on to dispel some of the myths that some Canadians may believe about refugees: that they are terrorists or opportunists wishing to take resources from other Canadians. Richard's sympathetic portrait of his neighbours shows readers how similar refugees are to them, rather than how different they are. He explains that refugees on welfare would rather be working but are prevented from doing so because of the time it takes to the government to process their requests. Just as most Canadians do, his neighbours work hard once they do find jobs and try to live within their means.

Richard's three concrete examples of his neighbours' life-and-death experiences contrast sharply with the rights, comforts, and safety that Canadians take for granted. He acknowledges readers' potential disbelief but reiterates that such events do happen in other countries, as he has learned. Consequently, he urges readers to accept the Roma refugees' claims of persecution and trust the immigration process to discover anyone trying to enter the country under false pretenses. As well, he reminds readers that every nation, even Canada, has honest and dishonest citizens.

In the next section of the essay, Richard refutes two counter-arguments his opposition might raise: the fear that refugees take jobs from Canadians and that refugees could somehow damage the Canadian way of life. In response, Richard cites his neighbours' willingness, whatever their status might have been in their homeland, to take low-paying jobs that many Canadians do not want. He then explains that refugees have no interest in importing the very terrors they themselves are fleeing from. This acknowledgment of conflicting viewpoints uses logic rather than logical fallacies to show shortcomings of possible counter-arguments. By having the courage to raise the other side's arguments and show why they are incorrect, Richard adds powerful support to his point of view.

Richard concludes with a plea that readers offer refugees the same compassion they feel for other people in the world who are suffering. He asks readers to consider the difficulty of leaving one's homeland and starting over. Finally, he reinforces his argument by reminding readers of what he has learned about hatred and how it reflects on the person, and by extension, the nation, that allows hatred to flourish. His concluding sentence points to action his readers can take to put an end to racism against both immigrants and refugees, and his essay is a graphic example of one citizen's effort to do just that.

Practising Writing Argument Essays

Write an essay to convince your readers of one of the following assertions:

a. All college students, regardless of age, ethnic background, or social status, are (or are not) caught "between worlds."
b. Skateboarders should (or should not) be prosecuted if they pursue their sport on public streets.
c. Year-round school is (or is not) a viable solution to cutting education costs.
d. Music videos should (or should not) be subject to the same rating system as movies are.
e. Pam Withers (p. 54) is correct (or incorrect) in saying that "boycotting male babysitters is a poor substitute for carefully screening a caregiver of any gender."
f. Brenda Austin-Smith (p. 66) is (or is not) correct in her position that the Internet is hostile to women.
g. The rising threat of AIDS, as outlined in "Love and Fear in the Age of AIDS" (p. 75), is (or is not) a significant problem that warrants an intensive information campaign at your college.
h. Regional politicians should (or should not) be free to change place names in order to follow "politically correct" thinking of their time, as in the example in "'Negro' Name Change Protested" (p. 143).

Readings That Use Argument

Essays in this text that use argument to persuade readers to change their beliefs or behaviour include the following:

"Welcome to FamilyValuesWorld!" p. 9
"Men as Success Objects," p. 50
"The Babysitters Club: No Boys Allowed," p. 54

Final Tips for Argument

- Recognize your purpose (argument or proposal).
- Identify your audience, consider their perspective, and prepare your appeal. Avoid insulting or attacking them.
- Word your thesis carefully to provoke thought or action.
- Outline your argument so it is focused and organized.
- Support all claims with convincing evidence and reasoned analysis.
- Anticipate objections and differing viewpoints, and show why your argument is stronger even if the others have some merit.
- Guard against logical fallacies; they weaken any argument.
- Make sure your conclusion brings satisfying closure to your argument. Avoid tacking on any new points.

ANALYSIS: PROCESS, PROBLEM, AND SUBJECT

When you analyse anything—a film, an instructor's performance, an experiment in a chemistry lab, or even your roommate's mysterious casserole—you are taking the whole apart to examine its components. This, in turn, lets you understand how the parts contribute to the entire work. The purpose of an **analysis** is not merely to take the process, problem, or subject apart, but to see the *value* of the individual parts and to appreciate their *interaction* in creating the whole.

When to Use Analysis

You analyse constantly, perhaps without knowing you are going through any formal steps. For example, if you are giving a party, you may have an unconscious order or process. You will wait to hear who is coming before you shop for food, clean before you decorate, and stock the coolers before your friends arrive. The order of these steps is important. Further, you know that each individual step is important to achieving a successful whole—a great party—and that if any step is neglected (like no ice for the cooler), the party may flop.

Written analysis involves the same attention to order and details, regardless of the academic field. In fact, you will find that written analysis is assigned in every academic discipline. Whether you are dissecting a frog in biology, interpreting a painting in art history, examining a poem in English, reviewing curriculum in education, exploring a management problem in business, or studying a discrimination problem in law, you will be expected to write analytical papers.

These papers will be specifically targeted to the subject you are studying, but three basic types of analytical assignments predominate: analysis of a process, a problem, or a subject. Sometimes these distinctions blur, depending on your purpose and audience. For example, you might write a set of directions for dissecting a frog, describe how frogs are usually dissected, or write about the problems that students have in biology courses. All of these papers involve breaking the whole into parts and examining the parts to show readers their importance to the whole.

ANALYSIS OF A PROCESS

A paper that examines a **process** explains how to do something or how the process itself is carried out: for example, perform a swimming pool rescue, get a classmate to ask you out, train for a marathon, cook using a wok, avoid loaning your favourite jacket, develop and print a roll of black and white film, pay car insurance while earning minimum wage, or get a roommate's friend to move out.

How to Write a Process Analysis
Brainstorming for a Topic

If a topic has not been assigned, brainstorm for possibilities. Consider what you know how to do that others don't (such as how to make a perfect quiche) or what you would like to learn in order to explain that process to readers (such as how to create a dried-flower arrangement). Don't overlook the unusual: how to wallpaper the inside of your car, how to chart a cross-country flight for the least amount of money, or how to get your little brother to do your chores. You might also want to research how other people do things: how communities implement recycling projects, how laws are passed in Parliament, how a new course becomes part of your college's curriculum, or how marketing firms predict consumers' willingness to try new products. Remember that a process analysis paper doesn't need to be dull or tedious. These papers can be lively if you use ingenuity and a little prewriting energy.

Drafting a Paper

If you are writing a paper that tells your readers how to do something, or one that describes how something happens, these tips will help:

1. Determine whether or not the chronology is important. For some processes, the sequence of the steps is critical (performing a swimming pool rescue), while for others it isn't as important (getting a classmate to ask you out).

2. If the chronology is important, list the steps and re-examine your list to make sure readers will be able to follow the logic of your arrangement.

3. Write each step completely, including all the necessary information and removing confusing or irrelevant details. Group steps into stages, if possible. For example, processing a black and white film is one stage made up of a series of smaller steps requiring particular equipment and chemicals; printing the contact sheet is a separate stage requiring different equipment and chemicals. Together, the steps lead a student photographer through the film processing to creation of a finished print.

   Imagine yourself in your readers' position, trying to follow your instructions for something they have never done.

4. Write a thesis that clearly asserts your point:

   Thesis: Creating dried-flower arrangements is satisfying and lucrative.

   Thesis: Following the proper sequence of steps will facilitate a swimming pool rescue.

5. Draft your essay by linking each step with appropriate transitions to move your readers smoothly through this process.

6. Rewrite and edit your essay so that the language is vivid and the directions are precise.

Example: Process Analysis

In the following essay, Walter Gajewski, a professional working in the academic computing field, describes the process of using e-mail.

E-Mail for Neophytes
Walter Gajewski

Communicating with friends and colleagues worldwide is no longer the exclusive tool of the "mad hacker." Students and faculty at most colleges now have access to e-mail--electronic mail--which combines the capabilities of the computer with those of the telephone line. Text, sound, and video movies can be transmitted, by way of phone lines, from one computer address to another.

To contact colleagues at distant locations, you need to have an account on a server at an organization like a business, hospital, or school, or else you must subscribe to a commercial Internet Service Provider such as HookUp, IDirect, InfoRamp, Spectra, or Sympatico. The Internet is a complex, worldwide network of thousands of computers that are accessible to professors, government researchers, industry--and you, if your home computer or computer lab at school has access to the Internet. Over the Internet, talk is cheap. No matter how many messages you send or how far you send them, your college or university does not pay anything beyond the fixed amount required to maintain its own portion of the Internet.

When you use e-mail, you need to have a specific account name, which is your e-mail "address." Before you can log on to your computer account, the computer will ask you to enter your secret password. (No one else should know or needs to know this password to send you mail.) Next, call up the mail utility software and wait to be asked for the "address" of the person or persons you are contacting. This could be one address, or it could be a word (an "alias") that represents a mailing list of thousands of addresses that you compiled ahead of time. After you enter the complete address, the computer will request the subject of your communication, and then the body of your message. This message you type in may be any length.

When you are finished, you simply give the command that indicates you are done. (This command varies depending on your software package.) The computer will ask if you want to send copies to anyone else. The computer then sends off your message. In a matter of seconds, your mail arrives at its destination anywhere in the world.

As important as speed is the fact that documents travelling directly from computer to computer remain as computer files rather than as a fixed printed page. Therefore, this document can be immediately edited without needing to be retyped into the computer. The ease and versatility of this process has made e-mail very popular today. But the possibilities for e-mail are just emerging. If you are interested in the future of interpersonal communication, make sure you check in the mail--the e-mail, that is.

Small-Group Discussion About the Process Analysis Essay

In small groups, discuss Gajewski's strategy.

1. How does Gajewski attract readers to his subject? Who is his intended audience?

2. Why does Gajewski incorporate definition in this analysis?

3. What is the process described? In what ways is chronology important to this analysis?

4. Cite specific details that Gajewski includes to encourage readers to consider using e-mail.

5. If you are computer literate, can you follow the description of this process to use e-mail? Are there any steps that need to be expanded or removed?

Practising Process Analysis

1. In small groups, write down the steps explaining how to do the following:
   a. find summer employment
   b. balance a diet to achieve good nutrition
   c. prepare a three-year-old to play in the snow
   d. stay awake in a dull lecture
   e. convince an unwilling landlord to make a repair
   f. use library computers to find a book or an article on immigrants seeking refugee status

   Spend time reaching accord within your group to ensure that all steps follow logically and that no necessary steps are left out. Aim for clarity and precision; remove words that obscure your directions. Any one of these analyses could be drafted into a collaborative paper.

2. Select and explain a process that you know well from the list below:
   a. how social cliques form
   b. how a camera or video camera works
   c. how a college orients its first-year students
   d. how glaciers form
   e. how Olympic teams are created
   f. how a batik is made

g. how pool, backgammon, or your favourite game or sport is played

h. how a musical piece is practised for performance

Write your explanation as precisely as you can so that readers can learn the process. Does your interest in the topic show in your description?

Readings That Use Process Analysis

Throughout this textbook, you will notice a number of sections that explain various processes: how to conduct an interview; how to cluster, list, and read actively; how to incorporate quoted material; how to write a thesis or an outline. These sections of *Between Worlds* may be useful to you as models of process analysis. They also underscore how important process is to teaching and learning.

The essay "Making a Difference" (p. 191) contains a modified version of the kind of process analysis discussed in this chapter.

Final Tips for Analysing a Process

- Review the order of the steps you have written to determine that your readers can follow your instructions or description.

- Examine the details you have given to remove any confusing instructions or irrelevant details.

- Put yourself in your readers' position to see if you have defined necessary terms and provided necessary details.

- Reread your work to see if appropriate transitions link the steps or the parts of your analysis.

ANALYSIS OF A PROBLEM

Another kind of analysis paper describes a **problem**; it may or may not offer a solution. The writer may trace the history of the problem, but chronology is not as vital to this type of analysis as it is in a step-by-step process analysis. It is critical in this type of analysis to establish the problem, examine its parts, and show how the parts are related to the problem as a whole.

When to Use Problem Analysis

More than any other single type of writing, problem analysis appears in every academic field and profession. Our daily newspapers, weekly news magazines, monthly periodicals, and scholarly journals all feature essays analysing issues. The writers of the readings in this textbook analyse a variety of problems: alcoholism, drug abuse, irresponsible parenting, closeted homosexuals, living between two cultures, stereotyping, isolation of people with disabilities, group conformity, work patterns, and racial, ethnic, and gender discrimination. In spite of the wide range of issues, writers of problem analysis share similar strategies when they examine an issue.

How to Write a Problem Analysis

Your initial job in any writing situation is to engage your readers, and nowhere is this more important than in problem analysis. Why should your readers care about stereotypes, the rights of the disabled, or any other subject that doesn't directly relate to them? It is your job to create reader interest, and you can do this in a number of ways. Sometimes a historical review of the problem will intrigue readers. Startling statistics or a bold anecdote should jar complacent readers out of apathy. Sometimes posing a direct question prompts readers to consider their responses and become involved in the topic—at least enough to read the work. After you have engaged your readers, decide how much background information they require in order to understand the problem. For example, if you are writing an analysis of changing interest rates, you will include less background material if you are writing the paper for your business class than for your English class.

Then, as in all analysis papers, you will need to decide the parts of the problem that you want to examine. You must describe the problem so that any reader can understand it. This might include a discussion of the severity of the problem, the numbers affected by it, which population is most affected, and the consequences if this problem is uncorrected. A detailed study of each aspect of the problem and how it relates to the other parts will constitute the body of your paper. You might speculate about the barriers to solving this problem (such as cost, frustration with earlier failures, indifference, or denial), if they are relevant to your analysis.

It is important that this analysis have a focus and a clear point or assertion. For example, if you are concerned about the fact that Canadians are on the job more than workers in other countries, it is not enough merely to identify the number of hours that Canadian employees work each week. Nor is it enough to show that they work more hours per week and more weeks per year than their European counterparts, or that they are not routinely given flexible work schedules so they can coordinate their family's needs with their work responsibilities. All of these important facts could support a point, but the point must be made.

You will need to clarify, in the form of a thesis or assertion, why the analysis of these facts is important: that Canadian workers are overworked, that Canadians have insufficient leisure time, that Canadian children grow up deprived of their parents, or any other point that you deem significant as a result of your analysis. But without a point, you have no paper.

Once you have determined your assertion, you are ready to outline, draft, and revise your paper. (See the student example of a problem analysis on eating disorders, pp. 239–61, for specific suggestions about outlining, drafting, and revising.)

Example: Problem Analysis

The essay in the Chapter 4 of the Reader entitled "Don't Let Stereotypes Warp Your Judgments" (p. 128), written by economist Robert L. Heilbroner, contains a unique perception of a common problem. Read Heilbroner's problem analysis and then answer the following questions.

Small-Group Discussion About the Problem Analysis Essay

In small groups, discuss Heilbroner's strategy:

1. How does Heilbroner attract readers? What is his introduction technique?
2. What does Heilbroner perceive as the real problem of stereotyping? Where does his assertion appear? How does Heilbroner convince readers that stereotyping is a problem if they have never felt victimized by stereotyping?
3. How does Heilbroner analyse the severity of the problem? According to Heilbroner's analysis of the problem, which populations are engaged in stereotyping, and how widespread is this? Evaluate the quality of his support and how he uses it.
4. Explain why Heilbroner moves into a process analysis mode to propose a solution to the problem of stereotyping.

Practising Problem Analysis

Problem analysis assignments appear after many of the works in the Reader. In addition to those that reflect the theme of being "between worlds," you might write an analysis of any of these problems:

a. limited inexpensive housing available for college students
b. policies at work or school that seem poorly conceived
c. a family's inability to communicate

d. athletes' use of drugs
e. unnecessary packaging of everyday products
f. overdrinking and overeating in our society

Readings That Use Problem Analysis

Essays in this book that are examples of a problem analysis include the following:

Final Tips for Analysing a Problem

- Engage your readers to convince them of the importance of the problem.
- Provide sufficient background information for your intended audience.

- Make sure that your thesis expresses why your analysis of the problem is important.
- Reread and revise to ascertain that you have adequately discussed the parts of the problem that require analysis, and that you have related those parts to the problem as a whole.

ANALYSIS OF A SUBJECT

Another type of analysis paper is one that examines a **subject**—a painting, poem, sculpture, car, contract, course, or short story. An analysis paper may also focus on a particular aspect of the subject—the composition of a painting, an image in a poem, the proportions of a sculpture, the motor of a car, the exceptions of a contract, the requirements of a course, or a character in a short story. These papers, too, involve breaking the subject into parts and closely examining them to show readers the importance of the parts to the subject as a whole.

When to Use Subject Analysis

Instructors expect analysis when their assignments and exam questions contain words such as *explain, interpret, describe, explore why, show how, explicate, discuss, relate,* or *trace.* If you have been asked to examine an art object, explain an economic plan, explicate a particular work of literature, explore why a company's health plan needs review, show how a historical treatise influenced a movement, trace a legal decision, analyse a political candidate's platform, or describe a community's park system, you are required to examine the parts—or a part that has been assigned—and show how that part or those parts relate to the whole.

How to Write a Subject Analysis
Brainstorming for a Topic

If a topic has not been assigned, brainstorm to find a subject that interests you or for which you have some information. While it might not make sense for someone without mechanical aptitude to decide to analyse what is under the hood of a Volkswagen Jetta or for a mechanical engineering student to analyse "The Love Song of J. Alfred Prufrock," don't select a subject that is too familiar. The purpose of any writing assignment is discovery, and nothing will help you understand a subject better than careful analysis.

Drafting a Paper

Examine carefully the subject that you have selected or that has been assigned. Question the significance of the work, responding to it with a fresh perspective. Don't assume that because it is a famous work of art or literature, it is therefore worthy of analysis. Determine for yourself why the subject is worth the time that you will devote to examining it.

If you have not been assigned a particular part to analyse, make a list of as many aspects or parts of the subject as you can. Then consider which parts are most significant and which you can most productively examine. In some cases, the success of your paper and how you will be evaluated will be determined by your ability to limit your selection to particularly provocative or relevant aspects. Ultimately, your job will be to show the significance of the parts or a particular part in relation to the entire work.

As introductory material, before you begin your analysis of the parts, describe the whole subject briefly. Remember that description is not the same thing as analysis, but realize also that your readers can't care about the parts without knowing something about the whole. Depending on the subject of your analysis, this introductory description might involve a historical context (of a treatise, bill, contract), an overall physical description (of a sculpture, painting, motor, person), or a summary (of a novel, short story, play, poem, bill, contract).

Write your minute description and detailed perception of the parts that you perceive to be the most significant for an understanding of the work. As you write an analysis of each part, keep your eye on the whole. Whether you are analysing an art form, literary work, or object, you will need to return to your subject repeatedly to be sure that you are seeing or reading it thoroughly and carefully. You will not be able to write an analysis of a painting quickly glimpsed or a poem read only once.

Focus your paper with an assertion that shows your perception of the parts in relation to the subject that you are analysing. Expressing your perception in the form of a thesis will keep both you and your readers on target.

Character Analysis
When to Use Character Analysis

Because literary analysis is frequently assigned in English courses, and because narratives are often read in college composition classes, we include here a **character analysis** to demonstrate the process of analysing a subject. Character analysis can be used to study someone you know or someone in a text—a narrative, a poem, a short story, a novel, a play, or a biography. In history, psychology, art, and education courses, you may be asked to analyse the traits of a particular person in order to understand the time period, the created work, or the behaviour of important figures.

How to Write a Character Analysis

Whether you are examining a subject from life or print, you will want to observe and record telling details—those that reveal something significant about the person. As you study a character, you will accumulate lots of facts, some that you will discard as irrelevant and others that you will decide are indicative of the person's character. From these facts, you will be able to make assumptions about your subject's personality and character. In fact, the heart of your analysis will depend on inference—that is, a hypothesis that you formulate about character based on the facts that you have observed.

PREWRITING FOR A TEXT-BASED CHARACTER STUDY

As you actively read the narrative or biography, list specific examples of speech, behaviour, and thought that reveal the character. Read the text with an alert eye, pulling examples, important phrases, and key lines for your list. Mix facts and your responses or inferences about them as you go along. You do not need to evaluate each example as you write your list; you will sort, eliminate, and reword examples later.

LISTING INFORMATION FROM A BOOK

If you are keeping notes for a biographical study and are using a full-length book, you might find it useful to keep separate index cards for each character trait that you observe while you are reading. Record the page numbers each time you see that trait reappearing. By the time that you have completed a 300- or 400-page biography, you may have 15 or 20 different "inference cards," each with a different trait written at the top and each with many recorded page numbers. The cards that have similar traits can be grouped, the traits with few page numbers can be ignored, and the traits that look most useful for a character study can then be shaped into focus points for the paper. The page numbers on the cards that will form the focus points for the paper should be written into paraphrased and quoted note cards. These cards can then be arranged for a draft. This system of note taking, a variation of listing, is especially useful for longer texts.

LISTING INFORMATION FROM A SHORT STORY

If you are taking notes from a short text—a poem, play, or short story—you can use lined paper for your list. Here is how a list of character traits describing Grandmama, the central character in Wayson Choy's short story "The Jade Peony" (p. 17), might look:

- refuses to go to the hospital when she is sick (p. 17)
- works out the details of her will (p. 17)
- says "I am too stubborn" to father (p. 17)
- reaches for grandson Sek-Lung's hand (p. 17)
- taught Sek-Lung juggling tricks when he was six (p. 18)
- skilled at making windchimes (p. 18)
- embarrasses family by scavenging in back alley (p. 18)
- lies about later scavenging trips to appease family (p. 19)
- prepares pieces for windchimes in secret (p. 19)
- searches for "special pieces" of glass in a burnt-out church (p. 19)
- controls family argument about learning languages by complimenting members and then saying "We are all Chinese" (seems manipulative yet firm in her beliefs) (p. 20)
- teaches Sek-Lung how to make windchimes (pp. 20–21)
- calmly tells Sek-Lung that when she trembles, her body is fighting death (p. 21)
- shops for special silk (p. 21)
- says the jade peony is the colour of her spirit (p. 21)
- blushes when she remembers her girlhood admirer (p. 21)
- she and Sek-Lung work together on her final windchime (pp. 21–22)
- says chime cannot make any sound until she dies (p. 22)
- believes she will become a ghost and return (p. 22)
- says to Sek-Lung, "I will always be with you" (p. 22)
- dies in basement of the hospital (p. 23)

GROUPING AND ARRANGING

The grouping of like ideas on the list may be the next step in the prewriting of your character analysis. Find examples that belong together—usually because they support the trait that you have inferred about the person—and rewrite your list or number the examples on your list to reflect the commonality that prompts you to place the details together. If the reason the details belong together comes to you, or you realize that the details support a character inference, write down your idea.

Here is how the grouped list of details about Grandmama might look:

Character Traits	Inferences
• refuses to go to the hospital when she is sick • embarrasses family by scavenging in back alley • lies about later scavenging trips to appease family • prepares pieces for windchimes in secret	rebellious
• controls family argument about learning languages by complimenting members and then saying "We are all Chinese" (seems manipulative yet firm in her beliefs)	manipulative
• reaches for grandson Sek-Lung's hand • taught Sek-Lung juggling tricks when he was six • teaches Sek-Lung how to make windchimes • she and Sek-Lung work together on her final windchime • says to Sek-Lung, "I will always be with you"	loving and caring
• blushes when she remembers her girlhood admirer	sentimental or easily embarrasssed
• says chime cannot make a sound until she dies • believes she will become a ghost and return	superstitious
• works out the details of her will • says "I am too stubborn" to father • calmly tells Sek-Lung that when she trembles, her body is fighting death	strong facing death

Listing and grouping may take some time, but by listing the details of character that are important, and by grouping items on the list that are analogous, you will have done a considerable amount of preparation for your paper. You will have concrete examples to support your assertions, and you will have a systematic arrangement of inferences that you can supplement with other examples from the text that you might have missed in your first list.

Arranging and Thesis Construction

Consider how you will arrange your character traits and the specific examples that support the traits. What do you want to emphasize in your analysis? Consider ending your character analysis with the trait that you find most significant or most indicative of character. By using your most emphatic point in the terminal spot in your paper, you will have a natural conclusion—one that gets at both the heart of your subject and the theme of the short story.

Perhaps the place to start is with the most obvious feature of the subject for analysis, because it will take less effort to convince your audience of your perception if your readers share your perception. In the case of Grandmama, her advanced age and approaching death are probably the dramatic starting points for the analysis.

DETERMINING A THESIS

You need to have a thesis for your character study, whether or not you include it in your paper. You can determine one by using the character traits that you perceived during grouping. Remember that your thesis expresses a view about a limited subject, such as Grandmama's character. If you have many observations on your prewriting list, you are well on your way to determining your thesis.

Here are some possibilities for thesis statements for the character analysis of Grandmama. Remember, each writer's perceptions and preferences will determine the thesis and the order in which the information will be presented.

1. Grandmama appears to be a rebellious old woman, but she is also strong and caring about her family and its Chinese heritage.
2. Because Grandmama is so rebellious, it is surprising to find sensitive, loving qualities in her character.
3. Grandmama is a loving old woman whose caring commitment to her favourite grandson is masked by the rebellious exterior she shows the rest of her family.
4. Although Grandmama rebels against her family's rules, her behaviour is a sign of her strong will as she faces death.

Example: Character Analysis

As you read this character analysis, notice that in addition to a thorough examination of the separate qualities of her subject's character, student Victoria Hogan returns to the essence of the entire work to bring closure to her study.

First and Second Childhoods
Victoria Hogan

The phrase "She's in her second childhood" is often used to explain senile behaviour in the elderly. It is true that their concern about poor health can make the elderly appear more self-centred than they had been in earlier years. However, the phrase has a more positive connotation in the case of the character Grandmama in the story "The Jade Peony" by Wayson Choy. Although Grandmama chafes at her family's rules like a rebellious child, her behaviour is a sign of her strong will, in the face of death, to pass on her love and Chinese traditions to her favourite young grandson.

Grandmama's strength is apparent from the first time we meet her, eighty-three years old and very sick. She endures terrible coughing fits at night that do not respond to traditional herbal remedies, and she prepares to finalize her will. Knowing that at this point in her life she cannot hide from death, she admits, "'I am too stubborn. The only cure for old age is to die'" (17). When her hand trembles, she calmly says to her young grandson Sek-Lung, "'That is my body fighting with Death. He is in this room now'" (21). Her courage to face her inevitable end counteracts his panic and soon he is absorbed in the activity she is teaching him, the creation of windchimes.

It is this activity that necessitates Grandmama's rebellious behaviour. Her regular visits to local back alleys to scavenge through garbage cans for "a treasure trove of glass fragments and castaway costume jewellery" (18) embarrass her family too much. The solution is to lie about the outings she and Sek-Lung are having, to call them "shopping trips" (19) when the only browsing they are doing is through the garbage of people in neighbourhoods so far away the family won't suspect. Accomplices, Grandmama and Sek-Lung prepare their "splendid junk" for the windchimes in secret, and they keep them under Grandmama's bed, well-hidden from the rest of the family (19).

Grandmama may appear rebellious, yet an important incident in the story indicates that there is a larger reason than simple defiance behind her actions. During a family squabble about the need for learning the Mandarin Chinese language, she manipulates the situation. She compliments Stepmother and Kiam to ease the tension, and then states firmly, "'We are all Chinese'" (20). Grandmama reminds her family that they may be living in Canada, but their Chinese background must not be abandoned. This is why she must teach Sek-Lung how to make traditional windchimes as she learned to, even if their "shopping trips" go against the family's wishes. Being the youngest, the least judgmental, and always in her company, Sek-Lung is the most receptive to her teachings.

Along with learning the skill of making windchimes, Sek-Lung absorbs Grandmama's superstitions. Their final, sacred, and carefully prepared windchime is not to make a sound until after Grandmama's death. Father is then to put it in Grandmama's window, the old woman tells her grandson, "'so that my ghost may see it, and hear it, and return. I must say good-bye to this world properly or wander in this foreign land for-ever'" (22). Her love for Sek-Lung in life, demonstrated by her reaching for his hand to comfort them both when she is sick (17) and teaching him the old ways, will be repeated even after her death. She reassures him, saying, "'I will always be with you, Little Sek-Lung, but in a different way . . . You'll see'" (22). The things she has taught him will live on in him.

Grandmama may be in her second childhood, breaking the rules and having a six-year-old as her favoured companion, but she uses that stage of her life to teach Sek-Lung a life les-son during his first childhood: the importance of love and strength in the face of inevitable death. If she must occa-sionally rebel to ensure she has taught him well, she will do so, and he will be the beneficiary of her love for him.

Work Cited

Choy, Wayson. "The Jade Peony." Between Worlds: A Reader, Rhetoric, and Handbook. First Canadian Edition. Ed. Susan Bachmann, Melinda Barth, and Karen Golets Pancer. Don Mills: Addison Wesley Longman, 1998. 17-23.

Small-Group Discussion About the Character Analysis

In small groups, discuss the strategies Victoria employs in her character analysis. Consider these questions:

1. What is the strategy of Victoria's introductory paragraph?

2. What is the thesis of this character study?

3. How does Victoria convince readers that her character inferences are sound?

4. How is each paragraph individually focused? How is each paragraph related to the essay as a whole?

5. How does Victoria give her readers an understanding both of the parts of Grandmama's character and of their relationship to her as a whole? How does Victoria's character analysis contribute to your understanding of the short story as a whole?

Practising Character Analysis

In small groups, select one of the following:

1. Write a list of character traits that describe Saliha, from "Ajax Là-Bas" (p. 110). Group the details that belong together, arrange the details, and write an assertion—a thesis—that would be workable for a character analysis.

2. Write a list of character traits that describe Aspasia Kaplaneris, the author of "Earthbound . . . for Now" (p. 139). Group the details that belong together, arrange the details, and write an assertion—a thesis—that would be workable for a character analysis.

Essay Assignments for Subject Analysis

Practise writing an analysis of one of the topics below:

a. a favourite painting or a photo from a magazine
b. the lyrics to a piece of music
c. a piece of laboratory, electronic, or exercise equipment
d. the setting or music in a particular film
e. a controversial campus policy
f. the image of wolf willow in "In Search of Whitemud" (p. 160)
g. the narrator in Tom Wayman's poem "Factory Time" (p. 172)
h. Leah in "Kiss Me" (p. 81)

Readings That Use Subject Analysis

Works in this text that analyse a subject include the following:

"Here's to Family Feasting," p. 4
"Respect and Balance in Our 'Tribe,'" p. 6
"Paper Boy," p. 24
"Fathers, Sons and Hockey" p. 26
"The Business of Being Half and Half," p. 98
"In Search of Whitemud," p. 160

Final Tips for Analysing a Subject

- Study your subject thoroughly so that you understand how and why it is a worthwhile topic for analysis.
- Choose the most significant parts of the subject to analyse. List specific details and group qualities that belong together.
- Examine those parts in considerable detail, showing how they are both discrete and interrelated.
- Focus on an assertion that needs to be proven by analysis.

- In your introduction, briefly describe the whole so that your readers have some context for your study.
- Throughout your essay, stay aware of the whole as you discuss the separate parts.

SUMMARY

Summarizing is a skill we all use in our daily lives. Whenever we tell our friends about our recent holiday, recap the highlights of a sports event, or prepare a résumé for a job application, we are picking out the most important points, organizing them, and communicating them to an audience. If you can summarize what you have read in writing, you are able to prove to yourself or an instructor that you understand both the content of the reading and the way the writer has arranged the material. Summarizing is therefore an important college reading and writing skill.

Summaries are not the same as paraphrases. A **summary** is a condensation of a longer work that highlights the thesis and main points. On the other hand, a paraphrase is a restatement, in your own words, of another author's sentence or sentences. Where a summary is much shorter than the original text, a paraphrase is about the same length as the original. (For more on paraphrases, see pp. 251–54.)

When to Use a Summary

You may use summarizing as a learning tool, collecting summaries of assigned readings in any class as study guides for examinations, or you may be asked in some classes to hand in summaries to show that you have read and understood journal articles or essays. As well, research essays may require you to write short summaries of larger works.

How to Write a Summary

This section will guide you through the process of writing a full summary appropriate for the kinds of summary assignments you might expect to receive in most classes. These steps are also the first you will take if you are asked to summarize an essay and then evaluate it.

First, read the work actively, marking directly on the copy (if possible) the obvious sections within the text. Underline the thesis, if one is explicitly stated, as well as any key points or examples you see as you read. Be sure to note any unfamiliar words and check their meaning in a dictionary. If you misinterpret the meaning of a word, you risk misinterpreting the entire essay's meaning.

Then reread the text. On a separate sheet of paper, write a few sentences summarizing each section of the work that you have marked in the margins of the original. As you are making your notes, try to focus on the ideas the author is presenting rather than the actual words. Your final summary should be in your own words, but a particularly memorable phrase or expression will resist paraphrasing. Include this memorable language in your summary within quotation marks.

In your own words, write the author's thesis, or what you infer to be the central assertion of the entire essay. You may write a general thesis or one that forecasts the points the writer will use to support his or her assertion. Try to incorporate the essay's title and author with your explanation of the thesis in the summary's first sentence.

Next, write a draft that starts with the thesis (even if the writer has delayed the central assertion of the work) and contains the few sentence summaries you wrote for each of the sections of the text. Use the full name of the author of the work the first time you mention him or her. Then use only his or her last name in other places in your summary so that readers of your work are reminded who had the ideas in the original text. Even if the essay was written in the past, use the present tense when you write a summary, since the ideas exist and are being discussed now, in the present. Switch to the past tense only if the meaning requires it.

Reread your draft to be sure of the following:

- Your thesis reflects the author's full point.
- Each section has its own assertion (topic sentence) and sufficient support from the original.
- Your summary parallels the original in tone and, if possible, order.
- Your summary is accurate, objective, complete, and in your own words. *Objective* means that none of your feelings about the text are reflected in statements or tone. *Complete* means that you have covered the main points of each section of the original essay.
- Any phrases or sentences that are not in your own words are paraphrased or set within quotation marks if they are taken directly from the original.
- Reread your summary and check for spelling, mechanical errors, and sentence correctness. Insert necessary transition words and phrases to indicate the connections between ideas.

Example: Summary

Here is an example of a summary of Moira Farr's essay "Welcome to FamilyValuesWorld!" (p. 9) by student Nikki Foster.

```
                 Summary of "Welcome to FamilyValuesWorld!"
                               Nikki Foster
```

In her essay "Welcome to FamilyValuesWorld!" Moira Farr writes that the currently popular term <u>family values</u> depends on a narrow and unrealistic definition of what a family is. This definition originates from the media's idealized images of family rather than real Canadian families in the 1990s. Advocates of family values moralize that "Families are Good" (11) and the stereotypical nuclear family is the only valid model. Yet Farr argues that all families are not necessarily good ones, and the image of the family-values family is deceptive. It's possible that a family that matches the stereotype only appears to be good, while a genuinely good family could "look like nothing the planet's ever seen before" (12).

The author includes two examples of dysfunctional families to support her point that every family is not necessarily good. Mikal Gilmore, brother of convicted murderer Gary Gilmore, wrote a powerful and personal book about his family that presents a universal truth: parents often inflict the same kind of abuse on their children that they themselves suffered at the hands of their own parents. In the second example, Farr discusses an outwardly typical Canadian family that agreed to be videotaped in their home. The resulting documentary film, "The Trouble With Evan," teaches another truth: parents with seriously inadequate parenting skills often raise seriously troubled children. Both of these examples show that even in a traditional nuclear family, dysfunction is as possible a legacy from one generation to the next as health.

Despite the family-values promise, membership in a traditional family alone cannot guarantee happiness and fulfilment. Having the courage to face everything we have learned in our own family is what can help us create a more successful self-image; understanding our family truths is what can help us to improve family life. Farr's essay urges us to find the truth in our own family rather than increasing our efforts to conform to a stereotype.

Analysing the Summary

In preparing her summary, Nikki realized that Moira Farr's thesis is implied rather than stated in one sentence near the beginning of the essay, so she had to read the entire essay carefully to find Farr's main point. Nikki also had to decide which details were the most important and which she would have to leave out, because her instructor required a summary limited to about 350 words. She decided to divide the essay into four parts: a long introduction, a section discussing Mikal Gilmore's family, a section discussing Evan's family, and a concluding section offering solutions to the problem of accepting the reality of families.

Nikki's summary begins with the name of the essay and author, and a definition of *family values* that is central to readers' understanding of Farr's argument. She goes on to discuss Farr's thesis, that family values is a misleading concept. Nikki uses two short quotations in her opening paragraph; she found that each of these quotations resisted paraphrasing in her own words. Notice that despite the many lively examples Farr includes in the first part of her essay, Nikki had to focus only on Farr's thesis in order to keep her summary concise.

Nikki's second paragraph combines the Gilmore and Evan examples to illustrate Farr's point that membership in a nuclear family does not guarantee stability in children. She explains the significance of the examples to Farr's thesis at the end of her second paragraph: nuclear families are not immune to the dysfunctional behaviours often attributed to nontraditional families. Notice how Nikki writes in the present tense when she writes about the ideas raised in Farr's essay. When she is narrating events that happened in the past, such as the book Mikal Gilmore wrote or the videotaping that Evan's family agreed to, she correctly uses the past tense.

The final paragraph of Nikki's summary explains Farr's reasoning that facing the reality and understanding the truth of family life is the only way we can find out what might have gone wrong and learn from those mistakes. The distillation of Farr's thesis in Nikki's final sentence gives the summary a sense of closure. Overall, Nikki summarizes a challenging essay in a way that is both comprehensive and comprehensible.

Practising Writing Summaries

1. Write a paragraph-long summary of Nikki Foster's summary above.
2. In small groups, read either "The Shackles of Everyday Lies" (p. 34), "The Babysitters Club: No Boys Allowed" (p. 54), "The Business of Being Half and Half" (p. 98), "Adding Weight to an Image of Beauty" (p. 152), or "Life After Cable" (p. 188). As a group, outline the thesis and main points you would include if you were to write a one-paragraph summary of the essay.
3. In pairs, read "Making Big Deals out of Little Deals" (p. 72), "Did You Ever Have to Make Up Your Mind?" (p. 123), or "Need, Want, Deserve" (p. 184). Separately, write an outline of the essay's thesis and the main points. Then compare your outlines. Check each other's outline for accuracy, objectivity, completeness, and conciseness. Decide what changes, if any, need to be made to your own. Then write a one- or two-paragraph summary based on your revised outline.
4. Read "The Beauty Myth" (p. 57), "Quebec" (p. 117), "Don't Let Stereotypes Warp Your Judgments" (p. 128), or "A Plea for the Physical" (p. 175), and write a 300-word summary of the essay.

Final Tips for Summaries

*   As you read the work you are to summarize, mark the thesis, key points, sections of the work, and unfamiliar words.
*   Write notes about the ideas in the essay using your own words.
*   Begin your summary with a statement of the essay's thesis.
*   Develop the summary, remembering to be accurate, objective, and complete, as well as concise.
*   Check that the text of your summary is in your own words and that you have kept direct quotations to a minimum.

WRITING AN ESSAY EXAM

An in-class essay exam will require you to retrieve information that you know and to present it in an orderly way and with sufficient development that your instructor will be convinced that you know the material. Following is a six-step strategy that will help you present information that you know.

A Six-Step Strategy

1. Read the question more than once.
2. Determine what the question specifically requires you to do. Have you been asked to *define, list, summarize, compare or contrast, explain,* or

analyse? See the list following for definitions of words that are commonly used on essay exams.

3. Briefly outline the material that will satisfy the question you were asked. Do not spend much time on this step; the outline can be brief, with only key words or phrases to remind you of material that you need to include.

4. Write a thesis that will focus your answer and possibly forecast the areas you will develop in your response to the question.

5. Write the essay.

6. Reread your answer to correct errors in spelling and grammar. Use a dictionary if you are permitted to bring one to the exam. Do not plan to rewrite; you will seldom have sufficient time. If you recall material that would improve your essay, indicate that you have an insertion and write the added material on another sheet of paper.

It is most important that you understand exactly what the question requires you to do. For example, if the test question asks you to *list* the chemical elements commonly called salts, you are to enumerate—present in a list or outline form—the specific chemical elements called salts. An essay is not required, would be inappropriate, and might cost you points. If the question asks you to *compare and contrast* two subjects, and you only show how the subjects contrast, you have missed part of the question—how the subjects compare. The following chart will help you understand what is expected on exams.

Key Words Used on Exams

Word	Meaning and Example
analyse	break into elements or parts and examine
	• "Analyse the job of the Speaker of the House of Commons."
	• "Analyse the use of the term 'affirmative action' in Crail's short story 'Affirmative Action.'"
compare	look for and bring out points of similarity, qualities that resemble each other
	• "Compare the narrators' search for self-identity in Rita Joe's poem 'I Lost My Talk' and M. Nourbese Philip's poem 'What's in a Name?'"
contrast	stress the dissimilarities, differences
	• "Contrast the roles of the provincial and federal governments."

define	give the meaning of a word or concept
	• "Define the term *archetype*."
describe	give an account
	• "Describe the Aztec civilization at Teotihuacan."
	or give a process
	• "Describe the method for providing emergency first aid to an accident victim."
	or give a word picture
	• "Describe Tom Thomson's painting *The West Wind*."
discuss	examine, and consider from different points of view
	• "Discuss the use of pesticides in controlling mosquitoes."
explain	make clear, interpret, tell the meaning of, tell how
	• "Explain how the actions of people can, at times, trigger a rainstorm."
justify	show good reason for, give evidence to support your position
	• "Justify the public naming of the accused in rape cases."
relate	show correlation, how things are connected
	• "Show the relationship of early childhood education to elementary school academic success."
summarize	give the main points or facts in condensed form, omitting details
	• "Summarize the plot of *Othello*."
trace	in narrative form, describe the progress, development, or history of events
	• "Trace the opening of the Canadian West through the construction of the Canadian Pacific Railway."

If you understand the meaning of words used in exams, you will not lose points or time by pursuing a direction that will fail to give you full credit for the information that you know.

An Outline for an In-Class Essay

Any of the practice assignments on page 354 could be posed as in-class essay exams. First we present a brief sample outline that would lead to a focused in-class essay. Try outlining answers to the practice assignments to improve your skills and as a study review of the essays that you have read.

Question: *Summarize* and *discuss* the important issues raised in Janice Giavedoni's "Jerry Lewis and the MDA Telethon: Is It Really That Bad?" (p. 136).

1. Message of MDA Telethon reinforces stereotypes: the disabled are "pathetic cripples," "weak," "ineffectual," to be pitied.

2. Message of Lewis's language destroys self-image
   ex. - "half a person"
   ex. - "Well, they can't walk down the street, can they?"
   ex. - promises to make things "perfect"

3. Message of Lewis's film clips perpetuates stereotypes
   ex. - "happiness" is "short-lived" on hearing child's diagnosis
   ex. - the disabled cannot be left alone
   ex. - daughter can never go out, doomed to feel "pathetic and pitiable"

4. MDA Telethon projects feelings of inadequacy on disabled people that are not there
   - do not feel guilty, miserable, desperate for a cure
   - disabled lives are worth living
   - Janice Giavedoni exemplifies a well-adjusted, active, normal disabled person

Each of the four areas contributes to the summary of Giavedoni's issues. Each of the numbered points would be treated in a separate paragraph, with the key words noted in each section to become part of the specific development and exemplification in the discussion of Giavedoni's grievances against Lewis and his telethons. Point 4 would probably be an effective conclusion to the in-class essay. The thesis might forecast that, according to Giavedoni's criticism of Jerry Lewis, the language and film clips on the MDA Telethon are the central factors perpetuating damaging stereotypes of people with disabilities.

Practising Outlining for In-Class Essays

1. Define *irony* and describe three specific examples of irony in Archibald J. Crail's short story "Affirmative Action" (p. 145).

2. Summarize and discuss Pam Withers's point in "The Babysitters Club: No Boys Allowed" (p. 54).

3. Based on W.H. Auden's essay "Work, Labour, Play" (p. 170), write an essay in which you contrast his descriptions of a "labourer" and a "worker."

4. Analyse the images in Tom Wayman's poem "Factory Time" (p. 172).

CHAPTER 10
Writing the Research Paper

Assigned by many instructors and loved by few students, the research paper has a worse reputation than it deserves. Like most tasks that at first seem overwhelming—packing the car to go away to school, or preparing for a party—the research paper needs time and organization. The steps suggested here, and the model of a student paper in this section, should help you handle the project.

PLANNING THE RESEARCH PAPER
Time Schedule for the Research Paper

Even if you had outstanding luck in high school and welded a research paper together in an amazing overnight session, your college professor probably won't be forgiving of the "solder drips" of hasty welding, and you may find your course grade threatened by a poorly prepared research paper. Instead, admit to yourself that the research paper requires your attention through a number of steps, all of which you can handle.

Further, the paper may allow you to experience the pleasure of discovering some new interest and information. If your instructor gives you some choice in your topic, take advantage of this opportunity to find out more about something that you really do want to learn more about. Instead of selecting a topic that is familiar or seems easy, pursue one that intrigues you, one that is worth the time and energy that you will devote to the investigation.

Some instructors assign due dates for the various stages of the paper. If yours does not, try dividing the time between the assigned date and the due date into four approximately equal parts. For example, if you have two months for the preparation of this paper, each stage will have two weeks. If you have one month, you can give each stage a week of your time.

Stage 1

- *Determine the topic* that interests you and satisfies the paper assigned. Allow a few days for this, but do not let yourself postpone that first decision for longer than a few days.
- Go to the library and *begin your search* for materials. Be sure to meet the reference room librarian—the researcher's best friend. Ask the librarian if your topic has additional subject headings that you should be aware of so that you can do a *complete* search while you are in the library. Use computer databases and whatever other sources are available. Check that you have all the necessary bibliographic information for the type of source you are using. Some students like to make bibliography note cards for each source. (See the model note cards on pp. 360–61.)

Stage 2

- *Read and take notes on* the material that you have found. Be prepared to photocopy longer or more complex printed material. As well, be prepared to copy onto your own computer disk or print directly from a CD-ROM database, an on-line service, or the Internet. If you take notes in the library on material that you do not intend to photocopy and take home with you, write direct quotations in your notes and paraphrase these later, when you know how much material you want to use. If you are taking notes by hand, keep accurate records of titles, authors, and page numbers so that you do not need to return to the sources to find information that you need for correct documentation. (This step will be discussed more completely on pp. 360–61 and 364–65.) As you take notes, think about how you might focus your paper.

Stage 3

- *Determine a working thesis* and write an outline for the paper.
- *Write a draft* of your paper and meet with your instructor or writing-centre staff for feedback before you begin the revision.
- *Revise* your draft, strengthening the thesis, improving the arrangement, using more emphatic support, improving word choice and transitions, and clarifying any writing that your reader found ambiguous or weak.

Stage 4

- If you have handwritten your draft, *type* your paper. Prepare the works-cited page and, if your instructor prefers one, a cover sheet with the title and your name, section, instructor's name, and date. (See the model on pp. 368–84, which is based on the Modern Language Association (MLA) style. Instructors in disciplines other than English may require a different style. We include both the MLA and the American Psychological Association (APA) documentation methods later in this chapter.)

- *Proofread your manuscript* from cover page through the works-cited page. Neatly correct all typing and other errors that you discover. If you have a major correction—for example, an entire sentence omitted when you typed from your draft—you may need to retype the page. If you have written your paper on a computer, editing will be considerably easier.

If you divide the research paper assignment into parts, you will not be overwhelmed by the task. You may discover that the time allotted for a certain stage is not realistic for you. For example, you may realize that you need longer to draft and revise your paper and less time for Stage 4; this may be true if you are working on a word processor. However, think how comfortable you will be if you still have 25 percent of your time for that final preparation of your manuscript.

GATHERING LIBRARY MATERIAL
Getting Started

Shannon Powell's instructor required a research paper that was more developed, and used more sources, than the shorter documented papers that had been assigned in her composition course. Shannon's assignment was to respond more fully to one of the subjects included in the Reader of *Between Worlds*. Shannon considered the topics that had been discussed in class, and she realized that she wanted to learn more about the world of people with disabilities.

Her initial response to the research paper may have been posed in the form of questions: What are the problems people with disabilities have in how they are perceived by others? In working? In their social lives? What has been done to help them? What kind of legislation exists to help people with disabilities? How do they feel about their condition?

With these questions in mind, Shannon went to her college library.

Meet the Librarian

The week before the research paper was assigned, Shannon's composition instructor arranged a class library tour. The reference librarian showed the students how to use the computer terminals and indexed guides to find the information they would need for their research assignments.

Many colleges offer workshops on how to access library resources. Your college librarians can show you not only how to find books and periodicals, but also how to use the microfilm machines, CD-ROM and on-line databases, and the Internet. You should never feel embarrassed to ask for help and instruction. As technology changes and new ways of disseminating information are developed, students and instructors alike will need the help of library staff to learn how to use the available resources.

Finding Information

Before you begin your search for information, ask a librarian for information about the library. Each library has its own computer cataloguing system for books, periodicals, and other materials. Every time you use a new library or begin a different research project, ask the librarian which type of search he or she would recommend for the books that you need, and which type of search for the periodicals. Many students leave libraries empty-handed or with few sources because they have not used the correct search, or because they have not entered all the appropriate headings.

Reference librarians should not be expected to do your work for you, but you will find that they know more ways to discover material than you can imagine. For example, a student's search for information on the men's movement yielded nothing when "Men's Movement" was entered into the computer. The reference librarian knew to use "Psychology—Men" to find that material. Reference librarians can also show you how to use the *Library of Congress Subject Headings* or electronic indexes to find the best descriptive words for topics, called *key words* or *descriptors*, that can help you with your search.

Your library has information on just about every topic; if you are not finding what you need, you may be using an incorrect heading or misspelling a term. Computers are helpful, but it often takes a human being— a librarian—to show you how to access that help. Better than always giving you the answers, most librarians will also show you the *process* for finding the information for your research.

Using Electronic Sources

Until recently, students wishing to find current information for research essays had to search in printed periodical indexes for the titles of articles related to their topic, and then locate the periodical on their library's shelves. Increasingly, however, libraries are subscribing to electronic databases in addition to, or instead of, traditional printed indexes. These electronic databases are available on CD-ROM or through on-line computer services, and they list periodical articles much the same as printed indexes do.

Today's electronic databases make research more efficient because of the speed and expanded search options they offer, not to mention the wider range of periodicals a single electronic source can carry. Many electronic databases also carry full-text reprints of articles from traditional print sources. Rather than having to look on the shelf for the relevant periodical or order the periodical from another library, students can print a copy of the article's text from the library's computer system or download the text onto a disk and view it on their computer at home. The Internet is another electronic source available to, and popular with, student researchers.

Evaluating Sources

Your topic will determine the kinds of supporting material you will need in your paper. If your topic requires up-to-date information (news events, current legislation, technological or medical data, or recent statistics), you will want to consult periodicals. As the term implies, they are issued periodically, and therefore they are timely. Periodicals such as newspapers, magazines, and journals are available in traditional print form, although increasingly, libraries are subscribing to electronically published periodicals as well, which provide full-text reproductions of articles.

If your writing does not require current information, or if it necessitates an overview (of legislative changes, economic patterns, fashion trends, art, or political movements), you may want the depth and perspective that books provide. In addition, don't neglect videos, films, government reports, vertical files, questionnaires, and interviews as potential sources of information.

Increasingly, the Internet is becoming a popular medium for student research. However, be careful about the quality of sources you use from the Internet. Unlike information in traditional paper sources such as periodicals and books, information from the Internet is not necessarily reviewed for accuracy by an editorial board before being posted. If you focus your Internet research on databases published by respected organizations, such as colleges, universities, government agencies, and established businesses, the information you gather is most likely to be accurate. In most cases, it is possible to use the Internet to research the credentials of experts who are cited in Internet publications before you decide to use their work in your essay.

Sample Bibliography Cards

Shannon started by recording on index cards the bibliographic information that she would need to document her sources. Because she used cards instead of a sheet of paper, Shannon was able to arrange the cards alphabetically when the time came to prepare her works-cited page. If your library provides you with a printed copy of the bibliographic information for books and periodicals that you are using for your essay, you may decide to use those sheets, arranging them in alphabetical order by author's last name when you write your works-cited page.

Here are **sample bibliography cards** for the note-taking phase. Notice that Shannon added the library call number for the book, in case she had to borrow it again later:

For a book

```
362.      Peggy Hutchison
40971     "Social, Recreation, and Leisure Opportunities"
Dialo     from Dialogue on Disability: A Canadian
          Perspective.
          Ed. N.J. Marlett, R. Gall, and A. Wight-Felske.
          Vol. 1. The Service System
          Calgary: U of Calgary Press, 1987
          pp. 47-60
```

For a periodical

Malcolm Peat

"Attitudes and Access: Advancing the Rights of People
with Disabilities"

<u>Canadian Medical Association Journal</u>

1 March 1997

pp. 657-59

<u>CBCA</u>, CD-ROM

SilverPlatter, 1997

Shannon began the reading and note-taking process after she had collected the books and had photocopied the pages of the periodical articles that were available and seemed most relevant to her subject. In earlier class assignments, Shannon had practised summarizing and paraphrasing the main ideas of works that she used. She had also practised finding and extracting the best parts of a writer's work to use in quoted form in her own writing. As well, she had learned about the MLA system to document her sources. Because Shannon had worked with incorporating other writers' ideas and language into her material, she understood how to avoid the problem of **plagiarism**.

Plagiarism

Using someone else's ideas or language as your own, accidentally or deliberately, is a serious offence that schools may punish with expulsion. If you are desperate to complete an assigned paper, using somebody else's work may seem like a good idea to you. *Don't do it.* Failing a course or risking expulsion from school cannot be a sensible decision. Talk to your instructor about your anxieties, and then determine that you will do the work with integrity.

Plagiarism most often occurs inadvertently. Often it occurs because of sloppy note taking, poor record keeping, or even ignorance. You can avoid this problem by carefully recording, from your earliest notes on, the source of every idea—even in summary or paraphrased form—and of every key word or phrase of another writer that you are using. Plagiarism also occurs if you incorrectly begin or end the quotation marks that designate the quote you are incorporating into your text. Further, if you change or omit *anything* in the text that you are quoting, you need to use brackets (see p. 459) or an ellipsis (see p. 457–58) to signify to your readers that you have made a change. Plagiarism also occurs if you incompletely or inaccurately cite the source of material that you have used. Make certain, even from the first note-taking sessions, that you have correctly recorded *all* the information that you will need for your works-cited page. Examples of inadvertent plagiarism are shown below, so that you can avoid this error in your own work.

Inadvertent Plagiarism

Plagiarism occurs if a quotation is not used or documented correctly. Read the original text below, from Michael Ignatieff's "Quebec" (p. 119), and the incorrect uses of the quotation following the excerpt:

> It seems extraordinary, in retrospect, that I should have supposed that we—the Québécois and I—actually knew each other well enough to constitute any kind of community at all. That childhood memory of the cemetery was actually closer to the truth. Yet is it a memory of mine or a fantasy? I had better confess that I didn't always remember it as I have told it now. For years, I thought I had actually fought the Frenchies. I believed I had seen the big rough French boys, storming down from the heights of the cemetery, chasing us back into Juliana Road with a hail of ball bearings. Now I am quite sure: we never even saw them. They were phantoms to me, as I was to them, and phantoms they have remained.

Identify the incorrect uses of the material in each of the examples below:

1. Michael Ignatieff questions whether he and the Québécois ever knew each other well enough to constitute any kind of community at all.
2. Ignatieff clearly remembers "the big rough French boys, storming down from the heights of the cemetery" and says they were "like phantoms" (119).
3. An Anglophone wants to confess that he's not sure if his recollection of being attacked by some rough French boys is a memory or a fantasy.
4. Ignatieff marvels that "we--the Québécois and Anglophones--actually knew each other well enough to constitute any kind of community at all" (119).

EXPLANATION OF ERRORS

1. In his mistaken notion that he has "only paraphrased," this writer has failed to place quotation marks around Ignatieff's words "knew each other well enough to constitute any kind of community at all." Also, the student has not documented with parenthetical information the source of the material that he has taken from Michael Ignatieff. Even if the student were to use only the phrase "constitute any kind of community at all," the words are Ignatieff's and must be documented.

2. This writer has misrepresented Ignatieff. The original expresses the idea that Ignatieff *believed* he had been attacked by some French boys, but Ignatieff goes on to explain that this belief was incorrect, and that he had never actually seen the French boys at all. The student writer has written a combination of paraphrase and quotation that does not correctly express Ignatieff's point.

3. The writer here has attempted a paraphrase of Ignatieff's words that stays too close to the original in repeating "confess," "rough French boys," "memory," and "fantasy," without using quotation marks, and that fails, in any case, to attribute and document the source of the idea.

4. This writer has made a change in Ignatieff's's quoted material in order to clarify Ignatieff's words in the context of the student's essay, but the writer has failed to use brackets to inform the reader that there are some changes in the quoted material. This is how the sentence should look:

    > Ignatieff marvels that "we—the Québécois and [Anglophones]—actually knew each other well enough to constitute any kind of community at all" (119).

You may feel that there are too many ways for you to make mistakes when you use another writer's ideas or words in your essays. Follow these steps to avoid inadvertent plagiarism: carefully copy material from another source, compare your quoted material to the original, and verify that you have been accurate in the use of quotation marks, brackets, and parentheses. Double-check your paraphrases as well. Your words must accurately capture the meaning of the original author's idea, without repeating sections of the original passage. If you follow these steps, you will avoid the inadvertent plagiarism that threatens your integrity as a writer and flaws the writing that you produce. (For more on quoting and paraphrasing, see pp. 249–54.)

With the goal in mind of paraphrasing and quoting carefully those relevant sections of her collected texts, Shannon began making note cards for her paper.

Sample Note Cards

The **note cards** that Shannon wrote during Stage 2 of her paper preparation looked like these:

Original text: ". . . the focus of the Saskatchewan government's approach to accommodation has been to improve the physical accessibility of government-owned and -leased buildings . . ."

Paraphrased note card

Case Studies in *Effective Practices*

p. 191

The Saskatchewan government is striving to ensure that its workplaces be made physically accessible.

Original text: "Like a lot of government bureaucracies, we haven't done a good enough job of letting the public know what services we do provide."

Quotation note card

"Special Seating There for Those Who Need It"
Al MacRury, p. A4
According to Gabe Macaluso, head of the Hamilton Entertainment and Convention Facilities Inc., "Like a lot of government bureaucracies, we haven't done a good enough job of letting the public know what services we do provide."

Notice how Shannon introduces the quotation on her note card with the name of the person who made the original comment in the article by Al MacRury. This information will remind her whose comment it is and will help her cite her source accurately in her essay. Full details of the source will be on her bibliography note cards.

Developing a Working Thesis

While she read from her collection of materials and took notes, Shannon began to focus on her subject in a sharper way. She realized that there were a number of ways to approach the subject of disabilities, but that she was especially interested in three: legislation that recognizes the needs of people with disabilities, their access to employment, and their access to the same social opportunities as the able-bodied. Her working thesis looked something like this:

> **Working Thesis:** People with disabilities are achieving some gains in employment and leisure opportunities, but they still suffer social isolation and indignities.

Shannon talked with her instructor about her working thesis and the rough outline of the three parts that she planned to write. After discussing her plan and what she had found in her research, Shannon and her instructor concluded that she did not have enough current information about the social isolation of people with disabilities, and that despite a compelling quotation from one of her research sources, her own casual observations would be insufficient for a well-developed research paper. The instructor suggested that Shannon approach the special resources centre on campus to arrange interviews with disabled students who would be interested in talking about their social situations. Further, both the instructor and Shannon concluded that they knew very little about legislation concerning people with disabilities, and both realized that readers would want to know something about this legislation.

Gathering Additional Information: The Interview

Before she started the first draft of her paper, Shannon returned to the library to collect information on the legislation that gives people with disabilities access and assures their rights. She made summary note cards of the legislation that had been passed, as well as what had been proposed but not yet passed.

Shannon also contacted the director of her campus special resources centre and collected names and telephone numbers of students who he thought would enjoy talking with her. She needed an extra few days to arrange to meet and talk with these individuals. Shannon conducted three interviews with students with disabilities, hoping to use their experiences to support her research. More than reflecting their perspectives, she was able to catch their actual voices in print.

Preparing for the Interview

In order to catch voices to use in your paper, you need to do some prior work. You will want to think through exactly what additional support you hope to gain from the interview. It helps to prepare an icebreaker question or two to put your interviewees at ease. If you suspect they may be guarded or unwilling to reveal the information you need—particularly for an argument essay, where they may represent the opposing position—you should order your questions so that the milder ones come first. Once the interviewees are engaged in conversation, it will be easier to get them to answer more hard-hitting questions.

Your questions should be written down in the order that you plan to ask them. If you number each, you can use these same numbers as you record the answers during the interview so you don't have to rewrite the question, or even the topic, when you are taking notes.

Conducting the Interview

Although you have prepared questions and ordered them, you may find that the answers cause you to skip to another question or to think up a question on the spot. Your ability to respond with follow-up questions and encouragement ("Why do you think that happened?" "How did you respond?") may determine the depth of the interview. Such follow-up questions may prompt the subjects to move from predictable responses to ones that are fresh and candid.

As you take notes, concentrate on getting down key phrases and controversial claims. Shannon recorded this from one of her interviewees: "Some people are prejudiced and ignore us. That makes me angry." Shannon put quotation marks around exact words so she could remember which words were her subject's and which she added or paraphrased. As you interview your subjects, don't hesitate to ask them to clarify points or expand on ideas so you can get the necessary information.

Some interviewers use portable tape recorders as a backup to capture precise words, but tape recorders haven't replaced notebooks. Relying on tape recorders can be disastrous if the machine malfunctions or the tape turns out to be inaudible. Even if the tape is clear, it is tedious to sit through an hour or two of taped conversation in order to transcribe the key quotations. Before you leave, remember to ask about additional sources or reference materials (reading materials, brochures, and names of other specialists).

Because these people are giving you some valuable time for the interview, it is essential that you offer to meet where and when it is convenient for them. Arrive on time, don't overstay your welcome, and prepare your questions before the meeting. Remember to be courteous and to show appreciation for their time and help at the end of the interview and, later, with a follow-up thank-you note.

Transcribing the Interview

Immediately after the interview, write out or type up the questions and answers while the session is still fresh in your mind. If you discover you have missed any important material or may have misunderstood a point, call your interviewee immediately for a clarification.

When you integrate the interviewees' comments into your paper, be careful to quote exactly and to represent the context of the statement accurately. Misusing quotations or distorting their intended meaning destroys your integrity as a writer. Shannon found that her conversations with people with disabilities provided insights that her readings could not. The strength of her argument, however, could not rely only on interviews. For her final essay, she used a range of sources—including books, a newspaper column, some government reports, a journal article, a newsletter from the library's vertical file, documents obtained over the Internet, and even a radio interview—to develop her argument.

SAMPLE STUDENT PAPER

Shannon Powell's full paper is included here. The numbers on the manuscript correspond to the numbers of the explanations on the facing page. These explanations will guide you through the details Shannon had to consider as she wrote up her research and documented it using MLA style.

Shannon Powell

English 1A Sec. 6336

Prof. Douglas

November 3, 1997

Access and Acceptance:

Enabling a Canadian Minority

Stereotypes, especially about people with disabilities, can be difficult to combat. In 1981, a
British writer who has <u>grand mal</u> epilepsy listed some
of the damaging beliefs and contradictory assumptions
made about him and other people with disabilities. He
wrote:

> We are held to be visually repulsive; help-
> less; pathetic; dependent; too independent;
> plucky, brave, and courageous; bitter, with
> chips on our shoulders; evil (the "twisted
> mind in the twisted body"); mentally
> retarded; endowed with mystical powers, and
> much else. (Sutherland 58)

Today many people with disabilities are working dili-
gently to resist the labels others have forced on
them. They and their able-bodied friends and colleagues know that one of the best ways to banish damaging stereotypes is to ensure that Canadians from
this minority group participate fully in day-to-day
life; it is important that they be seen as <u>people</u>
first and people with disabilities second. However,
it is highly unlikely that such progress can been
accomplished without the help of a sympathetic political and social climate. In order to achieve the
acceptance that most able-bodied Canadians take for

Explanatory Notes for the Research Paper

The numbers on these explanatory notes correspond to the numbers in the margin of the research paper.

1. *Form.* Shannon types her last name and the page number of her manuscript in the upper right corner of *each* page of her paper. She leaves a 2.5-centimetre margin on the sides, top, and bottom of each page of her paper.

2. *Heading.* According to the MLA, you do not need to use a separate sheet of paper for a title page. If your instructor prefers one, include the information required here and print it on the lower right corner or centred on a plain sheet that will precede the first page of your manuscript.

   To follow MLA form, begin your *heading* on the first page of your manuscript, 2.5 centimetres from the top of the first page and flush with the left margin. Include your name, the course number and section, your instructor's name, and the date on separate lines, double-spacing between them. Double-space again and centre your title, and then double-space between your title and the first line of your manuscript. Do *not* put quotation marks around or underline your title.

3. *Holding the paper together.* Secure the pages of your paper with one paper clip, as MLA advises, or with a staple, as many instructors prefer.

4. *Title.* Your title should engage your readers by establishing an appropriate expectation for what the paper is about, and it should please your readers' ears as well as eyes. If your readers "stumble" while reading your title, you need to revise it. Shannon's title establishes the focus of her paper, the wish for "access" and "acceptance." Notice that she uses the strong word "enabling" and engages readers' curiosity about which "Canadian minority" she will discuss.

5. *Long quotation.* Shannon's opening paragraph includes a long quotation. She introduces the quotation with some background information about the author that sets the context for her readers. Since the quotation is longer than four typed lines, it is double-spaced and set off from the main body of the essay with a double indent, and the quotation marks are omitted. To document the source, Shannon encloses the last name of the author and the page where she found the sentence. Readers who want more information about the source will find it on Shannon's works-cited page at the end of the essay. Notice that for a long quotation, the period is placed at the end of the quoted material, before the parenthetical information.

granted, people with disabilities need their legislators' and the public's commitment to ensure them the same access to employment and social opportunities that all citizens enjoy.

Outside of Canada, the issue of disabled rights has been gaining increased attention. Following the United Nations Decade of the Disabled, from 1983 to 1992, the General Assembly of the United Nations "adopted a set of standard rules . . . to ensure that disabled people were accorded the same rights, freedoms, and obligations as other members of society" (Peat par. 3). While these rules are not compulsory, they "express a strong moral and political commitment" to the principle that people with disabilities should have equal opportunities with other citizens (Peat par. 3). The United States government demonstrated such commitment when it passed the Americans with Disabilities Act in 1990, an enormous piece of legislation that strives to ensure that all citizens have equal access to the opportunities and institutions that the able-bodied take for granted (ODA, "Fact Sheet" par. 15).

In Canada, the Charter of Rights and Freedoms forbids discrimination based on a person's mental or physical disability. However, many commentators believe that more specific legislation is needed to ensure the active removal of subtle and unfair "physical, technological, bureaucratic, legal, or attitudinal" barriers as well as prevention of new ones (ODA, "Fact Sheet" pars. 2-3). Canada's Federal Task Force on Disability Issues released a report in

6. *Short quotation and summary.* In this section of the paper, Shannon combines quoted and summarized material from an electronic source. Since pagination in electronic sources does not match page numbers in a corresponding print version, Shannon gives the paragraph number, rather than the page number, after the name of the author. Notice the ellipsis in the middle of the quotation to indicate that Shannon has left out part of the original text. Readers can assume that the summarized material is also from Peat, since that is the only source cited here. When the parenthetical reference following a short quotation, paraphrase, or summary is placed at the end of the sentence, the period appears outside the closing parenthesis.

7. *Paraphrased material.* Shannon ends this paragraph with a brief paraphrase from a source she found on the Internet. Since she has two sources from the Ontario Disabilities Act (ODA) Committee, she differentiates this one by adding the Internet document's title "Fact Sheet." The document is divided into paragraph-long sections, so Shannon indicates paragraph 15, the section she has paraphrased, with the abbreviation "par. 15."

8. *Paraphrase and short quotation.* Here Shannon begins with more information from the ODA Committee's "Fact Sheet," in this case from the Internet document's second and third paragraphs, which she identifies as "pars. 2–3."

October 1996 proposing the establishment of a Canadians with Disabilities Act. The report admits that the issue of systemic discrimination, which is "the unintended effect of a program, policy, or law that otherwise appears to treat everyone equally," needs to be addressed (27). So far, though, no such law has been presented to Parliament.

In Ontario, a private member's bill, the Ontarians with Disabilities Act, was introduced by Ontario MPP Gary Malkowski in 1994, but it was lost when the 1995 provincial election was called ("Ontarians with Disabilities Act" 1). A group of individuals and community organizations named the Ontarians with Disabilities Act Committee is lobbying the current provincial government to fulfill its 1995 election promise that a revised version of Malkowski's bill would be passed in its first term of office (ODA, "Fact Sheet" par. 8).

If they are slow to act on access at a legislative level, some governments are gradually making improvements in the area of access to employment in their own offices. To increase access to employment in the Saskatchewan public service, for example, managers work with that province's Disabilities Directorate to identify positions for applicants with disabilities. As well, help is available for students with disabilities to prepare for potential government jobs. Government policy requires that workplaces be physically accessible. As well, technical devices for employees' use, such as computers, are available on permanent loan; maintenance and repair expenses for

9. *Short quotation*. Since the next quotation comes from a different source, Shannon introduces it by stating the name of the group that issued the report from which the quotation is taken. Mentioning the corporate author this way clarifies where the information comes from and means readers are not interrupted later with a long reference in the parentheses at the end of the quotation. Shannon adds only the appropriate page number in parentheses here.

10. *Summarized material*. To show where she found the information about Malkowski's bill, Shannon cites a copy of a newsletter kept in her college library's vertical file. No author is given, so Shannon identifies it by its title, enclosed in quotation marks, in her in-text citation. The newsletter's pages are numbered, so she is able to include the page number as well.

11. *Summarized material*. Shannon's in-text citation refers readers to a paragraph she has summarized from an Internet document she referred to earlier in her essay.

these devices are covered by the employer (Canada, Consultation Group 191).

Some businesses are also trying to integrate people with disabilities in their workforce rather than shutting them out. For example, in 1992, 7.2 percent of Scotiabank's full-time workforce and 6.4 percent of its part-timers were people with disabilities who have achieved equal access (Canada, Consultation Group 23). Compared to the 295 people with disabilities (or 2.4 percent of its total workforce) working for the Saskatchewan government in 1993, the bank's percentage is impressive (Canada, Consultation Group 186). Of course, Scotiabank employs more than twice as many people as the Saskatchewan government does, and in offices across the country. Since the percentage of Canadian citizens with disabilities is over 15 percent (ODA, "Fact Sheet" par. 2), it is reasonable to assume that eventually both the public and the private sector will try to raise their percentage of employees with disabilities closer to this national average.

A survey conducted across Canada in March 1997 indicates that the public is becoming more supportive of legislation to improve access for people with disabilities. For example, on the issue of equal access to employment, 75 percent of the people interviewed in Ontario supported legislation that would remove and prevent barriers to the workplace, and 84 percent reported that "bringing disabled people into the workforce would benefit society" (ODA, "Results"). The more people with disabilities can find their way

12. *Summarized material.* Shannon indicates that this material comes from page 191 of a document issued by the Canadian government's Consultation Group on Employment Equity for Persons with Disabilities. Shortening the name to Consultation Group differentiates it from the other government group whose work she consulted.

13. *Statistic acknowledgment.* Shannon notes the percentage of full-time and part-time employees with disabilities working for Scotiabank and the Government of Saskatchewan. She documents these figures with a reference to her source and the pages where she located these figures.

14. *Uncommon knowledge quoted.* Since few readers are likely to know what proportion of Canada's population has disabilities, Shannon documents the source of this information with a parenthetical reference to the ODA "Fact Sheet" she found on the Internet, along with the paragraph where this statistic is given.

15. *Survey results.* Shannon summarizes part of the results of a survey and quotes one of the questions so readers get a sense of what kinds of questions were asked. Since the document combines paragraphs and inset lists of statistics, she was uncertain about how to show in which section she found this information. The document is fairly short, so rather than include a possibly misleading paragraph number, she decided to limit this citation to the document name alone. Interested readers should easily be able to find the pertinent section in the original Internet document.

into the workforce, the more they will contribute to the economic life of the country, by earning wages, paying taxes, and consuming the same products and services as their able-bodied neighbours.

Besides being seen as contributing members of society, people with disabilities need to be seen as participating members of society. One way of accomplishing this is by improving access to social activities that able-bodied Canadians often take for granted. Hamilton is one Ontario city that takes its responsibility toward its disabled citizens seriously. For example, its concert hall, Hamilton Place, has ten seats designated for physically disabled patrons along with another ten for companions or attendants. Free headphones are available for the hearing-impaired, and both they and people with vision impairments are eligible for seating close to the stage at the concert's lowest ticket price. At Copps Coliseum, Hamilton's equivalent of Toronto's Maple Leaf Gardens, people in wheelchairs who want to attend a hockey game, ice show, or rock concert can easily use the nearby elevator to access one of the 56 seats positioned near the ice surface or stage especially for them. Attendants accompanying physically disabled patrons are not charged (MacRury A4). Gabe Macaluso of Hamilton Entertainment and Convention Facilities Inc., which operates Hamilton Place and Copps Coliseum, adds that there have been few complaints about accessibility and that the city has a "'standing subcommittee which monitors issues involving disabled consumers'" (qtd. in MacRury A4).

16. *Summarized material and citation.* Shannon summarizes in her own words some of the efforts being made to improve access for people with disabilities in Hamilton, Ontario. She documents the source of her information with the author's last name and the page number of the newspaper article where she found the information.

17. *Short quotation within the article.* A spokesperson is quoted within the article that Shannon read about people with disabilities and their access to entertainment facilities. She identifies the speaker in the introduction to the quotation. In her parenthetical reference, she uses the abbreviation "qtd. in" (for "quoted in"), followed by the source and page where the quotation can be found.

Nevertheless, Macaluso is aware that even if an organization has taken steps to improve access, it can't assume all is well. He notes: "'Like a lot of government bureaucracies, we haven't done a good enough job of letting the public know what services we do provide'" (qtd. in MacRury A4). Such sensitivity to the needs of people with disabilities and the willingness to look for improvements is a model for other public agencies and private businesses to follow.

However, no matter how much access to such leisure facilities Canadians with disabilities have, according to Peggy Hutchison, a professor who studies recreation and integration,

> it is not enough to assume, as some do, that participation in recreation activities can fill the gap left by unemployment. . . . Issues such as quality of social relationships, the opportunity to contribute to the community in a valued way, the degree to which a person has control of his or her life, and many other issues contribute to a person's quality of life. (50)

In other words, all people, with or without disabilities, share the same desire for a satisfying life, which includes both access to employment and acceptance in everyday social situations.

Yet while no longer blatantly discriminated against, people with disabilities often continue to suffer the burden of social bias. Even those remarkable individuals who are able to triumph over physical barriers have trouble surmounting social barriers

18. *Long quotation.* This excerpt from an essay by Hutchison runs to more than four typed lines, so Shannon follows the MLA guidelines for long quotations. Since she introduces this quotation with the author's full name, she cites only the page number in parentheses.

Shannon had to leave out more than one sentence from the original in order to focus on the sections that are most pertinent to her thesis. The four periods indicate to readers that the word "unemployment" falls at the end of one sentence in the original source. The other three periods indicate that one or more sentences have been deleted from the original before the new sentence starting with "Issues such as quality."

that the able-bodied have not had to face. Susan
Rodde, who has cerebral palsy, confirms that in most
social situations, "we, the physically challenged,
have to be the icebreakers." Otherwise, at parties
and social gatherings, the disabled person is often
isolated or ignored. Unfortunately, the "ice" does
need to be broken because many people feel uncomfortable around disabled or disfigured people, and so
far, the responsibility for making social contact
lies with the disabled person (Rodde). Because they
may feel vulnerable, able-bodied people tend not to
form close relationships with people with disabilities, and some even refuse casual contact. Rebecca
Acuirre, who also has cerebral palsy, says that she
recently asked a stranger in a mall what time it was,
and he kept walking as though he didn't hear her.
"Some people are prejudiced and ignore us. That makes
me angry," she says. How can these prejudices be
abolished? "We need more exposure," says Acuirre,
adding that the more opportunities she has to participate in the same social activities as the able-
bodied, the more she finds she is accepted.

Life-long able-bodiedness is not guaranteed; an
accident or even normal aging processes can affect
our physical capabilities in ways we can't predict.
David Lepofsky, a Toronto lawyer who specializes in
disability cases, told a radio audience recently that
"all of us who are listening today may be able to hear
but may need sign interpreters some time, or we may
have other disabilities in the future." Lepofsky's
words are an important reminder that access could

19. *Short quotation and paraphrase from an interview.* Because there are no page numbers associated with interviews, Shannon has two options available to indicate the speaker. She can include the person's name in the introduction to the quotation, or enclose only the last name of the person interviewed in parentheses.

20. *Second in-text reference to a source.* The first time Shannon mentions one of her sources, Rebecca Acuirre, in the body of her essay, she uses her interviewee's full name. In second and subsequent in-text references, Shannon uses Acuirre's last name alone, according to MLA style.

21. *Short quotation from an interview.* Shannon's final quotation comes from a radio interview she was able to record. Since she introduces the name of the speaker, she does not need to include a parenthetical reference. Interested readers will see Lepofsky's name in the works-cited list at the end of the essay.

well become a personal issue for us one day, rather than just an abstract concept that affects <u>other</u> people.

As improvements in legislation and public attitudes continue to make new opportunities accessible to people with disabilities, the gap between the majority and the minority will close. Ideally, these developments will permit all people to be viewed in terms of their capabilities rather than their disabilities, and the dream people with disabilities have of access and acceptance will become a reality.

WORKS CITED

Acuirre, Rebecca. Personal interview. 21 Oct. 1997.

Canada. Consultation Group on Employment Equity for Persons with Disabilities. Case Studies on Effective Practices in the Employment of Persons with Disabilities. Ottawa: Government of Canada, 1994.

---. Federal Task Force for Canadians with Disabilities. Equal Citizenship for Canadians with Disabilities: The Will to Act. Ottawa: Government of Canada, 1996.

Hutchison, Peggy. "Social, Recreation, and Leisure Opportunities." Dialogue on Disability: A Canadian Perspective. Ed. N.J. Marlett, R. Gall, and A. Wight-Felske. Vol. 1: The Service System. Calgary: U of Calgary Press, 1987. 47-60.

Lepofsky, David. Interview by Andy Barrie. Metro Morning. CBC Radio One. 10 Oct. 1997.

MacRury, Al. "Special Seating There for Those Who Need It." Hamilton Spectator 24 March 1997: A4.

Ontarians with Disabilities Act (ODA) Committee. "Fact Sheet." Ontarians with Disabilities Act Committee. N.d. On-line. Integrated Network of Disability Information and Education. Available: http://indie.ca/oda/factsheet.html. 15 Oct. 1997.

---. "Results of Lou Harris Poll." Ontarians with Disabilities Act Committee. 1997. On-line. Integrated Network of Disability Information and Education. Available: http://indie.ca/oda/survey.html. 15 Oct. 1997.

"Ontarians with Disabilities Act." <u>OMOD Issues</u> May 1996.

Peat, Malcolm. "Attitudes and Access: Advancing the Rights of People with Disabilities." <u>Canadian Medical Association Journal</u> 1 Mar. 1997: 657-59. <u>CBCA</u>. CD-ROM. SilverPlatter. 1997.

Rodde, Susan. Telephone interview. 22 Oct. 1997.

Sutherland, Allan T. <u>Disabled We Stand</u>. London: Souvenir Press, 1981.

22. *The form for the list of sources used in the text.* The heading "WORKS CITED" in capitals is centred 2.5 centimetres from the top of the page. The first cited work is typed two lines beneath the heading. The entire list is double-spaced. The list is alphabetically arranged by the author or speaker's last name or by the first word in the title of an unsigned article. The entry begins at the left margin. If it is longer than one line, its second line is indented five spaces from the left margin. (More complete information about MLA form is on pp. 386–405.)

23. Entry for a personal interview. The date of the interview is noted.

24. Entry for a government publication.

25. Entry for another government publication authored by a different group.

26. Entry for an article in an anthology with three editors. Notice that the name of the author of the article is listed first. In this publication, only the editors' first initials, rather than first names, are given.

27. Entry for a radio interview.

28. Entry for a signed article in a daily newspaper. There is no period between the title of the periodical and the date. Notice the "A" prior to the page number to indicate the section of the newspaper in which the article appeared.

29. Entry for a document written by an association and obtained from the Internet. The letters "N.d." mean that the document does not include a date of electronic publication; the "N" is capitalized because the abbreviation follows a period. The final date is the date the document was accessed on the Internet.

30. Entry for a second document by the same association and obtained from the Internet. The date "1997" indicates the year the document was published. The final date is the date the document was accessed on the Internet.

31. Entry for an unsigned article from a newsletter. Newsletters are treated the same as periodicals.

32. Entry for a signed article from a scholarly journal. Although originally published in print, Shannon found the full text of this article on a CD-ROM database. The information following the page numbers of the original print version of the article gives the name of the database, the medium, the vendor, and the year of electronic publication.

33. Entry for a personal interview.

34. Entry for a book.

DOCUMENTING THE RESEARCH PAPER: MODERN LANGUAGE ASSOCIATION (MLA) STYLE

Whenever you use the words, information, or ideas of another writer—even if in your own words as a summary or paraphrase—you must credit the source. Formerly, writers gave credit to their sources by using numbers that referred to notes at the bottom of the page or at the end of the manuscript on a separate sheet of paper. In contrast to this older method, the new MLA style guide liberates the writer from hours of tedious work. Instead of using superscripts and footnotes or endnotes, you will place the necessary information in parentheses immediately following the quoted or paraphrased passage.

The forms illustrated below will show you exactly how to provide the necessary information for documenting both printed and electronic sources. The fourth edition (1995) of the *MLA Handbook for Writers of Research Papers* is the source of this information, and it is certainly the guide that your college English instructors will want you to use.

Writing Parenthetical Citations

Your in-text citation should give just enough information so that your reader can find the origin of your material on the works-cited page at the end of your paper. Here are sample parenthetical citations to illustrate MLA format.

Author Not Named in the Text

Incorporate your source material by introducing the quotation with your own words. When you haven't included the author's name in your text, you must note in parentheses the author's last name and the page or pages of your source.

> Shifting immigration patterns have changed Canadian demographics and have thus made us more aware of diversity in the workplace. Until recently, "Canada's society was relatively homogeneous, but as the Canadian population became more diverse, issues of unfair treatment became more evident" (Wilson 5).

Author Named in the Text

One effective way to introduce your paraphrased or quoted material is to include the author's name within your text, especially if the author is an authority on the subject; your parenthetical citation will be brief and less intrusive, containing only the page number by itself.

> According to Trevor Wilson, a specialist in diversity management and employment equity,
>> The issue of diversity has arisen largely as a result of significant changes in the Canadian population and in the work force. For many years, Canada's society was relatively homogeneous, but as the Canadian population became more diverse, issues of unfair treatment became more evident (5).

MLA style requires quotations longer than four typed lines to be indented ten spaces and written without quotation marks. Remember that such quotations, like your main text, should be double-spaced.

The first time you mention an author in the text of your essay, use his or her full name; in subsequent references to the author, use the last name only.

> Wilson argues that organizations that adopt "a diversity strategy--to recognize and acknowledge differences" among their employees--attract the most skilled and talented members of the work force (18).

Two Works by the Same Author

If your paper contains two different works by the same author, your parenthetical reference will need to give an abbreviated form of the title, with the page number, so that readers will know which work you are using in that particular section of your paper.

> Ben Mattlin deplores the pity for the disabled that Jerry Lewis's yearly telethon evokes ("Open Letter" 6). Mattlin also exposes the hypocrisy in depicting people with disabilities as superheroes. He points out that "courage and determination are often necessary when living with a disability. But there's nothing special in that, because there's no choice. Flattering appraisals sound patronizing . . ." ("Beyond Reasonable Doubts" 5).

A Work with Two or Three Authors

If the work was written by two or three authors, use each of their names in your text or in the parenthetical citations.

> In their discussion of political differences between First Nations peoples and the government of Canada, Ovide Mercredi and Mary Ellen Turpel analyse the lessons of the 1990 Oka conflict: "The crisis facing our country showed all of us the value and importance of human respect, kindness, and justice--the value of drawing upon these virtues before relations break down, because breakdowns are likely" (49).

> Some commentators have suggested that the 1990 conflict at Oka taught us some valuable lessons: "The crisis facing our country showed all of us the value and importance of human respect, kindness, and justice--the value of drawing upon these virtues before relations break down, because breakdowns are likely" (Mercredi and Turpel 49).

A Work with More Than Three Authors

If your source was written by more than three authors, you may use only the first author's last name, followed by "et al." and the page number, in parentheses, or you may list all the authors' last names in the text (or with the page number in parentheses). Once you have chosen one format, it is important to use it consistently.

> In <u>Women's Ways of Knowing: The Development of Self, Voice, and Mind</u>, the authors note that there are many women who "believed they were stupid and helpless. They had grown up either in actual physical danger or in such intimidating circumstances that they feared being wrong, revealing their ignorance, being laughed at" (Belenky et al. 57).

> In <u>Women's Ways of Knowing: The Development of Self, Voice, and Mind</u>, the authors note that there are many women who "believed they were stupid and helpless. They had grown up either in actual physical danger or in such intimidating circumstances that they feared being wrong, revealing their ignorance, being laughed at" (Belenky, Clinchy, Goldberger, and Tarule 57).

> In <u>Women's Ways of Knowing: The Development of Self, Voice, and Mind</u>, Belenky, Clinchy, Goldberger, and Tarule note that there are many women who "believed they were stupid and helpless. They had grown up either in actual physical

danger or in such intimidating circumstances that they feared being wrong, revealing their ignorance, being laughed at" (57).

Author's Name Not Given

If the author is anonymous, use the complete title in your text or an abbreviated form of the title with the page number in the parentheses.

The obituary for Northrop Frye in the Winnipeg Free Press describes him as the "internationally renowned critic who hated small talk but dazzled thousands with his words" ("Critic" 27).

Association, Corporate Author, or Government Publication

Either name the corporate author in your text, or include an abbreviated form in the parentheses. If the name is long, try to work it into your text to avoid an intrusive citation.

Health and Welfare Canada advises early childhood educators that they "have an underlying responsibility to educate an often uninformed public about the capabilities of handicapped children for developmental growth and independence" (25).

Literature: Novel, Play, Poem

NOVEL

Because some classic works appear in various editions, it is important to give the chapter number or part in addition to the page number to help your reader find the reference you are citing.

In the novel Pride and Prejudice, Elizabeth Bennet's self-centred cousin Mr. Collins proposes to her, not with a declaration of love, but with a list of what he believes are legitimate reasons for marriage:

> My reasons for marrying are, first that I think it a right thing for every clergyman in easy circumstances (like myself) to set the example of matrimony in his parish. Secondly, that I am convinced it will add very greatly to my happiness; and thirdly--which I perhaps ought to have mentioned earlier, that it is the particular advice

and recommendation of the very noble lady whom I
have the honour of calling patroness. (80; ch.
19)

Here the page number is followed by a semi-colon and the chapter number.

For modern novels, cite the source with the author's name and page number or page number only.

Choy's description of Sekky's experience at Strathcona
School in 1941 is a litany of contrasts: "At recess, our
dialects and accents conflicted, our heights and handicaps
betrayed us, our skin colours and backgrounds clashed, but
inside Miss E. Doyle's tightly disciplined kingdom we were
all--lions or lambs--equals" (184).

PLAY

In William Shakespeare's <u>Othello</u>, Emilia sounds like a
twentieth-century feminist when she claims that "it is
their husbands' faults" if their wives have affairs
(4.3.89-90).

Here the numbers indicate the passage is from Act 4, Scene 3, lines 89 to 90.

POEM

The narrator in Lorna Crozier's poem "Paper Boy" summarizes
her childhood bond with her brother and the importance of
their relationship in the final lines: "he, as much as my
mother, / giving me this life" (36-37).

Here the numbers indicate the passage is taken from lines 36 to 37. The slash (/) with spaces on either side separates the end of one line of poetry from the beginning of the next line.

Indirect Source

When you use the words of a writer who is quoted in another author's work, try to incorporate the name of the original author of the quotation in the text of your essay. Begin the parenthetical citation with the abbreviation "qtd. in" followed by the last name of the author of the source you consulted and the appropriate page numbers where you found the indirect quotation. (If you do not incorporate the original author's name in your text, it should appear at the beginning of the citation, before the source.)

Women and men both cite increased "freedom" as a benefit of divorce. But Catherine Kohler Riessman discovered that women meant that they "gained independence and autonomy" while men meant that they felt "less confined," "less claustrophobic," and had "fewer responsibilities" (qtd. in Tanner 40-41).

More Than One Work

If you want to show that two works are the sources of your information, separate the references with a semicolon.

Two recent writers concerned with men's issues observe that many women have options to work full time or part time, stay at home, or combine staying at home with a career. On the other hand, men need to stay in the corporate world and provide for the family full time (Allis 81; Farrell 90).

Electronic Sources

Acknowledge electronic sources in your text the same way you would cite any printed book or article. The only difference is that, rather than citing a page number, you cite the relevant paragraph number(s) to indicate the exact location of the material in the electronic text. Note in parentheses the author's name, write the abbreviation "par." or "pars." and then give the paragraph number(s).

Employment trends in Canada are changing: "By 1993, part-time jobs accounted for almost a quarter of all jobs in Canada, and 35% of them--760,000--were held by people who said they wanted but couldn't find full-time jobs" (Taylor par. 15).

If you have introduced your quotation, paraphrase, or summary with the author's name, include only the paragraph reference in the citation.

Morrissy's editorial points out that because of developments in telecommunications, the confidence of entrepreneurs, and revised trade arrangements with the rest of Canada, New Brunswick's "economy is at a turning point in its history" (pars. 2-6).

Preparing the Works-Cited Page

Whenever you note in parentheses that you have used someone else's material, you will need to explain that source completely in the works-cited list at the end of your manuscript. The **works-cited list** includes all the sources you have cited in your essay. (A **works-consulted page** includes all the sources you used in your research, whether you have cited from them or not.) At one time such pages were called a bibliography. However, since the word *bibliography* implies books, seeming to exclude the electronic and other sources in current use today, MLA style no longer calls this list a bibliography. To see how this page will look, refer to the works-cited page of the student research paper, on pages 383–84. Notice that all entries are double-spaced.

Because the complete source is listed only in the works cited, it is essential that each entry conform exactly to standard form so that readers can easily locate your source. Most of the forms that you will need are illustrated below.

Elements of a Citation from a Book

```
              1                          2
      ┌──────────────┐  ┌──────────────────────────────────────────┐
  6 │ Cannon, Margaret.  The Invisible Empire: Racism in Canada.
      │     ┌─────┐  ┌──────┐  ┌────┐
      │     Toronto: Random, 1995.
              3          4        5
```

1. Use the author's full name—last name at the beginning—followed by a comma and then the first name and any middle name or initial. Omit any titles (Dr., Ph.D., Rev.). End with a period and one space.
2. Include the book's full title, including any subtitles. Underline the title (or italicize if you can) and capitalize the first and last words as well as all important words. If there is a subtitle, separate the main title and the subtitle with a colon and one space. Place a period after the title and leave one space.
3. Give the publication information, beginning with the city of publication, followed by a colon and one space. If more than one city is listed for the publisher, give only the first.
4. Include the name of the publisher, followed by a comma. Shorten the name to remove "and Co." or "Inc." Abbreviate long names. (The "Random" in the above example refers to Random House.)
5. Give the date of publication and end with a period.
6. Any line after the first line is double-spaced and indented five spaces.

Books

ONE AUTHOR

Cannon, Margaret. The Invisible Empire: Racism in Canada.
    Toronto: Random, 1995.

TWO OR THREE AUTHORS

Mercredi, Ovide, and Mary Ellen Turpel. In the Rapids:
    Navigating the Future of First Nations. Toronto:
    Viking, 1993.

Notice that any authors' names after the first author are written with the first
name before the last name.

MORE THAN THREE AUTHORS OR EDITORS

Henry, Frances, et al. The Colour of Democracy: Racism in
    Canadian Society. Toronto: Harcourt Brace, 1995.

or

Henry, Frances, Carol Tator, Winston Mattis, and Tim Rees.
    The Colour of Democracy: Racism in Canadian Society.
    Toronto: Harcourt Brace, 1995.

With more than three authors, you have the choice of shortening the entry to
provide only the first author's name, followed by the Latin abbreviation "et
al." (which means "and others"), or you may provide all of the names.

AUTHOR WITH AN EDITOR

Shakespeare, William. King Lear. Ed. Alfred Harbage.
    Baltimore: Penguin, 1969.

Cite the name of the author first and then, after the title of the work, give the
editor's name, preceded by "Ed."

BOOK WITH AN EDITOR AND NO AUTHOR CITED

Peabody, George, ed. Best Maritime Short Stories. Halifax:
    Formac, 1988.

If the book does not have an author, cite the editor's name, followed by "ed."
(or "eds." if there is more than one editor).

SELECTION FROM AN ANTHOLOGY OR COLLECTION

```
Dumont, Marilyn. "The Halfbreed Parade." Miscegenation
     Blues: Voices of Mixed Race Women. Ed. Carol Camper.
     Toronto: Sister Vision, 1994. 195.

Bradshaw, Chris. "Walkability." Beyond the Car: Essays on
     the Auto Culture. Ed. Sue Zielinski and Gordon Laird.
     Toronto: Steel Rail, 1995. 165-70.
```

Give the author and title of the selection, using quotation marks around the title. Then give the underlined title of the anthology. If the anthology has an editor, note the name or names after "Ed." Give the page numbers for the entire selection as shown above.

TWO OR MORE SELECTIONS FROM THE SAME ANTHOLOGY

```
Angus, Charlie. "The Battle over Gun Control: Marking the
     Divide Between Rural and Urban Canada." Bachmann,
     Barth, and Golets Pancer 197-98.

Bachmann, Susan, Melinda Barth, and Karen Golets Pancer.
     Between Worlds: A Reader, Rhetoric, and Handbook.
     First Canadian Edition. Don Mills: Addison Wesley
     Longman, 1998.

Chodos, Robert. "Being a Jew at Christmas." Bachmann,
     Barth, and Golets Pancer 94-97.
```

To avoid repetition, give the full citation for the book once, under the editor's last name. Then all articles are listed alphabetically under the individual authors' names, followed by the title of the work. After each title, put the editor's name as a cross-reference to the complete citation, ending with the page numbers.

TWO OR MORE BOOKS BY THE SAME AUTHOR(S)

```
Findley, Timothy. Famous Last Words. Toronto: Clarke Irwin,
     1981.

---. Headhunter. Toronto: HarperCollins, 1993.
```

Give the name(s) for the first entry only. After that, in place of the name(s), type three hyphens, followed by a period and one space and then the next title. The three hyphens always stand for exactly the same name(s) as in the preceding entry. The titles of the author's works should be listed alphabetically.

CORPORATE AUTHOR

> Andres Wines Ltd. <u>New Horizons: Annual Report March 31, 1996</u>. Winona, ON: Andres Wines, 1996.

Use the name of the institution, association, or corporation as the author even if it is also the name of the publisher. If the place of publication could be unfamiliar to readers, include an abbreviation of the province or country.

GOVERNMENT PUBLICATION

> Canada. Health and Welfare. <u>Children With Special Needs: A Guide to Integration</u>. Ottawa: Health and Welfare Canada, 1980.

State the name of the government first, followed by the name of the branch issuing the publication.

AUTHOR NOT NAMED

> <u>The Canadian Oxford Dictionary</u>. Toronto: Oxford UP, 1998.

If a book has no author noted on the title page, begin the entry with the title and alphabetize according to the first word other than "a," "an," or "the." "UP" is the abbreviation for University Press.

OTHER THAN FIRST EDITION

If you are citing an edition other than the first, place the edition number between the title and the publication information.

> Benson, Eugene, and William Toye, eds. <u>Oxford Companion to Canadian Literature</u>. 2nd ed. Toronto: Oxford UP, 1997.

REPUBLICATION

> Montgomery, L. M. <u>Anne of Avonlea</u>. 1909. Toronto: Ryerson, 1942.

If you are citing a work that has been published by different publishers, place the original date of publication (but not the place or publisher's name) after the title. Then provide the complete information for the source you are using.

TITLE WITHIN THE TITLE

> Gilbert, Stuart. <u>James Joyce's</u> Ulysses. New York: Vintage, 1955.

If the title of the work that you are using contains another book title, do not underline the original book title or place it in quotation marks.

If the title of the work that you are using contains a title that is normally enclosed in quotation marks (a short story or poem), keep the quotation marks and underline the entire title, extending the underlining or italics to include the final period and closing quotation mark: *Dare to Eat a Peach: A Study of "The Love Song of J. Alfred Prufrock."*

MULTIVOLUME WORK

> Brown, Russell, and Donna Bennett, eds. <u>An Anthology of Canadian Literature in English</u>. 2 vols. Toronto: Oxford UP, 1982-83.

If you have used two or more volumes of a multivolume work, state the total number of volumes in the work. Place this information ("2 vols.") between the title and publishing information.

> McCall, Christina, and Stephen Clarkson. <u>The Heroic Delusion</u>. Toronto: McClelland and Stewart, 1994. Vol. 2 of <u>Trudeau and Our Times</u>. 2 vols. 1990-94.

If you are using only one volume of a multivolume work, give the title of that volume after the author's name, and then give the publishing information. After the publishing date, note the volume number, the title of the collection, and the number of volumes in the collection. If the volumes were published over a period of years, indicate the dates.

TRANSLATION

> Tremblay, Michel. <u>Hosanna</u>. Trans. John Van Burek and Bill Glassco. Vancouver: Talonbooks, 1974.

When citing a work that has been translated, give the author's name. After the title, give the name of the translator or translators, preceded by "Trans."

INTRODUCTION, PREFACE, FOREWORD, OR AFTERWORD

> Williams, David M. Foreword. <u>Diversity at Work: The Business Case for Equity</u>. By Trevor Wilson. Etobicoke: Wiley, 1996. xv-xvii.

If you are citing material from an introduction, preface, foreword, or afterword written by someone other than the author of the book, give the name of the writer and designate the section he or she wrote. Notice also that "Foreword" above is without underlining or quotation marks. After the title of the work, "By" precedes the author's name.

If the author of the introduction or preface is the same as the author of the book, give only the last name after the title.

```
Lorinc, John. Author's Note. Opportunity Knocks: The Truth
    About Canada's Franchise Industry. By Lorinc.
    Scarborough: Prentice Hall, 1995. xi.
```

ARTICLE IN AN ENCYCLOPEDIA OR OTHER REFERENCE BOOK

```
Adams, Peter. "Arctic Archipelago." The Canadian
    Encyclopedia. 1988 ed.
```

```
"Baie Verte." Encyclopedia of Newfoundland and Labrador.
    1981 ed.
```

If there is an author of the edition or article, alphabetize by last name. Otherwise, alphabetize in the works-cited page by the title of the entry.

Periodicals: Journals, Magazines, and Newspapers

JOURNAL WITH CONTINUOUS PAGINATION

```
Turner, Linda. "Time Out with Half-Time: Job Sharing in the
    Nineties." Canadian Journal of Counselling 30 (1996):
    104-13.
```

Journals sometimes paginate consecutively throughout a year. Each issue, after the first one, continues numbering from where the previous issue ended. After the title, give the volume number and then the publication year in parentheses, followed by a colon and the page numbers.

JOURNAL THAT PAGINATES EACH ISSUE SEPARATELY

```
Hardwick, Julie. "Widowhood and Patriarchy in Seventeenth-
    Century France." Journal of Social History 26.1
    (1992): 133-48.
```

If the journal numbers each issue separately, give the volume number, a period, and the issue number (as in "26.1" above) after the title of the journal.

MONTHLY OR BIMONTHLY MAGAZINE

> Regush, Nicholas. "Brain Storms and Angels." <u>Equinox</u> Aug.
> 1995: 62-73.

Notice that in a monthly or bimonthly periodical, the month of publication is abbreviated, and no volume or issue numbers are given.

In this example, the pages given are consecutive, which means that the article begins on page 62 and ends on page 73. Often, an article may be printed on nonconsecutive pages; it may begin on one page but may be interrupted by other articles. If so, write the number of the first page followed by a plus sign and a period.

> Kimber, Stephen. "When the Casinos Came to Town."
> <u>Chatelaine</u> June 1997: 40+.

WEEKLY OR BIWEEKLY MAGAZINE

> Caragata, Warren. "Crime in Cybercity." <u>Maclean's</u> 22 May
> 1995: 58-60.

DAILY NEWSPAPER, SIGNED ARTICLE

> Ruttan, Susan. "Cigarettes Are Highly Addictive Killers."
> <u>Calgary Herald</u> 27 Sept. 1995: B1.

DAILY NEWSPAPER, UNSIGNED ARTICLE OR EDITORIAL

> "Canada, the Unfinished Country." Editorial. <u>Globe and Mail</u>
> 1 July 1996: A10.

If the newspaper is divided into numbered or lettered sections, give the section designation before the page number, as in "A10" above.

TITLED REVIEW

> Lawson, Guy. "Outcasts Provide a Life Lesson." Rev. of <u>The
> Timekeeper</u>, by Trevor Ferguson. <u>Toronto Star</u> 27 Apr.
> 1996: L15.

UNTITLED REVIEW

> Rooke, Constance. Rev. of <u>Mobile Homes</u>, by Noel Hudson. <u>The
> Malahat Review</u> Sept. 1986: 153-54.

Electronic Sources

At one time, a library's holdings consisted mainly of books and printed periodicals. Today, most libraries also subscribe to electronic databases, information issued either on a CD-ROM or through an on-line service transmitted to the library's computer system. Students also use the Internet from the library's computer or from home when they are searching for information. In this section we discuss how to prepare MLA-style entries on your works-cited page for electronic sources.

Elements of a Citation from a CD-ROM or On-Line Service

Many electronic databases index and carry full-text electronic reproductions of articles that appeared in print elsewhere. CD-ROM databases are updated regularly to include work published in print since the last electronic publishing date. *Canadian Business and Current Affairs (CBCA), Canadian NewsDisc, Computer Select, Compact D/, General Periodicals Ondisc (GPO),* and *Business Periodicals Ondisc (BPO)* are examples of this type of database. Services that both index and publish material through their on-line databases include EBSCOhost, Dialog, Lexis-Nexis, Educational Resources Information Center (ERIC), CompuServe, and America Online.

In general, a citation of a source found on a CD-ROM or on-line service follows the same format as a corresponding traditional print source, with one important addition. The last part of the citation adds specific information about the electronic source, including the name of the database, its format (CD-ROM or on-line service), the vendor or supplier of the database, and the date of electronic publication (for CD-ROM) or date of access (for on-line service).

Researchers are still developing a standardized method for citing electronic sources. One guide, entitled *Electronic Styles: A Handbook for Citing Electronic Information* (1996), by Xia Li and Nancy B. Crane, is considered to be the most comprehensive. Li and Crane also offer regularly updated formats on their Web site, which can be accessed at http://www.uvm.edu/~ncrane/estyles.

If your electronic source is missing any of the details included in the following examples, cite as completely as possible whatever information is available. Remember that your purpose is to acknowledge the author and give adequate information so readers can easily access the material you used in your research.

```
        1                          2
┌─────────────────┐  ┌───────────────────────────────────
Leach, Norvin.  "New ActiveX API to Ease PC Access for
─────────────────────────────────┐  ┌──────────────────┐
                    3                          4
Disabled." PC Week 22 July 1996: 10. Computer Select.
  5              6              7
┌───────┐ ┌──────────────┐ ┌──────────┐
CD-ROM. Computer Select. Aug. 1996.
```

1. A citation from a CD-ROM or on-line service begins like a traditional print source. Use the author's full name—last name at the beginning—followed by a comma and then the first name and any middle name or initial. End with a period and one space.

2. Give the title of the material you have cited (in quotation marks or underlined, as necessary). Put a period inside the quotation marks for a title of an article or after the title of the work if it is a complete document, and leave one space.

3. If applicable, state the print source (for example, the book or periodical from which the material was taken), the volume, issue, and/or date (followed by a colon and one space), and the page number(s) for the article in the printed source, followed by a period and one space.

   The next section of the citation contains information pertaining specifically to the electronic nature of the source used to access the information:

4. State and underline the title of the electronic database, followed by a period and one space.

5. State the publication medium (CD-ROM or On-line) followed by a period and one space.

6. Include the name of the vendor, supplier, or computer service, followed by a period and one space.

7. For a CD-ROM, give the date of electronic publication, that is, the date that the CD-ROM was issued. For an on-line service, give the date you accessed the on-line publication. MLA prefers abbreviations for the name of the month. Follow this information with a period.

CD-ROM: SIGNED ARTICLE FROM A DAILY NEWSPAPER

```
Laxer, Daniel J. "English and French Share More Than They
    Realize." Montreal Gazette 29 June 1997, final ed.: A9.
    Canadian NewsDisc. CD-ROM. SilverPlatter. Aug. 1997.
```

After the date of print publication, put a comma and the edition of the newspaper, if applicable, followed by a colon.

CD-ROM: UNSIGNED ARTICLE

"Higher Success Ratios for Small Businesses." <u>Manitoba</u>
<u>Business</u> June 1994: 29-30. <u>CBCA</u>. CD-ROM. SilverPlatter.
Aug. 1996.

If the electronic database does not include the author's name, begin your citation with the title of the article.

CD-ROM: ABSTRACT

Some regularly updated CD-ROM databases are primarily indexes that list the title and publication information for the printed source. This type of CD-ROM database does not carry a full-text reproduction, so it is up to the researcher to find the article elsewhere. However, these databases often include a summary, called an *abstract*, of the article listed. Be careful to differentiate between a full-text reproduction of an article and an abstract. If you cite from an abstract, be sure to include that information in your citation between the printed source page numbers and the title of the electronic database.

Jongbloed. L., and A. Crichton. "A New Definition of
Disability: Implications for Rehabilitation and Social
Policy." <u>Canadian Journal of Occupational Therapy</u> 57.1
(1990): 32-38. Abstract. <u>CINAHL</u>. CD-ROM. SilverPlatter.
Aug. 1996.

CD-ROM: SINGLE-ISSUE CD-ROM (OR DISKETTE)

This type of database is published once and may be updated, but not necessarily on a regular basis. Encyclopedias, dictionaries, and company or government reports issued on CD-ROM (or sometimes on diskette) fall into this category. Since this electronic source is similar to a book, cite from it as you would from a book. Notice, however, that the publication medium follows the title of the electronic source. If your source is on disk, note "Diskette" after the title of the work (rather than CD-ROM).

"Labrador Boundary Dispute." <u>The 1997 Canadian Encyclopedia</u>
<u>Plus</u>. CD-ROM. Toronto: McClelland and Stewart, 1997.

ON-LINE SERVICE: ARTICLE FROM A JOURNAL WITH CONTINUOUS PAGINATION

Horton, Richard. "Women as Women with HIV." <u>Lancet</u> 345
(1995): 531-32. <u>Lexis-Nexis</u>. On-line. Lexis-Nexis. 21
Nov. 1996.

ON-LINE SERVICE: ARTICLE FROM A JOURNAL THAT PAGINATES EACH ISSUE SEPARATELY

> Taylor, Linda E. "Flexible Workstyles." <u>Canada and the World Backgrounder</u> 60.5 (1995): 20-24. <u>EBSCOhost</u>. On-line. EBSCOpublishing. 6 Nov. 1996.

ON-LINE SERVICE: ARTICLE FROM A WEEKLY MAGAZINE

> Chisholm, Patricia. "The Role of the Parents." <u>Maclean's</u> 12 Aug. 1996: 13. <u>EBSCOhost</u>. On-line. EBSCOpublishing. 6 Nov. 1996.

Elements of a Citation from the Internet

Documenting sources you have found on the Internet can be problematic, partly because information posted on the Internet is always changing, and partly because information from the Internet does not follow a uniform format and does not give standard publication information the way printed books and periodicals do. Always give as much information as possible in your works-cited entry. That way, as long as the material remains on-line, readers have enough information to retrieve it themselves at a later date.

The following suggestions for citing sources found on the Internet are based on Li and Crane's MLA-style guidelines. (See p. 399 for information on their book.)

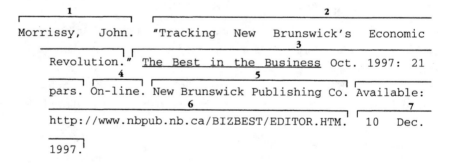

1. A citation from a source found on the Internet begins like a traditional printed source. Use the author's full name—last name at the beginning—followed by a comma and then the first name and any middle name or initial. (For material that does not identify an author, begin your entry with the title, as you would for an unsigned work from a traditional print source.) End with a period and leave one space.
2. Give the title of the material you have cited (in quotation marks or underlined, as necessary). Put a period after the title (inside the closing quotation

mark, where applicable) and leave one space.

3. If the material you have cited is part of a larger work, state and underline the name of the electronic work from which the material is taken. Include the date of electronic publication; use the abbreviation "N.d." if no publication date is given. For periodical articles, state the number of paragraphs followed by the abbreviation "pars." (This takes the place of the page numbers you cite for the printed source, since page numbers do not apply to Internet documents.) Leave one space.

Occasionally, the material you cite will be reproduced from a printed source that has a different title from the electronic source; for example, an article on AIDS prevention from a medical journal may be reprinted on an Internet site provided by a social service agency. In this case, the printed source's title and publication information (volume, issue, date, and page number(s), if available) should appear *before* the information on the electronic source.

4. Indicate the medium—"On-line"—followed by a period and one space.

5. Include the name of the information supplier, followed by a period and one space.

6. State "Available" followed by a colon and the Uniform Resource Locator (URL) for the Internet source. Be careful to type this Internet address exactly as it appears on your source, including upper and lower case. Put a period at the end of the URL and leave a space. (When searching for sources, remember that this period is *not* a part of the Internet address.)

7. Note the date you accessed the material, putting the day, the month (abbreviated if possible), and the year, followed by a period.

INTERNET: INDIVIDUAL WORK

```
Bode, Thilo. Address by Dr. Thilo Bode, International
    Executive Director of Greenpeace, to the General
    Assembly of the United Nations. N.d. On-line.
    Greenpeace    Canada.    Available:    http://www
    .greenpeacecanada.org/bode.htm. 29 Oct. 1997.
```

This citation is the electronic version of a text for a speech. The Internet source does not indicate any corresponding print version.

INTERNET: ARTICLE FROM A MAGAZINE

```
Evans, Jeff. "Paranoid as You Wanna Be: Protecting Your
    Computer Assets." The Computer Paper. Nov. 1997: 41
    pars. On-line. Canada Computer Paper. Available:
    http://www.tcp.ca/1997/9711/9711pro/paranoid/
    paranoid.html. 8 Nov. 1997.
```

For periodical articles, count the number of paragraphs and include this information after the volume and/or date.

INTERNET: NO AUTHOR GIVEN

> "General Description of Centre." <u>Faculty of Management, Centre for Technology Studies</u>. N.d. On-line. University of Lethbridge. Available: http://home.uleth.ca/man-cts/ctrdesc.htm. 13 Jan. 1998.

The document cited here does not include an author's name, so the entry begins with the information that is available. Since the material does not have a formal title, the running title at the top of the Internet document is cited as the title of the work. A complete description of the provider of this information as well as the URL will ensure that interested readers can access this information.

INTERNET: CORPORATE AUTHOR

> Ontarians with Disabilities Act (ODA) Committee. "Fact Sheet." <u>Ontarians with Disabilities Act Committee</u>. N.d. On-line. Integrated Network of Disability Information and Education. Available: http://indie.ca/oda/factsheet.html. 15 Oct. 1997.

In this citation, a group is considered to be the author. It is also possible to consider this entry as being by an unnamed author. In this case, the name of the committee would appear only as the name of the larger Web site on which the document "Fact Sheet" appears.

> "Fact Sheet." <u>Ontarians with Disabilities Act Committee</u>. N.d. On-line. Integrated Network of Disability Information and Education. Available: http://indie.ca/oda/factsheet.html. 15 Oct. 1997.

Whenever you are unsure about how to cite from an Internet source, err on the side of caution, and give as much information as possible.

Other Sources

INTERVIEW

> Acuirre, Rebecca. Personal interview. 21 Oct. 1997.

FILM OR TELEVISION PROGRAM

> The Sweet Hereafter. Dir. Atom Egoyan. With Ian Holm, Sarah
> Polley, Tom McCamus, and Bruce Greenwood. Alliance
> Communications, 1997.

If you want to refer to a particular individual involved with the film, cite that person's name first.

> Holm, Ian, actor. The Sweet Hereafter. Dir. Atom Egoyan.
> With Sarah Polley, Tom McCamus, and Bruce Greenwood.
> Alliance Communications, 1997.

Organizing the Works Cited

The works cited are always arranged alphabetically, according to authors' last names. If there is no author named, then the work is listed according to title. If the title begins with "A," "An," or "The," keep the article where it is but alphabetize the title according to the second word.

All sources—whether book or article—are arranged together in one list. Do not have a list of books and then a list of articles. *Do not number the sources in your bibliography*. Double-space between all lines; the second line and subsequent lines of each entry are indented five spaces. See the works-cited page in the model student research paper (pp. 383–84).

DOCUMENTING THE RESEARCH PAPER: AMERICAN PSYCHOLOGICAL ASSOCIATION (APA) STYLE

Although most English instructors will require MLA form for documenting sources, instructors from other disciplines may prefer APA form. Check with your instructors to see which of the two forms they prefer. These two styles are very different; don't confuse them. The fourth edition (1994) of the *Publication Manual of the American Psychological Association* is the source of the following information.

Writing Parenthetical Citations

The main difference between MLA and APA forms is that in APA parenthetical citations, the date of publication and sometimes the page number of the source are included. The punctuation, therefore, is also different.

According to APA form, parenthetical citations for both printed and electronic sources follow the same format. If you introduce quoted material with the author's name, follow the author's name with the date of publication in parentheses. At the end of the quotation, include the page number (for a printed source) or the paragraph number (for an electronic source) in parentheses.

> In Ben Mattlin's study (1991) of the media and people with disabilities, he approves Christopher Burke's role as a "competent, high-functioning, integral part of his family" (p. 8).

Notice that the date of the study is included within the introduction to the quotation, and then the page number is abbreviated with "p." within the final parentheses.

If you do not use the author's name when you introduce the quoted material, place the author's name, the date, and the page number in parentheses at the end of the quoted material. Use commas between the items in the parentheses.

> One critic approves Christopher Burke's role as a "competent, high-functioning, integral part of his family" (Mattlin, 1991, p. 8).

If you are quoting a journal article from an electronic source, include the paragraph number rather than a page number in parentheses.

> Jeff Evans suggests that the best "defence in protecting your computer assets is to always, always, always make backups of your computer data, and store them in a safe place" (1997, paragraph 10).

If you paraphrase the material rather than quote from it, include the author's last name and the date of publication either in your text or in parentheses at the end of the summarized material. Do not include the page number.

> According to Ben Mattlin (1991), actors with disabilities are playing important roles in television dramas.

> One writer who has examined the media's treatment of people with disabilities reports some positive changes in television (Mattlin, 1991).

Below are specific examples of common situations you may need to document in APA form.

A Work with Two Authors

If your material was written by two authors, name both in the introduction to the material or in the final parentheses each time you cite the work. In the parentheses, use "&" rather than "and."

> Rachlis and Kushner (1994) examine Canada's health-care system and propose reforms that some readers may find controversial.

> Two writers have proposed controversial reforms of Canada's health-care system (Rachlis & Kushner, 1994).

Author's Name Not Given

If the author of the material that you are using is not given, either use the complete title in your introduction to the material or use the first few words of the title in the parenthetical citation with the date.

> One obituary for Canada's most famous literary critic, Northrop Frye, described him in contradictory terms, as a shy superstar ("Critic Frye," 1990).

Corporate Author

If you are using a work with a corporate or group author with a particularly long name, write out the full name the first time you use it, followed by an abbreviation in brackets. In later citations, use just the abbreviation.

> The manual recommends that scientific researchers choose a clear and objective writing style, since creative writing techniques can "confuse or disturb readers of scientific prose" (American Psychological Association [APA], 1994).

Indirect Source

If you use work that is borrowed from another source, you need to acknowledge that you did not use the original source.

> Actor Henry Holden relates his own experience with social discrimination by noting that he is "not generally accepted by nondisabled people in social situations" (cited in Davidson, 1987).

Preparing the References Page

In APA form, the alphabetical listing of works used in the manuscript is entitled "References." (In MLA form, this listing is called "Works Cited.") Here are some general guidelines for the references page:

- Double-space the entries. The first line should be indented five spaces, and all subsequent lines should be flush with the left margin.
- Alphabetize the list by the last name of the author or editor. If the work is anonymous, alphabetize by the first word of the title other than "a," "an," or "the."
- All authors' names should be listed last name first, followed by a comma and initials for first and middle names. Do not use "et al." Use an ampersand ("&") rather than the word "and."
- Include the year of publication in parentheses. If the article is from a periodical published monthly or daily, write the name of the month in full.
- For the titles of books and articles, capitalize only the first word of the title and of the subtitle, as well as all proper nouns.
- Underline (or italicize) the titles of books and journals. Do not underline or use quotation marks around the titles of articles. Capitalize the names of periodicals as they are normally written. Underline the volume number of periodicals.
- Give the full names of publishers, excluding "Inc." and "Co."
- Use the abbreviation "p." or "pp." before page numbers in books and newspapers, but not in other periodicals. For inclusive page numbers, include all figures ("365–370," not "365–70").

Books

ONE AUTHOR

Cannon, M. (1995). The invisible empire: racism in Canada. Toronto: Random House.

TWO OR MORE AUTHORS

Mercredi, O., & Turpel, M. E. (1993). In the rapids: Navigating the future of First Nations. Toronto: Viking.

EDITOR

Peabody, G. (Ed.). (1988). Best Maritime short stories. Halifax: Formac.

WORK IN AN ANTHOLOGY

Bradshaw, C. (1995). Walkability. In S. Zielinski & G. Laird (Eds.), <u>Beyond the car: Essays on the auto culture</u> (pp. 165-170). Toronto: Steel Rail.

TWO OR MORE BOOKS BY THE SAME AUTHOR

Findley, T. (1981). <u>Famous last words</u>. Toronto: Clarke Irwin.

Findley, T. (1993). <u>Headhunter</u>. Toronto: HarperCollins.

AUTHOR NOT NAMED

<u>The Canadian Oxford dictionary</u>. (1998). Toronto: Oxford University Press.

LATER EDITION

Benson, E., & Toye, W. (Eds.). (1997). <u>Oxford companion to Canadian literature</u> (2nd ed.). Toronto: Oxford University Press.

MULTIVOLUME WORK

Brown, R., & Bennett, D. (Eds.). (1983). <u>An anthology of Canadian literature in English</u> (Vol. 2). Toronto: Oxford University Press.

Clarkson, S., & McCall, C. (1990-94). <u>Trudeau and our times</u> (Vols. 1-2). Toronto: McClelland & Stewart.

TRANSLATION

Tremblay, M. (1974). <u>Hosanna</u>. (J. Van Burek & B. Glassco, Trans.). Vancouver: Talonbooks.

Periodicals: Journals, Magazines, and Newspapers

JOURNAL WITH CONTINUOUS PAGINATION

Turner, L. (1996). Time out with half-time: Job sharing in the nineties. <u>Canadian Journal of Counselling, 30</u>, 104-113.

JOURNAL THAT PAGINATES EACH ISSUE SEPARATELY

Hardwick, J. (1992) Widowhood and patriarchy in seventeenth-century France. <u>Journal of Social History, 26</u>(1), 133-148.

MAGAZINE

Regush, N. (1995, August). Brain storms and angels. *Equinox*, 62-73.

DAILY NEWSPAPER, SIGNED ARTICLE

Ruttan, S. (1995, September 27). Cigarettes are high-ly addictive killers. *Calgary Herald*, sec. B, p. 1.

DAILY NEWSPAPER, UNSIGNED ARTICLE OR EDITORIAL

Canada, the unfinished country. (1996, July 1). *Globe and Mail*, p. A10.

TITLED REVIEW

Lawson, G. (1996, April 27). Outcasts provide a life lesson [Review of *The timekeeper*]. *Toronto Star*, p. L15.

Electronic Sources

Xia Li and Nancy B. Crane's *Electronic Styles: A Handbook for Citing Electronic Information* (1996) and their regularly updated Web site can offer you more detailed information about citations for electronic sources. The address for their Web site is http://www.uvm.edu/~ncrane/estyles.

The following suggestions for citing electronic sources are based on Li and Crane's APA-style guidelines.

CD-ROM: FULL-TEXT ARTICLE

Leach, N. (1996, July 22). New ActiveX API to ease PC access for disabled. *PC Week* [CD-ROM], 13(29), 10. Available: Computer Select/Item: 18 502 585 [1996, November 6].

Notice that the first part of the citation follows the APA guidelines for print publications. The main differences for electronically published work are the inclusion of the medium enclosed in square brackets and the word "Available" followed by a colon and the supplier. Include the item number for the work if it is given in your electronic source, followed by the date of access in square brackets.

CD-ROM: ABSTRACT

Jongbloed, L., & Crichton, A. (1990). A new definition of disability: Implications for rehabilitation and social policy. <u>Canadian Journal of Occupational Therapy</u> [CD-ROM], <u>57</u> (1), 32-38. Abstract available: SilverPlatter/CINAHL/ Item: 1990104655 [1996, November 20].

To indicate that this work is an abstract, the word "Abstract" is included before "available." As well, the supplier's name is followed by the name of the electronic database.

CD-ROM: SINGLE-ISSUE CD-ROM OR DISKETTE

Labrador boundary dispute. (1997). In <u>The 1997 Canadian Encyclopedia Plus</u> [CD-ROM]. Available: McClelland and Stewart [1997, September 6].

ON-LINE SERVICE: ARTICLE FROM A JOURNAL WITH CONTINUOUS PAGINATION

Horton, R. (1995). Women as women with HIV. <u>Lancet</u> [On-line], <u>345</u>, 531-532. Available: Lexis-Nexis [1996, November 21].

ON-LINE SERVICE: ARTICLE FROM A JOURNAL THAT PAGINATES EACH ISSUE SEPARATELY

Taylor, L. E. (1995). Flexible workstyles. <u>Canada and the World Backgrounder</u> [On-line], <u>60</u>(5), 20-24. Available: EBSCOpublishing/EBSCOhost/Item: 9505050144 [1996, November 6].

ON-LINE SERVICE: ARTICLE FROM A WEEKLY MAGAZINE

Chisholm, P. (1996, August 12). The role of the parents. <u>Maclean's</u> [On-line], 13. Available: EBSCOpublishing/ EBSCOhost/Item: 9608157734 [1996, November 6].

INTERNET: INDIVIDUAL WORK

Bode, T. (No date). <u>Address by Dr. Thilo Bode, international executive director of Greenpeace, to the General Assembly of the United Nations</u> [On-line]. Available: http://www.greenpeacecanada.org/bode.htm [1997, October 29].

This document does not include a date of publication, so the entry "(No date)." follows the author's name.

INTERNET: ARTICLE FROM A MAGAZINE

Morrissy, J. (1997, October). Tracking New Brunswick's economic revolution. The Best in the Business [Online], 21 paragraphs. Available: http://www.nbpub.nb.ca/BIZBEST/ EDITOR.HTM [1997, December 10].

Evans, J. (1997, November). Paranoid as you wanna be: Protecting your computer assets. The Computer Paper [On-line], 41 paragraphs. Available: http://www.tcp.ca/1997/ 9711/9711pro/paranoid/paranoid.html [1997, November 8].

INTERNET: NO AUTHOR GIVEN

General description of centre. (No date). Faculty of Management, Centre for Technology Studies [On-line]. University of Lethbridge. Available: http://home.uleth.ca/ man-cts/ctrdesc.htm [1998, January 13].

In this example, the University of Lethbridge is listed as service provider. For Internet citations, always give as much information as you can to help others find your source.

Other Sources

PERSONAL INTERVIEW

Interviews that you conduct yourself are not listed in APA references. Instead, use an in-text parenthetical citation. If the subject's name is in your text, use this form: "(personal communication, October 21, 1997)." If the subject's name is not in your text, use this form: "(R. Acuirre, personal communication, October 21, 1997)."

FILM

Egoyan, A. (Director). (1997). The sweet hereafter [Film]. Toronto: Alliance Communications.

PART III
The Handbook

This handbook is designed to help you use words and control sentences in order to write convincing, error-free papers. You can use this handbook to draft and revise your essays, as well as to understand the comments that your instructors write in the margins of your papers.

We do not believe that you need an extensive background in grammar in order to write clearly or well. But we are convinced that control of grammar and punctuation will give you power over both your ideas and your readers.

You may believe that you make numerous mistakes in your papers; indeed, the prevalence of circled words and marginal notes on some may seem overwhelming. If you and your friends were to examine all of your papers, however, you would discover that you likely do not make a great number of *different* errors so much as you repeat the *same kind* of error many times. For that reason, we have isolated the common recurrent errors for discussion and correction.

This handbook begins with a short chapter, "How Sentences Work." This chapter is deliberately succinct; in it we try to meet your needs without telling you more than you ever wanted (or needed) to know about the elements of a sentence. Chapter 12, "Common Errors," precisely identifies and describes those recurrent errors that typically appear in student papers. Chapter 13, "Punctuation," will help you eliminate guesswork and punctuate accurately.

In Chapter 14, "Avoiding Faulty Word Choice," you will learn how well-chosen words can strengthen your essays. To determine quickly whether your word choice is sound, you can use the alphabetical list of troublesome words in Chapter 15, "Avoiding Commonly Confused Words." Finally, Chapter 16, "Exercises: Editing to Correct Errors," offers a selection of editing exercises you can use to practise recognizing and correcting grammatical errors.

As you are revising your drafts, you can use this handbook whenever you feel uncertain about your grammar or mechanics. When your papers are returned, you can use it as a guide to error correction by matching your instructor's marginal notes to the symbols used in this book. Ultimately, this handbook is designed to empower you without overwhelming you.

EDITING SYMBOLS

The following symbols may be used by your instructor to indicate errors in your paper. You may also use these symbols when you proofread a paper to denote changes you will want to make in your drafts or to mark errors in your classmates' papers.

∧	insert (missing word or punctuation)	⊂	close up space
⩘	insert comma	⤶	new paragraph
∾	reverse (letters or words)	no⤶	no paragraph
ℐ	delete (punctuation or word)	≡	capitalize
#	add a space	/	use lower case

Sentence errors, discussed in Chapter 12, are commonly indicated by the following symbols:

frag	fragment	*shift*	inconsistency in text
ros or *r-o*	run-on sentence	*mixed*	mixed construction
fs	fused sentence	*mm*	misplaced modifier
cs	comma splice	*dm*	dangling modifier
ref	pronoun reference	*//*	faulty parallelism
verb	verb form error	*P*	faulty punctuation
agr	agreement		

Symbols used to correct word choice errors, discussed in Chapters 14 and 15, and other symbols to designate common errors include the following:

cliché	cliché, an overused or trite expression
dialect	not standard English usage, or a regional, occupational, or ethnic word not appropriate in the context used
d or *dic*	diction, inappropriate level
id	idiomatic, not standard Canadian usage; the problem often appears in preposition use
jarg	jargon, or an occupational word inappropriate for formal writing
nonst.	nonstandard; may indicate idiomatic use, jargon, or slang
sl or *slang*	the level of the word choice is inappropriate
trite	overused expression, as a cliché
wd ch	word choice; a general term that may indicate any of the more definitively marked errors on this list
w/w	wrong word; a general term that may indicate a word confused with another word, slang, jargon, improper word, or idiom
x	obvious error; may refer to any of the above
awk	awkward
coh	lacks coherence
?	confused meaning
red	redundant
sp	spelling error
trans	stronger transition needed
wdy	wordy

In addition to denoting errors, your instructor may indicate strong writing and good points by using this symbol:

✓	excellent point and word choice

CHAPTER 11
How Sentences Work

Understanding how sentences work will give you the vocabulary you need to discuss your writing, as well as to correct errors that have been noted in your papers. Such knowledge will also increase your power and versatility as a writer. By eliminating some of the guesswork that can hamper student writers, this handbook can help give you the tools and confidence to write with conviction.

As you probably know, a sentence is a group of words that expresses a complete thought. Almost all sentences in English contain a subject and a verb. The basic unit containing a subject and a verb is called a clause, although not all clauses are sentences. (For more on clauses, see pp. 422–23.) Some sentences may have a verb only—such as *Beware!*—where the subject "you" is implied but not stated. However, one-word sentences like this one are rare in written English.

In key examples throughout this section, we have underlined the subject once and the verb twice to help you identify them quickly.

SUBJECTS

A **subject** is who or what a clause is about.

Ryan draws constantly.
[Subjects may precede verbs.]

There is a grin on Ritu's face.
[Subjects may follow verbs.]

Noun as Subject

The subject of the clause may be a **noun** or a **pronoun**. A noun can be

- *a person:* athlete, Susan Aglukark, veterinarian
- *a place:* Lake Athabasca, bike path, the Citadel
- *a thing:* computer, hammock, Harley-Davidson
- *a quality/idea/activity:* wit, peace, dancing

Pronoun as Subject

A **pronoun** takes the place of a noun and can also function as the subject of a clause. Pronouns can be

- *personal:* I, you, he, she, it, we, they

    They reviewed their lecture notes.

- *indefinite:* all, any, anybody, anything, each, either, everybody, every-one, neither, nobody, none, no one, nothing, one, some, somebody, someone, something

    Everybody needs to recycle.

- *demonstrative:* that, this, such, these, those

    Those are the sale items.

- *relative:* who, whom, whoever, whomever, whose, which, whichever, that, what

    The order that is ready is the deluxe pizza.

    [In this example, *that* is the subject of the dependent or relative clause. The subject of the independent clause is *order.* (For more about clauses, see pp. 422–23.)]

- *interrogative:* who, whom, whoever, whomever, whose, which, that, what

    Who recommended this awful film?

Compound Subject

Subjects may be compound, as in these sentences:

    Julie and Joe restore old automobiles.
    The dietician and nurses gave the patients new menus.
    Here are questions and assignments for each reading.
    Books, newpapers, and magazines collected on his desk.

OBJECTS

Direct Object

Nouns or pronouns function as the subject of a clause. However, nouns and pronouns can appear elsewhere in a sentence. A noun or pronoun that receives the action of the verb is called a **direct object**. In the sentence "Julie and Joe restore old automobiles," the noun *automobiles* answers the question, "What do Julie and Joe restore?" *Automobiles* is thus the direct object of the verb *restore*. Similarly, in the sentence "Julie and Joe restore them," the object form of the pronoun *them* is the direct object of the verb *restore*. (See p. 431 for more on pronoun forms.)

Indirect Object

A noun that identifies to or for whom or what the action of the verb is performed is the **indirect object**. In the sentence "The dietician and nurses gave the patients new menus," the noun *patients* answers the question, "To whom were the menus given?"

Object of the Preposition

A noun that follows a preposition (see list on p. 420) is called the **object of the preposition**. In the sentence "Books, newspapers, and magazines collected on his desk," the noun *desk* is the object of the preposition *on*.

Objects may provide important information in a sentence, but they are not necessary in order to have a clause. Verbs, however, are essential.

VERBS

A **verb** is what the subject does, is, has, or has done to it. The verb may be more than one word (*may be coming*). The verb also changes form to agree with the subject (*he **drives**; they **drive***) and to indicate time (*he **drove**, he **has driven***). Regular verbs form their past tense by adding *-ed*, but there are a number of irregular forms like *drive* that have special forms.

Action Verbs

An **action verb** specifies what the subject does, has, or has done to it. The action does not have to be physical in any sense: *meditate* is an action verb. Other action verbs include *dance, think, laugh, provoke, erupt,* and *suggest.*

> Enzo's humour <u>relaxes</u> everyone.
> Dr. Schnarr <u>wrote</u> an insightful study of Rudy Wiebe's work.

State-of-Being Verbs

A **state-of-being** or **linking verb** specifies what the subject is. State-of-being verbs include the following: *is, are, was, were, am, feel, seem, be, being, been,* *do, does, did, have, has, had.* These can be main verbs or helping verbs. For more on helping verbs, see the following section.

```
Dylan is interested in Canadian history.
```
[*is* as main verb]

```
Evan is playing volleyball this year.
```
[*is* as a helping verb]

Helping Verbs

The **helping verb** is always used with a main verb. Helping verbs include *can, will, shall, should, could, would, may, might,* and *must.*

```
The designated driver will get everyone home safely.
They should have requested assistance.
```

ADJECTIVES AND ADVERBS

Many sentences contain modifying words that describe the nouns and verbs. **Adjectives** modify nouns (*corroded* pipes, *hectic* schedule) and pronouns (the *curious* one). **Adverbs** modify verbs (*cautiously* responded), adjectives (*truly* generous), adverbs (*very* slowly), and word groups (*Eventually,* he entered the room). Adverbs answer the questions *how? when? where?* and *why?* They often end in *-ly,* but not always.

The following sentence contains both adjectives and adverbs. Can you identify each?

```
According to Professor Shalinsky, angry young men often
will vent their frustrations on vulnerable, weaker beings--
typically children or women.
```

The adjectives *angry* and *young* modify the noun *men;* the adjectives *vulnerable* and *weaker* modify the noun *beings.* The adverbs *often* and *typically* modify the verb *will vent.*

Adjectives and adverbs can provide valuable details, but they can be overused. Being descriptive doesn't require a string of adjectives and adverbs. Often a strong verb gives a more precise picture in fewer words:

```
The drunken man walked unsteadily and unevenly from the
bar.
The drunken man staggered from the bar.
```

The verb *staggered* is vivid and precise. The pile-up of adverbs in the first sentence is wordy and imprecise. Such tightening often improves writing and saves space for more necessary depth and development.

PHRASES

A **phrase** is a group of words that acts as a noun, verb, adjective, or adverb. Since a phrase does not contain both a subject and a verb, it cannot stand alone as a sentence. This is particularly helpful to know in order to avoid fragments.

Prepositional Phrases

A **prepositional phrase** always starts with a **preposition** (a word that shows relationships in time and space) and ends with the **object of the preposition**. The most common prepositions are listed below:

about	beside	from	outside	toward
above	besides	in	over	under
across	between	inside	past	underneath
after	beyond	into	plus	unlike
against	but	like	regarding	until
along	by	near	respecting	unto
among	concerning	next	round	up
around	considering	of	since	upon
as	despite	off	than	with
at	down	on	through	without
before	during	onto	throughout	
behind	except	opposite	till	
below	for	out	to	

Some prepositions, such as *along with*, *as well as*, *in addition to*, *next to*, and *up to* are more than one word long.

The object of the preposition is always a noun or pronoun:

<u>Vickie</u> <u>finds</u> the best deals **at garage sales**.

During intermission, <u>Becky and Tessa</u> <u>went</u> **for popcorn.**

At home, <u>Anne</u> <u>babysits</u> **for her daughter during the day**.

[In the last sentence, *at home*, *for her daughter*, and *during the day* are all prepositional phrases. Note how much easier it is to locate the subject and verb when the prepositional phrases are eliminated.]

Verbal Phrases

These phrases look like verbs, but they do not function as the main verb of the clause. Verbal phrases may serve as subjects, objects, adjectives, and adverbs. Two main types of verbal phrases are **infinitive phrases** and **-ing phrases**.

Infinitive Phrases

If the verb is preceded by *to* (*to ski*), the verb is in the **infinitive form**. It helps to recognize infinitives because they cannot be the main verbs.

Most <u>professors</u> <u>like</u> **to challenge** students.

To think <u>is</u> **to question.**
[Infinitives can function as subjects.]

-ing Phrases

A word ending in *-ing* may look like a verb, but it needs a helping verb or a main verb elsewhere in the sentence. Notice how *working* serves a different function in each of the following sentences (only in the first sentence is it part of the main verb):

Ludmila is **working** as an art director.

Working as an art director <u>requires</u> overtime hours.
[When *-ing* words function as subjects, they are called **gerunds**.]

The **working** <u>artist</u> exhibited her paintings.
[When *-ing* words function as adjectives, they are called **participles**.]

Words and phrases with *-ing* can often lead writers to believe they have a complete sentence—that is, at least one independent clause—when they may have only a fragment. For example, "In the evening after arriving home from work" is not an independent clause; it simply consists of three phrases.

One way to determine if there is an independent clause, and therefore a sentence, is to draw a line through each phrase:

~~In the evening after arriving home from work~~, Bill retreats ~~to his studio for hours to play piano~~ and ~~to compose new songs~~.

What is left is the subject and verb of the sentence.

Now that you can recognize the most important parts of a sentence, you can better understand how clauses work and how they can be combined.

CLAUSES

A **clause** is a group of words with a subject and main verb. A sentence is always a clause, called an **independent clause**, because it contains both a subject and a verb and is a complete thought. However, every clause is not necessarily a sentence—a concept that many students find puzzling. A **dependent clause**, for example, has a subject and a verb, but is grammatically incomplete and cannot therefore stand alone as sentence. The difference between these two basic types of clauses is discussed below.

Independent (or Main) Clauses

The **independent clause** has a subject and main verb and can stand alone:

    Daniel is remodelling his apartment.

    Alyssa loves singing with Robert and Susie.

    The poet invited Chantal and Keith backstage.

Dependent (or Subordinate) Clauses

The **dependent clause** has a subject and main verb but cannot stand alone. Dependent clauses begin with one of these **subordinate conjunctions**:

after	how	what, whatever
although	if, even if	when, whenever
as, as if	in order that	whereas
as long as	since	whether
as soon as	that, so that	which, whichever
because	unless	while
before	until	who, whom, whose

Whenever a clause begins with one of these words (unless it is a question), it is a dependent clause. If we take an independent clause such as

    We jogged

and put one of the subordinate conjunctions in front of it, it becomes dependent (and therefore a fragment):

    After we jogged

    Because we jogged

To make a complete sentence, we need to add an independent clause (or delete the subordinate conjunction):

    After we jogged, we went for a swim.

    Because we jogged, we justified eating brownies.

Dependent clauses can function as adjectives, adverbs, or nouns in a sentence:

The film student **who won the award** graduated with honours.
[Dependent clause functions as an adjective.]

Whenever Josie eats peanut butter, she gets the hiccups.
[Dependent clause functions as an adverb.]

We all hoped **that Donovan Bailey would win.**
[Dependent clause functions as a noun, object of the verb *hoped*.]

What my parents don't know can't hurt them.
[Dependent clause functions as a noun, subject of the negative verb phrase *can't hurt*.]

Every sentence must have at least one independent clause in it.

SENTENCE VARIATION

If you know how to control and combine clauses, you can vary your sentences for greater emphasis, more clarity, and less monotony. The four basic sentence types are illustrated below.

Simple Sentences

Simple sentences contain one independent clause:

Ron's support delighted us.
Walter spent hours with his sons each night.

Compound Sentences

Compound sentences contain two independent clauses. There are only two ways to punctuate a compound sentence:

1. A **comma** followed by a coordinating conjunction (*and, but, for, or, nor, yet, so*):

   We arrived at the cabin, **so** they left.

2. A **semicolon** by itself (or it may be followed by a word like *nevertheless* or *however*):

   We arrived; they left.
   We arrived; **therefore,** they left.

Notice that the writer's decision to use a coordinate conjunction or a semicolon is not arbitrary. If the writer wishes to clarify or emphasize the relationship between the two clauses, he or she will use a coordinate conjunction (such as *so*) or a conjunctive adverb (such as *therefore*). If the writer prefers not to define the relationship between the clauses, then the semicolon by itself is more appropriate.

Complex Sentences

Complex sentences contain one independent clause and one or more dependent clauses. Below, the dependent clauses are in boldface.

> <u>Marian</u> <u>spent</u> two weeks at camp every summer **when <u>she</u> <u>was</u> a girl**.
>
> **Because <u>she</u> <u>was</u> so sociable,** <u>she</u> <u>made</u> many friends.

Notice that when the dependent clause comes first in the sentence, a comma is placed between the dependent and independent clauses.

Compound–Complex Sentences

Compound–complex sentences contain two or more independent clauses and one or more dependent clauses. The dependent clause or clauses may be at the beginning, at the end, or between the independent clauses. Here one dependent clause begins the sentence, and another ends the sentence:

> **Although <u>Jane</u> <u>is</u> a senior citizen,** <u>she</u> <u>swims</u> competitively, and <u>we</u> <u>are</u> all impressed **that <u>she</u> <u>has</u> <u>won</u> so many medals**.

In the following sentence, the dependent clause is between the two independent clauses:

> <u>Tammy</u> <u>studied</u> **before <u>she</u> <u>went</u> to work each night,** but <u>she</u> <u>still</u> <u>felt</u> anxious about the exam.

Writing Sentences

1. Underline the subjects and verbs in the following sentences. Then determine whether each sentence is simple, compound, complex, or compound–complex.

> I loved summer camp. When my dad drove the car into the driveway, my heart pounded with excitement. The other campers were arriving at the same time, so I wanted to see my old friends. At the main building, we signed in and picked up my cabin number. My parents started walking me

to my cabin, although I skipped down the path far ahead of them. The counsellors were waiting for us there. In the cabin, I chose a top bunk if one was still available, and I chattered to the other girls until my parents said goodbye. As soon as they left, I was off to the craft room or the waterfront. The fun lasted for two wonderful weeks.

2. Using details from the last essay that you discussed in class, write your own sentences to illustrate each sentence type: simple, compound, complex, and compound–complex. Then underline all subjects once and all verbs twice to make sure you have the necessary clauses. Manipulating these sentence types will help you vary your sentences and combine your ideas more smoothly.

CHAPTER 12
Common Errors

In the next three chapters, we examine common errors that appear most frequently in student papers. These errors are listed below, with the symbols instructors use to note these errors in the margins of your papers:

frag	fragment	*mixed*	mixed construction
ros (fs)	run-on sentence (fused sentence)	*mm*	misplaced modifier
cs	comma splice	*dm*	dangling modifier
ref	pronoun reference	*//*	faulty parallelism
verb	verb form error	*P*	faulty punctuation
agr	agreement	*wd ch*	faulty word choice
shift	inconsistency in text		

FRAGMENTS

Although sentence fragments are used frequently in fiction and advertising copy to simulate spoken English, the sentence fragment is considered nonstandard in formal writing. Fragments may confuse the reader, and they make your writing seem choppy and your ideas disconnected.

frag   A **fragment** is a group of words that, for some reason, cannot stand alone as a complete sentence. The reason may be any one of the following:

1. The word group may lack a subject.

frag
> While the students prepared their final exams, they sunbathed at the same time. **Became involved in discussions that distracted them from their studies.**
> [Add a subject.]

> While the students prepared their final exams, they sunbathed at the same time. Soon <u>they</u> <u>became involved</u> in discussions that distracted them from their studies.

2. The word group may lack a complete verb.

> Arriving before the concert began, we enjoyed the excitement in the air. **The band tuning up before their opening song.**
> [Add a helping verb.]

> Arriving before the concert began, we enjoyed the excitement in the air. The band was tuning up before their opening song.

3. The word group may lack both a subject and a verb.

> I value my piano teacher. **A bright and patient woman.** She encourages perfection even while she tolerates my mistakes.
> [Attach the fragment to the independent clause before or after it.]

> I value my piano teacher, a bright and patient woman. She encourages perfection even while she tolerates my mistakes.

> **or**
> I value my piano teacher. A bright and patient woman, she encourages perfection even while she tolerates my mistakes.

4. The word group may contain both a subject and a verb but be simply a dependent clause.

> Many students use the Internet as a source for research essays. **Which is why our college library is installing a new computer system.**
> [Avoid starting any sentence with *which* unless you are asking a question.]

> Many students use the Internet as a source for research. This is why our college library is installing a new computer system.

> **or**
> Because many students use the Internet as a source for research, our college library is installing a new computer system.

Another example of such a fragment is the following:

> **Although rap music has been criticized for its violence and harsh language.** Rap really reflects the tension in the cities rather than causes it.
> [Connect the fragment to the independent clause.]

> Although rap music has been criticized for its violence and harsh language, rap really reflects the tension in the cities rather than causes it.

As noted earlier, writers may deliberately use a fragment for emphasis or to mimic conversation, but these uses are always controlled and planned. Otherwise, fragments make an essay confusing or choppy. Sometimes the simplest solution is to connect the fragment to an independent clause that is either right before or after it.

RUN-ON SENTENCES AND COMMA SPLICES

ros
fs
cs

Run-on sentences (sometimes called **fused sentences**), or sentences flawed with a **comma splice**, occur when a writer perceives that the thoughts in two complete sentences are related but fails to join the thoughts appropriately. Sometimes the writer makes the mistake of inserting a comma between the independent clauses, creating a comma splice. No punctuation at all between the independent clauses creates a run-on (or fused) sentence. Both errors occur because the writer sees a relationship between sentences and isn't sure what to do to show the relationship.

The "sentence" that follows is one anyone might say, and a writer might be tempted to write:

ros

        It snowed for days the skiers were ecstatic.

The writer has clearly perceived a relationship between the joy of the skiers and the weather conditions. But the word group is incorrectly punctuated and is a run-on or fused sentence.

The writer may decide to "correct" the error by inserting a comma between the two independent clauses:

cs

        It snowed for days, the skiers were ecstatic.

The comma is inadequate punctuation, however, for separating the independent clauses. That "correction" results in the sentence fault called a **comma splice**, which is noted as "cs" in the margin of a paper.

Correcting Run-on Sentences and Comma Splices

The methods below illustrate alternatives for correcting run-on sentences. Notice that the five choices are all grammatically correct, but each places different emphasis on the two clauses and may change the meaning of the sentence.

1. Separate the independent clauses with a period:

        It snowed for days. The skiers were ecstatic.

2. Use a comma plus a coordinating conjunction (*and, but, for, or, nor, yet, so*) between the independent clauses:

```
It snowed for days, and the skiers were ecstatic.
```
or
```
It snowed for days, yet the skiers were ecstatic.
```
or
```
It snowed for days, so the skiers were ecstatic.
```

3. Use a semicolon between the independent clauses:

```
It snowed for days; the skiers were ecstatic.
```

4. Change one independent clause into a dependent clause:

```
Because it snowed for days, the skiers were ecstatic.
```
or
```
The skiers were ecstatic because it snowed for days.
```

Notice that when the dependent clause begins the sentence, a comma separates it from the main clause. Conversely, when the independent clause begins the sentence, there is no comma before the dependent clause that concludes the sentence. See page 422 for a list of words that begin dependent clauses.

5. Use a semicolon after the first independent clause, and then a conjunctive adverb (see below) followed by a comma:

```
It snowed for days; consequently, the skiers were ecsta-
tic.
```
or
```
It snowed for days; nevertheless, the skiers were ecsta-
tic.
```

Conjunctive Adverbs

Conjunctive adverbs include the following:

accordingly	finally	likewise	similarly
also	furthermore	meanwhile	specifically
anyway	hence	moreover	still
besides	however	nevertheless	subsequently
certainly	incidentally	next	then
consequently	indeed	nonetheless	therefore
conversely	instead	otherwise	thus

Style and Meaning

Grammatical correction of a run-on sentence is not the only concern of the writer. Style, emphasis, and meaning also should be considered when you are deciding which conjunction to use. Notice the difference in emphasis in the following examples:

```
It snowed for days. The skiers were ecstatic.
Because it snowed for days, the skiers were ecstatic.
```

In the first correction, the writer asks the reader to infer the relationship between the skiers' being "ecstatic" and the fact that "it snowed for days." In the second example, the cause-and-effect relationship is defined clearly. Look at the following simple sentences, which have been incorrectly combined to form a run-on sentence, and notice what happens to the meaning, emphasis, or relationship between the independent clauses when different corrections are employed:

ros   Renée pitched the team won.

1.   Renée pitched. The team won.

The writer has stated facts in the two sentences but has not defined a relationship between them.

2.   Renée pitched, and the team won.

A mild relationship is suggested by connecting the two events with *and*.

```
Renée pitched, so the team won.
```

The relationship between the team's victory and the person who pitched is defined in this construction using *so*.

```
Renée pitched, yet the team won.
```

The use of *yet*, which signals something contrary to expectation, changes the relationship between the independent clauses in this example. The word *yet* tells readers that in spite of the fact that Renée pitched, the team won.

3.   Renée pitched; the team won.

The semicolon does not define the relationship between the two independent clauses, although a subtle relationship is suggested by the writer's using a semicolon instead of a period. The semicolon is a compromise punctuation symbol. It is stronger than a comma, but it is not as complete a stop as a period.

4.   Whenever Renée pitched, the team won.
     The team won because Renée pitched.
     Although Renée pitched, the team won.
     The team won unless Renée pitched.

The dependent clause, whether it begins or ends the sentence, defines the exact relationship between the two clauses in the sentence. Clearly, the subordinate conjunction chosen has everything to do with the meaning of the sentence.

5.   Renée pitched; therefore, the team won.
     Renée pitched; nevertheless, the team won.

Again, the conjunctive adverb defines the precise relationship between the two clauses of the sentence. For the purpose of connecting two short independent clauses, most writers would find the combination of semi-colon and conjunctive adverb and comma too cumbersome. A coordinating conjunction with a comma would probably be a better method of linking the two clauses.

PRONOUN REFERENCE

Pronouns are words that take the place of nouns. In most cases, pronouns are an advantage to the writer because they permit reference to nouns named without the writer's having to repeat the noun or find a clear substitute (or synonym) for it. Ambiguity, vagueness, or confusion can result, however, if *ref* the writer has not used pronouns responsibly. The marginal symbol "ref" indicates a problem with the **pronoun reference**.

This chart shows the form personal pronouns take:

	Subjective	**Possessive**	**Objective**
Singular	I	my, mine	me
	you	your, yours	you
	he	his	him
	she	her, hers	her
	it	its	it
Plural	we	our, ours	us
	you	your, yours	you
	they	their, theirs	them

Indefinite pronouns include *all, any, anybody, anything, each, either, everybody, everyone, everything, neither, nobody, none, no one, nothing, one, some, somebody, someone,* and *something.*

Pronoun problems occur when readers do not know what noun is referred to by the noun substitute, the pronoun.

1. Sometimes the pronoun used could refer to either of two nouns:

ref

> When Karen told Pat the news, she burst into tears.

She can refer to either Karen or Pat. The ambiguity must be resolved for readers:

> Pat burst into tears when Karen told her the news.
> **or**
> Karen burst into tears when she told Pat the news.

2. Sometimes the subject is implied by the writer but is not stated in the sentence. The pronoun does not clearly refer to any given noun, and confusion results for readers:

ref

> For years, Pete carried rocks from the quarry, and **it** strained his back.

It cannot refer to the plural *rocks*, and the singular noun *quarry* didn't "strain his back." The writer probably means "this work" or "the constant hauling of heavy rocks." The writer needs to make that clarification in the sentence:

> For years, Pete carried rocks from the quarry, and **this work** strained his back.

3. Indefinite pronouns can also pose a problem for writer and readers if the singular form of the indefinite pronoun is inconsistent with the meaning of the sentence or the gender of the pronoun is assumed by the writer to be a generic *he.* Generally, a singular pronoun should be used with an indefinite pronoun:

> **Each** boy on the football team has **his** own locker.
> **Anybody** who has **her** doubts about the value of natural childbirth should take a Lamaze course.

If the writer is certain of the singular intention and gender of the subject, no problems arise in determining the form of the possessive pronoun and no reader will be offended. If the indefinite pronoun has a plural meaning, however, the grammatical necessity of a singular possessive pronoun may result in an inappropriate use of a generic *his*, or a repetitive use of *his or her*, or the temptation to use the awkward form *his/her*.

Here is an example of the problem:

ref

```
Everybody applying for a part-time job on campus should
report to his counsellor.
```

Everybody is a singular pronoun and requires a singular possessive pronoun: *his* or *her*. *Their* is plural and can't be used in this sentence. But should the writer assume the generic *his*? Readers might object that the implication of the sentence is that only males may apply for a part-time job on campus. A similar misunderstanding would occur if the writer opted for *her* as the singular possessive pronoun. If this were a single-sentence statement, as in a school bulletin, the writer might choose *his or her* for a correct and clear mandate. But the repetitive use of *his or her* can be a burden in a longer essay.

Learn to find alternatives. A plural noun and plural possessive pronoun will take care of the problem, so rewrite the sentence:

```
All students applying for a part-time job on campus
should report to their counsellors.
```

You may also want to see "Sexist Language" (pp. 465–66) in Chapter 14 for further discussion of pronoun choices.

VERB FORM ERRORS

verb The marginal note "verb" indicates an error in the form of the verb. Such errors may be agreement problems, unnecessary shifts, or mixed constructions, all of which are discussed in more detail in this chapter.

English verbs have four forms:

Present	Past	Past Participle	Present Participle
walk	walked	walked	walking
snore	snored	snored	snoring
shop	shopped	shopped	shopping
buy	bought	bought	buying
throw	threw	thrown	throwing

To create past and past participle forms of regular verbs such as *walk*, *snore*, and *shop*, add *-ed* or *-d* to the present form. As their name implies, irregular verbs such as *buy* and *throw* have irregular past, past participle, and present participle forms. Irregular verb form errors are common, so check your dictionary for the correct forms for these verbs.

verb   `Marlene `<u>`swum`</u>` the race in record time.`
             `Marlene `<u>`swam`</u>` the race in record time.`

verb   `The witness `<u>`sworn`</u>` to tell the truth.`
             `The witness `<u>`swore`</u>` to tell the truth.`
             or
             `The witness `<u>`has sworn`</u>` to tell the truth.`

Verb form errors may also occur because the writer leaves off the *-s* ending on third-person singular verbs is the present tense. Some dialects drop this *-s* ending in speech; however, in written English the final *-s* must be included.

verb   `He `<u>`live`</u>` in a small town called Oakburn.`
             `He `<u>`lives`</u>` in a small town called Oakburn.`

AGREEMENT

agr The marginal note "agr" means that there is an agreement problem; the subject and the verb do not agree in number. Both subject and verb should be singular or both should be plural.

      `The `<u>`sun`</u>` `<u>`rises`</u>` in the east and `<u>`sets`</u>` in the west.`
      `Most birds fly south for the winter.`

Some sentences, especially those that have groups of words separating the subject and verb, may present agreement problems. Some conditions to be aware of are listed below.

1.   A prepositional phrase does not influence the verb of the sentence:

      `The `<u>`birds`</u>` in the nest `<u>`need`</u>` food from the mother bird.`
      `The first five `<u>`days`</u>` of our holiday `<u>`are going`</u>` to be the most exciting.`
      `Her `<u>`secretary`</u>`, in addition to her staff, `<u>`prefers`</u>` the new computer.`

Notice that by removing the prepositional phrases from your consideration, you will use the correct verb form for the subject of the sentence.

2.   Subjects connected by *and* usually have a plural verb:

      `The student's academic `<u>`load`</u>` **and** work `<u>`time`</u>` `<u>`keep`</u>` him busy.`

a. When the compound subject (nouns connected by *and*) is regarded as a unit, the subject is regarded as singular and has a singular verb:

<u>Peanut butter and jelly</u> <u>remains</u> Raul's favourite lunch.

b. If the double nouns refer to the same person or thing, the verb is singular:

Melinda's <u>home and studio</u> <u>is</u> 215 Thompson Street.

c. When *each* or *every* precedes the multiple nouns, use a singular verb:

<u>Each</u> instructor, student, and staff member <u>prefers</u> the new insurance plan.

d. When nouns are connected by *or* or *nor*, the verb agrees with the noun closer to it:

Your student ID or room <u>key</u> <u>guarantees</u> the loan of sports equipment

Your student ID or room <u>keys</u> <u>guarantee</u> the loan of sports equipment.

Neither the police officer nor his <u>cadets</u> <u>were attend-</u><u>ing</u> the lecture.

Either the band or the <u>comedian</u> <u>provides</u> the program notes.

3. Most indefinite pronouns have a singular verb, even if the pronoun seems to convey a plural sense. Indefinite pronouns include *anybody, anyone, each, either, everybody, everyone, everything, neither, none, no one, someone,* and *something*. Notice how each indefinite pronoun is used in the following sentences:

<u>Each</u> of the cast members <u>has</u> two free tickets for guests.

<u>Everybody</u> <u>endures</u> the stress of two final exams a day.

<u>Everyone</u> on the school board <u>votes</u> at each meeting.

Have you read Irving Abella's book <u>None</u> <u>Is</u> <u>Too</u> <u>Many</u>?

All, any, or *some,* however, may be singular or plural depending on what the pronoun refers to:

<u>All</u> of the pizza <u>is gone</u>.

<u>All</u> of the books <u>are shelved</u>.

4. Collective nouns (like *band, family, committee, class, jury,* and *audience*) require a singular verb unless the meaning of the noun is plural, or individuality is to be emphasized:

> The <u>jury</u> <u>presents</u> its decision today.
>
> The <u>jury</u> <u>are</u> undecided about a verdict.

5. Even when the subject follows the verb, the verb must be in the correct form. The following sentences open with a construction called an **expletive**. Expletives begin with *there is* if the true subject following the expletive is singular or *there are* if the true subject is plural:

> There <u>is</u> too little <u>time</u> to organize the campaign.
>
> There <u>are</u> many <u>reasons</u> why I was unable to finish this assignment on time.

6. Titles require singular verbs:

> *Lives of the Saints* <u>is</u> the book we will read next.
>
> <u>Jacoby and Associates</u> <u>is</u> the accounting firm on the corner.
>
> <u>Succulents</u> <u>is</u> the section of the nursery Carlos prefers.

7. Nouns describing academic disciplines—like *economics, statistics,* or *physics*—and diseases that end in an *s*—like *mumps* and *measles*—and *news* are treated as singular nouns:

> <u>Physics</u> <u>challenges</u> Maria, but she does well in the course.
>
> <u>Measles</u> usually <u>attacks</u> only the children who have not been immunized.

SHIFTS

shift The marginal note "shift" marks an inconsistency in the text in person, number, or verb tense.

Shifts in Person and Number

Shifts in person and number sometimes occur because you are not certain from what point of view to write or because you move from one perspective to another without being conscious of the change. You may begin with the idea of addressing a general audience—"someone"—and then decide to address the reader as "you." Or you may begin with a singular reader in mind and switch to a plural sense of "all readers." If you start to write from one perspective and switch to another, a distracting shift occurs:

shift

If <u>someone</u> in the group writes a paper, <u>they</u> may present it.

If a <u>person</u> writes a paper, <u>he or she</u> may present it.

or (better)

If <u>people</u> write papers, <u>they</u> may present them.

shift

The <u>vegetarian</u> learns to prepare interesting and nutritious meals with vegetables and grains, but then <u>you</u> have to assure <u>your</u> friends that <u>you</u> are getting enough protein.

If <u>you</u> are a vegetarian, <u>you</u> learn to prepare interesting and nutritious meals with vegetables and grains, but then <u>you</u> have to assure <u>your</u> friends that <u>you</u> are getting enough protein.

or

<u>Vegetarians</u> learn to prepare interesting and nutritious meals with vegetables and grains, but then <u>they</u> have to assure <u>their</u> friends that <u>they</u> are getting enough protein.

Shifts in Verb Tense

Shifts in verb tense will confuse a reader about the time the action of your sentence takes place. You have probably heard oral story-tellers shift from one tense to another. Eventually you may have figured out the course of the narration, perhaps by asking the speaker to clarify the time of the action. But a shift in tense is particularly distracting in writing because you can't ask a writer for a clarification of the text. Notice how the verb tense in the following example shifts from the past to the present:

shift

Shortly after we <u>arrived</u> at the picnic site, it <u>started</u> to rain. So we <u>pack</u> up the bread, salami, and fruit and <u>rush</u> to the cars.

Here is the correction for verb tense consistency:

Shortly after we <u>arrived</u> at the picnic site, it <u>started</u> to rain. So we <u>packed</u> up the bread, salami, and fruit and <u>rushed</u> to the cars.

Use the present tense throughout to write a summary or a description of a literary work such as this one of Margaret Laurence's novel *The Diviners*:

Morag Gunn first meets Skinner Tonnerre by chance, when she was trying to overcome her fear of crossing the old rope bridge across the river outside Manawaka. Skinner rocks the bridge, and although Morag insisted that she wasn't afraid, he knows she is. Ten years later, when Morag is trying to find the courage to end her marriage to Brooke, she again met Skinner by chance, on a street in a run-down area of Toronto.

Morag Gunn first meets Skinner Tonnerre by chance, when she is trying to overcome her fear of crossing the old rope bridge across the river outside Manawaka. Skinner rocks the bridge, and although Morag insists that she isn't afraid, he knows she is. Ten years later, when Morag is trying to find the courage to end her marriage to Brooke, she again meets Skinner by chance, on a street in a run-down area of Toronto.

Shifts in Voice

Just as a shift in number or tense can be distracting, a shift from one voice to another can confuse or distract your readers. Use the active voice or passive voice consistently.

When the subject of a sentence does the action, the sentence is in the **active voice**:

Lester brought the pasta salad.

When the subject receives the action, the verb is in the **passive voice**. Notice that the passive voice is less effective than the active voice because it is less direct:

The pasta salad was brought by Lester.

When the active and passive voice are combined, the sentence is inconsistent in voice and would be marked with a "shift" in the margin of the paper:

Lester brought the pasta salad, and the soft drinks were brought by Mike.

Lester brought the pasta salad, and Mike brought the soft drinks.

In some cases, the passive voice is necessary because what might be the subject of the sentence is unknown or unimportant:

The car was hijacked last week.

Because the hijacker is apparently unknown, the sentence is in the passive voice, with the action being done to the car, the subject of the sentence.

```
The researcher was granted additional funds to complete the
study of the effects of second-hand smoke.
```

The name of the agency that granted the researcher the funds for the study may be unimportant to the writer of this sentence; the important point is that the researcher has the funds for the project.

Passive voice constructions may create suspicion that the writer is deliberately hiding information:

```
The city council was voted unlimited travel funds.
```

Clearly, the city resident who reads that sentence in the local paper would want to know who did the voting, and why the newspaper failed to name the subject of the verb voted. Use the active voice whenever you know and wish to identify the "doer" of a particular act.

MIXED CONSTRUCTIONS

xed The marginal note "mixed" indicates that there are sentence parts that don't go together. The sentence may start with one subject and shift to another, or the verb may not fit the true subject of the sentence. The sentence also may begin with one grammatical construction and end with another. The problem, then, is a misfit in grammar or in logic, so the sentence is confusing to the reader:

xed
```
Although he is active in the men's movement doesn't mean
he is a misogynist.
```

In this sentence, the writer tries to make the dependent clause "Although he is active in the men's movement" the subject of the sentence. The writer probably intends *he* to be the subject of the sentence; rewriting the sentence to show this and selecting a correct verb for the subject will eliminate the confusion:

```
Although he is active in the men's movement, he is not a
misogynist.
```

Confused Sentence Parts

Each of the following mixed sentences contains a confusion between sentence parts. In some cases, the writer has started with one subject in mind and has ended the sentence with a different or implied subject. In other cases, the grammatical form of the first part of the sentence is inconsistent with the end of the sentence. Most often the revision involves correct identification of the true subject of the sentence and then the selection of an appropriate verb.

mixed   Among those women suffering with eating disorders, they are not always bulimic.
    Not all women with eating disorders are bulimic.

mixed   By prewriting, outlining, drafting, and revising is how he wrote good papers.
    He wrote good papers by prewriting, outlining, drafting, and revising his work.

mixed   The subject of ecology involves controversy.
    Ecology involves controversy.

Faulty Verb Choice

In some sentences with mixed meaning, the fault occurs because the subject is said to do or to be something that is illogical.

mixed   A realization between the academic senate and the dean would be the ideal policy on plagiarism.

The sentence says that "a realization" would be "the ideal policy," which is not exactly what the writer means. Correction of the faulty use of the verb *would be* will clarify the sentence:

    Ideally, a policy on plagiarism would be decided between the academic senate and the dean.

    or

    Ideally, the academic senate and the dean would realize the necessity for a policy on plagiarism.

In speech, *is when* and *is where* are common constructions for defining words, but these are mixed constructions and should be corrected in writing.

mixed   Acquiescence **is when** you give in to your oppressor.
    Acquiescence means to give in to an oppressor.

mixed   A final exam **is where** you show comprehensive knowledge.
    On a final exam, you show comprehensive knowledge.

MISPLACED (AND DANGLING) MODIFIERS

MM The marginal note "mm" means **misplaced modifier**. A **modifier** is a word, phrase, or clause used to describe another word in the sentence. The modifier should be as close to that word as possible, or the meaning can be confusing or unintentionally humorous.

MM
```
Attacking our canary, I caught the cat.
```

Written this way, "attacking the canary" appears to describe "I" rather than "cat." Such a misplaced modifier can be easily corrected by rearranging the phrase so it describes "cat":

```
I caught the cat attacking our canary.
```

Sometimes there may not be a word for the modifier to describe. In these cases, the sentence needs to be rewritten:

dm
```
At the age of 12, my family hiked through Gros Morne
National Park.
```

Here the writer probably does not mean that his or her family was 12 years old, but this sentence does not contain a word for the opening phrase to describe. Therefore, "at the age of 12" is called a **dangling modifier** (noted as "dm" in the margin) because it fails to refer logically to any word in the sentence. Dangling modifiers can be corrected by the following methods:

dm

1. Keep the modifier as it is and add a word for the modifier to describe:

   ```
   At the age of 12, I hiked through Gros Morne National
   Park with my family.
   ```

2. Turn the modifier into a dependent clause so that the meaning is clear:

   ```
   When I was 12, my family hiked through Gros Morne
   National Park.
   ```

Often the modifier is not simply "dangling" but is oddly placed in the sentence so that the meaning is absurd:

MM
```
You will value the difficult classes you took semesters
from now.
Semesters from now, you will value the difficult classes
you took.
```

MM
```
Yuko's blind date was described as a 190-centimetre-tall
musician with a long ponytail weighing only 60 kilograms.
Yuko's blind date was described as a 60-kilogram, 190-
centimetre-tall musician with a long ponytail.
```

Misplaced words can turn even the most serious dissertation into a comedy of errors. Occasionally an instructor may simply write "awk" (awkward) or "confusing" or "reword" in the margins when the error is actually a misplaced modifier. Becoming aware of the importance of the placement of each word or phrase in a sentence can help you detect and prevent such comical and confusing meanings before you prepare your final draft.

FAULTY PARALLELISM

To achieve clarity, emphasis, and harmony in writing, use parallel construction for parts of sentences that you repeat. The "parts" may be single words, phrases, or clauses. Therefore, when you write any kind of list, put the items in similar grammatical form (all -*ing* words, all infinitives, and so on). Instead of writing "He likes hiking and to ski," you should write "He likes hiking and skiing" or "He likes to hike and to ski."

//   If **faulty parallelism** is noted in the margin of your paper, you have not kept the parts of your sentence in the same grammatical form.

Single Words

//   The movie entertained and was enlightening.
       The movie was **entertaining and enlightening.**

Phrases

//   Ausra enjoys telling complicated jokes, performing the latest dances, and exotic food.
       Ausra enjoys **telling complicated jokes, performing the latest dances,** and **eating exotic food.**

Dependent Clauses

//   The instructor reminded the students that papers must be submitted on time and to prepare reading assignments before class.
       The instructor reminded the students **that papers must be submitted on time** and **that reading assignments must be prepared before class.**

Independent Clauses

//   "I came, I did some learning, and I triumphed," announced the jubilant graduate.
       "I came, I learned, and **I triumphed,"** announced the jubilant graduate.

Correlative Conjunctions

You can also achieve greater clarity, emphasis, and balance by using parallel constructions with correlative conjunctions (paired terms such as *not only . . . but also, either . . . or,* and *neither . . . nor*):

We discovered fast walking is good for health and also for friendship.
We discovered that fast walking is good **not only** for health **but also** for friendship.

Rachel doesn't work as a waitress any longer, and neither does Donna.
Neither Rachel **nor** Donna works as a waitress any longer.

CHAPTER 13
Punctuation

p   "P" in the margin of an essay indicates some sort of error in punctuation. Because the comma is the most frequently used punctuation symbol, most errors occur in comma use. Commas usually function to separate elements within a sentence, but they also have standard uses in dates, addresses, and multiple-digit numbers. Below are models of the standard uses of the comma, with brief explanations to help you avoid comma errors.

THE COMMA

1. Use a comma *before a coordinating conjunction* joining independent clauses. (Coordinating conjunctions are *and*, *but*, *for*, *or*, *nor*, *yet*, and *so*. See also p. 423.)

> The college has slashed its budget, so student activity fees will increase this year.
>
> Many men want to take paternity leave when their babies are born, but most companies are not prepared for the requests.

Short independent clauses may not need a comma with the conjunction, but if there is any doubt about the need or clarity, use the comma.

> He arrived so I left.
> He arrived, so I left.

2. Use a comma *to separate introductory elements* from the rest of the sentence.

> To register for aerobics classes, bring your student identification card.
>
> If car insurance costs continue to rise, Vanessa may have to sell her sports car.
>
> Exhilarated, the climber reached the summit.
>
> By the next century, most college graduates will be in service-related careers.

3. Use a comma *to separate items in a series.*

> The college bookstore has been criticized for selling sexist magazines, cigarettes, and greeting cards of questionable taste.
>
> Triathlons require quick running, swimming, and cycling.
>
> The requirements for ownership of the condominium include a bank-approved loan, a satisfactory security rating, and a willingness to comply with the homeowners' rules and procedures.

4. Use a comma *between coordinate adjectives* if there is not a conjunction. Coordinate adjectives are adjectives that modify the same word equally.

> The shady, blooming, fragrant garden welcomed the walkers.
>
> A shady and fragrant garden welcomed the walkers.

If the first adjective modifies the second adjective, do not use a comma.

> That home's most interesting feature is a white oak staircase.
>
> Professor Pierce's exams require complicated mathematical computations.

5. Use commas *to set off nonrestrictive word groups.* Nonrestrictive elements describe nouns or pronouns by giving extra or nonessential information. The nonrestrictive element could be removed from the sentence without sacrificing the accuracy of the sentence.

> Neepawa, which is located 170 kilometres west of Winnipeg, was the model for Margaret Laurence's fictional town of Manawaka.
>
> Wayson Choy's first novel, *The Jade Peony*, won a Trillium Award.
>
> The Rolls Royce, its silver hood ornament gleaming in the sun, was completely out of gas.

6. Do *not* use commas with restrictive word groups. Restrictive elements limit the meaning of words or provide vital (or restricting) information.

> The entrées **on the left side of the menu** are suitable for diners who prefer low-cholesterol diets.

The sentence gives the information that *only* the entrées on the *left side* of the menu are low in cholesterol. Presumably, the other items on the menu are not especially for clients who prefer low cholesterol.

Our son **who lived in New Brunswick** studies Canadian history.

For a family with sons residing in different provinces, the restrictive clause is essential and commas should not be used.

Customers **using credit cards** collect free airline mileage.

Again, the lack of commas shows that the information is restrictive. Only those customers who use credit cards will collect airline mileage; customers who pay by cheque or cash do not.

7. Use commas *to separate transitional or parenthetical expressions, conjunctive adverbs, contrasting elements, and most phrases* from the main part of the sentence.

> Silk, for example, can be washed by hand.
>
> Jana's great-grandfather, as the story goes, was one of the organizers of the 1935 Regina Riot.
>
> A medium avocado contains 324 calories; therefore, it is not an ideal fruit for people watching their weight.
>
> Darren, unlike his brother Stephen, can be reasonable.
>
> Her photography program completed, Elaine opened a studio in Charlottetown.

8. Use commas *to set off expressions and questions of direct address, the words* yes *and* no, *and interjections.*

> Sorry, Professor Martiniuk, only two of those books are available.
> You will complete the income tax forms, won't you?
> Yes, most readers prefer the new MLA documentation form.
> Oh, I can't decide if we really need a lawyer.

9. Use commas *for dates, addresses, and titles.*

> James Joyce was born on February 2, 1882, St. Bridget's Day and Groundhog Day, too.
>
> The special delivery letter was sent to 1430 Victoria Avenue East, Brandon, Manitoba.
>
> Will Wood, Ph.D., has been offered a job with a multinational software company.

10. Use commas *to set off direct quotations.*

> As Richard Ellman notes, "Stephen Dedalus said the family was a net which he would fly past."
>
> "I too believe in Taos, without having seen it," wrote D.H. Lawrence to Mabel Luhan.

11. Do *not* use a comma to separate a verb from its subject or object. The following examples show *incorrect* uses of the comma:

p   Fast walking around a track, can be painless but effective exercise.

p   Christine explained to Mario, that studying for the exam was more important than playing video games.

12. Do *not* use a comma between compound elements if the word groups are not independent clauses. The following examples show *incorrect* uses of the comma:

p   Frank can prepare a multicourse meal, and bake bread on the same day.

p   Valerie understands that the Landscape Ontario conference is in January, and that she will need to miss some classes to attend it.

13. A comma should *not* be used to separate an adjective from the noun that follows it. The following examples are *incorrect* uses of the comma:

p   It was a sunny, warm, and windless, day.

p   A massive, polished, ornately carved, buffet stood in the dining room.

THE APOSTROPHE

An apostrophe is used most frequently to form **contractions** and **possessives**.

Contractions

When two words are merged into one, the apostrophe takes the place of any missing letters:

does n<u>o</u>t	doesn'_t
it <u>is</u>	it'_s
should <u>have</u>	should'_ve
I <u>woul</u>d	I'_d

Contractions tend to make writing seem more conversational and informal; therefore, contractions are often avoided in formal writing and in research papers. Remember that the apostrophe takes the place of the missing letter and does not ever belong in the break between the two words:

couldn't [**not** could'nt]

Other instances where apostrophes indicate a missing letter or letters are commonly found in informal writing, particularly in dialogues from narratives and fiction:

```
around          'round
until           'til
1950s           '50s
playing         playin'
```

Again, such forms are typically reserved for writing that is intended to sound conversational.

Possessives

Possessive nouns indicate belonging or ownership and are typically placed immediately before whatever is owned. Rather than write "the trumpet of Jason" or "the office of his doctor," we eliminate the *of* and move the owner in front of the possession:

```
Jason's trumpet
his doctor's office
```

Sometimes such ownership is loosely implied:

```
tonight's party
Thursday's test
one day's sick leave
two weeks' vacation
```

But, in a sense, the party really does "belong" to tonight (not tomorrow) and the test "belongs" to Thursday (not Friday). Similarly, the sick leave is "of one day" and the vacation is "of two weeks." Clearly, the possessive form here makes the writing smoother and less wordy.

To indicate possession, obey the following guidelines:

1. Add -'s if the possessive noun does not end in *s*, whether it is singular or plural:

    ```
    Sophie's jokes
    Ben's request
    the men's movement
    the children's enthusiasm
    ```

2. Add -'s if the possessive noun ends in *s* and is singular:

    ```
    James's routine
    Yeats's poetry
    ```

You may find a variation of this second rule so that "Yeats's poetry" may be written "Yeats' poetry." Both ways are acceptable.

3. Add only an apostrophe at the end of the word if the possessive noun ends in an *s* and is plural:

```
those actors' salaries
five students' projects
the Wilsons' generosity
```

Joint Possession

When two or more people possess the same thing, show joint possession by using *-'s* (or *-s'*) with the last noun only:

```
We relaxed at Al and Dorothy's cabin.
Ahmed and Jess's help was appreciated.
```

Individual Possession

When two or more people possess distinct things, show individual possession by using *-'s* (or *-s'*) with both nouns:

```
Andy's and Beth's marketing surveys aren't completed
yet.
The instructors' and the students' questions were both
fascinating.
```

Compound Nouns

If a noun is compound, use *-'s* (or *-s'*) with the last component of that noun term:

```
My brother-in-law's woodworking is very professional.
Barbara and Tom took their sisters-in-law's advice.
```

Indefinite Pronouns

Indefinite pronouns are those that refer to no specific person or thing: *everyone, anyone, no one,* and *something.* These pronouns also need an apostrophe to indicate possession:

```
We asked everybody's opinion of the film.
Is someone's safety in jeopardy?
```

Possessive Pronouns

Possessive pronouns are already possessive and need no apostrophes:

my, mine	our, ours
your, yours	their, theirs
her, hers	whose
his	
its	

Whose car should we drive?
I would prefer to ride in **yours** rather than **theirs**.

Plurals of Numbers, Letters, Words, and Abbreviations

Traditionally, -'s has been used to form the plural of numbers mentioned as numbers, letters mentioned as letters, words mentioned as words, and abbreviations:

They all marched in two's.
He earned three A's this term.
Their hurray's were all we needed to hear.
We must be sure to check their ID's.

However, common usage is now to leave out the apostrophe where the result will not confuse readers:

They all marched in twos.
Their hurrays were all we needed to hear.
We must be sure to check their IDs.
She was nostalgic for the 1960s.

Some reminders:

1. Make sure a noun is possessive (and not merely plural) before you use an apostrophe. The noun *passengers* does not "own" anything in the following sentence; therefore it is a simple plural.

    The ~~passenger's~~ *passengers* were not allowed to smoke.

2. Possessive pronouns need no apostrophes.

    The crowd expressed ~~it's~~ *its* pleasure.

    That responsibility is ~~her's~~ *hers*.

3. Many instructors prefer that their students not use contractions in formal writing and research papers.

THE PERIOD, QUESTION MARK, AND EXCLAMATION MARK

The most obvious use of the period is to mark the end of a sentence—unless the sentence is a direct question or needs an exclamation mark:

```
Do you remember learning punctuation rules in school?
Yes, and it all seemed so easy then!
```

Because the exclamation mark is used for strong commands and emphatic statements, it should not be overused. Further, an exclamation mark is never used with a period, a comma, or another exclamation mark.

Don't use a question mark for an indirect or implied question:

```
I wonder if I ever had trouble with punctuation in elemen-
tary school.
```

Use the period for abbreviations:

```
Mr. Mrs. Ms.        Dr. Rev. Capt.     B.Sc. M.A. Ph.D.
B.C. A.D.           A.M. P.M.          i.e. e.g. etc.
(or B.C.E and C.E.)
```

Use only one period if the abbreviation falls at the end of a sentence:

```
Most archaeologists believe that groups of people known as
Paleoeskimos first settled in the Arctic around 2000 B.C.E.
```

Notice that no period is used with postal abbreviations:

```
PEI     NS     AB     YK
```

Do not use periods with acronyms (words that are made from the first letters of many words and are pronounced as words):

```
NATO     UNICEF
```

Usually no period is used in abbreviations of the names of organizations or schools:

```
CBC     RCMP     CUN     NHL     WLU
```

THE SEMICOLON

The semicolon is most often used to connect two independent clauses:

> Students who have been granted a student loan may defer pay-
> ment of their fees; students who are ineligible must pay
> their fees before registration.

Notice that the semicolon is used in place of a period to show that the two independent ideas—clauses that could stand alone as separate sentences—are *related*. The semicolon suggests the relationship without defining it.

The semicolon is also used after an independent clause and before some transitional phrases (like *on the other hand* or *in contrast*) and after conjunctive adverbs (such as *therefore, however*, and *furthermore*; see the list on p. 429).

> Newcomers to Canada often enjoy material advantages that they
> lacked in their native lands; on the other hand, they often
> feel spiritually deprived in their new country.
>
> Professor Smiley will accept late papers; however, he reduces
> the grade for each day the paper is late.

The semicolon is used for separating items in a list if the punctuation within the list includes commas:

> The characters in Archibald J. Crail's story "Affirmative
> Action" include Marius, the protagonist; Christine and
> Rhonda, the senior clerks in his accounting section; and
> their supervisor.

THE COLON

A colon is used to introduce and call attention to a statement, to introduce a list, and to introduce a quotation if the quotation is at the end of a sentence. It is also used in bibliographic forms, in reporting time, and in separating main titles from subtitles. In the first set of uses, a colon is usually preceded by a main clause (a word group containing a subject and verb). The main clause does not need to be followed by a complete clause.

> Jakeet was thrilled when he learned what he had won: an
> entrance scholarship to the college's performing arts program.
> [introduces a statement]

To apply for a Canadian passport you must submit the following: a completed application form, two passport photos of
yourself, proof of Canadian citizenship, and a cheque for $60.
[introduces a list]

Kerry Banks points out the lack of role models for new fathers
in the 1990s: "Pressured by society to be different from our
own fathers and struggling to achieve domestic equilibrium with
our wives, we cannot help but feel anxious" (38).
[introduces a quotation]

Don Mills: Addison Wesley Longman
[bibliography]

Between Worlds: A Reader, Rhetoric, and Handbook
[title and subtitle]

The train departs at 5:30 in the morning.
[time]

In some cases, a colon should not be used. For example, do not place a
colon between a subject and a verb, between a verb and its complements, or
between a preposition and its object:

p   The animals in that section of the zoo include: panthers,
     leopards, lions, and tigers.

p   The courses he needs to take for his first semester in nurs-
     ing are: Health Assessment, Human Physiology, Introduction to
     Psychology, and Writing Skills for Health Science.

p   Don't put luggage on: the bed, the desk, or the reclining
     chair.

THE DASH

The dash (which is sometimes created by typing two hyphens with no spaces
around or between them) is used sparingly for dramatic emphasis, to call
attention to material the dash sets off. Sometimes the dash is used in places
where a colon could also be used, but the dash is considered more informal.
Because the dash indicates a sudden shift in thought and is used for dramatic emphasis, it should not be overused. In formal writing a comma, colon, or
period may be more appropriate punctuation symbols.

We all believe that protecting the environment is a priority today--but we still drive our cars rather than using
public transportation.

Here the dash is used to emphasize the contrast between what "we all believe" and what we do. A comma could also be used in this sentence.

> Both successful women and less-successful women have the same goal--to "marry up"--so men still have a constant psychological need to be successful at work.

Dashes are used here to set off the definitive information, the "same goal" the writer believes women have. Commas could have been used, but dashes achieve more emphasis.

The dash may also be used in the same manner as the colon to announce a dramatic point:

> Jakeet was thrilled when he learned what he had won--an entrance scholarship to the college's performing arts program.

QUOTATION MARKS

Quotation marks are used to enclose direct quotations, some titles, and occasionally words defined or used in a special way. Quotation marks are used in pairs.

A **direct quotation** is noted with quotation marks. A direct quotation states in exact words what someone has said or written:

> Kate Braid insists, "Computers offer only the crackle of keys, the strain of arms and neck in a single position for as long as you can hold it. This is not physical connection. This is torture" (180).

An **indirect quotation** notes what has been said in a paraphrased or indirect way. No quotation marks are needed:

> Kate Braid argues that our dependence on technology is creating in us an unnatural aversion to the physical side of life.

A **quotation within a quotation** requires the use of standard quotation marks around the outside quotation and single quotation marks around the interior quotation:

> Trudy Parsons, who is HIV-positive, worries that "Newfoundland has an HIV-infection rate among teens that is four times the national average. 'These kids still think that it is a gay men's disease and they can't get it,' she says" (76).

Commas and periods are placed inside quotation marks:

Sonnet L'Abbé jokes that the difference between Canadians and Americans is that "we have more cold and fewer guns."
"Our pride in being Canadian should stem from a pride in what we are," believes Sonnet L'Abbé.

Semicolons and colons are placed outside quotation marks:

Charlie Angus says urban and rural Canadians can't agree on gun control laws "because the issue is really about two different cultures and realities"; in other words, while we are aware of the differences between English-speaking and French-speaking Canadians, we may forget that culture can vary across the urban and rural dimension as well.
Angus discusses what he calls "a marker of the great divide between rural and urban Canada": gun control.

Question marks go inside quotation marks if they are part of the quotation but belong outside of quotation marks if the quoted statement is being used as a question by the writer quoting the material:

The professor asked, "Who agrees with Charlie Angus's thesis?"
Does Angus advocate "easy access to assault rifles and hand guns"?

If you are quoting a conversation, begin a new paragraph for each speaker. Notice the punctuation of the quoted conversation in this excerpt from Bruce Halling's narrative (p. 294).

"Did you hear what happened to Ricky Liverpool?" one friend asked.
"Yeah," sighed the other friend as the door started closing.
"What happened?" I asked, feigning moderate interest.

If you are quoting poetry, integrate into your own text quoted single lines of poetry. Two or three lines of poetry may be brought into your text and enclosed in quotation marks, or they may be set off from your text, without quotation marks but indented ten spaces from the left margin:

The narrator in Lorna Crozier's poem "Paper Boy" recalls her childhood devotion to her older brother:

    How I loved to be with him
    even in the cold, even when
    he didn't want me there.

The narrator in Lorna Crozier's poem "Paper Boy" recalls her childhood devotion to her older brother. She says, "How I loved to be with him / even in the cold, even when / he didn't want me there."

The slash (/) is used to indicate the end of a line when poetry is incorporated into a text. (The use of the slash is described further on p. 460.) Set off poetry quotations of more than three lines and prose quotations of more than four lines.

Titles of short stories, songs, essays, poems, articles, parts of books, and episodes on television are enclosed in quotation marks:

"Ajax Là-Bas"
[short story]

"Four Strong Winds"
[song]

"Don't Let Stereotypes Warp Your Judgments"
[essay]

"I Lost My Talk"
[poem]

"Love and Fear in the Age of AIDS"
[article]

"Writing the Research Paper"
[chapter of book]

"Bad Is Good" on *Traders*
[television episode]

In special instances, quotation marks can be used to enclose words that are defined or used in a special way:

In Moira Farr's opinion, family values are not "valuable" at all, since the media-generated ideals seldom correspond to our experience of family life.

Do not use quotation marks around a word that you feel self-conscious about using. Instead, change the word or sentence:

The morning meeting is held to give the staff the "rundown" on the advertising goals for the day.
The morning meeting is held to explain that day's advertising goals to the staff.

THE ELLIPSIS

The ellipsis, a set of three spaced periods (. . .), informs the reader that something has been left out of a quotation. For example, a writer quoting material from Roy MacGregor's "Fathers, Sons and Hockey" might decide to leave out some material unnecessary to the text he or she is writing. Here MacGregor writes about the issue of class as it relates to the development of young hockey players:

> The great players of the past--Maurice Richard, Gordie Howe, Bobby Orr, Guy Lafleur, even Wayne Gretzky--all came out of the working class where a happy combination of idle time and few other distractions produced the best and most creative players for generations. (27)

Here the passage is revised using an ellipsis:

> The great players of the past . . . all came out of the working class where a happy combination of idle time and few other distractions produced the best and most creative players for generations. (27)

The decision to remove material and use the ellipsis must be governed by the writer's intent. But the ellipsis may not be used to remove anything that would change the meaning of the section that the writer is quoting. The names of particular players may not be relevant to the writer of the revised text, so the ellipsis is used as a convenient tool to shorten the quoted material and keep the emphasis where the writer wants it. The missing words in this case do not change the meaning of the original.

If you remove material from the quoted material at the end of the sentence, use a period before the three periods of the ellipsis. Here is an example of quoted material from Willa Marcus's essay "Need, Want, Deserve":

> Consider Gateshead. It's the biggest suburban shopping mall in Europe, and it comes complete with kiddy rides à la West Edmonton Mall. . . . In fact, you're in Newcastle-on-Tyne. (186)

If a parenthetical reference follows an ellipsis at the end of a sentence, use three spaced periods and then place the period to conclude the sentence after the final parenthesis:

> As Marcus points out, huge new shopping malls in Britain flourish "at the expense of High Street shops in smaller towns. . ." (187).

To avoid using the ellipsis too often, integrate carefully selected parts of quoted material into your text:

> Marcus wryly comments that when she and husband decided to buy their first car, they "deftly turned want into need" and told themselves they had already done their share for the environment by "doing without for eight years" (185).

By paraphrasing part of the quotation and integrating the author's text with your own, you can avoid both using lengthy quotations and overusing the ellipsis.

PARENTHESES

Use parentheses to separate a digression or aside from the main material:

> Their new car (which they usually parked in the driveway) was parked on the street.
>
> Because an increasing number of women (and men) are suffering from eating disorders, we must address the problem at our next Women's Issues conference.

Rules govern the use of punctuation within and outside parentheses. If a sentence requires a comma in addition to parentheses, use the comma after the second or closing parenthesis:

> During the Korean War (1950-53), the Canadian forces fought bravely at Kap'Yong.

If the information within the parentheses is a complete sentence, the final punctuation is enclosed within the parentheses:

> More information on gardens that require little water appears throughout the book. (See especially the chapters on cacti and native plants.)

Parentheses also are used in documentation to enclose the source of paraphrased or quoted information. In these cases, the terminal punctuation appears outside the parentheses:

> As Virginia Woolf says in *Orlando*, "Clothes have . . . more important offices than merely to keep us warm. They change our view of the world and the world's view of us" (187).

(For a more complete discussion of how parentheses are used in MLA documentation, see pp. 386–91, and for their use in APA documentation, see pp. 405–407.)

BRACKETS

Use brackets to enclose words or phrases that you have added to a quotation, to show any changes that you have made in quoted material, or to record your own comments about quoted material.

> Today, more attention is being paid "to the relationship between eating disorders [anorexia and bulimia] and the compulsive eating of many women."

In the preceding example, the writer has clarified a point for readers by defining within the quotation types of eating disorders. The brackets indicate that the words are not part of the original quotation.

> The Duke of Ferrara, in Robert Browning's poem "My Last Duchess," is disturbed that the Duchess "ranked [his] gift of a nine-hundred-years-old name / With anybody's gift."

In this example, the writer changed the original "my gift of a nine-hundred-years-old name" to fit into the text. To show the change from "my" to "his", the writer placed brackets around the change. The diagonal line (or slash) between "name" and "With" indicates the end of the line in the poem.

> The "Poison Pen Letters" greeting card says, "Everything has it's [sic] price . . . but I didn't know you came so cheap!"

This use of the brackets is to enclose *sic*, a Latin word meaning "in this manner." The "[sic]" used after "it's" in the above example indicates that the error of not using *its* is in the original, not an error introduced by the person quoting the original.

THE SLASH

The slash may be used sparingly to show options, like *pass/fail* or *Dean/Department Head*. Notice that there is no space between the word and the slash when the slash is used to show options.

The slash is also used to define the end of a line of poetry if the line is incorporated into a text. For example, notice how the writer incorporates some words from Rita Joe's poem "I Lost My Talk" into a poetry explication:

> The speaker in the poem ends with a gentle request: "Let me find my talk / So I can teach you about me."

The slash indicates where the line ends in the original work (which appears on p. 106). Notice that a space appears on either side of the slash when it is used to indicate the end of a line of poetry.

In bulletins, reports, and some business correspondence, the slash is used in the form *he/she* as in this sentence:

> The person who lost a ring in the library may claim it after he/she describes it to campus security.

In essays, you should avoid the form *he/she* by writing *he or she*, as in this sentence:

> The student who aspires to a career in health care may attain it if he or she is willing to work hard.

Both *he/she* and *he or she* can be avoided by rewriting the sentence:

> The person who lost a ring in the library may claim it by describing it to campus security.

> The student who aspires to a career in health care may attain it by working hard.

THE HYPHEN

The hyphen is used to divide a word or to form a compound word. To divide a word that will not fit on the typed or written line, separate the part of the word that will fit on the line with a hyphen at a syllable break, then conclude the word on the next line. The break must occur only between syllables and should not leave fewer than two letters at the end of the line or fewer than three letters at the beginning of the next line. The hyphen appears at the end of the first line, not at the beginning of the next line.

Notice how each error is corrected:

p

> Of all of the applicants for the job, she was the best teach-er for the class.

> Of all of the applicants for the job, she was the best teacher for the class.

A word can be broken between syllables if the break will leave at least two letters at the end of the line and three or more letters at the beginning of the next line. Because the syllables of *teach-er* will not fit that rule, the entire word must be moved to the next line.

p

> After his paper was completed, the frustrated student fo-
> und another critical article.
>
> After his paper was completed, the frustrated student
> found another critical article.

[A one-syllable word cannot be broken, so *found* must be moved to the next line.]

p

> Over the past twenty years, the average size of the fam-
> -ily has decreased in developed countries.
>
> Over the past twenty years, the average size of the fam-
> ily has decreased in developed countries.

[The hyphen is used only at the end of the first line.]

Divide compound words only where the hyphen already exists:

p

> He gave the family heirloom to his sis-
> ter-in-law.
>
> He gave the family heirloom to his sister-
> in-law.

p

> Histories of popular music describe the heart-throb-
> bing gestures of Elvis Presley.
>
> Histories of popular music describe the heart-
> throbbing gestures of Elvis Presley.

Hyphens are also used to form compound words that modify a noun:

> The grade-conscious students know how important time man-
> agement is.
> The award-winning play toured the country.

If the modifiers follow the noun, the hyphens are usually left out.

> The students are grade conscious.
> The play was award winning and toured the country.

Hyphens are used in spelled-out fractions and compound whole numbers from *twenty-one* to *ninety-nine*:

> Over one-half of the voters will stay home election day.
> Everyone hates that old school-bus song, "Ninety-Nine
> Bottles of Beer on the Wall."

Hyphens are used to attach some prefixes. Usually, prefixes are attached to a word without a hyphen: *preconceived, disinterested, unhappy*. But prefixes such as *ex-*, *self-*, and *all-*, prefixes that precede a capitalized word, and prefixes that are a capital letter usually require a hyphen—for example, *self-supporting*, *ex-champion*, *anti-European*, and *U-boat*. Sometimes, to prevent confusion, a hyphen is necessary to separate a prefix ending in a vowel and a main word that starts with a vowel—for example, *de-escalate*, *re-invent*, and *pre-advise*.

CHAPTER 14

Avoiding Faulty Word Choice

aying attention to the way other authors use words will help you improve your own vocabulary and therefore give you a wider range of options when you are trying to find the right words for your own writing.

If you like to use a thesaurus, do so with care. Some students are overly dependent on the thesaurus, thinking that the words in any grouping are interchangeable. This is not the case. Most words given as alternates under a head word may have a similar **denotative**, or general, meaning. However, their **connotative** meaning, the associations accompanying that word, will be quite different. For example, the words *house* and *home* have similar denotative meanings: a place where people live. On the other hand, their connotative meanings are quite different. A *house* is a type of building, whereas the word *home* evokes for most people additional meanings of safety, comfort, familiarity, and warmth.

wd ch   Poor word choice will weaken writing, and instructors will note these errors in the margins of papers. Specific examples of faulty word choice are cited in the alphabetically arranged list of commonly confused words (pp. 469–79). Other types of word choice problems are defined and exemplified in the rest of this chapter.

CLICHÉS

Clichés, or overused words or expressions, should be avoided because predictable language is stale. Expressions that were once novel and even colourful have lost their descriptive quality through overuse. Like a faded carpet, clichés no longer add colour to the space they occupy. If you can complete the following expression automatically, you know that you have an example of a cliché:

The bread was hard as a _____.

We searched all day, but it was like looking for a needle _____.

Good writing is clear, fresh, and vivid:

> The bread was as hard as aged camel dung and about as tasty.
> We searched all day, but it was like looking for a button in my mother's tool drawer.

SLANG, JARGON, AND COLLOQUIAL WORDS

In informal writing and conversation, we tend to use **colloquial** language (such as *mom* and *dad* instead of *mother* and *father*.) Some of our most vivid language is considered **slang** (highly informal, often coined words used in speaking) or **jargon** (the special vocabulary of people who have the same job, interest, or way of life). In fact, in conversation, if pretentious language were substituted for some of the commonly used colloquial words—*intoxicated* for *drunk* or *children* for *kids*—our conversations would sound stuffy or silly. Slang is often vigorous and colourful, but it is nonstandard and therefore unacceptable in most formal writing. The jargon that is acceptable in conversation or memos at work may be unintelligible to general readers. If you think your "cool," "laid-back," or "awesome" word choice is going to influence negatively your readers' feelings about your integrity as a writer, elevate your language and remove the inappropriate word.

ARCHAIC WORDS, EUPHEMISMS, AND PRETENTIOUS WORDS

Some **archaic words** that appear in literature, especially poetry, may not be appropriate for expository writing:

d ch
> Christine was **amongst** the Canadians who travelled to Quebec before the last referendum.
>
> Christine was **among** the Canadians who travelled to Quebec before the last referendum.

The word *amongst*, used in poetry, sounds inflated in expository texts.

Writers sometimes use **euphemisms**—substitutes for words perceived as offensive. One problem with euphemisms is they are often imprecise, as in this sentence: "We lost our grandmother last week." The reader might wonder if she is still wandering in the parking lot of the local mall. Use direct and precise language to communicate accurately.

Pretentious language is used by writers who believe it will make their work appear more refined or elegant. Avoid words like *facilitate* or *utilize* when *help* and *use* are adequate. Some pretentious words have persisted and reached cliché status: *viable* and *parameters*, for example.

REDUNDANCIES

The legal profession has contributed some double-talk like *aid and abet* to our language, and some other **redundancies** have persisted even though they are bulky or inane: *each and every*, *revert back*, *pre-plan*, *end result*, *temporary respite*, or *true fact*. You can see that *each* and *every* mean the same thing, so the words should not be used together. *To revert* means "to go back." And what is a fact if it isn't true? If you regard these redundancies as you would clichés—language that is predictable and imprecise—you will eliminate them from your writing.

SEXIST LANGUAGE

Language that demeans women or men is **sexist**. Most writers would know not to use *chick* or *broad* or *stud* or *hunk* in formal essays. More subtle but equally insidious sexist language also needs to be avoided:

d ch   The professor uses **his** wisdom to remain objective.
d ch   Each nurse is required to store **her** lunch in a locker.
d ch   A clever lawyer parks **his** car in the free lot.
d ch   The competent PTA president uses **her** gavel rarely.

Even a superficial look at job and lifestyle choices in the last decades would confirm the necessity of unbiased language in print. Nurses and lawyers are both female and male; nowhere is it prescribed that only women will be PTA presidents. Consider the choices illustrated below for freeing your papers of sexist language:

A professor uses wisdom to remain objective.
Professors use their wisdom to remain objective.

Nurses are required to store their lunches in lockers.
Each nurse is required to store his or her lunch in a locker.

Clever lawyers park their cars in the free lot.
A clever lawyer parks her or his car in the free lot.

Vary using *his or her* pattern with *her or his*, but avoid this very awkward construction as often as possible by using the article instead of a possessive pronoun, or by using a plural noun as the subject:

The competent PTA president uses the gavel rarely.
Competent PTA presidents use their gavels rarely.

Do not assume any job is gender specific. *Fireman* should be *firefighter*, *clergyman* should be *minister* or *member of the clergy*, and *mailman* should be *letter carrier* or *mail carrier*. Do not add *lady* to job titles; "She is a lady doctor" is as inane as "He is a male artist."

You can further free your writing from sexism by eliminating the generic use of *man* in examples like the following:

Mankind is more aware of stereotypes than it was a decade ago.

Humanity is more aware of stereotypes than it was a decade ago.

People are more aware of stereotypes than they were a decade ago.

Revising Word Choice

1. The following paragraph, drafted for an essay for a film course, has several word choice problems. The writer was trying to use words that would make her appear knowledgeable about the subject, but not overly formal. Consider the effect faulty word choice has on you as a reader and on your impression of the writer. Then revise the paragraph to remove redundancies, clichés, colloquialisms, and slang.

In today's society, when people rent a video, they wanna have a good time and enjoy themselves. Every year, tons of lousy movies are made and they flop in theatres, only to be shoved down people's throats in the video store. Some titles, however, are misleading as to their crapulence. The most common problem is a story that's about as exciting as watching paint dry. Those are the movies that put you to sleep. In other films, the characters are weak and poorly developed; in a scene where viewers are supposed to feel sorry for a character, they laugh so hard they choke on their popcorn or it shoots out their nose and back into the bowl. To be honest, there are fans for every type of movie, even the bad ones. As for those of you who like to rent a good, outstanding movie, don't hold your breath. They are few and far between.

2. The following paragraph was drafted by a student who depended on a thesaurus, rather than a dictionary, to find the right word. Does faulty word choice interfere with your understanding of the passage? In what ways? What impression do you think the writer is trying to give? Is he or she successful? Revise the paragraph to remove jargon, if you can, as well as euphemistic, sexist, archaic, and pretentious language.

A student such as myself can learn multitudinous disquisitions from a final-semester co-op placement. Whilst a co-op student in a sizable corporation, he can investigate product development practices and manufacturing procedures. As well, he can learn revenue-enhancing techniques from the company's top salesman. He can even spend time in the manpower office, learning how to implement restructuring methods and how to relieve employees of their duties. Fully cognizant of the organization's entrepreneurial orientation and corporate paradigm, the student can confidently take his place on the corporate ladder if he is fortunate enough to be hired by the aforementioned company after graduation.

CHAPTER 15
Avoiding Commonly Confused Words

There are a number of words that are often confused or misused by many writers, not just college students. Each of your authors learned something from the others about word choice as we compiled this list. Your audience and your intention will govern your word choice, but if you have an error noted in the margin of one of your papers, look here for an explanation in order to revise the language you used.

An examination of many different college handbooks shows us that instructors use a remarkable number and variety of possible marginal symbols to alert students to errors or confusion in word choice. Any of the following symbols may appear in the margin of a paper to alert the student to an incorrect word:

cliché	an overused or trite expression
dialect	not standard English usage, or a regional, occupational, or ethnic word not appropriate in the context used
d or dic	diction, an inappropriate level of language use, inappropriate word or slang
id	idiomatic, not standard Canadian usage; the problem often appears in preposition use
jarg	jargon, or an occupational word inappropriate for formal writing
nonst.	nonstandard; may indicate idiomatic use, jargon, or slang
sl or slang	the level of the word choice is inappropriate
trite	overused expression, such as a cliché
wd ch	word choice; a general term that may indicate any of the more definitively marked errors on this list
w/w	wrong word; a general term that may indicate a word confused with another word, slang, jargon, improper word, or idiom
X	obvious error; may refer to any of the above

It is important for you to ask your instructor for clarification of a marginal symbol if one is used that you do not understand. If one of your words is marked as a poor choice or an error, you may find the explanation here, and then you can easily revise your work.

COMMONLY CONFUSED WORDS

a, an Use *a* before words beginning with consonant sounds, including those spelled with an initial pronounced *h* (*a horse*) and those spelled with vowels that are sounded as consonants (*a one-hour final*, *a university*). Use *an* before words beginning with vowel sounds, including those spelled with an initial *h* (*an igloo*, *an hour*).

accept, except *Accept* is a verb meaning "to receive." *Except* is a preposition meaning "excluding" or "but."

> I *accept* your plan to tour Vancouver *except* for the concert in Stanley Park.

advice, advise *Advice* is the noun meaning "opinion of what to do." *Advise* is the verb meaning "to give opinion or counsel."

> I *advise* you to follow your counsellor's *advice*.

affect, effect *Affect* is usually a verb meaning "to influence." *Effect* is a noun meaning "result." In psychology, *affect* is used as a noun meaning "a feeling or emotion." *Effect* can be used as a verb meaning "to implement, or to bring about."

> The eyedrops do not *affect* his driving.
> Candles create a romantic *effect* in the dining room.
> An examination of *affect* is critical in understanding personality.
> Parliament must *effect* a change in the tax laws.

all ready, already *All ready* means "completely prepared." *Already* means "by now" or "before now."

> We were all *ready* for the trip, but the bus had *already* left.

a lot *A lot* is always two words, never *alot*.

all right *All right* is spelled as two words. (*Alright* appears in some dictionaries, but most readers still consider it a misspelling.)

all together, altogether *All together* means "in a common location," "in unison," or "as a group." *Altogether* means "completely" or "entirely."

> We are *altogether* certain that caging the rabbits *all together* is a mistake.

allusion, illusion   An *allusion* is "an indirect reference"; an *illusion* is "a deceptive appearance" or "a fantasy that may be confused with reality."

> Jennifer's use of biblical *allusions* gave the *illusion* that she was religious.

among, between   Use *between* when referring to two; use *among* for three or more.

> *Between* you and me, he is *among* the most creative students in the class.

amount, number   *Amount* refers to a quantity of something that cannot be counted. *Number* refers to items that can be counted.

> The *amount* of flour used depends on the *number* of cookies you want to bake.

anxious   *Anxious* means "apprehensive" or "worried." Often it is confused with the word *eager*, which means "anticipating" or "looking forward to."

> Yumiko was *anxious* about her tax refund because she was *eager* to buy a CD player.

a while, awhile   *A while* is an article plus a noun; *awhile* is an adverb.

> We spoke for *a while* and then parted.
> Wait *awhile* before you swim.

being as, being that   These terms should not be used for *because* or *since*.

> *Because* the lot is full, I parked on the street.

beside, besides   *Beside* is a preposition meaning "next to." *Besides* is a preposition meaning "except," as well as an adverb meaning "in addition to."

> The secretary sat *beside* his dean.
> Everyone *besides* the team rides the school bus to each game.
> Your expertise is needed; *besides*, you know how to have fun!

can, may   *Can* means "is able to." *May* indicates permission.

> You *can* talk on the telephone for three hours, but you *may* not in my house!

censor, censure *Censor* as a verb means "to suppress or remove objectionable material." *Censor* as a noun is "the person who suppresses the objectionable material." *Censure* means "to criticize severely."

> The librarian refused to work with citizens who *censor* the classics.
> A *censor* of the 1970s *censored* *The Diviners*!
> The city council needs to *censure* neon signs in Old Montreal.

cite, site, sight *Cite* means "to quote by way of example, authority, or proof." *Site* is "the location of." *Sight* is a "spectacle or view."

> The tourist *sights* were on the *site* of an ancient village as *cited* in the travel guide.

complement, compliment *Complement* means "to complete" or "something that completes or supplements another." *Compliment* is a noun or verb that means "to praise."

> His sensitivity *complements* her assertiveness.
> Most people see through false *compliments*.

conscience, conscious *Conscience* refers to one's sense of right and wrong. *Conscious* is an adjective that means "alert to or aware of."

> The jury member was *conscious* of his nagging *conscience*.

could of, should of, would of These are nonstandard forms for *could have*, *should have*, and *would have*. *Of* is a preposition, not a part of a verb.

> The trainer *should have* exercised his horse today.

double negative Double negatives to emphasize negativity are nonstandard in English.

> I didn't see anything [not *nothing*].
> The child could hardly [not *couldn't hardly*] control his tears.

due to *Due to* is acceptable following a linking verb but is considered less acceptable at the beginning of a sentence.

> Most minor injuries during earthquakes are *due to* panic.
> Because of [not *due to*] rain, the beach party was cancelled.

due to the fact that Use *because* to avoid wordiness.

each *Each* is singular (see p. 435).

effect See **affect, effect**.

e.g. This is a Latin abbreviation meaning "for example." It is sometimes confused with *i.e.*, which means "that is." Neither of these abbreviations should be used in the text of a manuscript, but they can be used in parenthetical expressions.

either *Either* is singular (see p. 435).

elicit, illicit *Elicit* is a verb meaning "to evoke." *Illicit* is an adjective meaning "illegal or unlawful."

> The lawyer was unable to *elicit* any information from her client about *illicit* drug sales in the neighbourhood.

emigrate from, immigrate to *Emigrate* means "to leave a country or region to settle elsewhere." *Immigrate* means "to enter another country and live there."

> When Pano *emigrated* from Turkey, he missed living near the sea.
> After the Second World War, many Italians *immigrated* to Canada.

eminent, imminent *Eminent* means "celebrated" or "exalted." *Imminent* means "about to happen."

> The *eminent* seismologist predicted that an earthquake was *imminent*.

especially, specially *Especially* means "particularly" or "more than other things." *Specially* means "for a specific reason."

> Marcel *especially* values working on cabinets. He's known for *specially* ordered fine pieces made from exotic woods.

etc. Avoid ending a list with the abbreviation *etc.* Writers often overuse it to suggest they have more information than they do. The Latin expression is *et cetera*, which means "and others" or "and other things." The expression is best avoided because it is vague. It is also often misspelled as "ect."

every day, everyday *Every day* means "each day." *Everyday* is an adjective meaning "daily or ordinary."

> *Every day* when she gets home from work, Samantha does her *everyday* chores.

everybody, everyone *Everybody* and *everyone* are singular (see p. 435).

except See **accept, except**.

---

farther, further *Farther* refers to distance. *Further* implies quantity or degree. *Further* is now widely accepted for both meanings.

> We drifted *farther* out to sea.
> He is *further* along in his research than his instructor expected.

fewer, less *Fewer* refers to items that can be counted. *Less* refers to measurable amounts.

> Nathan does *fewer* chores and therefore earns *less* money than his brother.

firstly *Firstly* is pretentious. Use *first*.

fun *Fun* is colloquial when used as an adjective and should be avoided.

> It was an amusing [not *fun*] movie.

further See **farther, further**.

good, well *Good* is an adjective; *well* is usually an adverb.

> *Good* work is almost always *well* rewarded.

hanged, hung *Hanged* refers to people. *Hung* refers to pictures and things that can be suspended.

> The criminal was *hanged* from the tree.
> The Parkers *hung* Debbie's recent paintings in the living room.

he, he or she (he/she), his or her (his/her) The writer should no longer assume that *he* is an acceptable pronoun for all nouns. Further, *he or she* and *he/she* are awkward. To avoid these constructions, use the plural or a specific noun instead of the pronoun. (See also pp. 432–33 and 465–66.)

> When a student works in a small group, *he or she* participates more.
> When students work in small groups, *they* participate more.

hisself *Hisself* is nonstandard. Use *himself*.

hung See **hanged, hung**.

i.e. This Latin abbreviation should be replaced by the English *that is*.

illusion See **allusion, illusion**.

imminent See **eminent, imminent**.

imply, infer *Imply* means "to state indirectly or to suggest." *Infer* means "to come to a conclusion based on the evidence given."

By covering his ears, he *implied* that he no longer wanted to listen.
We can *infer* that the Duke of Ferrara is an arrogant man because he refused to "stoop" to speak to his wife.

irregardless   *Irregardless* is nonstandard. Use *regardless*.

its, it's   *Its* is the possessive form. *It's* is the contraction for *it is* or *it has* (see p. 447).

It's too bad that Kyle and Andrea's cat has injured *its* tail.
It's been a bad day for their cat.

later, latter   *Later* refers to time. *Latter* refers to the second of two things named.

Initially many refugees were admitted to this country, but *later* the immigration policy restricted the numbers.
Both Rita MacNeil and Ashley MacIsaac come from Nova Scotia, but the *latter* tends to attract younger audiences.

lay, lie   *Lay* means "to place or put" and requires an object. (The past tense is *laid.*) *Lie* means "to rest or recline." (The past tense of *lie* is *lay,* and so the two words are sometimes confused.)

Evan *lay* the piano music on the bench before he left.
The dog will *lie* down exactly where he *lay* yesterday.

less   See **fewer, less**.

lie   See **lay, lie**.

loose, lose   *Loose* is an adjective meaning "unrestrained or unfastened." *Lose* is a verb meaning "to misplace" or "to be defeated."

If his bathing suit is too *loose,* Teij will *lose* it in the next wave.

lots, lots of   These words are too colloquial for formal writing. Use *many* or *much* instead.

mankind   Avoid this term, as its sexism offends many readers. Use *humans* or *humanity* or *humankind* instead.

It was one small step for the man who walked on the moon, but it was a giant step for *humanity*.

may of, might of   These are nonstandard forms of *may have* and *might have*.

maybe, may be *Maybe* is an adverb that means "perhaps." *May be* is a verb.

> *Maybe* the community will improve its social services, but that *may be* the only benefit of the turmoil.

media, medium *Media* is the plural of *medium*.

> Pablo Picasso created clay forms and sculptures in wood and wire, but paint is the *medium* for which he is best known. Perhaps the *media* should review his other art forms.

myself *Myself* is a reflexive or intensive pronoun and, like the other *-self* pronouns, should not be used in place of personal pronouns.

> I drove *myself* to the hospital because no one else was home.
> "I can do it *myself*!" the toddler protested.
> Juan ladled the chili for his father and me [not *myself*].

neither *Neither* is singular (see p. 435).

> *Neither* of us is available to babysit tonight.

nohow *Nohow* is nonstandard for *in any way*.

none *None* is singular.

> *None* of the alternatives seems reasonable.

nowheres *Nowheres* is nonstandard for *nowhere*.

number See **amount, number**.

of *Of* should not be used in constructions like *should of* or *would of* (*should have* or *would have*). *Of* is a preposition.

off of *Of* is not necessary with *off*. Use *off* alone or use *from*.

> The marbles rolled *off* the table and continued rolling around Devin's room.

O.K., OK, okay All three forms are acceptable, but in formal writing these expressions are inappropriate.

on account of A wordy way to write *because*.

owing to the fact that A wordy way to write *because*.

plus *Plus* is not appropriately used as a conjunction to join independent clauses. Use a standard coordinating or adverbial conjunction.

We celebrated Canada Day with hot dogs, corn on the cob, potato salad, and watermelon; in addition [not *plus*], we enjoyed the firework display at Lake Columbia.

precede, proceed The verb *precede* means "come before" (note the prefix *pre-*). The verb *proceed* means "go forward" or "move on."

Spanish 4 *precedes* Spanish 5, "Literature of Mexico."
To *proceed* without a contract would be foolish.

prejudice, prejudiced *Prejudice* is a noun; *prejudiced* is an adjective. Do not leave out the *-d* from the adjective.

Prejudice that starts in childhood is difficult to obliterate, and he was distinctly *prejudiced* against working mothers.

principal, principle *Principal* is a noun for the "chief official" or, in finance, the "capital sum." As an adjective, *principal* means "major" or "most important." *Principle* is a noun meaning "a law or truth, rule, or axiom."

The school's *principal* uses two *principles* for deciding the graduation speakers: which students have the best grades, and which students have the best *principles* to share with classmates.

proceed See **precede, proceed**.

raise, rise *Raise* is a verb meaning "to move or cause to move up," and it takes an object. *Rise* is a verb meaning "to go up," and it does not take a direct object.

The farmers who *raise* cows are concerned about the disease.
They *rise* early to attend to the livestock.

reason is because In speech, this expression is common. In formal writing, it is not appropriate. A clause using *that* is the preferred form.

The *reason* he paid his rent early was *that* [not *because*] he intended to be out of town on the first of the month.

reason why The expression *reason why* is redundant. *Reason* is sufficient.

The *reason* [not *reason why*] Jorge attends law school at night is not obvious to anyone but his family.

rise See **raise, rise**.

should of See **could of, should of, would of**.

sight See **cite, site, sight**.

since *Since* is sometimes used to mean *because*, but it is only clear as a conjunction in constructions having to do with time.

> Andy has been waiting *since* January for his tax forms.
> *Since* [or *because*?] you left, I've been dating others.

sit, set *Sit* means "to rest the weight of the body" as on a chair. *Set* means "to place."

> Helen wants you to *sit* on the black leather sofa.
> Rohit would rather you not *set* stoneware dishes on his cherry-wood table.

site See **cite, site, sight**.

somebody, someone *Somebody* and *someone* are singular (see p. 432).

sometime, some time, sometimes *Sometime* means "at an indefinite time." *Some time* is the adjective *some* modifying the noun *time*. *Sometimes* means "now and then."

> *Sometime* we should get together and play tennis.
> Byung Hee devoted *some time* to perfecting his pronunciation.
> *Sometimes* Ken discards every yolk from the eggs as he prepares his omelette.

supposed to, used to Don't neglect to use the *-d* ending on these often used and often misspelled words.

> He is *supposed to* [not *suppose to*] bring the wine for the dinner.
> Ariane became *used to* [not *use to*] Dee's indifferent housekeeping.

than, then *Than* is used in comparisons. *Then* is an adverb denoting time.

> There are many more calories in avocados *than* in apples.
> First Judy attended the school, and *then* she taught there.

their, there, they're *Their* is a possessive pronoun. *There* is an adverb denoting place. *They're* is a contraction of *they are*.

> *Their* plans for hang-gliding *there* in the park are apt to be postponed because *they're* not ready to pass the safety test.

then See **than, then**.

this here, these here, that there, them there Nonstandard for *this, these, that,* or *those*.

till, until, 'til *Till* and *until* have the same meaning and both are used. *'Til* is an unnecessary contraction of *until*.

thru *Thru* is a nonstandard spelling of *through* that should be avoided in all formal writing.

thusly Use *thus*, which is less pretentious.

to, too, two *To* is a preposition meaning "toward" and is part of the infinitive form of the verb (for example, *to run*). *Too* is an adverb meaning "overly." *Two* is a number.

> *Two* trips *to* the market in one day are not *too* many for a fine cook like Sasha.

toward, towards Either form is acceptable, but *toward* is preferred.

try and *Try and* is nonstandard; *try to* is preferred.

> *Try to* [not *try and*] meet Jordie before he locks up his bike.

unique *Unique* means "distinctively characteristic." It is an absolute adjective that shouldn't be modified by "most" or "very."

> A tuxedo shirt and jacket, bow tie, and Bermuda shorts create a *unique* [not *very unique*] style for a hot-weather prom.

until See **till, until, 'til**.

usage The noun *use* should be used whenever possible. *Usage* refers only to convention, as in *language usage*.

> The *use* [not *usage*] of computers has helped essay writing, but papers with proper *usage* have not increased because of expensive equipment.

used to See **supposed to, used to**.

well See **good, well**.

which, who *Which* is used for a thing or things, not for people. Use *who* for people.

> Rick Hansen, the Canadian wheelchair athlete *who* popularized the term *physically challenged*, also challenged us to rethink our perceptions of the disabled. His "Man in Motion" tour, *which* lasted 792 days, raised $20 million toward wheelchair sports and spinal cord research.

which, in which In most cases, ending a sentence with a preposition is natural and therefore considered to be grammatically correct for less formal writing.

> Salma found some boxes which she packed her books *in*.

However, some writers have been taught to avoid ending a sentence with a preposition. Instead, they use *in which*, a construction which is grammatically correct, although more formal.

> Salma found some boxes *in which* she packed her books.

Errors occur when students mistakenly include the preposition twice.

> Salma found some boxes *in which* she packed her books *in*.

while Do not use *while* to mean *although* if there is a chance of confusion for the reader. Like *since*, *while* should be reserved for time sense. Unless the point is to show that the actions occur at the same time, *although* is the better word.

> Nero fiddled *while* Rome burned.
> *Although* [not *while*] Irene continues to invest her small savings, Howard never resists a shoe sale.

who's, whose *Who's* is the contraction for *who is* or *who has*. *Whose* is a possessive pronoun.

> *Who's* going to return the library books?
> *Who's* been reading *Headhunter*?
> That depends on *whose* book is due.

would of See **could of, should of, would of**.

you The indefinite use of *you*, or even its use to mean "you the reader," can be incongruous or offensive and can be avoided.

> A generation ago, the fit hiker [rather than *you*] could find the ancient trail, but over the years erosion has destroyed that part of the cliff.
> It is common practice in some African tribes for prepubescent females [rather than *you*] to be scarified.

your, you're *Your* is a possessive pronoun. *You're* is the contraction of *you are*.

> *Your* savings will disappear if *you're* not careful.

CHAPTER 16
Exercises: Editing to Correct Errors

The prewriting, organizing, drafting, and revising stages of essay writing always take up most of the time you have allotted for the writing process. However, an essay is not truly finished until you have proofread and edited the draft for errors in sentence structure, grammar, spelling, and punctuation.

Here we offer some exercises to familiarize you with common grammatical errors and ways of correcting them. The exercises are arranged so that you can progress from practising on single sentences to finding and correcting errors in longer passages.

Our goal in this chapter is to show you how to apply proofreading and editing skills to your own essays. Errors that your instructor points out in your writing are opportunities for you to learn about the details of the English language and to discover how to correct your own work. We encourage you to develop your editing skills further and to master your own most common errors by trying some of the following exercises.

FRAGMENTS

1. Find and underline the sentence fragment errors in the following sentences and explain why the fragment is not a complete sentence. Then revise the sentence fragment errors to form complete and grammatically correct sentences. Do not revise sentences that are grammatically correct.

> **Example:** Denise was late for class. <u>Because her car's battery was dead.</u>
>
> **Reason:** *Because her car's battery was dead* is a dependent clause beginning with the subordinate conjunction *because*. A dependent clause must be attached to an independent clause to form a complete sentence.
>
> **Correction:** Denise was late for class because her car's battery was dead.

a. The little girl noticed that her ice cream had fallen out of the cone. And immediately began to cry.

b. Since the pay was so good, Ivan decided to take the job as a night security guard. Hoped to find the stamina to stay awake all night.

c. Tyler's neighbours are avid cross-country skiers. Every weekend during the winter they make the long trip to their cottage. Which is near some of the best cross-country trails in the province.

d. During our trip through the Alberta badlands, we were fascinated by the hoodoos. Strange columns of rock. They are formed by a combination of wind and rain erosion and can be several metres high.

e. On average, Canadians spend over five hours a day on leisure activities. Watching TV or videos for at least half that time.

f. Although the computer information systems program is demanding. Graduates have no difficulty finding satisfying jobs in their field.

g. Whenever my roommate sees a stray animal, he wants to bring it home. I remind him that pets aren't allowed in our building. If we adopt a pet, we'll have to move.

h. We arrived at the arena early. To see the players warming up before the game.

i. Most people know that it's not safe to drink and drive. Yet many of these same people consume alcohol and then operate their boats. A practice just as dangerous.

j. I value my friends for their honesty, empathy, and trustworthiness. Qualities which help me through good and bad times, and qualities I try to offer to them in return.

2. Correct the sentence fragment errors in the following sentences. Use methods that will connect the ideas properly and clarify meaning.

a. Competitive diving is a sport. That demands dedication. My friend Shelly is a good example of an athlete devoted to her sport.

b. If Shelly is invited to a party on a Friday night, but has a practice at six o'clock the next morning. She has to decide which is more important. She usually turns down the invitation.

c. Training takes up a considerable amount of time. Novice divers practise. Up to four hours a week. Competitive divers, on the other hand. As much as twenty hours a week. Or even more before a diving meet.

d. Diving is risky. Shelly says learning a difficult dive such as a triple somersault. Positioning her body so she enters the pool cleanly and without injuring herself can be a challenge.

e.	Some divers have hit their heads on the board or pool deck. While they are practising a new dive. Yet they, like Shelly, keep coming back for more. Because diving is a sport where the competition is between the diver and herself, as much as between competitors. Shelly says that when she finally masters a new dive, she feels an energy and self-confidence that are hard to describe.

3.	Correct the sentence fragment errors in this draft of a student's essay by adding the missing subject and/or verb or by joining the sentence fragment to another sentence.

Families today are smaller than in the past. My father was one of ten children in a closely knit family. Growing up in a small three-bedroom house in Toronto. You may not believe this, but all of the children in his family were born in October except for one. My Aunt Carla who was born in July. She is the black sheep in her family. Not just because of her birthday. Aunt Carla is the only one who moved away from the city. Saying she wanted to be free to do things her way. After she finished college, she packed up her small car and set out for Yellowknife, in the Northwest Territories.

No one believed she would stay away for long. Her parents thought she'd miss them too much. And since she was the only one in the whole family who always resisted work. Her brothers and sisters joked that she'd be home as soon as she ran out of gas or money. Whichever came first. However, she surprised them all, because three months after she had left she wrote to say she had a good job and was saving all her money to buy some property. Where she could build a house.

My father says they were all amazed. When an envelope addressed to the family arrived in the mail. Inside was a photo of Aunt Carla with a huge grin on her face, standing in the doorway of a house still under construction. Written on the back the words "My house. My way!" She was actually building a house and doing most of the work herself.

All this happened twenty years ago. She still lives in the house. Alone except for her dog, Midnight Sun. Aunt Carla comes to visit us every October. When we have a big family reunion to celebrate everybody's birthday, even hers. We're always sad when she leaves for home, but we all admire her for living her way.

RUN-ONS AND COMMA SPLICES
Run-Ons

1. Correct any run-on errors you find here in at least two different ways. What changes in emphasis do you notice for each version?

> **Example:** No one in my family would ever choose a career in health care we tend to faint at the sight of blood.
> **Correction 1:** No one in my family would ever choose a career in health care, because we tend to faint at the sight of blood.
> **Correction 2:** No one in my family would ever choose a career in health care. We tend to faint at the sight of blood.

Correction 1 emphasizes the reason the family members would not choose that field. Correction 2 emphasizes the family tendency to faint at the sight of blood.

a. I think we should mow the lawn this morning the weather forecast is calling for rain this afternoon.

b. Electronic mail has made communication easier people can easily keep in touch with friends and colleagues around the world.

c. My grandmother was a warm and loving woman. She never learned to speak English and I didn't speak Czech we were always able to understand each other.

d. Most students find the first week of college disorienting and stressful by the end of the semester they are right at home.

e. Rohan likes Canadian football his brother prefers the American game.

f. Exhausted but jubilant, the runners crossed the finish line one by one they had finished their first marathon.

g. Every August Lashonda and her friends take the train from Windsor to Toronto for Caribana the weekend is the highlight of their summer.

h. When you go to the library remember to take these books they are due today.

i. South Porcupine, which grew during the 1909 gold rush, was incorporated as a town in 1911 a serious fire destroyed much of the town that same year.

j. Derek and Eileen decided to spend part of their summer holiday volunteering they helped at a day camp for disabled children and found the experience so rewarding that they want to go back next year.

2. Correct the run-on errors in the following sentences. Choose a method that will connect the ideas effectively and clarify meaning.

   a. Today, students dream of finding the ideal job dreaming is not enough.
   b. In order to get the job you want, you must focus on your objectives you must find out what kind of education and experience the job requires.
   c. Develop your communication skills employers are impressed by applicants who are confident speakers and competent writers.
   d. Selling your talents to a potential employer may be easier than you think as long as you are motivated, enthusiastic, and willing to learn.
   e. Try to remember that success comes with hard work there is no guarantee if you are patient and persistent, the job of your dreams could become a reality.

3. Correct the run-on errors in this draft of a student's essay. Try to vary your correction methods.

Until a few years ago, the shopping habits of Canadians differed considerably from those of Europeans. In general, Canadians shop for groceries in large supermarkets once a week Europeans shop in smaller specialty stores, such as bakeries, on a daily basis and may even have dairy products delivered to their homes. Canadian shoppers had the convenience of one-stop shopping Europeans had the culinary advantage of buying fresh food every day, and the social advantages of both getting to know their retailers personally and meeting their neighbours in the shops.

As supermarkets become popular in Europe, many Europeans are taking up the North American habit of a weekly grocery-shopping trip. This change benefits large chain stores and their workers it also has the potential to hurt the small-business owners of delicatessens and fruit and vegetable shops some social commentators have also suggested that as patronage of small stores declines, so will the unique European sense of community. This may be true however I can't imagine the French gourmet being satisfied with a mass-produced baguette or the British food expert content with a leg of lamb on a styrofoam tray wrapped in plastic wrap. Dedicated lovers of good food from all social classes will continue to chat with their neighbours and local retailers about the quality and availability of food and about the weather and latest football scores.

Comma Splices

1. Correct any comma splice errors you find here in at least two different ways. What changes in emphasis do you notice for each version?

> **Example:** I spent the long weekend with my brothers, we played poker most of the time.
> **Correction 1:** I spent the long weekend with my brothers. We played poker most of the time.
> **Correction 2:** I spent the long weekend with my brothers, so we played poker most of the time.

In Correction 1, each sentence states a separate fact, with no direct connection between them. Correction 2 implies that time the brothers spend together is usually devoted to poker, and this occasion was no exception.

   a. Visitors to Canada want to see our most well-known sights, Niagara Falls and Banff usually top the list.
   b. Learning a second language is relatively easy for young children, adults can take up to seven years to become fluent.
   c. Vaso's car-repair shop is always busy, he has spent several years building his reputation for customer service.
   d. The lake may look frozen, it is not safe to skate on it yet.
   e. Please be sure to complete this questionnaire by next Friday, we need time to compile the results.
   f. The bus was late, Viresh was worried about being late for the test.
   g. Raking leaves together is one of our family's favourite fall activities, the children love jumping in the leaf pile once we're finished.
   h. By five o'clock in the morning Patrick still had more studying to do for that afternoon's exam, he vowed never to leave studying to the last minute ever again.
   i. In the weeks leading up to the Olympic games, athletes become increasingly concerned about injuries and sickness, they don't want ill health to keep them from competing.
   j. Canadians use different words to describe the same thing, for example, a *pond* in Ontario is a *slough* in Saskatchewan, a *slough* on the West Coast is a marshy saltwater inlet.

2. Correct the comma splice errors in the following sentences. Where possible, choose methods that will show how the ideas are connected.

   a. Food allergies are becoming more common, when extending an invitation for dinner, sensitive hosts ask their guests if there are any foods they can't eat.

b. As well, some people have dietary restrictions because of their religious practices, for example, neither Jews nor Muslims eat pork.

c. Vegetarianism is gaining popularity, it's important to ask guests if they eat other animal products such as eggs, cheese, or fish.

d. Once I was making a Caesar salad for a friend, without realizing that the anchovies in the dressing were something she couldn't eat.

e. I was about to add the anchovies when she mentioned that fish was not part of her vegetarian diet, I actually enjoyed this version of my Caesar salad recipe as much as my usual one.

3. Correct the comma splice errors in this draft of a student's essay. Try to vary your correction methods.

Models and movie stars earn enough money to hire personal trainers and install weight rooms in their homes, they need to look their best. You might want to follow their fitness lead, but not everyone can afford such luxuries. It is possible to live a healthy lifestyle on a shoestring budget, however, many college students have a state-of-the-art facility within a few steps of the residence. Taking advantage of your school's athletic facilities can help you look and feel like a million on a shoestring budget.

Exercising is a great way to stay in shape, it's also a great way to get rid of those inevitable frustrations. Many students find working out to be a great stress reliever. The athletic staff can set up a training program to help you get started, being properly taught how to use the weights and other equipment is very important. Injuries are common, but they can be avoided if you get the proper help when you are starting out. Some colleges offer badminton or squash lessons, others have organized aerobics classes. Some colleges have pools for swimming enthusiasts. All these activities offer full workouts and are lots of fun.

Living on a strict student budget can be very difficult, that doesn't mean you have to deny yourself a healthy lifestyle. In most colleges, use of the athletic facilities is included in your tuition fees. So you can't use expense as an excuse any more. Join in and have fun, I guarantee you'll feel good and look good if you just do it.

PRONOUN REFERENCE

1. Correct the unclear pronoun references in the following sentences two different ways. Explain the difference in meaning for each version.

> **Example:** Sally reminded her daughter that her grandmother's birthday was next week.
> **Correction 1:** Sally reminded her daughter that Sally's grandmother's birthday was next week.
> **Correction 2:** Sally reminded her daughter Emma that Emma's grandmother's birthday was next week.

In Correction 1, the change shows that Sally's grandmother's birthday is coming up. In Correction 2, adding the daughter's name helps clarify that it is the daughter Emma's grandmother whose birthday is coming up.

a. Paul's cousin said he had won an all-expenses-paid trip to Australia.

b. The driving instructor told Terry she was ready to take her driving test, so she called to book the date and time.

c. Whenever Morris asks to borrow Henry's tools, he feels uncomfortable.

d. Madeline wondered if her friend would tell her mother about her failing grade in chemistry.

e. Norman wanted to tell Raymond about the surprise party, but he knew he wouldn't be able to keep the secret from his girlfriend.

2. Correct the vague pronoun references in the following sentences two different ways. Explain the difference in meaning for each version.

> **Example:** They say that the abnormal weather pattern called El Niño is caused by changes in trade winds.
> **Correction 1:** Scientists say that the abnormal weather pattern called El Niño is caused by changes in trade winds.
> **Correction 2:** An article I read in the newspaper explained that the abnormal weather pattern called El Niño is caused by changes in trade winds.

Correction 1 replaces the vague pronoun "they" with a plural noun "scientists." This change emphasizes that people have done the research on El Niño. In Correction 2, the revision focuses on the source of the information, a newspaper article.

a. Stefan says he is transferring from the graphic design program to computer engineering, even though it will not be easy.

b. Dermot couldn't understand how to program the VCR until I wrote them out.

c. You must have good interpersonal communication skills to become a successful peer tutor. This helps the student you are tutoring.

d. Violent images in film and television have a negative effect on young people. It makes violence look exciting.

e. When Angelina was a teenager, her mother constantly pestered her to clean up her room, but this eventually changed.

3. Improve the pronoun references in the following sentences by clarifying indefinite pronouns where possible or correcting pronouns inconsistent with their antecedents. Try to correct each sentence two different ways. Make any other changes that are necessary to ensure the sentence is grammatically correct.

> **Example:** If anyone is late for the opening scene of tonight's performance of *Oedipus Rex*, she will not be admitted until intermission.
>
> **Correction 1:** If you are late for the opening scene of tonight's performance of *Oedipus Rex*, you will not be admitted until intermission.
>
> **Correction 2:** If ticket holders are late for the opening scene of tonight's performance of *Oedipus Rex*, they will not be admitted until intermission.

a. Every piano student who practises on a daily basis does well on her Conservatory exam.

b. Anyone who has ever tried to get rich at a casino also knows how easy it is to lose his money.

c. No one should be afraid to make a report to his employer if they have been sexually harassed on the job.

d. Everyone in this town has his opinion about the registration of firearms.

e. Each of the guests has brought her culinary specialty for the vegetarian potluck dinner.

4. Correct the pronoun reference problems in the following passage from a student's freewriting exercise. Revise or clarify the pronouns as necessary without changing the overall sense of the passage.

What does it take to become a good parent? This is the question that is on everyone's mind at one point in his life. Some assume that it involves buying their child everything he wants. I have noticed that all some children need to do is cry, beg, and pout to get what they want. They give in to the child the minute they begin to fuss. This teaches the child to whine whenever he wants something. I believe it is best to give in to a child only when he is behaving well. This teaches the child that good behaviour gets rewarded. It also helps him to grow up without being spoiled.

VERB FORM ERRORS

1. Correct the verb form errors in the following sentences. Use your dictionary to find the correct form if necessary.

   a. We done our homework and then we went to the movies.
   b. Matt should have went to the bank to deposit his paycheque.
   c. Hussein brang his children to the company picnic.
   d. Have you ever swam across this lake?
   e. After my friends had ate all the pizza, they spended the rest of the evening complaining about how full they were.

2. Correct the verb form errors in the following paragraph from a student's journal.

   In one article I read, the author says that at one time, few fathers spended time with their children. Once their first child was on the way, most men become serious about providing money for their family, and so, just as their fathers had did, they dived into their work whole-heartedly. These men seen their primary role as breadwinners. For earlier generations, that was the behaviour expected of fathers. Today, the author says, men who have maked the decision to become fathers see their role differently. They realize how important they are to their child's emotional well-being. This doesn't mean they have forgot about their financial responsibility. The author explains that men today believe that the time they spend with their children is more important to their child's upbringing than a big bank balance.

AGREEMENT

1. Correct the subject–verb agreement errors in these sentences to ensure that the subject and the verb are either both singular or both plural, as the meaning requires.

   Example: My dog Woody and my cat Polly tolerates each other.
   Correction: My dog Woody and my cat Polly tolerate each other.

a. Going to the movies have always been a passion of mine.

b. Parents of a newborn baby usually suffers from lack of sleep.

c. The film *Double Happiness* tell the story of a Chinese-Canadian woman trying to establish her identity.

d. Saul, Joan, Scott, and Melanie plans to travel to Prince Edward Island together next summer.

e. Marvin's part-time job as an attendant in a nursing home and his volunteer work at the senior citizens' community centre gives him all the experience he need to become a compassionate gerontologist.

f. Janet's pride and joy are her collection of antique quilts.

g. Macaroni and cheese tops the list of Drew's favourite casseroles.

h. Every artist, musician, and writer are encouraged to participate in the summer arts festival.

i. A valid driver's licence or two credit cards is required to cash a cheque at the hotel's front desk.

j. Neither the babysitter nor the children is listening to the lifeguard's warning.

k. Each of the contestants hope to win; neither want to lose.

l. Everything in Mr. Gerrard's cabin, including the kitchen sink, were purchased from second-hand stores.

m. Nobody like waiting at a bus stop in a snowstorm.

n. Some of the assignments has been handed in late.

o. All of my housework are done for this week.

p. Fifty dollars are too much to pay for a bottle of wine.

q. The occupational health and safety committee meet monthly in the board room.

r. The swim team prefer to practise in the early morning.

s. A majority of students favour the reduction of tuition fees.

t. The Anti-Poverty League believe that every man, woman, and child deserve the basic necessities of food, clothing, and shelter.

u. There has always been teenagers who rebels against authority.

v. Are mumps a common illness these days?

w. Meningitis are a potentially lethal infection that strike children and young people.

x. First published in 1945, *Two Solitudes* explore the theme of two cultures sharing a single nation.

y. Of all the courses Harriet has ever taken, statistics remain her least favourite.

2. Correct the subject–verb agreement errors in the following passage written by a music student. The passage is meant to be a description of something happening at the present time, so all verbs should be in the present tense.

Opening night for this season's symphony concert series have arrived. The audience applaud as the conductor step through the door at the left of the stage and approaches the podium in front of the orchestra. She turn toward the adoring crowd, and then smiles and bows. As the applause subside, she face the orchestra and pause to look at the musical score in front of her. The violinists at her left and the viola, cello, and bass players on her right is waiting to begin. Each of the musicians look expectantly at her. Then raising her baton, she signal the players to pick up their instruments. The audience is ready for an evening of beautiful music. However, a cellular phone begins to ring, and everyone in the hall turn to glare at the offending patron, who rummage through his coat pockets, looking for the phone, which continue its irritating sound. The conductor is unperturbed. With a wave of her hand, she leads the orchestra into a series of tones that are the same pitch and in the same rhythm as the cellular phone's incessant ringing. Confused, many patrons in the hall begins to give each other quizzical looks. I look at my program and read that the first piece is entitled "Tribute to Technology in the New Millennium." The description in the program explains the composer's masterpiece. It appears that the audience are present for the première of the world's first concerto for cellular phone and orchestra.

3. Correct the subject–verb agreement errors in the following paragraph.

This week, a group of students at my college are organizing an event called "Buy Nothing Day." The purpose of this event are to make people aware of lifestyle options that does not depend on excessive spending and overconsumption of consumer products. The students is part of the international voluntary simplicity movement whose goal are to promote a simpler way of life. The students spoke to our economics class last week and said that North American consumer culture advocate a "shop till you drop" mentality in people that not only contribute to pollution and the depletion of natural resources, but also make us feel unsuccessful if we cannot afford the latest fashions or gadgets. During "Buy Nothing Day," displays will be set up in the main concourse at school. These displays advocates trading, sharing, recycling, and learning to do without as the preferred lifestyle choice for the next millennium. The organizers is hoping that their efforts shows people that what we need and what we want are two different things, and that happiness can come from sharing rather than consuming.

SHIFTS
Shifts in Person and Number

1. Correct the shifts in person and number in the following sentences.

   a. If anyone puts their finger in an electrical socket, they will get a shock.

   b. Women suffering from eating disorders risk serious damage to your health.

   c. Everyone should try to use public transportation more and cars less, so we can reduce air pollution.

   d. You should be sure to take a first aid course because you never know when you might need to help someone in an emergency.

   e. A social services student learns how to communicate with their clients as well as how to spot any potential problems your client might have.

2. Correct the shifts in person and number in the following passage from a student's draft for a persuasive essay.

   The V-chip is a tiny computer chip that can be installed in your cable box or television and can be programmed to black out programs that people do not want their children to see. The technology that has brought parents the V-chip gives you an effective defence against the violence, sex, and coarse language that litter our television screens and pollute our children's minds. That is the opinion of promoters of the V-chip, who believe it will lead to a less violent society. However, we should be wary of these claims. You cannot expect a computer chip to be a miracle answer for parents who are too busy, lazy, or uninterested to spend time with their children and guide their television viewing wisely.

3. Revise the following passage from a student's writing journal in two different ways to correct the shifts in person and number. First, revise so the entire passage addresses the reader directly. Then, revise a second time so the entire passage is written using the third-person plural point of view.

For a hockey player to succeed, he must be dedicated to his sport. Dedication helps the whole team because it contributes to your team's spirit. You need to get to practice on time and never miss a game. Imagine a player who is not very dedicated. They show up for practice an hour late with no explanation. Their fellow players will grumble that you are not committed to winning. The team's morale can be affected by your poor attitude. A good player never stops trying, because if you do, it affects the whole team.

4. Underline the nouns and pronouns in the following freewriting exercise written by a student. Then correct the shifts in person and number.

Every English teacher has their own pet grammar peeve. Some hate sentence fragments, some despise sentences beginning with "but" or "and," and others go mad over apostrophe errors. One teacher I had would always complain to us that their lesson on commas had fallen on deaf ears. Then she'd patiently review the rules one more time. You can master one teacher's quirks, but then in one's next English course one will have a new teacher with their own "favourite" grammar errors. You can be sure they will be after you to check your writing for their pet grammar peeve. If there's one universal truth about English teachers, it's that they're passionate about their subject, and their pet peeves.

Shifts in Verb Tense

1. Correct the unnecessary tense shifts in the following passage, taken from a student's journal.

I was walking down King Street one day last summer when I see someone who looks like Jackie, my best friend in Grade 9. I was amazed to see her, because she had moved back to Cape Breton Island after we finish junior high school. That was five years ago. I didn't know she was back in town. I stop and I say, "Jackie, how are you?" She looks at me with a blank stare. For an awkward moment, I think that maybe I have the wrong person. Then her jaw dropped and she says, "Suzanne? I thought you left this hick town long ago. That's what Terry told me." We both hug each other and laugh that we nearly passed each other without speaking. We walked to the café on the corner and sit for an hour catching up on the news of the past five years. What a surprise it was to see her again.

2. Correct the unnecessary tense shifts in the following paragraph from a student's essay on Shakespeare's *Hamlet*.

Hamlet's grief over his father's death was complicated by his rage over his mother's quick marriage to Claudius. Hamlet loathed her for her disloyalty to his father's memory. What Hamlet knew, but what his immaturity kept him from admitting, was his mother's obvious need for a loving husband. He recalled his mother's dependence on his father and how "she would hang on him / As if increase of appetite had grown / By what it fed on" (1.2.143–45). However, Hamlet was unwilling to allow her to make her own choices or mistakes in finding someone new to care for her after her bereavement.

Shifts in Voice

1. Correct any unnecessary shifts in voice you find in the following sentences.

> **Example:** This restaurant serves Vietnamese food, although some Chinese and Thai dishes are also listed on the menu.
> **Correction:** This restaurant serves Vietnamese food, although it also lists some Chinese and Thai dishes on the menu.

a. At the community centre's summer day camp for preschoolers, the children can draw, paint, swim, and games can be played.
b. A Digital Versatile Disk player will also play CDs, so instead of buying two separate machines, only one is needed.
c. When you are learning to swing a golf club, you should keep your body balanced and at the same time your head should be kept down and your eyes should be focused on the ball.
d. Windows were broken, the police were called, and arrests were made after our next-door neighbour's annual New Year's party.
e. The prospective employee was told she should fill out the application form as soon as possible and that it should be mailed by Friday at the latest.

2. Correct any unnecessary voice shifts in the following process analysis written by a student.

For many students, a few harmless drinks the night before turn out to be a lot worse the next morning, when a hangover is experienced. If you need to cure a hangover, the first thing you should do is drink as much water or clear fluids as possible when you wake up. Even though you may have consumed a considerable amount of liquid the night before, by the next morning your body is dehydrated and needs to have its fluids replenished. However, limit yourself to nonalcoholic beverages because your hangover will be made worse by alcohol at this time. If an excruciating pain in your head, otherwise known as a headache, is noticed, you would be wise to take two extra-strength Tylenol tablets. Some people prefer to go back to bed and lie in a quiet, dark room to let the hangover subside. I recommend that you keep yourself busy while a hangover is being suffered. You will recover much faster if you are up and about than if you lie in bed all day. A recommended activity would be general housework, especially if last night's party was at your house. Do not rush, though; the housework should be done at a comfortable pace. I also advise you to get some fresh air by going for a walk in the park, although sunglasses may need to be worn if it is a sunny day. This precaution is necessary because the sun appears to be much brighter on hangover days, which could contribute to your headache. By the middle of the afternoon, you should be feeling almost like your old self again. At this time, your decision to drink to excess should be re-examined. I advise that such self-inflicted pain should be avoided.

MIXED CONSTRUCTIONS

1. Revise the following sentences so that the two parts of the sentence are consistent and logical.

> **Example:** Although removing children from abusive home environments will not solve the problem, but it is a good start in their rehabilitation.
> **Correction:** Removing children from abusive home environments will not solve the problem, but it is a good start in their rehabilitation.
> **Alternative Correction:** Although removing children from abusive home environments will not solve the problem, it is a good start in their rehabilitation.

a. Because matrimony has not been taken seriously and divorce rates are high does not mean that all marriages cannot survive.
b. Nowadays, by adding computer images to films is what makes the film more appealing to the viewer.
c. Whenever Dorota forgets her cellular phone at home is when she misses a phone call from an important client.

d.   An example would be if the plant is not receiving enough sunlight, uproot it and transplant it to a sunnier spot in the garden.

e.   The fact that having prepared the food in advance will make your dinner party run more smoothly.

2.   Correct the mixed construction errors in the following freewriting exercise written by a student.

When Friday finally comes, most people want to relax. Even if you live alone you can find ways to take good care of yourself and prepare for the rest of the weekend. Here are a few tips on how to unwind. When you get home is when you should phone your favourite restaurant and order your favourite meal. By asking the restaurant to deliver it in two hours will give you plenty of time to unwind before dinner. A soothing hot bath can be very serene and try a touch of aromatic essence in your bath, such as lavender, which is known for its calming qualities. Light a few candles and enjoy the soft light and while you are soaking in the warmth of your bath. After relaxing in the tub, change into some comfortable clothing and curl up in your most comfortable chair. If you like reading is a good time to get out a book and let the words on the page take you away from the cares of the day. When dinner arrives, pour a glass of wine for yourself to enjoy during your meal and putting soothing music on the stereo. After dinner, you may want to get some fresh air by going for a walk. It will clear your head and which can help you sleep better. Or you may want to pop a video into the VCR and escape with a good movie. But if you are totally relaxed by now is the time to slip into bed and sleep soundly and waking up refreshed and revitalized. The most important thing after a stressful week is to take time out for yourself.

MISPLACED AND DANGLING MODIFIERS

1.   Correct the misplaced modifier errors in the following sentences by moving the modifiers closer to the words they describe.

Example: Designed by Native craftspeople, Sherry loves this collection of silver and amethyst jewellery.
Correction: Sherry loves this collection of silver and amethyst jewellery designed by Native craftspeople.

a.   Advertisements for new cars can be seen on television, on billboards, and in magazines constantly tempting the consumer.

b. In most high schools, students who are late frequently are given detentions.

c. Caught by inconsistencies in his testimony, the judge convicted the defendant of the crime.

d. Grandpa loved listening to a show called *The Happy Gang* when he was a boy on the radio.

e. The manager sent the final report by courier to the clients that had been completed that day.

2. Correct the dangling modifier errors in the following sentences two different ways. First, revise by adding a word or words for the modifier to describe. Then correct the dangling modifier error by turning it into a dependent clause so the meaning is clear.

> **Example:** After taking all the facts into consideration, the final decision was easy to make.
> **Correction 1:** After taking all the facts into consideration, we found that the final decision was easy to make.
> **Correction 2:** After we took all the facts into consideration, the final decision was easy to make.

a. Waiting for a bus, a car crashed into the bus shelter.

b. When attending a concert, the price of a ticket can be higher than you want to spend.

c. Obtaining a business loan from a bank, a well-organized business plan is essential.

d. After cleaning my room, the dogs were whining at me to go for a walk.

e. Whether owning or renting, living in a house tends to be more expensive than living in an apartment.

3. Correct the misplaced and dangling modifier errors in the following paragraph from a student's essay.

Selecting an appropriate way of getting around town is vital when living in a busy city. Public transportation is available and it is also possible to buy a car. Being a student, a bike could be your preferred mode of travel because of your finances. Cycling is the best choice for any student living on a limited budget. The only real expense is the purchase price of the bicycle. If handy, it is possible to do all the maintenance yourself. There is no need to pay for a transit pass or gas and parking. You get to exercise on the way to your destination, save money, and even see different sights seated on your bike, because you can take a different route usually to get where you're going. Of course, if you live in Victoria, as I do, you don't have to worry about snowy winters. You might have a different opinion about transportation if you live in other parts of the country.

FAULTY PARALLELISM

1. Correct the examples of faulty parallelism in the following sentences.

> **Example:** When Scott left the comforts of home to attend college, he encountered expenses he had never considered before, such as tuition fees, money for his bus passes, long-distance phone calls, expenses for groceries, and rent.
> **Correction:** When Scott left the comforts of home to attend college, he encountered expenses he had never considered before, such as tuition fees, bus passes, phone bills, groceries, and rent.

a. My favourite courses are English and that course where we learned about World War II.

b. When you are revising your thesis statement, check that it is clear, provocative, and that it will convince your readers.

c. Spending too much time on the Internet can affect your family life, personal relationships, and your physical health can also be affected.

d. In this essay, the author discusses the ways a daughter's attitude toward her father changes during childhood, through the teenage years, and what it's like when she is an adult.

e. According to one theory of motivation, employees perform best when they are given respect, the responsibility they can handle, and recognition for their efforts.

2. Correct the faulty parallelism errors in the following passage from a student's freewriting exercise.

One of my friends decided to buy a small house because she was tired of living in a noisy apartment building. When Adrienne bought her house, she realized that she had more responsibilities, such as mowing the lawn, having to water the garden, and she had to shovel the snow in the winter. In addition to her telephone bill, she also had to pay the electricity bill, the monthly cable television payment, and the bill for the gas. Then there were her monthly mortgage payments and property tax instalments. Worst of all, whenever there was a problem with the house, such as a clogged drain, leaky faucet, or the fact that a window was broken, she had to call someone to do the repairs for her, because she didn't know how to do them herself. Still, she does not regret her decision to buy, because she now has the quiet life she wanted.

PUNCTUATION

The Comma

1. Add commas where necessary in the following sentences.

a. My camping trip to Riding Mountain National Park in Manitoba was relaxing but it was far too short.

b. Jacek finds tennis challenging so he spends as much time as possible practising his serve and return.

c. Abdul suffers from insomnia yet he manages to be cheerful every morning.

d. In two days Boris and Svetlana leave for their trip back to Russia.

e. Elated that she had won the scholarship Daniella called her boyfriend with the good news.

f. As he waited for the bus Al thought about how many hours a week he spent travelling to and from school.

g. Whenever our doorbell rings our old dog barks once shuffles to the door and stands waiting for us to open it.

h. If you want to take up skateboarding as a sport you can buy a complete board or you can buy a deck wheels bearings trucks kingpins bushings and hardware and put it together yourself.

i. Mina Shum David Cronenberg Denys Arcand Patricia Rozema and Atom Egoyan are the Canadian film directors David admires most.

j. The chef wanted to create a unique delectable unforgettable feast for her son's engagement party.

k. British Columbia's Gulf Islands located in the Strait of Georgia are known for their mild climate quiet coves and abundant wildlife.

l. The Royal Canadian Henley Regatta which is held in St. Catharines, Ontario every year is considered to be the foremost rowing competition in North America.

m. If you don't know much about computers your campus computer centre with its knowledgeable lab attendants and word-processing tutorials is the ideal place to begin your digital education.

n. The legitimacy of immunization the deliberate administration of a vaccine to prevent the patient from contracting a disease has been questioned by proponents of natural medicine.

o. Lacrosse is one sport that has been declining in popularity over the twentieth century.

p. The houses on the north side of the street have a better view of the mountains.

q. Gardeners with a sincere desire to preserve the earth avoid using chemical herbicides and pesticides.

r. Children who suffer from asthma should keep their rooms as uncluttered as possible.

s. The passengers tired from their long trip longed for a good night's sleep.

t. The passengers with Canadian passports were told to proceed to the customs clerks immediately.

u. Some cars such as Volkswagens have become collector's items.

v. The story's ending as we shall see is a happy one.

w. The prerequisite essay-writing course according to students who have taken it is more challenging than the advanced course they take in the second semester.

x. Sir Frederick Banting who discovered insulin along with Charles Best died in Newfoundland on February 21 1941.

y. If you go to Ottawa be sure to drive past Stornoway at 541 Acadia Avenue Rockcliffe Park the residence of the leader of the official opposition.

2. Correct the comma errors in the following essay written by a travel and tourism student.

Every year Canadian communities hold festivals to celebrate everything from historical events and cultural heritage to changes in the seasons. It's possible in fact to spend a year crossing the country from west to east in search of a celebration. For example you could begin in July with All Sooke Day on Vancouver Island. This festival celebrates the days of pioneer loggers with activities such as tree chopping log rolling and axe throwing. In August you could travel to Dauphin Manitoba for Canada's National Ukrainian Festival an event that attracts many visitors from across North America to take in performances by Ukrainian dancers and enjoy perogies and cabbage rolls. Kitchener–Waterloo Ontario hosts the popular Oktoberfest every October and you would be well advised to attend this week-long celebration of the bounty of the harvest and sample some of the beverages produced by local breweries. You could banish winter blues with a skating expedition along Ottawa's Rideau Canal followed by a steaming cup of hot chocolate and the freshly baked local delicacy called a beaver-tail during Winterlude. After that you would be wise to visit the world-renowned Quebec Winter Carnival in Quebec City so you could have your photograph taken with the event's mascot "Bonhomme Carnaval" in front of his ice palace. By the time spring rolls around you could conclude your national festival tour in Nova Scotia with a leisurely blossom tour through the countryside and final stop at one of the many "streetfests" during the Annapolis Valley Blossom Festival. There are celebrations galore in Canada so why not stay home and get to know the festivities in your own country this year?

The Apostrophe

1. Correct any apostrophe or possessive pronoun errors in the following sentences.

    a. Theyre going to Cuba next week.
    b. Its easy to learn how to fly a kite.
    c. Its been raining all day, so I doubt well be able to go sailing.
    d. The cat keeps scratching its ears.
    e. "Whose been eating my porridge?" said Papa Bear.
    f. Who's coat is this?
    g. We shoul'dve taken the bus to the stadium; we wouldve been there by now.
    h. Lowells dogs chewed the gardeners shovels and now their looking for they're water bowl.
    i. The teachers cafeteria is down the hall; youll find them in there having they're end-of-term staff meeting.
    j. Bobs car is newer than Chriss van.
    k. The door to the girls change room is locked.
    l. The childrens art work will be displayed in the foyer during Education Week.
    m. After a hard days work, he likes to go for a long run to wind down.
    n. Please be ready for tomorrow's test.
    o. We were invited to Lorraines and Clives cottage for the weekend.

2. Correct the apostrophe errors in the following passage from a student's freewriting exercise for a comparison-and-contrast essay.

    Both Ontario and Quebec have wonderful cities. Ontarios main urban area, Toronto, has many attraction's such as sports events, concerts, and theatres. Farther north, Ottawa is rich because of it's many historical government buildings and museums. The province of Quebec also has a lot to offer. Montreal is known for its fashion boutique's, night life, and jazz and comedy festivals. Quebec Citys rich history can be experienced in the lower town. Overall, Quebec City has a European atmosphere because of its old buildings and attractive shops and charming café's. The two provinces historical and cultural differences may contribute to political disputes, but they are both worthy destinations on every tourists' itinerary.

The Semicolon and the Colon

1. In the following sentences, add semicolons where they are needed.

> **Example:** As a full-time student and part-time gymnastics coach, Sean has little free time, nevertheless, he still finds time to visit his bedridden grandfather every weekend.
>
> **Correction:** As a full-time student and part-time gymnastics coach, Sean has little free time; nevertheless, he still finds time to visit his bedridden grandfather every weekend.

    a. Cobwebs traced a path across the window pane, dusty paperback books lined the shelf below.

    b. Ihor wants to find a summer job however, he isn't free to work until the middle of June.

    c. Customers who wish to pay by credit card may proceed to the information desk, customers who wish to pay cash may line up at the cashier's counter.

    d. Deciding to quit smoking is easy on the other hand, quitting is much harder.

    e. Music has always been the preferred art form of most teenagers, music videos take that art form to new levels.

2. In the following sentences, add colons where they are needed and delete any colons that are unnecessary.

> **Example:** My brother collects: baseball cards, antique bottles, jigsaw puzzles, and World War II memorabilia.
>
> **Correction:** My brother collects baseball cards, antique bottles, jigsaw puzzles, and World War II memorabilia.

    a. A diploma in electronic engineering can prepare you for a career in fields such as: robotics, data communications, and computer applications.

b. The author of this article says many fatherless children: live in poverty, fail school, and have psychological problems

c. Every driver should carry a winter storm kit consisting of the following: a flashlight, shovel, tow chain, booster cables, flares, matches, and candles.

d. The original members of Canada's Group of Seven were: the following Franklin Carmichael, Lawren Harris, Franz Johnston, Arthur Lismer, J.E.H. MacDonald, A.Y. Jackson, and F.H. Varley.

e. Kate Braid criticizes computers because they can't deliver the sensory stimuli she craves. "There is no crinkling of paper, no sharp smell of ink, no tight neatness of a newspaper freshly laid on your table, no satisfying weight of a good, thick book."

Practising Punctuation

Add commas, apostrophes, semicolons, or colons, as necessary, to the following paragraph. Also correct any possessive pronoun errors.

Volunteering can be one of the most rewarding experiences in a persons life it gives volunteers the chance to interact with people they might otherwise never meet and in ways that would not be available in they're paid employment. Opportunities for volunteer jobs are as broad as a prospective volunteers imagination. For example if you like to work with children it is possible to be a helper in a school. Dr. Frank Hogarth a retired professor who never had his own family now works as a math volunteer in his local junior high school Sarah Bluestein has organized a preschool for the young children of mothers who have recently moved to Canada. While the mothers are studying in their English as a Second Language classes their infants and toddlers are getting just as much attention in their own preschool. However you need'nt be at the end of your career to take on a volunteering challenge. Several local college students work as aides in a day program for children with developmental problems they are learning to share the children's joy in small successes. For example after many weeks of practice one child was able to put on her own coat without help for the first time another mastered setting the snack table with the cups and napkins placed properly in front of each chair a third child learned the rhythm of a song well enough to beat a drum in time to the music. As far as volunteering goes, these students agree with the advertising slogan "Just do it."

EDITING SUMMARY

As a final check on your editing skills, read the following draft written by a recreation student. It has a combination of the errors you practised correcting in this chapter.

People, who are thinking of taking up cycling as a sport, have two options and two corresponding types of bicycles available to them.

In recent years the thrill-seeking industry has been rapidly growing. Bringing with it the modern mountain bike. Mountain bikes are designed for off-road use. Its smaller wheel size and compact frame make hill climbing much easier. The hard-core mountain biker take to the hills of wooded areas. Speeding down steep descents and climbing vertical trails. Large and sturdy disk brakes are implemented because the mountain biker often has to avoid crashing into trees or flying off cliffs. In this discipline speed is compromised for good handling.

On the other hand handling is compromised for speed where the road-racing bike is concerned. Larger wheels allow the road bike to travel a greater distance per revolution. These wheels are also very thin. Which causes less drag. Which makes the road bike faster than the mountain bike. The same concept can be found in the road bike's crank which has a larger diameter than the mountain bikes crank. A road bikes frame are much larger than a mountain bikes, this difference is to give the road rider more comfort because they generally travel a much greater distance. The road bike is meant to be ridden on the road only. If a cyclist takes a road bike through off-road trails, it will surely be destroyed.

Sport cycling can be exciting nevertheless it makes sense for the newcomer to decide what kind of terrain and what kind of action they'll want before putting down that deposit on a new bike.

ACKNOWLEDGMENTS

Charlie Angus, "The Battle over Gun Control: Marking the Divide Between Rural and Urban Canada," *HighGrader Magazine*, Jan./Feb. 1995. Reprinted by permission of Charlie Angus, editor of *HighGrader Magazine*, Cobalt, Ontario.

W.H. Auden, "Work, Labour, Play," from *A Certain World* (Faber & Faber, 1971). Reprinted by permission of Curtis Brown, Ltd. Copyright © 1971 W.H. Auden, renewed.

Brenda Austin-Smith, "The Internet and Gender," *Canadian Dimension*, Feb./Mar. 1995. Reprinted with permission from *Canadian Dimension* (*CD*) magazine, 91 Albert St., Room 2-B, Winnipeg, Manitoba, Canada R3B 1G5. (204) 957-1519.

Kerry Banks, "As a Dad, Will I Do Right by My Daughter?" *Chatelaine*, June 1993.

Kate Braid, "A Plea for the Physical," *Canadian Forum*, June 1996. Reprinted by permission of the author.

Joy C., "The Phone Call," *Harvard Educational Review* 66.2 (Summer 1996), pp. 175–77. Copyright © by the President and Fellows of Harvard College. All rights reserved.

June Callwood, "Making a Difference," *Homemaker's Magazine*, Apr. 1989. Reprinted by permission of *Homemaker's Magazine*.

Kim Chernin, excerpt from *The Obsession: Reflections on the Tyranny of Slenderness* by Kim Chernin. Copyright © 1981 by Kim Chernin. Reprinted by permission of HarperCollins Publishers, Inc.

Robert Chodos, "Being a Jew at Christmas," *Compass: A Jesuit Journal*, Jan./Feb. 1992. Reprinted by permission of the author.

Wayson Choy, excerpt from *The Jade Peony* by Wayson Choy. Copyright © 1995. Published by Douglas & McIntyre. Reprinted by permission of the publisher.

Archibald J. Crail, "Affirmative Action," from *Fiery Spirits: A Collection of Short Fiction and Poetry by Canadian Writers of Black Descent*, ed. Ayanna Black. Reprinted by permission of the author.

Lorna Crozier, "Paper Boy," from *Inventing the Hawk* by Lorna Crozier. Used by permission of McClelland & Stewart, Inc., Toronto, *The Canadian Publishers*.

John DeMont, "Love and Fear in the Age of AIDS," *Maclean's*, 22 Feb. 1993. Reprinted by permission of *Maclean's*.

Joan Donaldson, "Singling Out Single Parents." First published as "Don't single out single parents" in the *Globe and Mail*, 17 Jan. 1996. Reprinted by permission of the author.

Pamela Erens, "Bodily Harm." First published in *Ms.* in 1985. Reprinted by permission of the author.

David Evans, "What Do Men Want?" *Chatelaine*, Nov. 1991. Reprinted by permission of the author.

Moira Farr, "Welcome to FamilyValuesWorld!" *This Magazine*, Dec./Jan. 1995. Reprinted by permission of the author.

Warren Farrell, "Men as Success Objects." First published in *Family Therapy Networker* in 1988. Reprinted with permission of Warren Farrell, Ph.D.

Madeleine Gagnon, "Respect and Balance in Our 'Tribe,'" *Compass*, Sept./Oct. 1994. Reprinted by permission of the author.

Janice Giavedoni, "Jerry Lewis and the MDA Telethon: Is It Really That Bad?" *Disability Today*, Fall 1994. Reprinted by permission of the publisher.

Lisa Gregoire, "On Jobs and Humility," *Globe and Mail*, 1 July 1996. Reprinted by permission of the author.

Lauren Griffin, "Making Big Deals out of Little Deals," *Compass*, Sept./Oct 1994. Reprinted by permission of Brit Griffin, Publisher, *HighGrader Magazine*.

Kenneth J. Harvey, "Life After Cable." Published as "It's dreary, it's cold, and they just killed our cable" in the *Globe and Mail*, 29 July 1996. Reprinted by permission of the author.

Robert L. Heilbroner, "Don't Let Stereotypes Warp Your Judgments." Reprinted by permission of Robert L. Heilbroner.

Michael Ignatieff, "Quebec," from *Blood and Belonging* by Michael Ignatieff. Copyright © Michael Ignatieff, 1993. Reprinted by permission of Penguin Books Canada Limited.

Shirley Jackson, "The Lottery," from *The Lottery* by Shirley Jackson. Copyright © 1948, 1949 by Shirley Jackson, and copyright renewed © 1976, 1977 by Laurence Hyman, Barry Hyman, Mrs. Sarah Webster, and Mrs. Joanne Schnurer. Reprinted by permission of Farrar, Straus & Giroux.

Rita Joe, "I Lost My Talk," from *Song of Eskasoni*. Copyright © Rita Joe. Used with permission of Ragweed Press, Charlottetown, PEI.

Aspasia Kaplaneris, "Earthbound . . . for Now." Reprinted by permission of the author.

Sean Kelly, "Discovering My Native Identity." Published as "A young man's discovery of his native identity" in the *Globe and Mail*, 6 July 1996.

Sonnet L'Abbé, "Hello, We're Not American!" *Globe and Mail*, 31 Jan. 1996. Reprinted by permission of the author.

Roy MacGregor, excerpt from *The Home Team: Fathers, Sons and Hockey* by Roy MacGregor. Copyright © Roy MacGregor, 1995. Reprinted by permission of Penguin Books Canada Limited.

Willa Marcus, "Need, Want, Deserve." Published as "I Worry That I Will Never Fully Master the Art of Shopping" in *Compass*, Jan. 91. Reprinted by permission of the author.

"'Negro' Name Change Protested," *Kitchener Waterloo Record*, 17 June 1996. Reprinted by permission of The Canadian Press.

Julia Nunes, "The Business of Being Half and Half," *Globe and Mail*, 10 Jan. 1996. Reprinted by permission of the author.

M. Nourbese Philip, "What's in a Name?" Reprinted by permission of the author.

Catherine Pigott, "Adding Weight to an Image of Beauty," *Globe and Mail*, 20 Mar. 1991. Reprinted by permission of the author.

Andrew Pyper, "Kiss Me," from *Kiss Me* by Andrew Pyper. Reprinted by permission of The Porcupine's Quill.

Robyn Sarah, "Maintenance," from *The Touchstone: Poems New and Selected*. (Anansi, 1992). Reprinted with the permission of House of Anansi.

"The Shackles of Everyday Lies," *Globe and Mail*, 24 July 1996.

Wallace Stegner, excerpt from *Wolf Willow* by Wallace Stegner. Copyright © 1955, 1957, 1958, 1959, 1962 by Wallace Stegner. Copyright renewed © 1990 by Wallace Stegner. Reprinted by permission of Brandt & Brandt Literary Agents, Inc.

Yeshim Ternar, "Ajax Là-Bas," from *Other Solitudes: Canadian Multicultural Fiction*, ed. Linda Hutcheon and Marion Richmond. Reprinted by permission of the author.

Judith Timson, "Long Day's Journey into Kitchen Clean-Up" from *Family Matters* by Judith Timson. Copyright © 1996 by Judith Timson. Published by HarperCollins Publishers. First published in *Chatelaine* (Dec. 1995) as "Here's to Family Feasting."

Tom Wayman, "Factory Time." Reprinted by permission of Harbour Publishing Co. Ltd.

Carl Wilson, "Did You Ever Have to Make Up Your Mind?" *Hour*, 1 Aug. 1996. Reprinted by permission of the author.

Pam Withers, "The Babysitters Club: No Boys Allowed," *Globe and Mail*, 29 Mar. 1996. Reprinted by permission of the author.

Naomi Wolf, excerpt from *The Beauty Myth* by Naomi Wolf. Copyright © 1990. Reprinted by permission of Random House of Canada Limited.

Sun-Kyung Yi, "An Accent on Learning English," *Globe and Mail*, 8 Apr. 1993. Reprinted by permission of the author.

INDEX

bibliography cards, 360–61
block method of comparison and contrast,
   314–15, 318–19
brackets, 362, 459
brainstorming, 218–20
   for causes and effects, 307–308
   for narration, 291–92
   for process analysis, 330–31
   for subject analysis, 338

cause and effect, 306–13
   argument in, 321
   organizing, 309
   transitions for, 270
character analysis, 339–47
   prewriting for, 340–42
   thesis for, 343
chronological organization, 241, 270–71, 331
circular arguments, 323
citations for research papers. *See* American
   Psychological Association (APA) style;
   Modern Language Association (MLA) style
clarity, 255–56
classification, 301–306
   and stereotyping, 305
   subtopics for, 302–303
clauses, 422–423. *See also* dependent (subordinate) clauses; independent (main) clauses
clichés, 463–64
clustering, 214–15, 291
coherence, 246–47, 268–76
collaborative learning, 218–20
collective nouns, 436
colloquial language, 223, 464
colons, 452–53
   quotation marks and, 455
comma splices, 428
commas, 444–47
   in compound sentences, 423
   parentheses and, 458
   quotation marks and, 455
comparison and contrast, 313–320
   argument in, 321
   block method of, 314–15, 318–19
   in definitions, 298
   point-by-point method of, 315, 318–19
   transitions for, 269
complex sentences, 424
compound nouns, 449
compound sentences, 423–24
compound subjects, 417, 434–35
compound–complex sentences, 424
conceding, in argument, 324
conclusions, 280–82
   in character analysis, 343

and introductions, 280–82
and thesis, 280–82
transitions for, 270
conjunctive adverbs, 429, 431, 446, 452
contractions, 447–48, 451
contradiction, in introductions, 279
contrast. *See* comparison and contrast
coordinate adjectives, 445
coordinating conjunctions, 423, 429, 444
correlative conjunctions, faulty parallelism and,
   443
cover sheet for research paper, 357
critical thinking, 233, 255–56

dangling modifiers, 441–42
dashes, 453–54
dates, commas and, 446
definition, 297–301
   classification in, 302
   incorporating, 298
   in introductions, 278–79
demonstrative pronouns, 417
dependent (subordinate) clauses, 422–23,
   424
   to correct run-on sentences, 429, 431
   faulty parallelism and, 442
   in fragments, 427
description, 285–89
   in definitions, 298
   in introductions, 277
   and narration, 290
   in subject analysis, 339
direct address, commas and, 446
direct objects, 417–18
direct quotations
   commas and, 446
   in introductions, 277
   quotation marks with, 454
documentation of sources. *See* American
   Psychological Association (APA) style;
   Modern Language Association (MLA)
   style
drafting an essay, 234–37
   using cause and effect, 308–309
   using narration, 292
   using process analysis, 331–32
   using subject analysis, 339
   using summary, 348
drafts
   evaluating, 237–38
   revising, 256–61

editing symbols, 414–15, 426, 468
either/or arguments, 323

electronic sources
   citing. *See* American Psychological Association (APA) style; Modern Language Association (MLA) style
   evaluating, 359–60
   using, 359
ellipsis, 362, 457–58
essay exams, 214, 351–54
   key words on, 352–53
   outline for, 353–54
essay format, MLA style, 369
et al., 388
euphemisms, 465
examples
   in definitions, 298
   transitions for, 270
exclamation marks, 451
expletives, 436

false analogies, 323
faulty parallelism, 442–43
faulty word choice, 463–79
format
   essay, MLA style, 369
   references page, APA style, 408
   works-cited page, MLA style, 385, 405
fragments, 426–28
freewriting, 210–12
fused sentences, 428–31

gaps in logic, avoiding, 275
gender, pronouns and, 432–33, 465–66
generalizations, hasty, 323
gerunds, 421
grouping, for character analysis, 341–42

heading, for research papers, 369
helping verbs, 419
hyphens, 460–62

illustrations
   in introductions, 278
   transitions for, 270
incubation, 220
indefinite pronouns, 417, 432–33, 435, 449
independent (main) clauses, 422–24
   in comma splices, 428
   commas and, 444
   faulty parallelism and, 442
   in run-on sentences, 428–31
   semicolons and, 452
indirect objects, 418
indirect quotations, 454
infinitive phrases, 421
-ing phrases, 421
interjections, commas and, 446

Internet. *See* electronic sources; American Psychological Association (APA) style; Modern Language Association (MLA) style
interrogative pronouns, 417
interviews, personal, 365–67
introductions, 276–80
   and audience, 276
   and conclusions, 280–82
   and thesis statements, 231, 276
introductory elements, commas and, 444

jargon, 464
journal writing, 212–14
   dialectical, 213

key words
   on essay exams, 352–53
   repetition of, 272, 274–75
   substitution of, 272–73

letters, plurals of, 450
library material, gathering, 357–60
linking verbs, 418–19
listing, 216, 286
   for character analysis, 340–341
logical fallacies, 322–23

main clauses. *See* independent (main) clauses
meaning, in correcting run-on sentences, 430–31
methods of developing essays, 283–354. *See also* analysis; argument; cause and effect; classification; comparison and contrast; description; definition; narration; summary
   combining, 283–85
misplaced modifiers, 441–42
mixed constructions in sentences, 439–440
MLA. *See* Modern Language Association (MLA) style
Modern Language Association (MLA) style, 386–405
   essay format, 369
   parenthetical citations, 249, 386–91
      association or corporate author, 389
      author named in text, 387
      author not named in text, 386
      author's name not given, 389
      electronic sources, 391
      government publication, 389
      indirect source, 390–91
      more than one work, 391
      more than three authors, 388–89
      novel, 389–90
      play, 390
      poem, 390

sentences, 416–25
    common errors in, 426–43
    complex, 424
    compound, 423–24
    compound–complex, 424
    confused parts, 440
    simple, 423
    symbols for errors, 414, 426
    variation, 423–24
series, commas in, 445
setting, in narration, 295

sexist language, 465–66
shifts
    in person and number, 436–37
    in verb tense, 437–38
    in voice, 438–39
sic, 459
simple sentences, 423
slang, 464
slash, 459–60
small-group discussion. *See* collaborative learning
sources
    acknowledging, 248–49
    evaluating, 359–60
    using for support, 247–54
"so what?" response, 233
spatial relationships, 241, 269, 271
standard English, 222, 223
state-of-being verbs, 418–19
statistics, in introductions, 279
stereotyping, 305
style, 222, 225–26
    in correcting run-on sentences, 430–31
subject analysis, 338–47. *See also* character
    analysis
subjective pronouns, 417, 431
subject(s), 416–17
    compound, 417, 434–35
    lacking in fragments, 426, 427
    noun as, 416
    pronoun as, 417
subordinate clauses. *See* dependent (subordi-
    nate) clauses
subordinate conjunctions, 422, 431
summary, 252, 347–51
    active reading for, 347
    distinguished from paraphrase, 252, 347
    thesis in, 348
synonyms, 272–73, 297

thesis, 228–33
    in argument, 320–21
    in character analysis, 343
    developing, 228–29
    as forecast of plan, 228, 231

"missing" or implied, 231, 292
in narration, 292
positioning, 231, 276
in process analysis, 336
recognizing, 229–30
revising, 230, 239
in summary, 348
supporting, 234–239
working, 235, 292
time relationships, 241, 269, 270–71
titles
    and agreement, 436
    commas and, 446
    quotation marks for, 456
tone, 223–25, 276
topic sentences, 244–45
topics
    for narration, 291–92
    for process analysis, 330–31
    for subject analysis, 338
transition(s), 269–71
    between paragraphs, 274–75
    terms, 269–70
transitional phrases
    commas and, 446
    semicolons and, 452

unity, of paragraph, 246

verb form errors, 433–34
verbal phrases, 421
verbs, 418–19
    action, 418
    agreement with subjects, 434–36
    faulty choice of, 440
    helping, 419
    lacking in fragments, 427
    linking, 418–19
    shifts in tense, 437–38
    state-of-being, 418–19
voice, 223, 225, 313
    active, 438–39
    passive, 438–39
    shifts in, 438–39

word choice, 222, 223, 225–26, 286
    faulty, 463–79
    symbols for errors, 415, 468
words
    compound, with hyphens, 460–62
    as words, plurals of, 450
works-cited page, 249, 360, 392, 405. *See also*
        Modern Language Association (MLA)
        style
    format of, 385, 405
works-consulted page, 392